NEW DIRECTIONS

African Americans in a Diversifying Nation

James S. Jackson
EDITOR

National Policy Association

Program for Research on Black Americans
University of Michigan

New Directions:
African Americans in a Diversifying Nation
NPA Report #297
Price: $24.95
ISBN 0-89068-152-X
Library of Congress
Card Catalog Number 00-102945

Copyright 2000
by the National Policy Association
A voluntary association incorporated under the laws
of the District of Columbia
1424 16th Street, N.W., Suite 700
Washington, D.C. 20036-2229

Printed in the United States of America

New Directions: African Americans in a Diversifying Nation

James S. Jackson
Editor

Foreword

The publication of this study, *New Directions: African Americans in a Diversifying Nation*, culminates NPA's six-year project on the critical issue of race relations in American society. Richard J. Schmeelk, then Chair of the National Policy Association Board of Trustees, proposed that NPA turn its research efforts to this issue. He believed that NPA's long experience in bringing together diverse groups to build common ground would be valuable in helping to bridge the racial divide in America. Mr. Schmeelk has been the major supporter of this undertaking as well as its leading advocate.

The issue of race relations in America has a long and tangled history. The Black/White dichotomy has been inextricably intertwined with the political, economic, and social development of America for more than two centuries. However, in the last decade of the 20th century, the issue assumed a new saliency with the growth of the Hispanic and Asian populations in the United States. This increase will continue to significantly affect the dynamics of race relations in the 21st century. *New Directions* reflects this new reality.

During the first phase of the project, NPA, together with the Joint Center for Political and Economic Studies, addressed one of the most contentious elements of public policy relating to race relations—affirmative action. Under the project, the impact of affirmative action in the workplace, in education, and in government contracting was examined, and recommendations for future directions in affirmative action policies were proposed. The NPA/Joint Center report, *Affirmative Action: A Course for the Future*, also informed the second phase of the project, a much broader examination of trends in race relations and policy implications for the future.

The framework for the broader study was established with the guidance of a Policy Advisory Group composed of distinguished scholars, public policy experts, and labor and business leaders. (For a listing of the members of the group, see "Acknowledgments.") Their contributions were invaluable in identifying the areas of focus for the study. The Policy Advisory Group also helped to guide the selection of scholars and provided substantive input to the chapter outlines. The agreed-upon goal of the study was to bring together research on the changes in the economic, political, and social status of African Americans over the past 40 years, to look toward future challenges posed by increasing diversity, and to formulate recommendations for public and private policy initiatives to promote equality of opportunity.

The Program for Research on Black Americans (PBRA) at the University of Michigan (UM) joined NPA as a cosponsor of the study in 1997. Dr. James S. Jackson, Director, Research Center for Group Dynamics and PRBA, and Daniel Katz Distinguished University Professor of Psychology, UM, became Principal Investigator for this effort and worked with an eminent group of scholars to produce the study.

New Directions presents significant and timely data on eight topical areas as well as thought-provoking recommendations for eliminating racial disparities and promoting greater awareness of the complexities arising from America's new diversity. Beginning with a review of current demographic data and an analysis of public attitudes on race and other policy issues, the study addresses income and wealth, education, health, family structure, politics, and criminal justice. It finds that the increasing diversity within the African American population indicates both progress and continuing challenges in each area. The study discusses the potential of several models of intergroup collaboration and the pitfalls of competition as all sectors of society seek to obtain the benefits of America's growing prosperity.

In the tradition of several seminal works in the past century, *New Directions* contributes to a greater understanding of race relations in contemporary America. W.E.B. DuBois's oft-quoted insight in his 1903 work, *The Souls of Black Folk,* that the problem of the 20th century would be the "color line" has indeed been proved true. In 1944, Gunnar Myrdal's *An American Dilemma: The Negro Problem and Modern Democracy* shed powerful light on the extent of racism in society as America approached mid-century. The National Research Council's 1989 work, *A Common Destiny: Blacks and American Society,* documented the dramatic changes for African Americans in the postwar years. The present study delineates America's progress in the final decades of the 20th century. It challenges all citizens, as the 21st century begins amid unparalleled economic, demographic, and social changes, to complete the unfinished business of providing equal opportunity for every American. It is our hope that this publication will contribute to the full achievement of that worthy goal.

Project Codirectors

Milton D. Morris
President,
Creative Futures International

Marilyn Zuckerman
Former Vice President,
National Policy Association

Acknowledgments

This study would not have been possible without the generous support and unfaltering commitment of Richard J. Schmeelk, Chairman of CAI Advisors & Co. and former Chair of the NPA Board of Trustees. The Priscilla and Richard J. Schmeelk Foundation was the principal contributor to this effort. NPA is also grateful to the following organizations for their support of the project: Shelley and Donald Rubin Foundation; U.S. Department of Labor; Ford Foundation (for the affirmative action study); Andrew W. Mellon Foundation; MCI Corporation; McDonald's Corporation; Chase Manhattan Foundation; Simpson Thatcher & Bartlett; and The Henry and Elaine Kaufman Foundation.

Members of the Policy Advisory Group, listed below, established the framework for the study and provided valuable input to the Principal Investigator and the authors:

Henry J. Aaron, Senior Fellow, The Brookings Institution;

Douglas Besharov, Resident Scholar, American Enterprise Institute;

Charles L. Betsey, Professor, Department of Economics, Howard University;

John J. Dilulio, Jr., Director, Partnership for Research on Religion and At-Risk Youth (PRRAY), Public/Private Ventures;

Anthony Downs, Senior Fellow, Economic Studies Department, The Brookings Institution;

Amitai Etizioni, University Professor, George Washington University;

Reynolds Farley, Research Scientist and Professor, Institute for Social Research, University of Michigan;

James Gibson, President, DC Agenda;

Charles V. Hamilton, Wallace S. Sayre Professor of Government, Columbia University (Retired);

Augustus F. Hawkins, Member, U.S. House of Representatives (Retired);

Norman Hill, President, A. Phillip Randolph Institute;

Joe W. Laymon, Director and Vice President of Human Resources for U.S. and Canada Services, Eastman Kodak Company;

Malcolm R. Lovell, Jr., Executive in Residence, School of Business and Public Administration, George Washington University;

Paula D. McClain, Professor of Political Science and Law, Duke University;

Robert B. McKersie, Sloan Fellows Professor of Management Emeritus, Massachusetts Institute of Technology;

Courtland Milloy, Columnist, *The Washington Post*;

Richard P. Nathan, Director, Nelson A. Rockefeller Institute of Government;

Constance Berry Newman, Former Under Secretary, Smithsonian Institution;

Rudolph A. Oswald, Economist in Residence, George Meany Center for Labor Studies;

Clarence Page, Columnist, *Chicago Tribune*;

Isabel Sawhill, Senior Fellow and Johnson Chair, The Brookings Institution;

Beth Shulman, Special Assistant to the President, United Food and Commercial Workers International Union;

Margaret C. Simms, Vice President for Research, Joint Center for Political and Economic Studies;

Reuben C. Warren, Associate Administrator for Urban Affairs, Agency for Toxic Substances and Disease Registry, U.S. Department of Health and Human Services; and

Richard Womack, Director, Department of Civil and Human Rights, AFL-CIO.

Martha Lee Benz, NPA Editor, contributed greatly in preparing the manuscripts for publication. She was ably assisted by Mary A. Haldeman, NPA Editorial Assistant.

The opinions expressed by the authors are their own and do not necessarily represent the views of their institutions, NPA, the University of Michigan, the Policy Advisory Group, or the project funders.

About the Authors and Editor

William A. Darity, Jr., is the Cary C. Boshamer Professor of Economics and Sociology at the University of North Carolina (UNC) at Chapel Hill. He is also Research Professor of Public Policy at Duke University. At UNC he has served as Director of the Minority Undergraduate Research Assistant Program, the Undergraduate Honors Program, and Graduate Studies. Dr. Darity's research focuses on inequality by race, class, and ethnicity; North-South theories of development and trade; history of economic thought and political economy; the Atlantic slave trade and the Industrial Revolution; and social psychology effects of unemployment exposure. He is coauthor of *Persistent Disparity: Race and Economic Inequality in the United States Since 1945* and *The Black Underclass: Critical Essays on Race and Unwantedness.*

Reynolds Farley is Research Scientist and Professor at the Population Studies Center of the University of Michigan's Institute for Social Research. He is also the Otis Dudley Duncan Professor of Sociology. His research interests focus on population trends in the United States, specifically racial trends and differences. Dr. Farley is author of *The Growth of the Black Population; Blacks and Whites: Narrowing the Gap?; and The New American Reality: Who We Are, How We Got Here, and Where We Are Going.* He is a member of the joint Russell Sage Foundation-Population Reference Bureau committee that will commission a series of scholarly monographs on findings from the 2000 census.

Darnell F. Hawkins is Professor of African American Studies, Sociology, and Criminal Justice at the University of Illinois at Chicago. He conducts research on topics that bridge the intersection between race/ethnicity and crime/justice. Dr. Hawkins has published numerous journal articles and essays on race, crime, and punishment in the United States. He is editor of *Homicide Among Black Americans* and *Ethnicity, Race, and Crime: Perspectives Across Time and Place.*

Cedric Herring is Professor in the Department of Sociology and in the Institute of Government and Public Affairs at the University of Illinois at Chicago. He was the founding Director of the Institute for Research on Race and Public Policy at the University of Illinois. Dr. Herring's research interests include social policy, labor force issues and policies, stratification and inequality, and the sociology of African Americans. Among his books are *Splitting the Middle: Political Alienation, Acquiescence, and Activism; African Americans and the Public Agenda: The Paradoxes of Public Policy;* and *Empowerment in Chicago: Grassroots Participation in Poverty Alleviation.*

Jennifer L. Hochschild is the William Stewart Tod Professor of Public and International Affairs at Princeton University, with a joint appointment in the Department of Politics and the Woodrow Wilson School of Public and International Affairs. She is also Director of the Center for Domestic and Comparative Policy Studies at Princeton. She is author of *Facing Up to the American Dream: Race, Class, and the Soul of the Nation; The New American Dilemma: Liberal Democracy and School Desegregation;* and *What's Fair: American Beliefs about Distributive Justice.*

James S. Jackson is Director of the Research Center for Group Dynamics and the Program for Research on Black Americans at the Institute for Social Research at the University of Michigan. He is also the Daniel Katz Distinguished University Professor of Psychology, Professor of Health Behavior and Health Education at the School of Public Health, Director of the Center for Afroamerican and African Studies, and Faculty Associate at the Institute of Gerontology. In 1990, he helped establish and continues to direct the African American Mental Health Research Program funded by the National Institute of Mental Health. His research interests and areas of publication include race and ethnic relations, health and mental health, adult development and aging, attitudes and attitude change, and African American politics. He is coeditor of *Family Life in Black America, Mental Health in Black America,* and *Aging in Black America.*

Thomas A. LaVeist is Associate Professor of Health and Public Policy in the School of Hygiene and Public Health at Johns Hopkins University. He is also Associate Professor in the Department of Sociology and Faculty Associate in the Hopkins Population Center. His research centers on broad issues such as the social and behavioral factors that explain race differences in health outcomes; the factors that influence access to and utilization of health services; and the impact of health and social policy on the health and quality of life of African Americans.

Paula D. McClain is Professor of Political Science and Law at Duke University. She was previously Professor of Government in the Woodrow Wilson Department of Government and Foreign Affairs at the University of Virginia. Her primary research interests are racial minority group politics, particularly interminority political and social competition, and urban politics, especially public policy and urban crime. Her most recent book is *Can We All Get Along? Racial and Ethnic Minorities in American Politics,* coauthored with Joseph Stewart, Jr.

Samuel L. Myers, Jr., is the Roy Wilkins Professor of Human Relations and Social Justice at the Humphrey Institute of Public Affairs, University of Minnesota, where he conducts research on racial economic inequality. Dr. Myers has authored numerous technical reports, journal articles, book chapters, essays, and opinion pieces. His books include *The Economics of Race and Crime; Faculty of Color in Academe: Bittersweet Success;* and *The Problem of Racial Economic Inequality: Trends and Prospects.*

Michael T. Nettles is Professor of Education at the University of Michigan. His research focuses on educational access, opportunity, and attainment for various population groups in America, state and national assessment, educational funding policies, and testing of students at all levels. Among his most recent publications are *Equity and Excellence in Educational Testing and Assessment* and *The Emerging National Policy Agenda on Higher Education Assessment: A Wake-up Call of Higher Education Researchers and Scholars.* Dr. Nettles is the first Executive Director of the Fredrick D. Patterson Research Institute of the United Negro College Fund. In that role he published the three-volume *African American Education Data Book* series and *Two Decades of Progress.*

Gary Orfield is Professor of Education and Social Policy at Harvard University and Director of the Harvard Project on School Desegregation. Dr. Orfield's research centers on civil rights, urban policy, and minority opportunity. Additional research areas include changing patterns of job opportunity, financial aid and college access, and civil rights enforcement in higher education. He is coauthor of *The Closing Door: Conservative Policy and Black Opportunity* and *Dismantling Desegregation* and coeditor of *Who Chooses? Who Loses: Culture, Institutions and the Unequal Effects of School Choice.*

Reuel R. Rogers is Assistant Professor of Political Science at Northwestern University. He recently completed his Ph.D. at Princeton University. His primary research interests are race, ethnicity, immigration, urban politics, and African American politics. He is author of "Black Like Who? Afro-Caribbean Immigrants, African Americans, and the Politics of Group Identity," in *Islands in the City: West Indian Migration to New York.* He has been a dissertation fellow with the Social Science Research Council and the Ford Foundation.

Joseph Stewart, Jr., is Professor of Political Science at the University of New Mexico. He has published works on civil rights policies and racial and ethnic politics in a variety of outlets. Three of his books have received a Gustavus Myers Award for "Outstanding Book on the Subject of Human Rights in the United States." His most recent books are *Can We All Get Along? Racial and Ethnic Minorities in American Politics,* coauthored with Paula D. McClain, and *Public Policy: An Evolutionary Approach,* coauthored with James P. Lester.

M. Belinda Tucker is Professor of Psychiatry and Biobehavioral Sciences at the University of California, Los Angeles, and a social psychologist. She has authored numerous articles on marriage and personal relationships and is coeditor of *The Decline in Marriage Among African Americans: Causes, Consequences and Policy Implications.* Dr. Tucker has directed landmark studies such as the National Women's Drug Abuse Project, the National Survey of Black Americans, and the Jamaica AIDS Project.

Chapter 1

Introduction and Overview

by James S. Jackson

Director, Research Center for Group Dynamics and Program for Research on Black Americans, Institute for Social Research, Center for Afroamerican and African Studies, and Daniel Katz Distinguished University Professor of Psychology, University of Michigan

INTRODUCTION

What will America look like in the 21st century? Who will be the "new" Americans? One aspect of this new look is certain: the United States will look dramatically different than at any time in its history. Large waves of immigration at the beginning of the 20th century transformed the United States. Immigration laws, public sentiment, and historical circumstances mainly limited that influx to White Europeans. However, the nation in the 21st century will reflect the presence of individuals from all regions of the earth. It is the nature and effects of the ever-growing race and ethnic diversity of the U.S. population that need to be addressed and understood today if the country is to realize a harmonious, productive future.

This chapter summarizes the perspectives and findings of a jointly sponsored project of the National Policy Association (NPA) and the Program for Research on Black Americans (PRBA) of the University of Michigan. Since 1996, NPA and PRBA have been working on an empirically based study, *New Directions: African Americans in a Diversifying Nation*, that analyzes the changes in the social and economic status of African Americans in the past four decades and in the relationship between Blacks and Whites in America. Highlights of racial issues, important junctures, and trends are presented in this chapter, with a view toward illuminating a more positive future.

The study has several major purposes. The first is to contribute to an understanding of the current and future individual and collective relationships of African Americans in a vastly different, multiracial country in the 21st century. The second purpose is to analyze the policies and strategies that have played a role in improving the status of African Americans. Third, the study aims to develop strategies and policies that address the challenges

ACKNOWLEDGMENTS
I would like to thank the 13 authors and coauthors of the chapters of this volume, *New Directions: African Americans in a Diversifying Nation*, whose work provided important material for the "Introduction and Overview." They are cited in the text as appropriate. I would also like to thank Nicholas A. Jones, Doctoral Candidate, Department of Sociology, University of Michigan, whose work also served as the basis of the current chapter. He is coauthor of the article, "New Directions in Thinking about Race in America: African Americans in a Diversifying Nation" (published in the National Policy Association's journal *Looking Ahead*, Vol. XX, No. 3, October 1998).

facing African Americans in a greatly transformed and ethnically and racially diversified America. The final purpose is to disseminate these findings to thought leaders, policymakers, and the public.

RACE IN AMERICA: THE PAST AND THE PRESENT

The history of the United States reflects a difficult struggle in defining who is and who is not to be included as part of the nation. This search continues to be arduous and, at times, contentious. For better or worse, race has been one of the most significant factors in U.S. history. Its importance is reflected in doctrines, laws, policies, ideologies, relationships, and daily lives. The legacy of the prominence of race in society is illustrated by the substantial racial inequalities that still plague the country (Fix and Turner, 1999).

Historical Disparities

What were the circumstances that characterized past differentials between Blacks and Whites in a historically largely dichotomous, polarized society? It is important to understand the context in which this question is raised: the racial and ethnic realities of the previous four decades.

Race relations between Blacks and Whites in America can be characterized in caste-like terms (Bell, 1993). The outcome of chattel slavery of the 17th, 18th, and 19th centuries was complete racial stratification. Whites of all ethnicities and immigrant status were at the top of the social and economic hierarchy, and Blacks were at the bottom. Large income gaps, differential earnings, employment and residential segregation, and separate schools and other public facilities characterized the Black-White situation in the period leading up to World War II. That period also included restrictive voting laws for Blacks, overt de jure and Jim Crow discrimination, high Black infant mortality, and low Black life expectancy (Frey, 1998; Franklin, 1997; Myrdal, 1944).

At the beginning of World War II, 90 percent of the Black population lived in poverty (Farley, 1996). U.S. economic growth from 1940 through the early 1970s had a profound influence on the economic prosperity of both Blacks and Whites. Inexpensive land, housing policies, the G.I. Bill, and related government policies and programs produced a favorable climate for large growth of the White middle class. According to Farley (Chapter 2, this volume), by 1970, approximately 70 percent of the White population could be classified as middle class. However, Farley also documents that even though the same policies and trends substantially reduced poverty among Blacks, the majority of African Americans have never been members of the middle economic class at any time in U.S. history. Race relations in America's past can be summarized as dealing with "America's dilemma" of the "Negro problem" (Myrdal, 1944). Established economically, politically, and socially as oppositional groups, Blacks and Whites existed in separate worlds (Farley, 1996).

America's Growing Diversity

Until about 40 years ago, the United States was essentially a Black-White country. Today, America is composed of people from all racial and ethnic backgrounds and nationalities. Two main factors have affected the growing diversity of America. The first is immigration. During the 1980s, 8.3 million legal immigrants, mostly from Asia and Latin America, entered the country. Another 4.3 million immigrated between 1990 and 1994. Figure 2-1 in Chapter 2 presents the changes in the racial composition of the United States during the past 60 years (Farley).

The second factor is the slowing birth rates of the two historically dominant racial groups in society, Blacks and Whites. There is consensus that Hispanics will replace African Americans as the single largest non-White minority group in the United States prior to 2010 (Farley; Harrison, 1998). By 2020, about one-third of the residents of the United States are expected to be Asian, Black, Latino, and Native American. However, these broad distinctions do not reflect the layers of complexity that will exist in a multicultural society (U.S. Bureau of the Census, 1996, 1997). Within each panethnic group are vast differences in language, religion, history, culture, and economic status. Thus, we must consider not only the variety of the groups that are emerging, but also the range of differences within them.

As a result of the broadening of the racial and ethnic makeup beyond Black-White in the last half of the 20th century, America faces, and will face even more in the future, many new issues. A Black-White framing of race and ethnicity will clearly no longer address issues of incorporation, democratic participation, economic equality, opportunity, and equity among groups and individuals (Hochschild and Rogers, Chapter 3, this volume).

Hochschild and Rogers note that the geographic areas where immigrants account for most of the demographic change will become increasingly multicultural, younger, and more bifurcated in their race and class structures. Other parts of the country, whose growth is more dependent on internal migration flows, will be far less multicultural in demographic makeup and will also differ in social and political dimensions. If Blacks continue to be concentrated in areas such as the South that historically have been poor, they will continue to live in poverty. Further, because the southern states are not heavily populated by other ethnicities, Blacks may not experience to the same extent as those groups changes in education (learning about other cultures), intermarriage (altering the face of ethnicity), social and job interactions, and other exposures that contribute to increasingly diverse life circumstances.

Continuing Disparities

Few doubt the total domination and exploitation of Blacks prior to the 20th century. However, Farley suggests that strong differences exist in academic circles concerning the nature of contemporary life for African Americans. One group within the current public debate about race holds that while some improvement has occurred, residential segregation and employment and housing discrimination continue to define racial inequalities (Yinger, 1995; Massey and Denton, 1993; Bobo, 1997). Another group of scholars contend that a great deal has changed and that race is no longer the main factor in determining life circumstances. They point to the narrowing of Black-White gaps on certain status outcomes and the growing variation in, for example, income and educational attainment within the Black population as indicators (Thernstrom and Thernstrom, 1997; Hernstein and Murray, 1994).

As noted above, the past institutionalized, unfair treatment of Blacks is widely accepted. But what are the circumstances that characterize current differentials between Blacks and Whites as the nation begins to experience unparalleled increases in racial and ethnic diversity along with unparalleled economic growth? Again, the context in which this question is raised should be clarified. Race relations have evolved from the tremendous social changes of the Civil Rights movement (Bell, 1993; Clark, 1993). That period was the most dramatic social revolution in the country's history. It witnessed the Supreme Court decision, *Brown* v. *Board of Education of Topeka* (1954), adoption of the Civil Rights Act of 1964 and the Voting Rights Act a year later, passage of a number of social policies often described as the "Great Society" programs, and development of affirmative action policies and programs. The period also witnessed dramatic progress by African Americans in the political arena as their voting levels increased and the number of elective offices they held soared (McClain and Stewart, Chapter 8, this volume). Nevertheless, many question whether the overall progress during those years was too little, given the anticipated potential of the era.

Key economic and social indicators reveal the magnitude of racial disparities existent throughout the nation. Demographic trends, income, education, and health factors, family structure, and political participation illustrate the enormous differences in life circumstances for Blacks and Whites. The chapters in this book analyze these and other indicators in depth; several fundamental areas are highlighted next.

Economic Conditions

Racial and ethnic groups in the United States show a consistent hierarchal ranking on crucial indicators of school enrollment, educational attainment, employment, occupational achievement, and earnings (Farley). Whites and native-born Asians are consistently at the top, while American Indians and Blacks rank at the bottom.

Employment opportunities have increased for minorities because of affirmative action mandates and equal employment opportunity laws, but informal segregation/discrimination has not disappeared. Increases in employers' demands for skills (Holzer, 1996) and a continuing gap in Black-White educational attainment (Nettles and Orfield, Chapter 5, this volume) contribute to racial differences in the labor market. Farley finds that the Black-White gap in unemployment was as large in the early 1990s as it was in 1970. Among women, the gap was even wider in the 1990s than in the past.

Figure 2-10 in Chapter 2 shows the average annual unemployment rates of Black and White men and women age 20 and over between 1960-99 (Farley). Throughout the economic upturn of the 1980s and 1990s, the unemployment rates of both Blacks and Whites decreased, leaving no convergence in the racial unemployment gap. There is little evidence of an improvement in the economic status of Black men and women since the Civil Rights period of the 1960s and early 1970s (Darity and Myers, Chapter 4, this volume).

Relative gains occurred in the median income of Blacks in the three decades after World War II, followed by a period of relative stagnation. Even though Black median family income increased from 1990 to 1998 compared with that of Whites, the Black-White gap in median family income in 2010 will be about the same as it was in the mid-1960s without a concerted effort to reduce this disparity (Farley).

These findings raise a major question: Are Blacks uniquely disadvantaged compared with other groups? In terms of household income, Farley finds that households headed by native-born Asians have the highest incomes, while Black and Native American households have the lowest. As Figure 2-14 in Chapter 2 demonstrates, in 1990, households headed by native-born Asians had incomes approximately 25 percent above those of Whites (Farley). Households headed by Blacks and Native Americans had about 35 percent less income than White households. In fact, Darity and Myers calculate that, based on an extrapolation of the rate of progress from 1970 to 1996, it would take 13 generations, or 300 years, for the gap in Black-White earnings to close.

Family Conditions

As noted by Tucker (Chapter 7, this volume), changes in the African American family over the past 40 years have played an enormous role in the lack of economic progress of Blacks (Austin, 1996; Franklin, 1997). The presence of single family households has greatly contributed to the poverty that strangles many Black communities (Huston, 1991; Maynard, 1997; Wilson, 1996). The demise of the family as an important social and financial institution has placed difficult burdens on other Black institutions such as the Black church, the oldest and probably most successful Black institution in the country (Lincoln and Mamiya, 1990). The stressors on Black family and community life, combined with the data on rates of incarceration (Hawkins and Herring, Chapter 9, this volume; Miller, 1996), have made it difficult for families to be formed and maintained (Tucker) and for material wealth to be accumulated within families and across generations (Darity and Myers).

Education Conditions

Integrated schools were mandated in the early 1970s, but racial disparities in test scores, achievement, and educational attainment persist (Nettles and Orfield). Today, there are numerous examples of these indicators of "differential schooling" between the haves and the have-nots. But it is even more striking that these disparities often fall along the color line (U.S. Department of Education, 1991).

Figure 2-8 in Chapter 2 presents the percentage of young Blacks and Whites age 18 to 24 who graduated from high school (receiving a diploma or high school equivalency—GED) between 1968 and 1997 (Farley). There has been racial progress, as seen in the relatively consistent decline in the Black-White gap in high school attainment rates. Farley reports that in the late 1960s, the ratio of Black to White receipt of high school diplomas for men was about 70 percent, but by the early 1990s it had increased to above 90 percent. The racial gap was even smaller among women. The trend toward a Black-White convergence in education through high school has continued over the long term.

College enrollment rates show a somewhat wider racial and gender gap. As demonstrated in Figure 2-9 in Chapter 2, the college enrollment rate of White male high school graduates steadily increased from 1980 to 1997, after declining in the 1970s. In the mid-1970s, there was close to racial parity in the college enrollment levels of men. However, no fall-off occurred in the 30 percent enrollment rate of Black men during the 1980-97 period, and their share attending college has been about 78 percent that of White men (Farley). Among women, record high numbers of both races attended college in the 1990s. For a short time in the 1970s, more Black high school graduates than their White counterparts were enrolled in college. But enrollment rates for White women began to grow more rapidly than the rates of Black women in the late 1970s, and the proportion of Black female high school graduates attending college in the past two decades has been about 85 percent that of White women (Farley).

Health Conditions

A major indicator of health is the mortality rate of populations (LaVeist, Chapter 6, this volume). Death rates are higher for Blacks than Whites at almost every age group until extreme old age (National Center, 1996). The death rate used as the key index of the nation's health is the infant mortality rate (the number of infants who die before their first birthday per 1,000 live births in a year). Recent public health efforts and developments in neonatal care have been directed at reducing infant deaths. These efforts have largely succeeded, and the infant death rate has steadily declined (see Figure 2-4 in Chapter 2). By 1997, record high numbers of Black and White babies were living beyond their first birthdays.

However, LaVeist notes that a salient feature of Black-White differentials in health is the higher Black infant mortality rate. Even though the death rates of Black and White babies have been decreasing, the deaths have occurred in a parallel fashion, so that the rate of Black deaths during the first year of life is more than double that of White deaths (Farley). The Black-White gap in infant mortality was as great in the early 1990s as it was in the early 1970s, and it is unlikely to decrease in future years without significant intervention.

Despite the investment of a large share of the U.S. gross national product (GNP) in health care, the United States has relatively high mortality rates compared with other developed countries (LaVeist). The life span in Japan is about three years longer than that of Whites in the United States, and the life span in Sweden and Canada is two years longer. Death rates in the United States are generally low compared with those in eastern Europe and developing countries. The infant mortality rate of Whites in the United States is similar to rates in some western European nations, but it is higher than rates in other countries, including Japan and Sweden (Farley).

The most striking statistics in the comparison of death rates internationally pertain to the ranking of African Americans. Black life expectancy is lower in the United States than life expectancy in any developed country, and Black infant mortality is the highest in a ranking of 25 developed and developing countries presented in Table 6-5 in Chapter 6 (LaVeist). A Black baby born in the United States is less likely to survive the first year of life than a baby born in Cuba, Chile, Bulgaria, or Poland.

Social Conditions

Residential segregation plays a major role in defining inequality in White and Black home ownership. Housing discrimination denies Blacks access to the economic benefits of home ownership in terms of resale value and wealth (Oliver and Shapiro, 1995). Home ownership not only increases wealth, but it also is of social and psychological value to families and individuals.

A number of reports document that while opportunities for Blacks to purchase homes are now more equal than they were in the past, audit investigations continue to demonstrate that potential Black buyers are shown fewer homes and in Black or only moderately integrated neighborhoods. They are also given less information about financing than Whites (Farley; Darity and Myers). In the late 1980s, Blacks applying for federal mortgages in Boston were refused more often than were White applicants of similar backgrounds (Munnell et al., 1992; Yinger, 1995).

In 1944, Myrdal detailed the harmful effects of racial residential segregation for Blacks. Blacks lacked access to the schools, parks, and facilities that were available to Whites, and White officials offered second-class services to Blacks without altering the level of services to Whites. According to Massey and Denton (1993), a system of extremely high residential segregation provides the major infrastructure for continuing Black-White racial stratification; it also limits education and employment chances for Blacks. Residential segregation contributes to a ghetto culture that is dysfunctional in the larger achievement-oriented society (Ogbu, 1978; Wilson, 1987).

Black neighborhoods are different from those of other minority groups and Whites. Figure 2-15 in Chapter 2 presents the racial composition of the typical neighborhoods of Blacks, Whites, Asians, and Hispanics in the 318 metropolitan areas defined for the 1990 census (Farley). Asians live in neighborhoods where more than 50 percent of the population is non-Hispanic

White, while Hispanics live in neighborhoods with about 40 percent White residents. However, Black neighborhoods have a relatively small White population.

Overall, White neighborhoods have better schools and city services, safer streets, and more effective political power than Black neighborhoods (Massey and Denton, 1993; Morenoff and Sampson, 1997; Kozol, 1991). Thus, Hispanics and Asians have greater potential for educational and social interaction with their prosperous White neighbors than Blacks (Farley).

CONCLUSION

In looking to the future, it is important to acknowledge that the United States has not been successful in addressing the issues of racial and ethnic incorporation, even framed simply in Black-White terms. While the circumstances of African Americans and the nature of Black-White relationships at the end of the 20th century were certainly better than during the periods of slavery, Reconstruction, Jim Crow, or pre-Civil Rights, there is much room for improvement (Clayton, 1996; Jaynes and Williams, 1989; Myrdal, 1944). How should America address the new problems that are sure to arise in an ethnically and racially diverse future? On the one hand, the country cannot continue to employ the strategies and policies utilized in the past and present, nor can it depend on the same narrow conceptualizations and thinking. On the other hand, the United States cannot be lulled into believing that the answers will materialize on their own. The positions of all people in a greatly diversifying nation need to be considered in attempting to achieve the harmonious multiracial, civil society envisioned in this volume.

A new national consensus is needed to build a coalition of groups in a uniquely ethnically and racially diversified America. Unlike the consensus of the 1960s that coalesced around the fundamental rights of citizenship (Smith, 1997), the consensus that is required in the 21st century must build on the democratic ideals of full participation, hard work, justice, and an abiding commitment to providing equal opportunity for all. It is this author's hope that the observations and conclusions of the authors in the following chapter will contribute to the development of this new consensus.

REFERENCES

Austin, R.W. Ed. 1996. *Repairing the Breach*. Dillon, Col.: Alpine Guild, Inc.

Bell, D. 1993. "Remembrances Past: Getting Beyond the Civil Rights Decline." In *Race in America: The Struggle for Equality*. Ed. H. Hill and J.E. Jones, Jr. Madison: University of Wisconsin Press, 73-82.

Bobo, L.D. 1997. "The Color Line, the Dilemma, and the Dream." In *Civil Rights and Social Wrongs*. Ed. J. Higham. University Park, Penn.: Pennsylvania State University Press, 31-55.

Brown v. *Board of Education of Topeka*. 1954. 347 U.S. 483.

Clark, K.B. 1993. "Racial Progress and Retreat: A Personal Memoir." In *Race in America: The Struggle for Equality.* Ed. H. Hill and J.E. Jones, Jr. Madison: University of Wisconsin Press, 3-18.

Clayton, O., Jr. Ed. 1996. *An American Dilemma Revisited: Race Relations in a Changing World.* New York: Russell Sage Foundation.

Darity, W.A., Jr., and S.L. Myers, Jr. 2000. "Languishing in Inequality: Racial Disparities in Wealth and Earnings in the New Millennium." In *New Directions: African Americans in a Diversifying Nation.* Ed. J.S. Jackson. Washington, D.C.: National Policy Association (NPA), Chap. 4.

Farley, R. 1996. *The New American Reality.* New York: Russell Sage Foundation.
———. 2000. "Demographic, Economic, and Social Trends in a Multicultural America." In *New Directions: African Americans in a Diversifying Nation.* Ed. J.S. Jackson. Washington, D.C.: NPA, Chap. 2.

Fix, M., and M.A. Turner, Eds. 1999. *A National Report Card on Discrimination in America: The Role of Testing.* Washington, D.C.: Urban Institute Press.

Franklin, D.L. 1997. *Ensuring Inequality: The Structural Transformation of the African American Family.* New York: Oxford University Press.

Frey, W.H. 1998. *Black Movement to the South and Regional Concentration of the Races.* Population Studies Center Research Report No. 98-412. Ann Arbor: University of Michigan, Population Studies Center.

Harrison, R. 1998. *What the Social Sciences Know about Race and Race Relations.* Paper presented at the American Sociological Association Conference on Race and Ethnicity in Washington, D.C.

Harrison, R.J., and C.E. Bennett. 1995. "Racial and Ethnic Diversity." In *State of the Union: America in the 1990s.* Ed. R. Farley. New York: Russell Sage Foundation.

Hawkins, D.F., and C. Herring. 2000. "Race, Crime, and Punishment: Old Controversies and New Challenges." In *New Directions: African Americans in a Diversifying Nation.* Ed. J.S. Jackson. Washington, D.C.: NPA, Chap. 9.

Hernstein, R.J., and C. Murray. 1994. *The Bell Curve: Intelligence and Class Structure in American Life.* New York: Free Press.

Hochschild, J.L., and R.R. Rogers. 2000. "Race Relations in a Diversifying Nation." In *New Directions: African Americans in a Diversifying Nation.* Ed. J.S. Jackson. Washington, D.C.: NPA, Chap. 3.

Holzer, H.J. 1996. *What Employers Want: Job Prospects for Less-Educated Workers.* New York: Russell Sage Foundation.

Huston, A. Ed. 1991. *Children in Poverty.* New York: Cambridge University Press.

Jaynes, G.D., and R.M. Williams, Jr. 1989. *A Common Destiny: Blacks and American Society.* Washington, D.C.: National Research Council.

Kozol, J. 1991. *Savage Inequalities.* New York: Crown Publishers, Inc.

LaVeist, T.A. 2000. "African Americans and Health Policy: Strategies for a Multiethnic Society." In *New Directions: African Americans in a Diversifying Nation.* Ed. J.S. Jackson. Washington, D.C.: NPA, Chap. 6.

Lincoln, C.E., and Mamiya, L.H. 1990. *The Black Church in the African American Experience.* Durham, N.C.: Duke University Press.

Massey, D., and N.A. Denton. 1993. *American Apartheid: Segregation and the Making of the Underclass.* Cambridge, Mass.: Harvard University Press.

Maynard, R.A. 1997. *Kids Having Kids: Economic Costs and Social Consequences of Teen Pregnancy.* Washington, D.C.: Urban Institute Press.

McClain, P.D., and J. Stewart, Jr. 2000. "An Overview of Black American Politics and Political Participation Since the Civil Rights Movement." In *New Directions: African Americans in a Diversifying Nation.* Ed. J.S. Jackson Washington, D.C.: NPA, Chap. 8.

Miller, J.G. 1996. *Search and Destroy: African American Males in the Criminal Justice System.* New York: Cambridge University Press.

Morenoff, J.D., and R.J. Sampson. 1997. "Violent Crime and the Spatial Dynamics of Neighborhood Transition: Chicago, 1970-1990." *Social Forces* 76:31-64.

Munnell, A., L.E. Browne, J. McEneaney, and G.M.B. Tootel. 1992. *Mortgage Lending in Boston: Interpreting HMDA Data.* Working Paper 92-7. Boston: Federal Reserve Bank of Boston.

Myrdal, G. 1944. *An American Dilemma: The Negro Problem and Modern Democracy.* New York: Harper and Row.

National Center for Health Statistics. 1996. *Monthly Vital Statistics Report* 44(7). Supplement February 29. Washington, D.C.: Government Printing Office (GPO).

Nettles, M.T., and G. Orfield. 2000. "Large Gains, Recent Reversals, and Continuing Inequality in Education for African Americans." In *New Directions: African Americans in a Diversifying Nation.* Ed. J.S. Jackson. Washington, D.C.: NPA, Chap. 5.

Ogbu, J. 1978. *Minority Education and Caste: The American System in Cross-Cultural Perspective.* New York: Academic Press.

Oliver, M.L., and T.M. Shapiro. 1995. *Black Wealth/White Wealth: A New Perspective on Racial Inequality.* New York: Routledge.

Patterson, O. 1997. *The Ordeal of Integration: Progress and Resentment in America's "Racial" Crisis.* Washington, D.C.: Civitas Counterpoint.

Smith, R.M. 1997. *Civic Ideals.* New Haven, Ct.: Yale University Press.

Thernstrom, S., and A. Thernstrom. 1997. *America in Black and White: One Nation, Indivisible.* New York: Simon & Schuster.

Tucker, M.B. 2000. "Considerations in the Development of Family Policy for African Americans." In *New Directions: African Americans in a Diversifying Nation.* Ed. J.S. Jackson. Washington, D.C.: NPA, Chap. 7.

U.S. Bureau of the Census. 1996. *Current Population Reports.* Series P60-193. Washington, D.C.: GPO.

———. 1997. *Current Population Reports.* Series P60, No. 198. Washington, D.C.: GPO.

U.S. Department of Education. 1991. *Digest of Education Statistics.* Washington, D.C.: GPO.

Wilson, W.J. 1987. *The Truly Disadvantaged: The Inner City, the Underclass, and Public Policy.* Chicago: University of Chicago Press.

———. 1996. *When Work Disappears: The World of the New Urban Poor.* New York: Alfred A. Knopf.

Yinger, J. 1995. *Closed Doors, Opportunities Lost: The Continuing Costs of Housing Discrimination.* New York: Russell Sage Foundation.

Chapter 2

Demographic, Economic, and Social Trends in a Multicultural America

by Reynolds Farley

Research Scientist and Professor,
Institute for Social Research, University of Michigan

INTRODUCTION

In June 1997, reports of waning support for school desegregation among African Americans in general and members of the National Association for the Advancement of Colored People (NAACP) in particular attracted much attention and shocked more than a few observers (Holmes, 1997). Since its founding in 1909, the NAACP had been a leading proponent of integration and was instrumental in the successful effort to have state-mandated school segregation declared unconstitutional. Although the NAACP later officially reconfirmed its support for integration, the controversy is indicative of growing Black disillusionment with the slow progress on racial issues. This disillusionment, also apparent in events surrounding the Rodney King beating and the O.J. Simpson trial as well as in the proceedings of President Bill Clinton's "Initiative on Race," reflects a common belief that the race problem is not going away (Hochschild, 1995).

As public debate about racial issues continues, a parallel discussion has been ongoing in academic circles. One side forcefully asserts that little has changed. It acknowledges some improvement in the living standards of African Americans, but maintains that persistent residential segregation, employment discrimination, and differences in economic standing show that racial inequality persists at extreme levels (Hacker, 1992; Massey and Denton, 1993; Yinger, 1995; Bobo, 1997). The other side argues that much has changed. It stresses the narrowing of Black-White gaps on selected outcomes and the increasing economic variation within the Black population as evidence that race is no longer the principal determinant of life chances (Thernstrom and Thernstrom, 1997).

The aim of this chapter is to shed light on this controversy by assessing what has changed and what has remained the same regarding racial differences in the United States. The focus is on several key indicators gathered in decennial censuses and other large surveys. Although primary attention is given to Black-White comparisons, America's increasing racial diversity necessitates the inclusion of Asian Americans, Hispanics, and American Indians where data and space permit. In examining racial trends, the analysis extends the author's earlier work (Farley, 1996, 1997). Federal statistics data allow a comparison of Blacks and Whites over a long time span, but describe other minorities for a brief span.

11

RACIAL COMPOSITION AND DEMOGRAPHIC CHARACTERISTICS

Figure 2-1 shows the racial composition of the United States over almost a 60-year span. In 1940 and again in 1960, America was primarily a Black-White country. That is no longer a valid characterization. During the past decade, the nation experienced a period of slow population growth for Blacks and Whites and very rapid growth for Asians and Latinos, resulting in a major change in racial composition. In the 1990s, the non-Hispanic White population—with its older age composition and below replacement-level birth rates—grew just 4 percent, and the non-Hispanic Black population increased only 14 percent. But the number of Hispanics grew by 42 percent, and the heterogeneous Asian population increased by 48 percent. Within the first decade of the 21st century, Hispanics will outnumber Blacks. The numerically dominant White population will decline in relative size, although it is far from certain that non-Hispanic Whites will ever become a minority group. The census of 2000 will not only provide new information about the nation's diverse composition, but it will also trigger much rethinking of how people classify themselves and others by race because it is the first

FIGURE 2-1

Population of the United States by Race, 1940-99

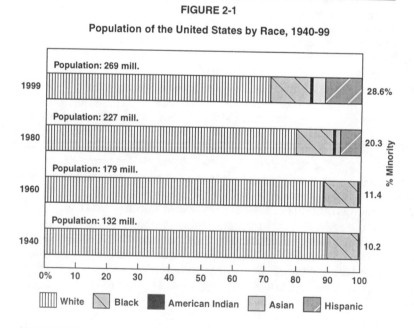

Note: Hispanics were not separately identified before the 1970 Census. Data for racial groups in 1980 and 1999 refer to non-Hispanics.

Source: U.S. Bureau of the Census (1940, 1960, 1997a, 1999a).

TABLE 2-1

Total Fertility Rates by Race, 1997

Race	Lifetime Births per Woman[1]
Hispanic	2.51
Non-Hispanic Black	2.21
American Indian	2.05
Asian	1.93
Non-Hispanic White	1.80

1. The number of children a woman would bear in her lifetime assuming the birth rates of 1997 remained unchanged.

Source: National Center for Health Statistics (1999b).

enumeration providing Americans the opportunity to identify with more than one race.

Age Distributions and Fertility Rates

Population pyramids in Figure 2-2 present age distributions in 1998. Native-born Whites were the oldest population with a lean pyramid and median ages of 35 years for men and 37 years for women, reflecting their recent history of low fertility. Native-born Blacks were a much younger population. The median age of African-American men was 9 years younger than that of White men, and the median age of Black women was 7 years younger than that of White women. Foreign-born Asians and foreign-born Hispanics had the distinctive age pyramids of recent immigrants—wide in the middle—because it is young adults who typically migrate to the United States to obtain an education, to seek better economic opportunities, or to escape political or religious oppression in their homelands. Native-born Asians and native-born Hispanics have unusually young age pyramids because young migrants often marry and start families shortly after arrival. The median age of 15 years for native-born Asians results from the recent immigration of young adults from India, China, and the Philippines.

The age composition of a population strongly influences its future growth rate. The older pyramids of Whites and African-Americans project slow population growth in the future, and the younger pyramids of Asians and Hispanics reveal their momentum for extremely rapid growth.

In addition to immigration, fertility rates explain the dissimilar age pyramids. Table 2-1 reports total fertility rates by race for 1997. The table indicates the number of children a woman would bear in her lifetime if 1997 birth rates remained unchanged (National Center for Health Statistics, 1999a, Tables 3, 8). Racial differences in birth rates are substantial, with Hispanic

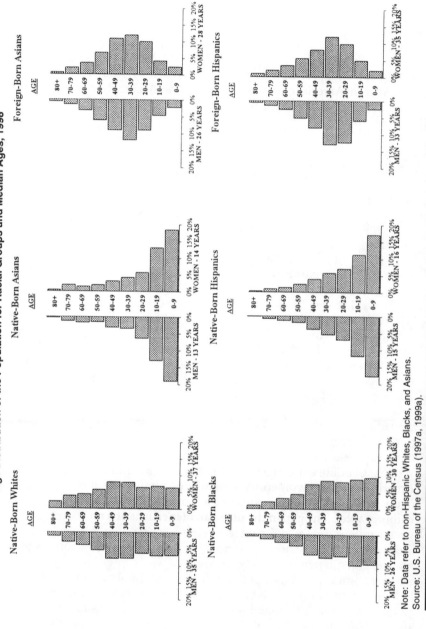

FIGURE 2-2

Age Distribution of the Population for Racial Groups and Median Ages, 1998

Note: Data refer to non-Hispanic Whites, Blacks, and Asians.

Source: U.S. Bureau of the Census (1997a, 1999a).

women now having the largest families and non-Hispanic White women the smallest. Childbearing rates of non-Hispanic Black women have changed from a relatively high fertility rate to one just above replacement level. In the mid-1960s, the African-American total fertility rate was in excess of four births per 1,000 women, but that rate was cut almost in half in the ensuing three decades.

For a population to have a zero growth rate, the total fertility rate for several generations must average about 2.1 births per woman. The 1997 fertility rates suggest slow population growth for Whites, American Indians, and African Americans, and eventually for Asians, but rapid growth for Hispanics. These rates also imply that childbearing differences will stimulate the growth of minority populations vis-à-vis the White population (see Figure 2-1). In 1997, the total fertility rate of African Americans was 23 percent greater, and the Hispanic rate 39 percent higher, than the birth rate of non-Hispanic Whites.

Mortality Rates

Figure 2-3 shows trends in the most frequently used index of mortality—the total number of years an individual could expect to live at birth if he or she experienced the death rates of a given year. Because women live, on average, six years longer than men, data are shown separately by gender. Reliable death rates for Asians, Hispanics, and American Indians are not available for dates in the past, so trend data are shown only for Blacks and Whites.

According to the top panel of Figure 2-3, the life expectancies of White and Black men increased from the end of the Great Depression through the mid-1950s, but had no further gains for about the next 15 years. Thereafter, the male life expectancy resumed its upward march. Indeed, more than 6 years have been added to the life span of White men since 1970, and they can now expect to live 74.3 years, the longest life span ever recorded for males in the United States. Mortality rates for Black men also fell after 1970, but that trend toward improvement slowed in the mid-1980s.

The distance between the two lines in Figure 2-3 indicating the Black-White gap in life expectancy does not show an optimistic trend for African American men or women. A similarly pessimistic pattern will be seen in many of the other comparisons of the status of Blacks and Whites presented in this chapter. The gap in the life span of men was at a minimum in 1961 (5.8 years) and gradually widened thereafter, especially from the mid-1980s on. This widening did not occur because the death rates of Black men increased, which, as just noted, was not the case; rather, the death rates of White men fell more rapidly than those of Black men. Currently, White males can expect to live 7.1 years longer than African-American males.

Between 1940 and 1970, racial change in mortality was much the same among women as among men, with life expectancies increasing for both races. As the bottom panel in Figure 2-3 illustrates, death rates continued to fall for Blacks and Whites, but after 1973 at a slightly faster rate among Black

FIGURE 2-3

Life Expectancies at Birth for Blacks and Whites, 1940-97

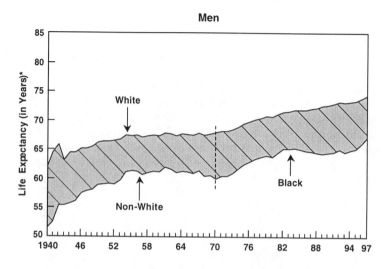

Men

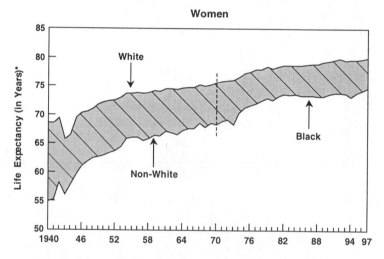

Women

*Life expectancy is the total number of years an individual could expect to live at birth if he or she experienced the death rates of a given year.

Note: Data for years prior to 1970 refer to non-Whites and Whites.

Source: National Center for Health Statistics (2000).

women, leading to a diminishing of the racial gap. Nevertheless, this gap has only modestly closed in the past 30 years. In 1967, the gap in the life span of women was 6.7 years; by 1997, it had dropped only 1.5 years. Men and women of both races now have longer life expectancies than in earlier years, but Black-White differences in length of life have clearly not declined.

The death rate most closely examined as a key indicator of the nation's health is the infant mortality rate—the number of infants who die before their first birthday per 1,000 live births in a year. Numerous recent public health efforts have succeeded in reducing infant deaths. In addition, developments in neonatal care permit the healthy survival of infants who, in the recent past, would have died shortly after birth. The chances of infant survival have also improved because of the increase in the educational attainment of Black and White mothers. The result has been a steadily declining infant death rate, as Figure 2-4 shows.

By 1997, the numbers of Black and White babies dying before their first birthday reached record lows. This is extremely good news. The discourag-

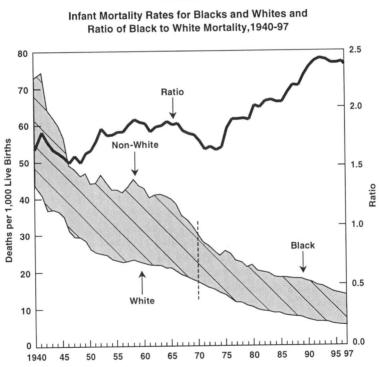

FIGURE 2-4

**Infant Mortality Rates for Blacks and Whites and
Ratio of Black to White Mortality,1940-97**

Note: Data for years prior to 1970 refer to non-Whites and Whites.

Source: National Center for Health Statistics (1984, 1999b).

ing news is that the Black-White gap in infant mortality was just as large in the 1990s as it was in the 1970s; indeed, the ratio of the Black-White infant mortality rate as depicted in Figure 2-4 was higher in 1997 than in 1940. Because the death rates of African American and White infants have been falling in a parallel fashion, Blacks continue to die during their first year of life at a rate more than double that of Whites. The gap in infant mortality will likely decline little in coming years.

How does mortality in the United States compare with other nations? Despite devoting 15 percent of all consumer expenditures to health care in 1998, the United States has relatively high death rates compared with similarly developed countries. Japan, Sweden, Canada, France, and Australia are among the advanced nations that have greater life expectancies at birth than Whites in the United States. In 1998, the expectation of life at birth in Japan was 80 years, 3 years longer than that of Whites in the United States, while in Sweden and Canada, it was 2 years longer. However, compared with death rates in eastern Europe and developing countries, the rates among Whites in the United States are generally low. The infant mortality rate of Whites in the United States—six deaths per 1,000 live births in 1998—compares favorably with the rates of developed countries such as Canada and France. But it is higher than the rates in Japan and Sweden, both with four infant deaths per 1,000 live births (U.S. Bureau of the Census, 1998a).

A comparison of the death rates of African Americans internationally shows startling statistics. The Black life expectancy in the United States of 71 years in 1997 was much lower than rates in other advanced countries—9 years lower than life expectancy in Japan and 8 years lower than that in Canada, Sweden, and France. Black infant mortality—14 deaths per 1,000 live births in 1998—was also higher than the rates in all developed nations and most developing countries, except Sri Lanka (16) and Mexico (26). These facts are especially troubling because some developing nations have gross national products that are only 20 percent of the U.S. GNP. The status of African Americans is well summarized by the fact that a Black baby born in the United States has less chance of reaching his or her first birthday than a newborn in Cuba, Chile, Bulgaria, or Poland.

Marriage and Living Arrangements of Children

African Americans and Whites also differ substantially in terms of the proportion who marry, age at marriage, number of children born to unmarried mothers, and divorce and remarriage rates. As a result, the races have significant differences in family living arrangements. Figure 2-5 shows the percentage of African American and White adults who were married and lived with a spouse in the recent past. Among Whites, this share declined moderately, falling from 68 percent in 1950 to 60 percent in 1998. In contrast, marriage among African Americans rapidly decreased, from 62 percent of Black adults, married spouse present, in 1950 to 36 percent at the end of the 1990s. At the prime adult ages, the differences are quite large. In 1999, 59 percent of White women age 25 to 54 lived with their husbands, whereas only

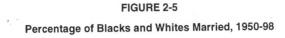

FIGURE 2-5

Percentage of Blacks and Whites Married, 1950-98

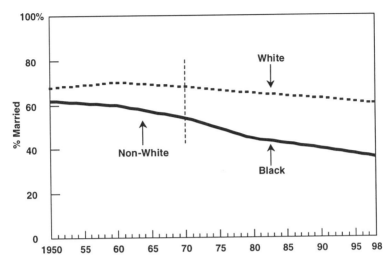

Note: Data after 1969 are for those 15 years old and older. Data for years prior to 1970 are for those 14 years old and older and refer to non-Whites and Whites.

Source: U.S. Bureau of the Census (2000a).

30 percent of African American women had this living arrangement (U.S. Bureau of the Census, 1999a). The Black-White gap in the proportion of adults who are married has steadily widened since the 1950s.

Closely linked to decisions about marriage are the living arrangements of children. Figure 2-6 summarizes the situation for racial groups in 1999. Asian and White children have a substantial advantage over other racial groups on this important social indicator. At the end of the 20th century, 82 percent of both native-born and foreign-born Asian children under age 18 were living with two parents, exceeding the 78 percent of non-Hispanic White children living with both parents. But only 38 percent of Black children resided with two parents in 1999; a higher proportion, 57 percent, lived with only their mothers.

Two parent families typically have greater economic resources for their children than single parent families. Children also benefit in other ways when they grow up with both parents. In comparing children from two parent families with those from single parent families, McLanahan and Sandefur (1994) found that they were less likely to drop out of secondary school, more likely to enroll in college, and less likely to be idle (neither enrolled in school nor working) in their late teens. Daughters from single

FIGURE 2-6

Living Arrangements of Children Under Age 18, 1999

Children Under Age 18

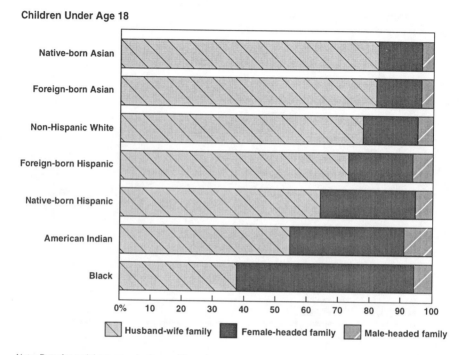

Note: Data for racial groups refer to non-Hispanics.

Source: U.S. Bureau of the Census (1999a).

parent families, net of other factors, were more likely to become teen mothers than were daughters raised in two parent families.

Although declining proportions of African Americans marry, an increasing number marry Whites. Figure 2-7 compares the percentage of Black and White husbands and wives who were married to a spouse of the other race in the period 1960-98. In 1970, three years after the U.S. Supreme Court struck down state laws prohibiting interracial marriages in *Loving* v. *Virginia,* only 1 percent of African American husbands had White wives. That proportion increased rapidly, and by 1998, more than 1 out of 25 Black husbands had White wives. During the 1990s, there was a particularly sharp increase in the percentage of Blacks, including Black women, marrying White spouses.

The growing frequency of Black-White marriages will undoubtedly produce a rapidly increasing number of interracial children. This growth may fundamentally alter the U.S. racial classification system because large

FIGURE 2-7

Frequency of White-Black Marriages, 1960-98

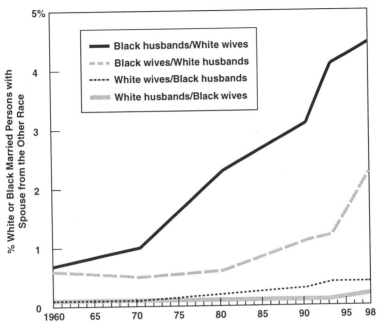

Note: This figure shows the percentage of Black husbands married to White wives and the percentage of White husbands married to Black wives. The number of Black men married to White women equals the number of White women married to Black men. However, the total number of married Black men is much smaller than the total number of married White women. Thus, even though the same individuals are involved, the percentage of Black husbands married to White wives is typically much higher than the percentage of White wives married to Black husbands.

Source: U.S. Bureau of the Census (1999b).

numbers of young people may identify with both races. The innovative racial question on the 2000 census will provide information about these demographic changes. This new trend may, in turn, help to break down the color line because the United States will soon have a large population of mixed or multiracial people. (For further information, see Harrison and Bennett, 1995, . 188-194; Farley, 1999, Figures 5-7, 5-8.)

Racial Stratification in Education and Employment

When key indicators of school enrollment, educational attainment, employment, occupational achievement, and earnings are examined, there is a consistent ranking of racial groups. Whites and native-born Asians are at the top, and African Americans and American Indians are at the bottom. But this is not the full story. Gender makes a large difference in the rankings, and Black women fare at least as well as White women on several important measures of earnings and income.

Figure 2-8 reports the percentage of male and female African Americans and Whites age 18 to 24 who received high school diplomas or General Educational Development (GED, high school equivalency) degrees from 1968 to 1997. In recent years, about 18 percent of all high school graduates obtained a GED rather than a four-year diploma (U.S. Department of Education, 2000). Unlike the trends for life expectancy and infant mortality, there are unambiguous signs of racial progress in this area as the Black-White gap in high school attainment has consistently declined. In the late 1960s, the percentage of Black males earning high school degrees was about 70 percent that of White males, but by the early 1990s, that proportion had risen to above 90 percent. The remaining gap is even smaller among women than among men. While parity has not been attained, the trend toward a Black-White convergence in education through secondary school has continued over the long term.

Different conclusions are drawn from an examination of college enrollment rates. Figure 2-9 reports the percentage of high school graduates age 18 to 24 enrolled in either a two- or four-year college from 1968 to 1997. The enrollment rates of White men spiked in the late 1960s when college offered an alternative to military service in Vietnam. After a long decline, the enrollment rates of White men began to climb in the 1980s, growing by 6 percentage points over the decade, and by the late 1990s they approached the elevated levels of the Vietnam era. For young Black men, there has been little fluctuation in college enrollment since the 1960s, with about 30 percent of Black high school graduates consistently attending college. For a few years in the mid-1970s, there was near racial parity in the college enrollment rates of men, resulting from the push to equalize opportunities for Blacks and few challenges to affirmative action. While the share of African American males enrolled in college did not change in the 1980s, it increased by 5 percentage points in the 1990s compared with a 2 percentage point growth in the rate of White males. The male Black-White ratio was about 78 percent from 1980 to 1997.

Among women, college enrollment rates have steadily risen, and record high proportions of both races pursued postsecondary degrees in the 1990s. For a brief period in the mid-to-late 1970s, a higher percentage of Black female high school graduates than similar White females were enrolled in college. However, in 1979, enrollment rates began to increase more rapidly for White women, rekindling the traditional disadvantage of Blacks on this indicator. Since the early 1980s, the percentage of Black female high school graduates enrolled in college has consistently been about 85 percent that of White females.

Given employers' increasing demand for highly skilled and educated employees (Holzer, 1996) and the persistent, though narrowing Black-White gap in educational attainment, racial disparities also likely exist in the labor

FIGURE 2-8

Percentage of High School or GED Graduates Age 18 to 24 and Ratio of Black to White Graduates, 1968-97
(Three-Year Moving Average)

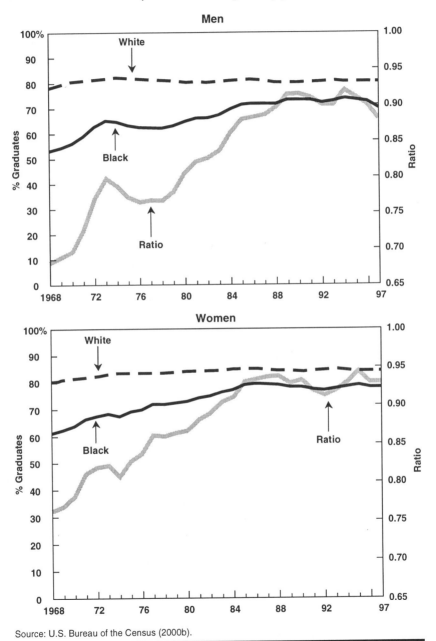

Source: U.S. Bureau of the Census (2000b).

FIGURE 2-9

Percentage of High School Graduates by Gender, Age 18 to 24, Enrolled in a Two- or Four-Year College and Ratio of Black to White, 1968-97

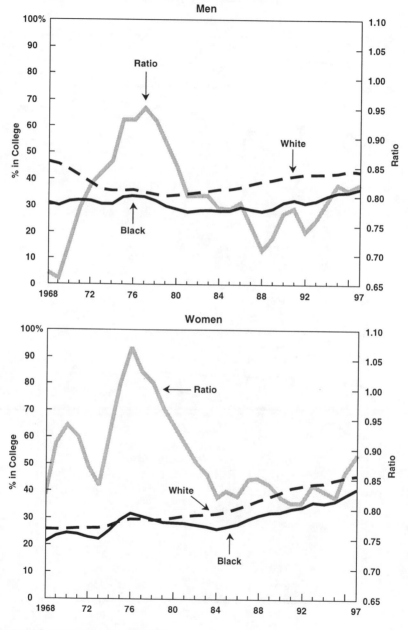

Source: U.S. Bureau of the Census (2000b).

market. An often used summary indicator of these disparities is the unemployment rate, one of the few indicators with reliable data over a long period. The labor force includes adults who had jobs or were looking for them; the unemployment rate indicates the percentage of men and women in the labor force who searched for a job in the past month, but did not find one.

There is both encouraging and discouraging news about African American unemployment rates. Figure 2-10 reports the average annual unemployment rates of Black and White men and women age 20 and older from 1960 to 1999. The Black-White ratio of unemployment rates rose sharply in recessions and plummeted when the business cycle returned to prosperity. For both genders, this ratio declined in the 1960s, a change attributable to the rapid economic expansion of that era and to the beneficial consequences of the Civil Rights Act and other federal efforts to equalize employment opportunities. With the emergence of industrial restructuring in the 1970s, the unemployment rates of African Americans increased faster than those of Whites (Wilson, 1987, 1996). Throughout the prosperous 1980s and especially in the even more prosperous 1990s, Black unemployment rates sank to low levels. But because the rates of Whites also decreased, there was no convergence in the racial unemployment gap. In most of those years, Blacks in the labor force were almost twice as likely as Whites to be unsuccessful in their search for a job.

Prosperity and Poverty

Numerous factors influence whether people are prosperous or impoverished, including family origin, investment in education, and employment status. As shown in this chapter, Blacks more often than Whites live in families headed by women, are not as likely as Whites to enroll in college, and are much more likely to be unable to find jobs. Taking these facts into account, how do African Americans rank in overall economic standing? The first trends examined compare Blacks to Whites because much of the nation's history involves these two races. Then the nation's major minority groups—African Americans, Asians, and Hispanics, as well as American Indians—are compared with Whites in 1990 and 1998.

Poverty was an area of policy concern throughout the 20th century, but there was no systematic attempt to measure it until President Lyndon B. Johnson declared a War on Poverty in 1964 (Katz, 1986; Trattner, 1989). Lacking an official measure, Mollie Orshansky of the Social Security Administration used U.S. Department of Agriculture estimates of minimally adequate food budgets for households of different sizes in the late 1950s and multiplied those food costs by three to determine an appropriate poverty line. Food costs, in other words, were assumed to account for one-third of household expenditures. That poverty number was used for three decades with annual adjustments for inflation, but not for changes in consumers' needs or actual purchases. In 1959, the U.S. Bureau of the Census developed estimates of the prevalence of poverty and since 1966 has estimated poverty rates each year. This rate has become a widely accepted and frequently cited

FIGURE 2-10

Average Annual Unemployment Rates of White and Black Men and Women Age 20 and Older and Ratio of Black to White Unemployment Rates, 1960-99

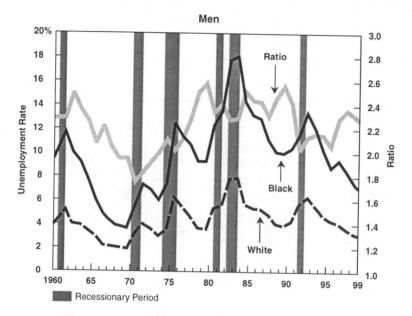

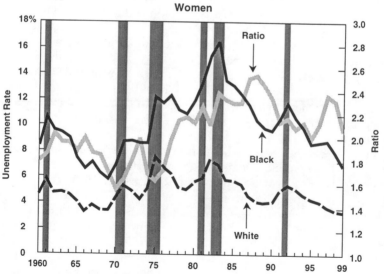

Note: Unemployment rates for years prior to 1972 refer to Whites and non-Whites.

Source: Council of Economic Advisers (2000).

index of the nation's economic status. By making assumptions about rates of inflation and using data from earlier censuses, poverty rates can be estimated beginning at the end of the Great Depression.

Comparing the Economic Status of Blacks and Whites

Figure 2-11 shows the distribution of African American and White populations by their poverty or prosperity status for six decades. In 1999, the

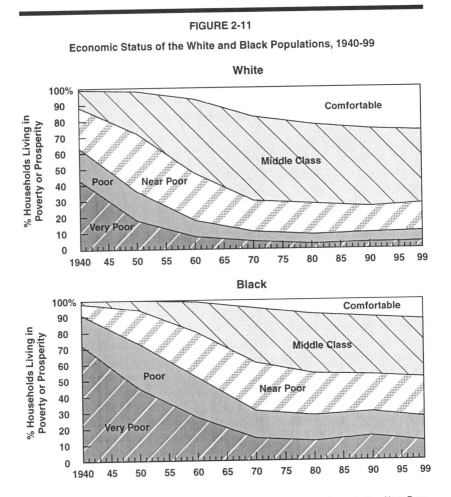

FIGURE 2-11

Economic Status of the White and Black Populations, 1940-99

Note: **Very Poor,** below 50 percent of poverty line; **Poor,** 50 to 99 percent of poverty line; **Near Poor,** 100 to 199 percent of poverty line; **Middle Class,** 200 to 499 percent of poverty line; **Comfortable,** 500 percent or more of poverty line.

Sources: U.S. Bureau of the Census (2000c); Farley (1996), Fig. 6-17.

poverty line for a household of four was $17,184 (U.S. Bureau of the Census, 2000c). Those classified as "very poor" live in households with cash incomes of less than one-half the poverty line (or a pretax cash income of under $8,600 for a household of four in 1999). The "poor" population equals the percentage of persons in households with cash incomes 50 percent to 99 percent of the poverty line, while those with incomes 100 percent to 199 percent of the poverty line are identified as "near poor." The "middle class" includes households with incomes two to five times the poverty line, and the economically "comfortable" live in households with incomes five or more times the poverty line.

At the outset of World War II, 91 percent of the African American population were impoverished, that is, very poor and poor, as were 63 percent of the White population. The tremendous economic growth that the United States experienced from 1940 until the energy crisis of 1973 radically changed that situation. Because of the beneficial economic trends and highly favorable government programs, including the GI Bill to educate veterans and housing policies that allowed Whites to invade and conquer the "crabgrass frontier" (Jackson, 1985), 70 percent of Whites could be termed economically middle class or comfortable in 1970. While the trends also substantially lessened the poverty rates of African Americans, only 40 percent of Blacks were in the middle class or comfortable in 1970. There has never been a period when the majority of Blacks were members of America's middle economic class. Throughout the country's history, more than one-half of all African Americans have lived in impoverished or near poor households.

Between 1973, when many employers began to restructure their labor forces, and the early 1990s, the story is much the same for Blacks and Whites—the growth of the middle economic class virtually stopped. Poverty did not greatly increase; rather, the era ended when more people joined the middle class each year than left it. To be sure, as the African American and White populations grew, the number of middle economic class households increased slowly from one year to the next. However, as a share of the total population, the middle class did not greatly change from the end of Richard Nixon's administration in 1975 until Bill Clinton's first term in 1993. Throughout that span, about 51 percent of the White population and 35 percent of the Black population could be termed middle class under the definition of an income between two and five times the poverty line.

A polarization of income distribution occurred among both races (Danziger and Gottschalk, 1995). For African Americans this meant an increase in the number of Black millionaires as well as persistent Black poverty. In quantitative terms, the Gini Index of Household Income Inequality for Black households went from 42 in 1970 to 46 in 1990 and then to 47 in 1998. Among Whites, the Gini Index increased from 39 in 1970 to 42 in 1990 and to 45 in 1998. The Gini Index is a frequently used measure of income concentration. It will approach its maximum value of 100 if all income is received by just a few households. If all households have similar incomes, the Gini Index will approach zero.

Economic changes and tight labor markets in the 1990s greatly improved economic conditions for the entire U.S. population, but the benefits were greater for African Americans on several indicators. The poverty rate for African Americans in 1999 was at a record low 27 percent, just slightly lower than the poverty rate for Blacks in the early 1970s. Thus, the impoverished Black population as a percentage of the total Black population was at a record low at the end of the 20th century. However, the relative size of the African American middle economic class did not increase, and the majority of Blacks still lived in impoverished or near poor households. Income polarization continued in the prosperous 1990s because the proportion of African Americans living in households with incomes at least five times the poverty line increased, and the Gini Index rose. One of the important trends of this era was the continued growth of a Black economic elite.

When other indicators of economic status are considered, modest improvements can be found for African Americans. Figure 2-12 reports trends in the per capita income of Blacks and Whites since the middle of the Civil

FIGURE 2-12

Per Capita Income of Blacks and Whites and Ratio of Black to White Income, 1967-98

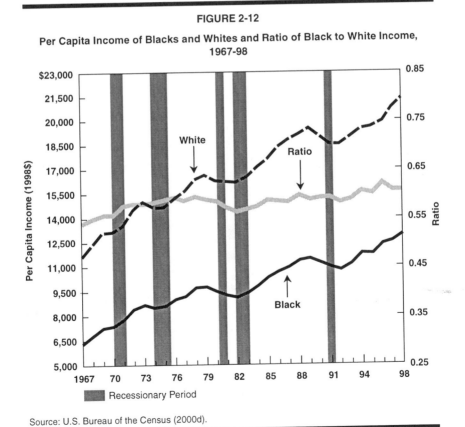

Source: U.S. Bureau of the Census (2000d).

Rights decade to 1998. The growth of income among African Americans continued throughout this period. However, the racial gap in per capita income closed only slightly in the 1990s because Whites also prospered. By the end of that decade, both Blacks and Whites had the highest per capita incomes ever, but the Black-White gap remained large—Black per capita income was 61 percent that of Whites.

The median income of Black and White families shows a familiar pattern. Between the early 1970s and the early 1990s, the family incomes of both races more or less stagnated, but began to rise in the mid-1990s. From 1990 to 1998, the median income of White families (in constant 1998 dollars) rose by 7 percent, while that of African American families increased by about 10 percent. Although Black and White families had higher median incomes than ever before, Black median income as a percentage of White median income rose from 54 percent in 1992 to 60 percent in 1998 (U.S. Bureau of the Census, 1998b). This increase left the income gap almost as large at the end of the century as it had been 30 years earlier.

Home ownership also illustrates changes in the economic status of African Americans and Whites in recent decades. Owning a home is often viewed as a key element in achieving the "American Dream." In addition, home ownership provides most families with their best opportunity to accumulate wealth (Oliver and Shapiro, 1995). Clearly, trends in home ownership mirror trends in income because a family's income strongly influences the ability to buy property. However, another important element in the ability to buy a home involves opportunities in the housing market. While there may be much less discrimination now than in the past, numerous audit studies report that Blacks looking for homes to buy are often treated differently than Whites: they are shown fewer homes, provided with less information about financing, or steered to Black or mixed neighborhoods. According to the authoritative study conducted by the Boston Federal Reserve Bank, African Americans who applied for mortgages from federally chartered institutions in that metropolis in the late 1980s were more likely to be turned down than were similar White applicants (Munnell et al., 1992; Yinger, 1995).

Given the racial gap in income and the persistence of discrimination in the housing market, it is not surprising that an ongoing, substantial gap exists in home ownership. Figure 2-13 reports the percentage of householders owning their homes. From the end of World War II to 1999, the majority of White households owned their residences; the majority of Blacks have never done so.

For both races, the proportion owning homes increased from 1940 to 1980 and then changed little until the 1990s. The percentage of homeowners increased presumably because of rising incomes and new efforts by federal agencies and private financial institutions to promote home ownership, especially among groups that traditionally rented. The share of White home-owners grew by 2 percentage points in the 1990s. That of Black homeowners rose by 3 percentage points, reaching a record high of 46 percent at the end of the decade. If current trends continue, within a decade or so, the majority

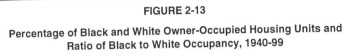

FIGURE 2-13

**Percentage of Black and White Owner-Occupied Housing Units and
Ratio of Black to White Occupancy, 1940-99**

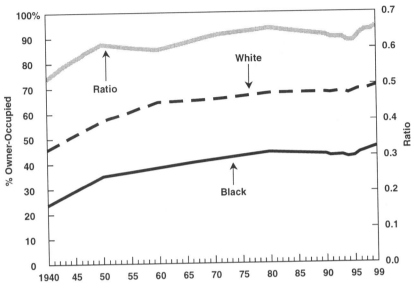

Source: U.S. Bureau of the Census (1982-92).

of African Americans may own their own homes, a status that Whites attained in 1945.

Comparing the Economic Status of Other Racial Groups

Are African Americans uniquely disadvantaged and Whites uniquely advantaged? This section considers the status of Blacks, Whites, Asians, Hispanics, and American Indians on three important indicators: household income; the racial composition of neighborhoods; and the poverty rate of children. The regional distribution of Blacks will also be discussed. The analysis is limited to the recent period because, in the past, small numbers of Asians and Latinos lived in the United States, and the federal statistical system seldom presented distinct information for these groups. Those of Spanish origin are considered comparable to a racial group and are removed from the other groups. Because place of birth makes a large difference in the economic circumstances of Latinos and Asians, those born abroad are distinguished from those born in the United States.

Figure 2-14 examines racial differences in household income. It reports the average income of minority households as a percentage of non-Hispanic White household income in 1990 and 1998 (in constant 1998 dollars). Infor-

New Directions

FIGURE 2-14

Income of Minority Households as a Percentage of White Household Income, 1990 and 1998

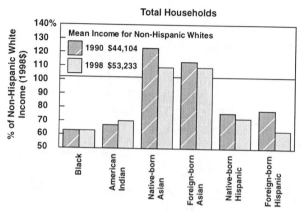

Total Households

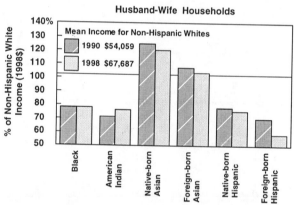

Husband-Wife Households

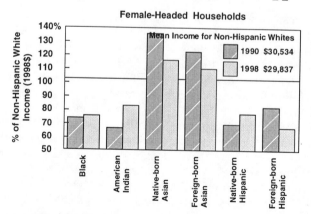

Female-Headed Households

Source: U.S. Bureau of the Census (1990, 2000d), Annual Demographic Files.

mation is shown for total households and for the two most common types of households—husband-wife households and those headed by a woman who has no husband living with her.

A familiar pattern is evident. In each type of household in both 1990 and 1998, those headed by native-born and foreign-born Asians reported the largest incomes. In total and female-headed households in 1998, African Americans and foreign-born Hispanics reported the smallest incomes. Foreign-born Hispanics also had the lowest income among husband-wife households. Households headed by native-born Asians had incomes about 25 percent above non-Hispanic Whites in 1990, while households headed by Blacks and American Indians had, on average, about 35 percent less income than White households.

Demographic factors help to explain the higher incomes of Asian households because husband-wife families make up a relatively large proportion of Asian households. Other factors accounting for the greater incomes of Asian households are their unusually large investments in education, the many hours that Asian women work, and the resulting high earnings of Asian women. Asian households, on average, also include more workers than other households (Farley, 1996, Chap. 6).

The second indicator of economic standing examined here is neighborhood racial composition. More than 50 years ago, Myrdal (1944, 618-622) described the deleterious consequences of racial residential segregation for African Americans. Not only did residential segregation deny Blacks access to the schools, parks, and municipal facilities enjoyed by Whites, it allowed prejudiced White elected officials to provide second-rate services to African American residents without harming White constituents. Massey and Denton (1993) argue that American "apartheid" continues to be the rigid backbone of the nation's system of racial stratification. In their view, residential segregation has the important intended and latent effects of truncating education and employment opportunities for Blacks. They argue that it also generates a ghetto culture and a Black linguistic style that is dysfunctional in America's achievement-oriented society. In other words, residential segregation fosters cultural practices that are not highly valued in the larger society (Wilson, 1987; Ogbu, 1978).

Figure 2-15 illustrates the racial composition of the typical neighborhood of Blacks, Whites, Asians, and Hispanics in the 318 metropolitan areas defined for the 1990 census. African American neighborhoods differ from those of other minority groups in the number of White residents. In 1990, Blacks resided in neighborhoods with a 29 percent non-Hispanic White population. In contrast, Asians lived in neighborhoods where, on average, 56 percent of the population were non-Hispanic Whites, and Hispanic neighborhoods included 40 percent non-Hispanic Whites.

If African Americans had incomes, wealth, and political clout equivalent to Whites, the residential segregation of African Americans into majority Black neighborhoods might not be a problem. With few exceptions, however, White neighborhoods have better schools, better city services, safer streets, and access to more effective political power than most overwhelmingly Black

FIGURE 2-15

Racial Composition of Neighborhoods in Metropolitan Areas, 1990

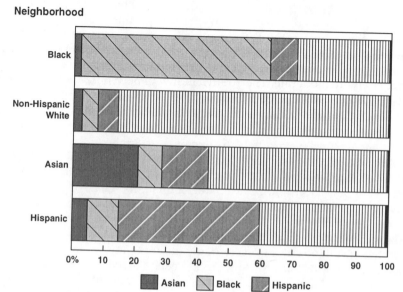

Note: Data refer to block groups in the 318 metropolitan areas defined for the 1990 census. In 1990, an average block group contained 210 occupied dwellings.

Source: U.S. Bureau of the Census (1990), Summary Tape, File A.

neighborhoods (Massey and Denton, 1993; Morenoff and Sampson, 1997; Kozol, 1991). The potential for assimilation with a prosperous, powerful White population appears to be much greater for Hispanics and Asians than for African Americans because Hispanics and Asians live in the same neighborhoods, often attend the same schools and churches, and usually receive the same city services as Whites.

While it is difficult to predict the racial composition of neighborhoods in the future, there are indications that racial residential segregation is gradually fading, albeit slowly. A recent analysis shows persistent and extensive patterns of small declines in Black-White residential segregation throughout the nation (Farley and Frey, 1994). Declines in residential segregation are larger in metropolises that attract many Black migrants from around the country: Orlando and Dallas in the South; Minneapolis in the Midwest; and Las Vegas, San Diego, Phoenix, Sacramento, and San Bernardino in the West.

Figure 2-16 illustrates long-term trends in the regional distribution of the African American population. Between 1940 and the 1960s, there was a massive outmigration of Blacks from the South, primarily to the Northeast and Midwest. This outmigration helped to reshape the nation's political institutions and to lay the foundation for the modern Civil Rights movement (Lemann, 1991). More recently, there has been a modest outmigration of African Americans from the Northeast and Midwest—where residential segregation levels are highest—back to the South where housing segregation is typically more moderate. The South has always been home to the majority of African Americans; even the great outmigration during World War II and the following decades did not alter this geographic pattern.

A final basis for comparing racial groups involves the economic status of children, using the five economic categories discussed earlier. These classifications range from very poor for those living in households with pretax cash incomes of less than one-half the poverty line to comfortable for those living in households with incomes that are at least five times the poverty line.

Prosperity and poverty for children under age 18 are summarized in Figure 2-17. Hispanic children born abroad were the most likely group to be impoverished in 1998—48 percent lived in households with incomes below 50 percent of the poverty line. Black and American Indian children each had

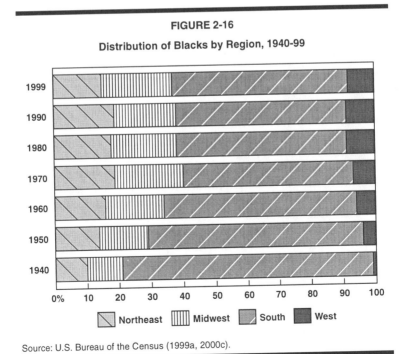

FIGURE 2-16

Distribution of Blacks by Region, 1940-99

Source: U.S. Bureau of the Census (1999a, 2000c).

FIGURE 2-17

Economic Status of Children Under Age 18 by Race, 1998

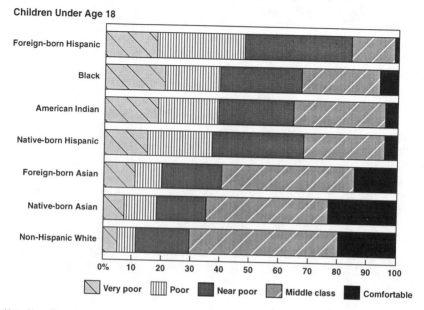

Note: **Very Poor,** below 50 percent of poverty line; **Poor,** 50 to 99 percent of poverty line; **Near Poor,** 100 to 199 percent of poverty line; **Middle Class,** 200 to 499 percent of poverty line; **Comfortable,** 500 percent or more of poverty line. The poverty line for a family of four was $16,660.00 in 1998. Data refer to non-Hispanic White, Black, and Asian populations.

Source: U.S. Bureau of the Census (1999a).

a poverty rate of 39 percent. Much less likely to live in impoverished environments were native-born Asian children, whose poverty rate was 18 percent, and non-Hispanic White children, with a poverty rate of 11 percent.

These data reveal large racial differences in the welfare of the nation's children, with the poverty rates of Black, Hispanic, and American Indian children more than three times the rate of White children. To the extent that childhood economic circumstances predict adult achievements (Duncan and Brooks-Gunn, 1997), these rates imply that the children of African Americans, Hispanics, and American Indians are especially disadvantaged, despite a decade of sustained economic growth.

CONCLUSIONS

Racial trends in the United States in the last half of the 20th century and their implications for developments in the new century can be summarized by focusing on four major trends.

The Extensive, Continuing Legacy of the Civil Rights Revolution

The Civil Rights movement effectively brought racial injustice to the nation's attention in the 1960s when Blacks and Whites joined together to address the racial hatreds that were deeply rooted in American society. When Congress debated Civil Rights legislation in that decade, there was still strong support for the idea that Whites were more qualified than Blacks to dominate politics, economics, and culture. There was extensive support for the principle of states' rights—the concept that the federal government had no power to tell states that they must racially integrate schools, that local parks must be open to both Blacks and Whites, that barkeepers and motel owners must serve African American customers, and that homeowners must sell or rent to Blacks. Twenty-seven senators voted against the Civil Rights Act of 1964, a law now celebrated as one of the major legislative triumphs of the century (Whalen and Whalen, 1985, 252-254). As recently as 1976, the Democratic Party's nominee for President defended the principle of "ethnically pure" neighborhoods, thereby seemingly supporting the right of one race to exclude the other.

Gradually, the nation accepted the idea that racial discrimination in public arenas violated state and federal laws. A number of national surveys demonstrated that the attitudes of Whites in the post-World War II era shifted from little support for the principle of equal racial opportunity to near-universal endorsement of the concept that racial discrimination is wrong (Schuman et al., 1997, Chap. 3). The nation was at least willing to grant to racial minorities the civil, political, and economic rights that Whites had assumed throughout history. Today, however, much less public support exists for programs that might quickly end racial disparities, such as busing students to integrate schools or initiating or maintaining affirmative action programs to guarantee jobs for minorities.

Debates about civil rights in the 1960s focused almost exclusively on the consequences of slavery and Jim Crow policies for African Americans. The debates also raised the crucial question of what personal characteristics could be considered in deciding who could migrate to this country, who could be admitted to a college or university, who could be employed or denied a job, and who could live where. If it is illegal to deny opportunities to African Americans simply because of their race, is it also illegal to turn down women merely because of their sex?

To the surprise of many, the Civil Rights Act prohibited discrimination against women in the labor force. Shortly thereafter, record high proportions of women began attending college and, later, professional and graduate schools. A feminization of higher education occurred in the last 30 years of the 20th century—higher proportions of women than men were enrolled in colleges, and the majority of college students were women. The 1980 and 1990 censuses showed major breakthroughs for women: their numbers greatly increased in occupations that had once been closed to them; their average earnings rose; and the gender gap in earnings declined (Spain and Bianchi, 1996). On most important indicators of occupational achievement and earnings, African American women reached near parity with their White peers in the late 1980s.

Beginning early in the last century, the nation's immigration laws favored the admission of northern Europeans and discouraged or prevented the entry of Africans and Asians. Few laws prevented the entry of Hispanics. The spirit of the Civil Rights decade led Congress to radically amend immigration policies in 1965 to minimize their racial implications. That change was promptly followed by an unexpectedly large flow of immigrants from Latin American, Asia, the Middle East, and Africa. Today, the annual volume of immigration rivals its level at the beginning of the 20th century. But only one immigrant in four arrives from Canada or Europe; the other three-fourths are Latinos, Africans, and Asians.

Other large groups have similarly benefited from the ideals of the Civil Rights decade. The Americans with Disabilities Act provides protection for people with physical and other limitations, thereby greatly increasing their opportunities for education and employment. There has also been the gradual emergence of some legal protections for gays, lesbians, and other groups previously facing discrimination because of their sexual identities.

The nation will not turn back to the pre-1960s era when mores made it permissible to screen out applicants and potential neighbors because of their skin color, religion, gender, or physical disability. America has achieved a level of understanding in which the principle of equal opportunity has been widely accepted and, to a significant but lesser degree, put into place.

The Ideal of Diversity Replacing Affirmative Action

Federal courts sought to integrate public schools in the 1960s and 1970s first by approving voluntary programs aimed at encouraging Black and White students to change schools to end segregation. When students did not voluntarily change schools, the courts gradually began to order the busing of students and the use of racial ratios to ensure that Black and White teachers taught in the same schools and that Black and White children learned together in the same classrooms. Those policies were unanimously upheld by the Supreme Court in its *Swan* v. *Charlotte-Mecklenburg* (1971) ruling.

During the late 1960s, the Office of Federal Contract Compliance (OFCC) sought information from employers about the racial and gender composition of their labor force and frequently found an absence of African Americans and women. The OFCC's attempts to increase minority representation were often unsuccessful because employers contended that their efforts to diversify employment accomplished little. The OFCC then requested employers to establish goals for hiring women and minorities in the near future. Those goals were gradually interpreted as affirmative action quotas because an employer failing to meet them could be subject to investigation and potentially costly litigation.

During the Nixon administration in the 1970s, federal resources were used to greatly increase the number of Black entrepreneurs. Nevertheless, Census Bureau surveys continued to show a dearth of African American businesses. In some industries such as construction, Blacks were only minutely represented. To overcome this racial pattern, Congress enacted the Public Works Employment Act in 1977, specifying that 10 percent of federal construction funding be spent with businesses owned by minorities or women if they satisfied federal requirements. The Supreme Court upheld this set-aside procedure in *Fullilove* v. *Klutznick* (1980). Rapidly thereafter, cities and states enacted similar laws, setting aside an even larger share of their disbursements for minority- and female-owned businesses. Universities also acknowledged the absence of minority students, especially in professional programs, and began to make race one factor in admission decisions. This policy was upheld by the U.S. Supreme Court in *Regents of the University of California* v. *Bakke* (1978).

To overcome the long-standing consequences of past discrimination, these laws and procedures specifically took race and gender into account. In an era in which equal treatment for all races was emphasized, it was inevitable that affirmative action policies would be challenged. Further, with the appointment of more conservative justices to the Supreme Court, state and municipal laws calling for minority set-asides were overturned (*Richmond* v. *Croson*, 1989) as were some universities' admission policies. The question of when race may be used to favor a group traditionally subject to pervasive discrimination has not been fully resolved, but affirmative action policies developed in the 1960s and 1970s are no longer widely supported.

The challenges to affirmative action, however, have occurred hand-in-hand with a growing belief in the value of diversity. Employers have come to accept the idea that their workforces should generally resemble the demographic composition of the local area or of their customers. Most educational, civic, and political institutions now have administrators who believe that their students and clients should, in demographic terms, resemble the entire population they serve, not just American-born Whites. Perhaps more progress will be made in bringing about racial equality with an emphasis on diversity than with court-mandated affirmative action policies.

The Implications of Demographic Change

As recently as 1960, the United States was primarily a Black-White nation. A small number of American Indians lived in the West, many in remote rural areas, and fewer than one million Asians were counted in that census. Because of differential birth rates and the tremendous impact of immigration, the nation's demographic composition is significantly different today, and it will change even more in the next five decades. The rapidly growing Spanish-origin population will numerically pass the Black population within 10 years.

Upon arrival, foreign immigrants often locate in only a few geographic areas, but shortly thereafter begin to spread across the United States in response to job and educational opportunities. One of the anticipated findings of the 2000 census is the substantial representation of Asians and Latinos in states and counties that were largely unaffected by immigration 10 to 15 years ago. Demographic diversity no longer characterizes just New York, Los Angeles, Chicago, Miami, Houston, and other ports of entry; it is found throughout the nation.

The country's racial composition will also be changed by the current high rates of interracial marriage. With Blacks increasingly marrying Whites, will most of their children claim African American as their race, or will they see themselves as White, mixed, or as members of some other racial category? The majority of native-born Asian women now marry Whites. How will their children identify themselves?

Official governmental statistics strongly influence how racial groups are viewed and how people classify themselves. These racial statistics are also used by federal courts and plaintiffs and defendants in litigation. From 1790 through 1990, the decennial censuses assumed that all people belonged to only one race. The census of 2000 allowed respondents to mark all the races that an individual or an individual's parents chose. How did mixed race couples report the race of their children? How did children with one Mexican and one Asian parent identify themselves? Did many or just a few people identify with several races?

Although discussion of race, Supreme Court decisions, and laws can no longer assume that America is a nation of just Blacks and Whites, the other consequences of current demographic shifts are not as clear. Will there be "rainbow coalitions" of Latinos, Asians, and African Americans effectively influencing elections and immigration policies? Will so many different races be reported—the census of 2000 will provide information for 126 distinct racial groups—that Americans will eventually decide that it is futile to measure race? It is easy to consider racial classifications of two to five distinct groups, but it is almost impossible to consider—and legislate for—126 different races. Will giving people the choice of reporting multiple races lead, in the long run, to a great reformulation of the concept of race or even to its disappearance?

Economic Growth as the Engine Driving Racial Change

Racial issues in the United States are intimately intertwined with employment and economic change. Much of the social and economic improvement of African Americans from the end of the Great Depression until the 1973 energy crisis can be attributed to the tremendous expansion of employment, the shift of Blacks from the rural South to the metropolitan North, and innovative federal and state programs that stimulated economic growth. Those programs helped to build schools and hospitals and created extensive transfer payments ranging from Social Security through expanded unemployment compensation to Aid to Families with Dependent Children. During World War II and for a quarter century thereafter, the nation's manufacturing, construction, and transportation industries created millions of jobs that could be filled by someone who lacked a high school diploma but who had a strong back and a dedication to hard work. The era in which

American Blacks made their greatest economic gains and substantially narrowed racial differences extended from the end of the Depression through 1973.

The briefly successful oil cartel as well as other macroeconomic shifts—including the rise of foreign competitors—drastically restructured the American labor market. High paying unionized jobs with generous fringe benefits became much more difficult to find as the economy went through a "quiet depression" in the late 1970s and early 1980s and then shifted to an emphasis on hiring workers with advanced training. For a quarter century beginning around 1970, the real earnings of men and women with a high school education or less declined, while the earnings of those with college and advanced degrees increased moderately (Levy, 1998). Because considerably more African Americans than Whites were represented at the lower end of the educational distribution, Blacks gradually fell behind on many important indicators.

The extensive economic expansion that began in 1991 may have introduced a new economic era. The census of 2000 and other sources will reveal much about whether the current boom with its exceptionally low unemployment rates has been beneficial for the nation's minorities, especially African Americans. Economic growth has created jobs at the upper and lower ends of the skills distribution. Immigrants lacking educational credentials have found jobs in the service sector and in low skill manufacturing work, while immigrants with advanced training have found employment in the fields of science, technology, and education.

Employers seem to be influenced by the new norm of diversity. In addition, the low unemployment rates undoubtedly have led them to consider applicants who would have been overlooked in previous times. In today's tight labor market, employers are strongly motivated to retain the workers they hire and to upgrade their skills.

For African Americans in the last decade of the 20th century, there were improvements in economic status and reductions in mortality. The median income of Black families rose to a record high in the late 1990s, and the poverty rate fell to an all-time low. Black unemployment rates are at their lowest levels since World War II. Because of the continued upward trend in educational attainment of Blacks, the Black-White gap in high school graduation may disappear in the foreseeable future.

These are favorable trends. But racial gaps in the late 1990s were still large with regard to infant mortality, life span, home ownership, and wealth holdings. Furthermore, among men much more so than among women, disparities in educational attainment, occupational achievement, and earnings remain substantial. The census of 2000 will likely reveal a new and moderately growing African American economic elite—individuals and families reporting college degrees, prestigious jobs, and substantial incomes, with many owning costly homes in prosperous, racially integrated suburbs. The census will also likely describe another major component of the African American population—those with limited education who hold the least desirable jobs and earn little, many of them living in the rural South or in underclass neighborhoods in the largest cities. They hardly benefited from the tremendous economic expansion of the 1990s. The presence of these two substantial, but distinct groups in the African American population make it a challenge to defend conclusions about whether the 1990s were the years in which the nation's traditional racial gaps began to close.

REFERENCES

Bobo, L.D. 1997. "The Color Line, the Dilemma, and the Dream." In *Civil Rights and Social Wrongs*. Ed. J. Higham. University Park: Pennsylvania State University Press, 31-55.

Council of Economic Advisers. 2000. Available from http://w3.access.gpo.gov/us budget/fy2001

Danziger, S., and P. Gottschalk. 1995. *America Unequal*. New York: Russell Sage Foundation.

Duncan, G.J., and J. Brooks-Gunn. 1997. *Consequences of Growing Up Poor*. New York: Russell Sage Foundation.

Farley, R. 1996. *The New American Reality*. New York: Russell Sage Foundation.

———. 1997. "Racial Trends and Differences in the United States 30 Years after the Civil Rights Movement." *Social Science Research* 26:235-262.

———. 1999. "Racial Issues in Residential Patterns and Intermarriages." In *Diversity and Its Discontents*. Ed. N.J. Smelser and J.C. Alexander. Princeton, N.J.: Princeton University Press.

Farley, R., and W.H. Frey. 1994. "Changes in the Segregation of Whites from Blacks During the 1980s: Small Steps Toward a More Integrated Society." *American Sociological Review* 59(1) (February):23-45.

Fullilove v. *Klutznick*. 1980. 448 U.S. 448.

Hacker, A. 1992. *Two Nations: Black and White, Separate, Hostile, Unequal*. New York: Charles Scribner's Sons.

Harrison, R.J., and C.E. Bennett. 1995. "Racial and Ethnic Diversity." In *State of the Union: America in the 1990s*. Ed. R. Farley. New York: Russell Sage Foundation.

Hochschild, J.L. 1995. *Facing Up to the American Dream: Race, Class, and the Soul of the Nation*. Princeton, N.J.: Princeton University Press.

Holmes, S.A. 1997. "At NAACP, Talk of a Shift on Integration." *New York Times* (June 23):A1.

Holzer, H.J. 1996. *What Employers Want: Job Prospects for Less-Educated Workers*. New York: Russell Sage Foundation.

Jackson, J.S. 1985. *Crabgrass Frontier: The Suburbanization of the United States*. New York: Oxford University Press.

Katz, M.B. 1986. *The Undeserving Poor: From the War on Poverty to the War on Welfare*. New York: Pantheon, Chap. 3.

Kozol, J. 1991. *Savage Inequalities*. New York: Crown Publishers, Inc.

Lemann, N. 1991. *The Promised Land: The Great Black Migration and How It Changed America*. New York: Alfred A. Knopf.

Loving v. *Virginia*. 1967. 338 U.S. 1.

Levy, F. 1998. *The New Dollars and Dreams: American Incomes and Economic Change.* New York: Russell Sage Foundation.

Massey, D., and N.A. Denton. 1993. *American Apartheid: Segregation and the Making of the Underclass.* Cambridge, Mass.: Harvard University Press.
McLanahan, S., and G. Sandefur. 1994. *Growing Up with a Single Parent: What Hurts, What Helps.* Cambridge, Mass.: Harvard University Press.
Morenoff, J.D., and R.J. Sampson. 1997. "Violent Crime and the Spatial Dynamics of Neighborhood Transition: Chicago, 1970-1990." *Social Forces* 76:31-64.
Munnell, A., G.M.B. Tootell, L.E. Browne, and J. McEneoney. 1996. "Mortgage Lending in Boston: Interpreting HMDA Data." *American Economic Review* 86(1):25-53.
Myrdal, G. 1944. *An American Dilemma: The Negro Problem and Modern Democracy.* New York: Harper and Row.

National Center for Health Statistics. 1984. *Vital Statistics of the United States, 1980.* II, Part A, Table 2.1.
———. 1999a. *National Vital Statistics Reports* 47(18) (April 29), Tables 3, 8.
———. 1999b. *Monthly Vital Statistics Reports* 47(19) Supplement (June 30), Table 27.
———. 2000. Available from http://www.cdc.gov/nchs/

Ogbu, J. 1978. *Minority Education and Caste: The American System in Cross Cultural Perspective.* New York: Academic Press.
Oliver, M.L., and T.M. Shapiro. 1995. *Black Wealth/White Wealth: A New Perspective on Racial Inequality.* New York: Routledge.

Regents of the University of California v. Bakke. 1978. 438 U.S. 265.
Richmond v. J.A. Croson Company. 1989. 488 U.S. 469.

Schuman, H., C. Steeh, L. Bobo, and M. Krysan. 1997. *Racial Attitudes in America: Trends and Interpretations.* Rev. ed. Cambridge, Mass.: Harvard University Press.
Spain, D., and S.M. Bianchi. 1996. *Balancing Act: Motherhood, Marriage, and Employment Among American Women.* New York: Russell Sage Foundation.
Swann v. Charlotte-Mecklenburg Board of Education. 1971. 402 U.S. 43.

Thernstrom, A., and S. Thernstrom. 1997. *America in Black and White: One Nation, Indivisible.* New York: Simon & Schuster.
Trattner, W.I. 1989. *From Poor Law to Welfare State: A History of Social Welfare in America.* 4th ed. New York: Free Press.

U.S. Bureau of the Census. 1940. *Sixteenth Census of the United States: Population: 1940.* II, Table 4. Washington, D.C.: U.S. Government Printing Office (GPO).
———. 1940-90. Public Use Microdata Samples from the censuses of 1940 to 1990.
———. 1960. *U.S. Census of the Population: 1960.* I, Part I, Table 44. Washington, D.C.: GPO.
———. 1982-92. *Statistical Abstracts of the United States, 1982-1992.* Washington, D.C.: GPO.
———. 1990. *U.S. Census of Population and Housing, 1990.* Public Use Microdata Sample. Washington, D.C.: GPO.
———. 1997a. *Statistical Abstract of the United States: 1997.* Table 19. Washington, D.C.: GPO.
———. 1997b. *Current Population Reports.* Annual Demographic Files (March), Public Use Microdata Sample. Washington, D.C.: GPO.
———. 1997c. Current Population Survey. Annual Demographic Files (March), Public Use Microdata Sample. Washington, D.C.: GPO.
———. 1998a. *Statistical Abstract of the United States: 1998.* Washington, D.C.: GPO.

————. 1998b. *Historical Income Tables—Families.* Revised November 6. Available from http://www.census.gov/hhes/income/histinc/

————. 1999a. *Current Population Reports.* Annual Demographic Files (March), Public Use Microdata Sample. Washington, D.C.: GPO.

————. 1999b. *Interracial Married Couples: 1960 to Present.* Published January 7. Available from: http://www.census.gov/population/socdemo/ms-la/tabms-3.txt

————. 2000a. Available from http://www.census.gov/population/socdemo/

————. 2000b. Available from http://www.census.gov/population/socdemo/school

————. 2000c. Available from http://www.census.gov/www/povty98.html

————. 2000d. Available from http://www.census.gov/hhes/income/histinc/

U.S. Department of Education. 1991. Tables 96, 97. Available from http://www.ed.gov/index.html

Whalen, C., and B. Whalen. 1985. *The Longest Debate: A Legislative History of the 1965 Civil Rights Act.* New York: New American Library.

Wilson, W.J. 1987. *The Truly Disadvantaged: The Inner City, the Underclass, and Public Policy.* Chicago: University of Chicago Press.

————. 1996. *When Work Disappears: The World of the New Urban Poor.* New York: Alfred A. Knopf.

Yinger, J. 1995. *Closed Doors, Opportunities Lost: The Continuing Costs of Housing Discrimination.* New York: Russell Sage Foundation.

Chapter 3

Race Relations in a Diversifying Nation

by Jennifer L. Hochschild

William Stewart Tod Professor of Public and International Affairs,
Princeton University

and Reuel R. Rogers

Assistant Professor, Department of Political Science,
Northwestern University

INTRODUCTION

"Diversifying" is indeed the key term for making sense of racial and ethnic relations in the United States.* The most basic form of diversification in contemporary politics is that of racial or ethnic background and identification of Americans. That divide is sometimes deepened by, but at other times submerged into, other divisions, such as class, gender, region, urbanicity, religion, ideology, or simply personal history or idiosyncrasy. At this point in American history, we can plausibly predict three mutually exclusive ways in which diversity might develop over the next few decades.

Pluralism

Conventional racial and ethnic identities are dissolving, at least around the edges, as groups come into close and complicated contact with each other. Intermarriage, residential and job integration, cultural blends, and intergroup political alliances are increasing. Class divisions within racial and ethnic groups, generational or nationality differences among recent immigrant groups, and ideological disagreements on particular policy issues also work to break down the divide among European Americans, African Americans, Hispanics, and Asian Americans. Groups will not dissolve into an anodyne melting pot, but individuals will have considerable leeway in deciding how and how much group identity matters to their lives.

Separation

Americans are moving toward mutual racial and ethnic separation, whether because groups choose to distinguish themselves from others or

---

* Because the topic of "race relations in a diversifying nation" is so huge and sprawling, we limit our focus to politics, that is, to conventionally defined political viewpoints, policy preferences, political coalition building (or the lack thereof), and strategies for electoral success. We reserve for another day (or other authors) sociological questions about intermarriage and residential integration, cultural questions about self-expression and artistic blending, and economic questions about class formation and occupational attainment.

45

because they are separated from others despite their intentions or even their awareness. Multicultural curricula and political programs sometimes emphasize differences and pride in distinctive identities more than shared interests or values. Disputes over redistribution through government programs sometimes turn into zero-sum contests among groups. The rapid growth of gated communities and the private provision of formerly public services allow some Americans to exclude others from their daily lives. Groups may not be overtly or even covertly hostile, but individuals' life chances will be largely shaped by the nature of the racial or ethnic group into which they were born.

Black Exceptionalism

Anglos, Asian Americans, and Hispanics are slowly becoming a single, intermingled population that will generally not include Blacks. The exclusion could be voluntary, forced on African Americans, or the result of an interaction between exclusion and separatist preferences. Intermarriage and residential integration are increasing dramatically among the first three groups, but not among the fourth. Second- and third-generation non-Black immigrants are moving into the middle class, while African Americans who have been in the United States for dozens of generations remain trapped, physically and economically, in inner-city ghettos and rural destitution. Conservative White politicians garner support among newly enfranchised immigrants in the largest U.S. cities, but seldom even try to appeal to traditional Black voters. Middle class Blacks and young Black adults increasingly endorse cultural forms of racial nationalism, even as they move into the economic mainstream. In short, life as an African American will be qualitatively different—although not always worse—than life as a member of any other racial or ethnic group. (For a similar prediction, see Gans, 1999.)

OVERVIEW OF CONCLUSIONS

In this chapter we do not present an overall conclusion as to whether pluralistic intermingling, ethnic separation, Black nationalism, or White defensiveness will predominate over the next few decades. Nor do we offer an overall judgment about the long-term possibilities for political coalition building among racial and ethnic groups. The structure of American racial and ethnic interactions is too complicated for summary judgments; the evidence is too mixed, or even contradictory. Most important, too many outcomes are contingent on choices not yet made and circumstances not yet faced. We will, however, offer more focused conclusions and draw some prescriptive lessons.

Two main results emerge from our analyses of survey data and coalition efforts among racial and ethnic groups in several cities.[1] First, it will be very difficult to develop and maintain stable coalitions across many groups and many issues *if* people persist in the preferences and perspectives they now express. The survey data show why stable coalitions across groups will be hard to maintain, and the case study evidence shows how hard such coalitions have been to maintain over the past few decades. Second, there is nevertheless much more opportunity to develop at least short-term coalitions than many observers of American politics now perceive. The survey data suggest where the coalitional possibilities lie; the case studies suggest how political activists might turn those possibilities into reality.

Our prescriptive lessons emerge from these conclusions. We begin from the premise that the first of the three pathways outlined above—pluralism and porous boundaries among groups—is the most desirable. Based on the evidence outlined here, the best way to achieve intergroup pluralism is to develop coalitions around issues other than racial and ethnic concerns. Fighting against discrimination will and should remain among the goals of a multiracial coalition, but it should probably not be at the forefront of such a coalition's political agenda.

To put the point more aphoristically, both survey and case study evidence suggests that the more a multiracial coalition focuses directly on issues of racial and ethnic equality, the less stable it will be and the more likely it will fragment into competitive factions. Conversely, the same evidence shows that the more a multiracial coalition focuses on issues that are *not* ostensibly about race, the greater its chance of persistence and success. These results obtain because, most of the time, issues of racial and ethnic equality come to have a zero-sum quality among people of color at least as often as between people of color and European Americans. In contrast, issues that focus on, for example, economic needs, community improvement, or family policies have at least the potential to benefit a wide range of people of all racial and ethnic identities, thereby generating more positive-sum gains cutting across racial and ethnic divides.

DIVERSIFICATION

In the 1980s, the United States absorbed 7.3 million immigrants, mostly from Asia and Latin America (at an annual rate of about 0.3 percent of the total population). Between 1991 and 1996, another 6.1 million immigrants entered the country (at an annual rate of about 0.4 percent of the population). An additional 5 million people live in the United States as undocumented immigrants (U.S. Bureau of the Census, 1998, Tables 5, 10). Assuming that ethnic and racial categories will remain fixed in the foreseeable future, Hispanics will replace African Americans as the single largest non-Anglo group in the United States by the end of the next decade or soon thereafter. As Chapter 2 of this volume, "Demographic, Economic, and Social Trends in a Multicultural America," shows, about one-third of the residents of the United States will be Asian, Black, Hispanic, or Native American by 2020, up from about 15 percent in 1960.

Within each of these panethnic groups lie deep differences in language, religion, history, culture, and economic status. Puerto Ricans usually speak English before they immigrate and are fairly familiar with U.S. customs and politics; other immigrants typically face much more dramatic cultural changes. People from Japan and China have been immigrating to the United States for 150 years; Samoans and Vietnamese have come only very recently. Protestant northern Europeans can expect to be welcomed; Moslem Middle Easterners should anticipate suspicion.

Geography interacts with demography to magnify diversity. Over the next few decades, cities and regions across the United States will have increasingly different racial and ethnic profiles. For example, in 10 of California's 58 counties, between one-third and two-thirds of the residents are Latino (mostly Mexican); in other counties, the Latino population is as low as 3 percent (Tolbert and Hero, 1996, 808). Most of the nation's fastest growing cities are in the West and Southwest, and their growth is attributable to immigration (Holmes, 1998). Currently, more than one-half of the residents of New York City are immigrants or children of immigrants (Moss et al., 1997). By 2025, in 12 states, non-Hispanic Whites will account for less than 60 percent of the residents; in another 12 states, they will make up more than 85 percent of the population (Frey and Farley, 1996).

In short, the United States is experiencing an unprecedentedly widespread "demographic balkanization," in which areas where immigrants account for most of the demographic change will become increasingly multicultural, younger, and more bifurcated in their race and class structures. Other parts of the country, whose growth is more dependent on internal migration flows, will become far less multicultural in their demographic makeup and will differ as well in other social, demographic, and political dimensions. What is new about this scenario is its geographic scope (Frey and Farley, 1996).

To what degree will demography and geography be destiny? In a majoritarian democracy like the United States, numbers matter greatly in any political calculus. As the largest racial minority group in the country and by virtue of sheer numbers, African Americans historically have made stronger claims on the attention of policymakers and elected officials than any other non-Anglo group. More particularly, Blacks' residential concentration in central cities has facilitated their political incorporation nationally and in some states. As the overall number of Asian Americans and Hispanics grows, especially in certain cities and states, the political standing of African Americans and Anglos will decline at least in relative terms if the political game is played out in zero-sum terms. But if Blacks and other non-Anglo groups are able to generate an alliance, and perhaps add a few liberal Whites, the list of winners and losers could change. In that case, there will be very different political dynamics in areas that remain predominantly White compared with areas that are demographically varied.

To diversification by race or ethnicity and location add a third form— economic. By conventional measures of income, education, or occupation, more than one-third of African Americans can now be described as middle class compared with more than one-half of Whites. This is an astonishing— probably historically unprecedented—change from the early 1960s, when Blacks enjoyed the "perverse egalitarianism" of almost uniform poverty in which even the best-off Blacks could seldom pass on their status to their children (Hogan and Featherman, 1978, 101). Today, there is greater disparity between the top and bottom fifths of Black Americans—in terms of income, education, victimization by violence, job status, and participation in electoral politics—than between the top and bottom fifths of White Americans. Consider, for example, the Gini ratio, a measure of income disparity between wealthiest and poorest; the closer it is to 1, the greater the inequality. Among Whites, the Gini ratio rose from 0.419 to 0.446 between 1990 and 1996; in the 30 years since 1967, it has risen 0.055 points. Among Blacks between 1990 and 1996, the Gini ratio rose from a higher base to a higher top—from 0.464 to 0.479. Inequality among Blacks in the 1990s has risen almost as much (0.047 points) as has inequality among Whites in the past three decades and from a higher starting point (U.S. Bureau of the Census, 1998b, Table B-3).

Latinos are undergoing a similar process of class dispersion. The Gini ratio rose from 0.424 in 1990 to 0.457 in 1996; since 1972 (the first year for which data are available), it has risen a dramatic 0.084 points (U.S. Bureau of the Census, 1998b, Table B-3; see also Institute, 1997). Comparable U.S. Bureau of the Census data are not available for Asian Americans, but several surveys clearly show variations within Asian nationalities. In Houston, for example, one-half of Filipinos enjoy household incomes over $50,000 (in 1994 dollars), compared with only one-fifth of Vietnamese (Klineberg, 1996, 13). Across the United States, the median family income of major Asian American groups in 1989 ranged from $30,500 among Vietnamese to $51,500 among Japanese.[2]

Poverty rates vary across, as well as within, the four main racial and ethnic groups. Throughout the 1990s, roughly 11 percent of Whites were poor, according to the Census Bureau. Comparable rates for Blacks averaged 31 percent; for Latinos, 29 percent; and for Asian Americans, 14 percent (U.S. Bureau of the Census, 1998b, Table C-1). Again, however, the poverty rates must be disaggregated; in the 1990s, for example, 30 percent of Samoans and Vietnamese were poor (Frey and Fielding, 1995; Lien, 1998, Table 1-2; Brackman and Erie, 1995; Wyly, 1997, Table 3).

Perhaps economics, not demography and geography, is destiny; that is, perhaps economic interests will swamp racial or ethnic identification or regional variations as the driving force behind intergroup relations over the next few decades. Common economic interests could, however, generate several distinct dynamics. Poor people might compete among themselves, perhaps along racial or ethnic lines, for scarce public resources and private jobs (Johnson and Oliver, 1989; Johnson et al., 1996; Miles, 1992; Sonenshein, 1996; Chen and Espiritu, 1989). Alternatively, they might unite to pursue common interests (Mollenkopf, 1997; Sonenshein, 1997; Schuck, 1993; Wilson, 1999). Well-off members of various groups might unite around a shared economic conservatism (Parent and Stekler, 1985; Welch, 1987; Tate, 1994, 38-45; Klineberg, 1996, Table 12), or split in contention over affirmative action, business set-asides, or simple competition over wealth and status.

Still other forms of diversity come into play in particular circumstances. Religion, gender, age, recency or timing of immigration, and individual political ideology are among the long list of factors that can overcome racial, geographic, or economic imperatives in determining an individual's policy views and willingness to enter into political coalitions. For example, third-generation Hispanics are not only economically better off than earlier generations, but they are also more culturally liberal and economically conservative (Klineberg, 1996, 15-21; Aguirre et al., 1989). Among some Hispanic groups, later generations and those who have lived in the United States longer resemble Black Americans in their views of racial discrimination more than do recent immigrants (Uhlaner, 1991; Garcia et al., 1996; de la Garza et al., 1992).

We noted earlier that the only safe generalization that can be made about race relations in a diversifying nation is that we should be excessively modest about making predictions. But we also proposed three paths that racial and ethnic relations might take over the next few decades. Next, we consider ways in which the various types of diversity just described map onto the possible pathways of pluralism, mutual separation, and African American exceptionalism.

COALITIONAL POSSIBILITIES

Agreement on Policy Preferences—Pluralism

Results of some surveys suggest that the pluralist model best describes citizens' political perceptions and views on crucial policy issues. There is little racial or ethnic disparity, for example, in judgments about the recent trajectories of American families. As Table 3-1 shows, all groups rank their

TABLE 3-1

Ranking of Concerns

"During the past 10 years, has (have) XX gotten better, worse, or stayed the same (*or* gotten easier or harder) for people like you (*or* families like yours)?"

Percentage saying "worse" or "harder," ordered by Whites' level of concern:

	Whites (N=802)	Asian Americans (N=353)	Latinos (N=252)	African Americans (N=474)
To get good jobs	56	56	50	60
The public schools	55	47	45	57
To find decent, affordable housing	55	48	55	49
For families to stay together	45	34	40	48
Health care	44	30	30	39

Source: *Washington Post* et al. (1995), 75-76.

concerns in the same order, with the exception of one inversion by Latinos. African Americans and Latinos are not overwhelmingly more distressed than members of the other two groups. Arguably, there is more of a vertical than a horizontal pattern; that is, there is more disparity in concern among the issues (health care is relatively unproblematic; job attainment is the most difficult) than across the groups.

The same pattern is evident in the way that citizens rank their desires for government action on particular policy issues (see Table 3-2). The issue of abortion generates a huge disparity between two racial groups—Asian Americans and Latinos. The issues of welfare and affirmative action also reveal substantial differences among groups. But overall, there are larger differences across the policy domains than among racial or ethnic groups. Most respondents endorse reform of the welfare system and balancing the budget. Respondents are split on reform of Medicare and income tax cuts, and only a minority of respondents endorse limits on business tax cuts, affirmative action, and abortion. In addition, the preference ordering across the four racial and ethnic groups is, with occasional exceptions, the same.

A final array similarly shows that even when members of various racial and ethnic groups consider policies to eliminate rather than to promote, they do not differ sharply from each other (see Table 3-3). Greater disparities exist in this set of preferences than in the previous set, with differences of 8 to 14 percentage points across at least two groups on most issues. (The only issue

---

TABLE 3-2

Policy Preferences for Congressional Action

"For each issue, please tell me if you think this is something Congress should do or should not do."

Percentage saying "strongly feel Congress should do," ordered by Whites' level of support:

	Whites (N=802)	Asian Americans (N=353)	Latinos (N=252)	African Americans (N=474)
Reform the welfare system	83	68	81	73
Balance the budget	82	75	75	79
Reform Medicare	53	58	59	58
Cut personal income taxes	52	46	55	50
Limit tax breaks for business	39	30	41	41
Limit affirmative action	38	27	30	25
Put more limits on abortion	35	24	50	32

Source: *Washington Post* et al. (1995), 73-74.

TABLE 3-3

Support for Spending Reductions

"A number of spending reductions have been proposed to balance the federal budget and avoid raising taxes. Would you favor or oppose making major spending reductions in . . ."

Percentage saying "favor major spending reductions," ordered by Whites' preferences:

	Whites (N=802)	Asian Americans (N=353)	Latinos (N=252)	African Americans (N=474)
Public assistance/welfare	63	55	53	45
Federal aid for cities	55	49	45	41
Food stamps	52	49	46	38
Defense	51	63	57	56
Tax credits for low income families	49	41	52	40
Public housing	49	41	49	37
Federal programs to create jobs and for job training	48	42	43	41
Legal aid for poor people	48	38	40	35
Federal aid for college loans	46	35	34	34
Medicaid	43	38	44	35
Medicare	39	44	34	33
Head Start	38	35	30	34
Social Security	37	42	34	35
Child health	34	35	30	31

Source: *Washington Post* et al. (1995), 8.

that generates huge disparities is welfare.) Whites are more inclined than at least two of the other groups to cut spending on all issues except defense, and African Americans are almost always less inclined to cut spending than all of the other groups. These results accord with the general finding that Blacks are the most liberal group and Whites the most conservative.

But even in this case, there is more variation between the top and the bottom of the list within each group than between the extreme positions on any single issue (except welfare) across groups. Furthermore, with a few exceptions (notably defense), respondents in all groups give roughly the same preference ordering for policies they would be willing to sacrifice. This is not a portrait of a citizenry sharply divided along racial and ethnic lines (Joint Center, 1997a, Table 4a).[3]

Focusing more narrowly on specific policy preferences for solving particular problems, we again see considerable convergence across racial and ethnic groups. Another survey shows, for example, all four groups agreeing that "education" is the "most important issue facing your community today," although varying degrees of urgency about other issues produced differences in the actual proportions focusing on education (U.S. Department of Justice, 1997, 115). Roughly speaking, all groups agree that drugs, crime, and gang violence are the next most important set of issues.[4]

Perhaps more surprising is that the groups mostly concur on how to solve the problems of crime and schooling. Consider crime policy first. Between 80 and 90 percent of Black, White, and "other" Americans agree that it is "extremely important" to spend tax dollars on "reducing crime" and "reducing illegal drug use" among youth. Since 1982, non-Whites have consistently been slightly more likely to agree that the United States spends too little money on "halting the rising crime rate" and "dealing with drug addiction" (U.S. Department of Justice, 1997, 141, 142-143, 144-145). Three-fourths of both Blacks and Whites agree that the penalties for powder and crack cocaine should be the same; 70 percent of Blacks and 80 percent of Whites support "3 strikes and you're out" laws (Joint Center, 1996, Tables A-5, A-6). Blacks, Whites, and Hispanics concur that "a juvenile charged with a serious property crime should be tried as an adult" (about 60 percent agreement), that "a juvenile charged with selling illegal drugs should be tried as an adult" (about two-thirds agreement), and that "a juvenile charged with a serious violent crime should be tried as an adult" (more than 80 percent agreement) (U.S. Department of Justice, 1997, 155). Among eight proposals offered on a 1996 survey, Blacks, Whites, and Hispanics identified "3 strikes," "money for youth programs," and "adding 100,000 more police officers" as the most effective ways to reduce crime (U.S. Department of Justice, 1996, 167). On only two issues—the hope that prison can rehabilitate prisoners and, especially, support for the death penalty—do non-Whites differ dramatically from Whites (Joint Center, 1996, Table A-7; U.S. Department of Justice, 1997, 155, 159-165).

Finally, consider attitudes toward education reform. More than 80 percent of Blacks, Whites, and Hispanics concur that it is "extremely important" to spend tax dollars on "educational opportunities for children" (U.S. Department of Justice, 1997, 141). Both African Americans and Whites are split on their views of vouchers (Hispanics evince the most enthusiasm for them) (Joint Center, 1996, Table B-3; Joint Center, 1997b, Table 7). Blacks, Whites, and Hispanics are almost equally supportive of a constitutional amendment to allow prayer in schools (Joint Center, 1996, Table B-4; Post-Modernity, 1996, Tables 10C, 47E).

The point should be clear: on important social and political problems, people of all racial and ethnic groups concur on what the problems are, how serious they are, and what many of the solutions should be. Where the population does not concur on the solutions—e.g., with school vouchers—the groups frequently resemble each other in the proportion supporting or opposing the given proposal. Thus, divisions over many policy proposals lie

TABLE 3-4

Perceptions of Discriminatory Treatment

"Among these groups, which one do you think faces the most discrimination in America today?"

Percentage choosing each group, ordered by Whites' responses:

	Whites (N=802)	Asian Americans (N=353)	Hispanics (N=252)	African Americans (N=474)
African Americans	51	62	42	**82**
Hispanic Americans	28	18	**40**	11
Asian Americans	14	**12**	11	5
Don't know	6	8	7	2

Source: *Washington Post* et al. (1995), 93.

along fault lines other than race or ethnicity such as political ideology, class, or urbanicity.

These are encouraging grounds for developing coalitions across racial and ethnic lines. Americans can be expected to continue to dispute vigorously policy proposals, but evidence suggests that many of the disputes will not fall along racial and ethnic lines. Therefore, the first of the three models described above, pluralistic intermingling, has some support: conventional racial and ethnic identities do not determine the anxieties and policy preferences of many, perhaps most, American citizens on numerous issues of deep importance to them.[5]

Disputes in Perceptions of Racial Discrimination— Racial and Ethnic Separation

The pluralist model is only one potential path for race relations in a diversifying nation. Consider the second plausible path—racial and ethnic separation and separatism. That possibility is revealed in responses to a query about relative degrees of discriminatory treatment (see Table 3-4). African Americans think that members of their group suffer most from discrimination by a very wide margin; Latinos think that members of their group suffer almost as much as African Americans. All groups, including Asian Americans, agree that Asian Americans do not win that dubious honor. (See National Conference, 1994, 87, 103, 119, 137; Klineberg, 1996, Table 14; *Los Angeles Times* Poll, 1993b, Ques. 19, for similar results.) Here are the seeds of coalitional trouble, at least between Blacks and Hispanics.

More detailed probing of arenas in which discrimination might occur produces the same pattern, with several crucial additions (see Table 3-5). Overall, African Americans perceive much higher levels of discrimination

TABLE 3-5

Discrimination in Key Arenas

"Which groups face discrimination in key arenas of life?"

Percentage choosing each group:

	Whites (N=1,093)	Asian Americans	Latinos (N=77)	African Americans (N=102)
Credit loans and mortgages				
African Americans	31	—	31	**69**
Latinos	31	—	**28**	60
Asian Americans	24	—	31	33
Promotion to management positions				
African Americans	44	—	40	**72**
Latinos	46	—	**48**	66
Asian Americans	36	—	33	39

	Whites (N=1,093)	Asian Americans (N=154)	Latinos (N=502)	African Americans (N=1,006)
Treatment by police				
African Americans	50	60	61	**81**
Latinos	46	54	**54**	72
Asian Americans	35	**53**	50	48
Portrayal in the media				
African Americans	45	37	46	**70**
Latinos	45	50	**44**	65
Asian Americans	40	**56**	43	44
Treatment in the legal system				
African Americans	37	37	47	**71**
Latinos	36	35	**43**	68
Asian Americans	35	**19**	35	45

Source: National Conference (1994), 73-75, 134, 136.

against non-Anglos than do the other groups, and they always believe that their own race faces the most discrimination. In addition, they always perceive more mistreatment of Latinos than Latinos themselves do; they are rather less concerned about Asian Americans. Latinos perceive essentially the same amount of discrimination against themselves and African Americans, and they see almost as much bias against Asian Americans. Asian Americans perceive their own race to suffer the most discrimination in one arena, similar levels as the other two groups in a second, and the least in a third. Whites generally see the least bias, and they make the smallest distinctions among the groups (see also Zubrinsky and Bobo, 1996, 353-354; *Los Angeles Times*, 1993b, Ques. 24-27; *Los Angeles Times*, 1997, Ques. 29-33).

In short, there is a clear racial/ethnic ranking of *how much* discrimination exists, but no clear racial/ethnic ranking of *who* suffers from it the most. In this context, any group's claim to unusually bad treatment will be subject to contest by the others—either because they deny the fact of bad treatment or because they deny that the first group suffers unusually from it.

Results of another survey question seeking comparisons across groups underline the tendency toward racial/ethnic separation or separatism (see Table 3-6). This item is less cognitive than affective; it speaks to self-image or aspirations for the future rather than to particular policy or political preferences.[6] Whites feel most in common with African Americans, who feel little in common with Whites. African Americans feel most in common with Latinos, who feel least in common with them. Latinos feel most in common with Whites, who feel little in common with them. Asian Americans feel most

TABLE 3-6

Comparisons of Affinity and Aversion

"Of these groups, if you had to say, which one do you feel you have the most in common with/ least in common with?"

Percentage choosing each group:

	Whites (N=1,093)	African Americans (N=1,006)	Latinos (N=502)	Asian Americans (N=154)
Feel most in common with:				
Whites	—	34	**55**	**50**
African Americans	**38**	—	25	12
Latinos	28	**45**	—	27
Asian Americans	19	19	6	—
Don't know; not available	15	2	14	11

	Whites	African Americans	Latinos	Asian Americans
Feel least in common with:				
Whites	—	**36**	21	21
African Americans	24	—	**36**	53
Latinos	**24**	19	—	13
Asian Americans	**36**	**36**	32	—
Don't know; not available	16	9	11	13

Source: National Conference (1994), 32.

in common with Whites, who feel least in common with them. Each group is chasing another that is running from it.

What these results imply for political coalitions depends on how the dynamic of coalition building is conceived. On the one hand, it is possible to generate, and may be possible to sustain, a coalition among people who feel little affinity for each other if their instrumental or ideological motivations are strong enough. This is the insight behind the cliché, "politics makes strange bedfellows," and there are numerous examples of the phenomenon (that, after all, is what makes the phrase a cliché). From that perspective, these results may be psychologically interesting, but they say little about potential political alliances to elect new officials or pass new legislation.

On the other hand, it is hard to generate, and especially hard to sustain, coalitions among people who feel little in common beyond a purely instrumental or ideological goal. As demonstrated below, coalitions do not develop fully enough to have significant impact over time unless participants are willing to take risks, are able to develop trust over time, and believe that they are fighting for a larger and shared purpose. The results of the survey question in Table 3-6 suggest that these elusive but essential emotional ties will be, to put it mildly, difficult to develop across racial and ethnic groups in the foreseeable future.

Disputes in Perceptions of Racial Discrimination—Black Exceptionalism

It is distressingly easy to demonstrate how far apart African Americans and Whites are on issues that explicitly evoke racial identity. Consider disparities in what might appear to be a simple description of fact, such as "How much racial discrimination exists in the United States?" Seldom do more than one-third of Whites believe that Blacks continue to experience racist treatment in jobs, housing, the media, or the criminal justice system (Gallup Organization, 1997; National Conference, 1994; *Washington Post* et al., 1995; Zukin, 1997, Chaps. 3, 4; Schuman et al., 1997, 158-159, 166-169). Blacks disagree. Twice as many Blacks as Whites agree that there is "a lot" of "discrimination and prejudice . . . against Blacks in the U.S. today," and more than twice as many claim that Blacks are treated "not well" or "badly" in their community (Joint Center, 1997a, Tables 1, 4, 6; Gallup Organization, 1997, Ques. 18; National Conference, 1994; *Washington Post* et al., 1995; Zukin, 1997, Chaps. 3, 4; Schuman et al., 1997, 260-265).

The same racial disparities are evident when people consider change over time rather than the current level of racial discrimination. Whites are increasingly convinced that racial equality is growing in the United States. In the mid-1960s, one-third or more (depending on the year and the wording of the question) believed that the nation was making progress in solving its racial problems; by the 1970s, more than one-half concurred; and by 1988, almost 90 percent of Whites thought that "in the past 25 years, the country has moved closer to equal opportunity among the races." By the mid-1990s, Whites had again become cautious. In one survey, only about 33 percent (compared with 12 percent of African Americans) asserted that discrimination against Blacks had decreased over the previous 10 years (Hochschild, 1995, esp. Chap. 3; *Washington Post* et al., 1995, Ques. 41a; Post-Modernity, 1996, Table 38). Nevertheless, Whites are consistently more likely to see progress than regression in racial equality.

African Americans, meanwhile, are becoming increasingly discouraged on the issue of change over time. The proportion of Blacks who see increasing racial equality declined from between 50 percent and 80 percent in the mid-1960s to between 20 percent and 45 percent in the 1980s.[7] In 1995, more than one-half of Blacks (compared with less than one-fourth of Whites) agreed that discrimination had worsened for their race over the previous decade; two years later, only one in five, compared with twice as many Whites, agreed that "the situation of Black people is better [than it was] five years ago" (Hochschild, 1995, Chap. 3; *Washington Post* et al., 1995, Ques. 41a; Joint Center, 1997a, Table 7; Post-Modernity, 1996, Table 4J).

One example demonstrates most clearly this striking divergence. From 1988 to 1993 (when David Dinkins was mayor), an increasing proportion of Black New Yorkers believed that race relations in their city were good, and a decreasing proportion of White New Yorkers concurred. In 1994, however (when Rudolph Giuliani became mayor), a majority of Whites who perceived any change thought that New York's race relations had improved recently; a majority of Blacks who perceived change thought that relations had worsened. Thus, no matter in what direction opinions about race relations move, Blacks and Whites follow opposite trajectories. Racial divergence, not merely growing Black pessimism, is the underlying phenomenon (Hochschild, 1995, 61).

Blacks and Whites disagree just as much on perceptions of how well Blacks are doing as on perceptions of discrimination. About 3 in 5 Whites believe that African Americans are as well off as or better off than Whites with regard to jobs, access to health care, and education; more than 2 in 5 Whites say the same with regard to income and housing. Again, African Americans disagree; only 14 percent to 30 percent accept the claim that Blacks are as well off as Whites, depending on the particular arena in question. Barely 3 in 10 Whites, compared with 7 in 10 Blacks, doubt that African Americans have as good a chance to live a middle class life as Whites do (*Washington Post* et al., 1995; Hochschild, 1995, 61-64; Zukin, 1997, Chaps. 2, 4).[8] Ironically, one of the few areas of perceptual agreement between the races shows both to be equally mistaken: both groups agree that Blacks make up about 25 percent of the U.S. population (*Washington Post* et al., 1995, Sec. 1). Blacks actually account for about 12 percent of the population.

The model of Black exceptionalism, however, includes the proposition that African Americans are distinct from Hispanics and Asian Americans as well as from Whites. The evidence on this broader point is more mixed. Hispanics typically fall in between Blacks and Whites on questions of race relations, whereas Asian Americans frequently resemble Whites (as far as can be differentiated from very scanty survey data).[9] For example, 3 in 10 African Americans, more than 4 in 10 Hispanics, and 6 in 10 Whites describe race relations in their community as excellent (Joint Center, 1997a, Table 1;

Zukin, 1997, Chap. 3). Few European Americans claim to face discrimination; many African Americans do; Hispanics and Asian Americans fall in between, with Hispanics closer to Blacks and Asians closer to Anglos (*Washington Post* et al., 1995, Ques. 4; Burns et al., 1998, Fig. 13; Klineberg, 1996, Table 14; *Los Angeles Times*, 1993b, Ques. 22). More than twice as many Black as White teenagers (46 percent versus 22 percent) claim to have been "a target of some racial or religious incident"; Hispanics fall exactly in between (at 32 percent) (Louis Harris and Associates, 1990, Table 47; Post-Modernity, 1996, Table 83B). Latinos are sometimes less convinced than African Americans that their own group faces discrimination. In one survey, 80 percent of Blacks, 70 percent of Hispanics, and 40 percent of Whites agree that "there is not enough attention paid to discrimination against Hispanics" (Joint Center, 1997a, Table 5; see also *Washington Post* et al., 1995, Ques. 11b; Zukin, 1997, Chap. 3; Uhlaner, 1991; Louis Harris and Associates, 1990, 34).

Perhaps the most important indicator of Black exceptionalism is the fact that African Americans attach more political significance to their racial identity than other groups do. More precisely, perceived racial interests strongly shape Blacks' political evaluations and choices, whereas other groups either see fewer racial/ethnic interests or do not use them to shape their policy values so strongly. (On Blacks, see Dawson, 1994; Kinder and Sanders, 1996; Tate, 1994; Bobo and Smith, 1994. On Hispanics, see Jones-Correa and Leal, 1996; Uhlaner, 1991). Thus, Blacks may be especially prone to avoiding coalitions with groups that do not seem to take their distinctive perceptions, preferences, and circumstances fully into account.

Shifting Agreements Across Policy Domains

So far there is evidence for pluralism, for group separation, and for African American exceptionalism. But these results reveal more than indeterminacy; they show that *the less that a survey question draws attention to race or ethnicity and the less that it asks people to measure their group against another, the less that they will split along group lines.* This makes sense analytically, but it leaves open a wide array of political possibilities. Under what circumstances is it possible—or desirable—to reduce citizens' attention to their racial or ethnic context and to increase their attention to something else? A final pattern of possibilities for coalition, and contestation, will help provide answers to that question.

Some issues are likely to pit two or three of the four groups against the others. Two are examined here, but others could be added.[10]

Affirmative Action

Hispanics support strong forms of affirmative action more than Whites do, but usually less than Blacks do. The evidence on Asian Americans is more volatile, both because sample sizes are usually too small for reliability and because Asian Americans are deeply conflicted about affirmative action. (Onishi, 1996). For example, in 1995, Whites were more likely to agree strongly than were Blacks, Asian Americans, and Hispanics that Congress should "limit affirmative action" (see Table 3-2 above). But on other affirmative action questions in the same survey, Asian Americans and Latinos always located themselves in between Anglos and Blacks, with Asian Americans closer to Whites and Latinos closer to Blacks (*Washington Post* et al., 1995; see also Joint Center, 1997a, Table 9; Zukin, 1997, Tables 4-5, 4-6; Post-Modernity, 1996, Table 10Q; Klineberg, 1996, Table 14; Bobo, 2000).[11] To summarize a huge array of data: Blacks are much more likely to support affirmative action for Blacks than are all of the other groups; Blacks and Latinos concur on strong though lesser support for affirmative action for Latinos; and all groups concur on relatively weak support for affirmative action for Asian Americans (National Conference, 1994, 86, 102, 118, 136; Burns et al., 1998, Fig. 12; Citrin, 1996, Table 1). Latinos and Whites favor affirmative action for the poor rather than for "people of a specific race or sex" slightly more than do the other two groups (*Washington Post* et al., 1995, Ques. 61).

From a political actor's perspective, the best evidence on support for affirmative action comes from exit polls after Californians voted in November 1996 on Proposition 209 to abolish the public use of affirmative action. The *San Francisco Examiner*, the *Los Angeles Times*, and Voter News Service conducted exit polls for Proposition 209, with similar results: roughly 60 percent of White, 26 percent of Black, 30 percent of Latino, and 45 percent of Asian American voters favored the proposition (Ness and Nakao, 1996, A1; *Los Angeles Times*, 1996, A29; Citrin et al., 1997a, Table 1). These results suggest greater support from Latino voters and less support from Asian voters for affirmative action than do surveys of the population as a whole. In an unsuccessful referendum to eliminate affirmative action in Houston, Texas, one year later, about three-fifths of White voters supported abolition compared with fewer than 10 percent of African American voters and about 25 percent of Latino voters (Mason, 1997).

Thus, a coalition among African Americans, Latinos, and occasionally Asian Americans in favor of at least limited forms of affirmative action is plausible, but not definite. Blacks care much more about the issue than do the other two groups; Blacks support its strongest forms more than do the other two groups; and Blacks are more committed to affirmative action for Blacks than are the other two groups. Evidence from particular disputes over affirmative action shows mutual support among two and sometimes all three of the non-Anglo groups as well as fierce zero-sum competition, depending on the location and the particular circumstances.

Immigrants and Immigration

Preferences with regard to immigration policy and views of immigrants show a different pattern. Although the data are again too sparse to be definitive, especially for Asian Americans, Latinos and probably Asian Americans are much more sympathetic to immigrants and much more supportive of policies to encourage more immigration than are African

Americans and Whites. Within that conclusion lies great variation—across surveys, over time, in different regions and cities, and across different nationality groups within a given ethnicity—which allows for different types of political mobilization. But the pattern suggests that an affirmative action coalition would break down rather quickly if its members shifted their attention to immigration.

A survey in Los Angeles shows the pattern clearly (see Table 3-7). Latinos and Asian Americans are consistently more likely to give responses sympathetic to immigrants than are Whites and African Americans. Latinos are the most liberal on immigration policy, followed by Asian Americans. African Americans and non-Hispanic Whites are least supportive of policies to encourage immigration and help immigrants. Other national and regional surveys show roughly the same pattern: African Americans and Whites are much less enthusiastic about immigrants and more restrictive in their preferences for immigration policy than are Latinos (*Los Angeles Times*, 1993a, Ques. 136, 137, 142, 143; *Los Angeles Times*, 1993b, Ques. 67; Fetzer, 1995, 12-14; Joint Center, 1997a, Table 6; Post-Modernity, 1996, Table 40A; General Social Survey, 1994, Ques. 514, 518A).[12] Surveys that include Asian Americans show a split on most but not all questions regarding immigrants and immigration policy between Latinos and Asian Americans, on the one hand, and Blacks and Whites, on the other (*Washington Post* et al., 1995; Klineberg, 1996, 32-33; Uhlaner, 1991, 360-365).

TABLE 3-7

**Residents of Los Angeles' Preferred Immigration Policy
by Race or Ethnicity, 1992**

High scores indicate attitudes more favorable to immigration

	Anglos (N=407)	African Americans (N=310)	Latinos (N=314)	Asian Americans (N=196)
Amnesty for undocumented residents	42	44	80	55
Additional spending to prevent illegal immigration	19	29	26	24
Require recent immigrant business owners to hire U.S. citizens	29	14	13	18
Reduce level of legal immigration	21	22	30	26
Policy index mean	2.62	2.53	2.88	2.74

Source: Bobo and Hutchings (1994), Table 1.

TABLE 3-8

**Effects of Recent Immigrants on Your Community
by Race or Ethnicity, 1997**

Percentage responding "better":

	Whites (N=800)	African Americans (N=229)	Hispanics (N=220)
Overall quality of life in your city or town	11	15	35
Quality of local public schools	8	9	34
Local crime situation	4	2	32
Local job opportunities for you and family	7	9	31
Local food, music, arts, culture	30	28	52
Local economy in general	20	21	39
Local politics and government	8	11	34

Note: Response alternatives were "worse," "not much effect," and "don't know."

Source: Princeton Survey Research Associates (1997), 70.

A recent national survey suggests why African Americans and Whites resemble each other and not Hispanics in their preferences for immigration policy. On every one of the seven opportunities they were offered, Hispanics found the effects of immigration on their community to be much more favorable than did the other two groups (see Table 3-8). Similarly, in 1995, more than one-half of the Black residents of Houston, Texas, declared that the impact of immigrants on their community was "bad" or "very bad," and only one-third judged that it was "good" or "very good" (Rodriguez, 1996, 118). In a survey at about the same time in Los Angeles, over one-half of African Americans and Whites agreed that if immigration to the United States continues at the present rate, members of their group would lose political influence and economic opportunity. Not surprisingly, only one-fifth of Latinos and one-tenth of Asian Americans expressed the same fears. Blacks were especially fearful of a direct zero-sum loss to immigrants (Johnson et al., 1996, Tables 1-3; *Los Angeles Times*, 1993a, Ques. 138-140). Concern about the health of the economy, alienation from society and polity, economic and political isolationism, fear of economic competition, and symbolic racism also contributes to anxiety about immigrants and immigration (Espenshade and Hempstead, 1996; Vidanage and Sears, 1995; Citrin et al., 1997b).

As with affirmative action, support for a ballot proposition is an illuminating supplement to survey data. In 1994, Californians voted on Proposition 187, which proposed to prohibit the use of public services such as schooling and health care by illegal immigrants. The proposition passed by a three-to-two margin. Averaging across exit poll data, we found that about 64 percent of Anglos, 52 percent of Blacks and Asian Americans, and only 27 percent of Latinos supported the proposition (Tolbert and Hero, 1996, 817; *Los Angeles Times*, 1994; *Migration News*, 1994; Campbell and Wong, 1998). Comparing survey responses with these voting results suggests that Asian American voters are less sympathetic to illegal immigrants than are Asian Americans overall and that voters in the other three groups roughly reflect the views of all members of those groups.

Finally, support for policies that indirectly address immigration shows the same pattern as support for immigration policies directly, thus widening the arena in which the "natural" alliance of African Americans and Latinos, or of people of color more broadly, is likely to be strained or broken. African Americans and Whites are much more likely than Latinos to agree that "being able to speak and understand English [is] an absolutely essential obligation of Americans" (Post-Modernity, 1996, Table 18D), and twice as many Blacks and Whites as Latinos strongly favor making English the official language of the Unites States (Post-Modernity, 1996, Table 10S; Fetzer, 1995, 23; General Social Survey, 1994, Ques. 512, 513). Surveys show that Latinos favor bilingual education programs in schools much more than do Whites and somewhat more than do African Americans (*Los Angeles Times*, 1993a, Ques. 134; Yankelovich Partners, 1995, Ques. 22; General Social Survey, 1994, Ques. 524).

Proposition 227, a measure to almost eliminate bilingual education in public schools, was approved in June 1998 by more than three-fifths of California's voters. The results show once again that Asian American voters are more conservative, or more assimilated, than are Asian Americans in general. But the rest of the votes follow roughly the pattern expected from the survey data: 67 percent of Whites, 48 percent of Blacks, and 37 percent of Latinos supported the measure (as did 57 percent of Asian Americans) (*Los Angeles Times*, 1998).

In short, a "rainbow coalition" of support cannot be expected for immigration policy any more than for affirmative action policy. Surveys suggest that such a coalition is within the realm of possibility and might, in some circumstances, be joined by well-educated and well-off Whites. But it would be difficult to sustain, especially if issues were framed in a way that entailed losses for some proportional to gains for others. Once again, dramatic fluidity is evident in coalitional possibilities.

Thus, based on survey data, a clear prediction of victory by one of the three initial models is not warranted for two reasons. First, the data yield too many complicated or inconsistent stories, for methodological or substantive reasons or both. Second, it is up to political actors who have not yet acted to determine which of the various possible groupings will in fact coalesce and whether issues that evoke antagonism or agreement will predominate. Race matters—but politics matters too.

COALITIONAL POLITICS ON THE GROUND

Surveys suggest possible coalitions; political activity creates or destroys real ones. Coalitions can be built on different bases and probably need to combine several to thrive. These bases include economic interests, a commitment to shared values, leaders willing to take risks to reach beyond their core supporters, interpersonal trust, and a conviction that the long-term benefits of a coalition will outweigh its short-term costs (Sonenshein, 1993, 1997).

Consider interests first. African Americans are the most liberal group on social and economic policy issues, seeking more government involvement and higher public expenditures on employment, health care, aid to the poor, education, and aid for urban infrastructures. This is an uncontested, familiar finding (see Table 3-3 above and Dawson, 1994; Tate, 1994; Hamilton and Hamilton, 1997). Latinos similarly favor "increased government spending on health and crime and drug control; education; the environment; child services; and bilingual education. They also overwhelmingly look to government to solve the problems that most concern them [and they] are notably more liberal than [Whites]" (de la Garza et al., 1992, 14). Some Whites and Asian Americans also support redistributive policies. Can this policy consensus be translated into a sustained coalition so that common interests override conflict over scarce resources?

To interests, add values. African Americans have historically been the group most committed to vigorous public efforts to attain racial equality and to show respect for distinctive group identities. This, too, is an uncontested and familiar finding. Most Latinos and some Whites and Asian Americans share these values. So the same question arises: can this ideological commitment be translated into a sustained coalition so that shared values override conflict over scarce status and differing views on how to put these values into practice?

Over the past few decades, leaders skilled at bringing together disparate and mistrustful groups have been in short supply. Mayor Tom Bradley of Los Angeles succeeded within his city; the Reverend Jesse Jackson has made valiant efforts to develop a rainbow coalition across the nation; and Mayor David Dinkins spoke eloquently of the "gorgeous mosaic" of New Yorkers. The Congressional Black Caucus and the Congressional Hispanic Caucus have overcome deep disagreements to work closely together, even on issues that mattered more to one than to the other of their constituencies. Nevertheless, moderate or conservative White politicians have recently proved far more adept at appealing to non-White immigrants. In New York, Los Angeles, Chicago, Gary, Philadelphia, and other cities, White conservatives have won enough support from Latino (and other) voters to replace or defeat Black liberal mayors (Sleeper, 1993; Mollenkopf, 1997; Sonenshein, 1997; Pinderhughes, 1997).

This pattern of defeat despite shared interests and values is partly explicable in terms of the other essential bases of coalition building—the willingness to take risks, the growth of interpersonal trust, and sufficient political strength to accept imminent losses for the sake of eventual gains.

Less abstractly, the current eclipse of Black-led coalitions has resulted partly from the distinctive history of earlier Black political successes. Blacks began to win urban elections, even where they remained a minority, when they both mobilized internally and cultivated alliances with liberal Whites. Latinos and Asian Americans were included in those coalitions only in subsidiary positions (Browning et al., 1990). But the standard biracial formula—implying a Black-White dichotomy and an axis of inclusion/exclusion—produces four problems for would-be Black leaders in the new environment.

First, the formula "posits the racial collectivity as its central agency and racial discrimination as its main analytical category" (Reed, 1999, 98). Exclusive emphasis on the problem of discrimination, while still useful in many political contexts, can deflect attention from new problems and policy concerns that African Americans share with newcomers. Second, it obscures intraracial stratification and thereby assumes allegiances within the Black population—or within other populations—that may not exist. Third, and conversely, the standard formula focuses too heavily on Black-White relations and thereby misses the opportunity to build alliances with other political actors (Skerry, 1993, e.g., 10, 370; Jennings, 1992, 44). Finally, it puts too much weight on winning positions from which Blacks have historically been excluded. This insistence on descriptive representation comes at the expense of other political and policy goals that can be shared across groups.

The biracial formula worked well in the 1970s and 1980s. But now, as Whites leave central cities and Hispanic and Asian immigrants take their places, Blacks who remain find that the terms of the political equation have changed. Whites still make up a plurality if not a majority of active voters and will remain disproportionately influential. However, traditional White redistributive liberalism is on the decline, giving way to concerns far less sympathetic to minority group claims, such as environmentalism, welfare dependency, trade policy, and crime control. Thus, even the Whites who remain in cities are less available for traditional Black-liberal White alliances (Kaus, 1992; Sleeper, 1997). Further, non-White constituencies in central cities will increasingly insist on more complex, multiracial coalitions.[13] In short, "the traditional way of conceptualizing racial-ethnic issues and strategies along a Black-White dichotomy will not be effective in mobilizing Puerto Ricans and other Latinos" (Falcón, 1995, 204), as well as Asian Americans and sympathetic Whites.

However, all is not lost. "While Puerto Ricans [and other non-Whites] do not respond neatly to this bipolar racial classification, the notion of being a non-White group is a strong one and, on this basis, there appear to be many areas of public policy consensus between large majorities of Puerto Ricans and Blacks" (Falcón, 1995, 204). The question is whether African Americans, other people of color, and like-minded Whites can surmount their partly outdated assumptions, mutual mistrust, and substantive disagreements enough to pursue their shared material and philosophical goals.

New York and Los Angeles are good cases for considering this question. Both cities have a substantial African American population that has achieved considerable political incorporation over the past few decades. Both cities boast increasingly heterogeneous populations, due mostly to immigration from Asia and Latin America. In both cities, African American political leaders have recently lost power to relatively conservative Whites. If these cases can be explained, the issue of when multiracial coalitions are, and are not, feasible should be clearer.

Multiracial Political Dynamics in New York City

Large numbers of immigrants continue to flock to New York City. Until the mid-1960s, most immigrants came from Europe, and most had arrived by the 1920s. Since 1965, however, the city has absorbed unprecedented waves of Caribbean, Asian, and Hispanic immigrants, so that, in combination with African Americans, non-Whites make up 57 percent of the population.[14]

By sheer numbers alone, Blacks, Hispanics, and Asian Americans in New York have the makings of a strong minority coalition. But numbers are not sufficient to accomplish such an enterprise. To begin with, voters differ from residents; there are twice as many White as Black registered voters, and almost four times as many White as Latino voters. In addition, the panethnic categories such as "Hispanic" and "Asian" obscure a politically salient fragmentation. New York's Hispanics include Puerto Ricans, Dominicans, Colombians, Cubans, and others. Black New Yorkers include native-born African Americans and a growing foreign-born population of African and Afro-Caribbean immigrants. Asian Americans include at least half a dozen nationalities—Chinese, Filipino, Korean, and Vietnamese immigrants from East Asia, and Indian, Bangladeshi, and Pakistani immigrants from South Asia—whose native languages are mutually unintelligible.

Nevertheless, New York's political culture and institutions display features that should encourage multiracial alliances. First, the city's Blacks and Latinos (specifically Puerto Ricans) have a long history of political mobilization, at least since the Depression.[15] Second, after years of under-representation in city government, the two groups have begun to approach legislative proportionality. "By 1992, Blacks and Latinos had come to hold 21 of 53 seats on the city council, 6 of the city's 14 congressional seats, 6 of 25 state senate seats, and 24 of the 60 assembly seats" (Mollenkopf, 1997, 99). Third, although Whites far outnumber Blacks and Hispanics in the general electorate, the disparity narrows considerably among registered Democrats. "Blacks are actually better represented among registered Democrats than in the voting-age population as a whole; Latinos are less underrepresented among Democrats than among registered voters as a whole" (Mollenkopf, 1994, 86). African Americans have attained significant leadership positions within the Democratic Party (which still controls local patronage and nomi-nation slates), and the two groups have formed a joint caucus in the state assembly.

The relatively low level of neighborhood-based conflicts between Blacks and new immigrants should also enhance the prospect for minority coalitions. New York has its share of interminority tensions, but they seldom reach the level of hostility seen in cities such as Los Angeles and Miami. (On

Los Angeles, see Baldassare, 1994; Gooding-Williams, 1993; Sonenshein, 1996; Davis, 1998. On Miami, see Grenier and Stepick, 1992; Portes and Stepick, 1993. On New York, see Mollenkopf, 1995, 1994; Waldinger, 1996.) Conflicts between Blacks and Korean merchants, for example, have spurred protests, vitriolic rhetoric, and scattered individual cases of violence, but not large-scale rioting or mass violence. Labor market competition between Blacks and new immigrants in New York has also been relatively subdued. With the important exception of the government sector and social services, African Americans and non-White immigrants largely concentrate in different sectors of the city's postindustrial labor market (Waldinger, 1996; Bailey and Waldinger, 1991). This division of labor may help to reduce tensions between African Americans and new immigrants if, as some argue, newcomers are taking jobs that native-born Blacks do not want.[16]

Finally, many Black New Yorkers and new immigrants share material interests that should provide the basis for an issue-oriented coalition. Until recently, they were largely excluded from the economic benefits of the postindustrial transformation that the city's economy has undergone. Thus, poverty rates among New York's Blacks and Latinos increased sharply in the 1980s despite the city's growing prosperity (Falcón, 1988, 174). In addition, the most rapidly growing and remunerative sectors of the postindustrial economy have generally excluded Blacks and other non-White groups. Marginality in a thriving economy brings further shared ills: higher rents in a tighter housing market, "very high unemployment rates, . . . extremely high dropout rates from the schools, and intense residential displacement due to factors such as disinvestment and gentrification" (Falcón, 1988, 174).[17]

How have New Yorkers fared in building multiracial coalitions, given this mix of shared interests, relatively sustained political involvement, and demographic disparities? In a word, poorly. Electoral coalitions between Blacks and other non-White groups have been infrequent, and those that have formed have proved ephemeral and susceptible to disruption. Between 1965 and 1973, Blacks joined Hispanics and liberal Whites to support Mayor John Lindsay's progressive administration. During his two terms, Lindsay set spending and service distribution priorities that favored the city's Black and Hispanic populations. He also experimented with new forms of minority political incorporation such as offices of neighborhood government (Mollenkopf, 1997). However, the experiment failed to take institutional root and lost ground in the subsequent conservative mayoral administrations headed by Abraham Beame and Edward Koch.

In 1985, the effort to create a progressive coalition took a different form. Non-White politicians sought to close ranks and mount an independent minority-based political initiative. About 40 Black political activists and elected officials convened the Coalition for a Just New York to select a candidate for mayor. Although Hispanic Congressman Herman Badillo aggressively courted the group and advocated issue positions in keeping with the group's agenda, several leading Black politicians were openly averse to endorsing a non-Black candidate, and the coalition passed on the opportunity. Not surprisingly, this open denial exacerbated tensions between the Black and the Hispanic communities. The coalition ultimately settled on Black Assemblyman Denny Farrell, who, by most accounts, was a weak choice and ran a deplorably ineffective campaign.

In this case, not only did the Black rejection of Badillo's overtures throw away an opportunity to "go along to get along"—essential to all coalitions (Stone, 1989)—but it also substituted a weaker for a stronger candidate. Ironically, Badillo's policy positions would have benefited African Americans as well as Hispanics, certainly more than did those of Ed Koch, the eventual mayoral winner. But Black leaders were unable to relinquish the implicit claim that Blacks historically have made to the most visible positions of leadership and to the right to define the policy agenda in minority-based coalitions. In analytic terms, they lacked sufficient trust and political strength to absorb short-term costs so as to take advantage of the interests and values they shared with New York's Hispanics.

In 1989, Blacks joined with Hispanics to elect David Dinkins as the city's first African American mayor. This venture seemed even more conducive to a stable coalition among people of color than the Lindsay experiment because Dinkins' electoral and governing coalitions were clearly organized and guided by minorities (along with some liberal Whites). Dinkins campaigned not only by seeking, successfully, to win virtually all African American votes, but also by making direct, purposeful appeals to Hispanics, Afro-Caribbeans, and other non-White constituencies. This strategy marked an important departure from the conventional Black-White electoral logic.

Under Dinkins' administration, the number of Black and Hispanic government officials increased, and relations between the police and the city's non-White residents improved modestly. But as in the 1970s, the coalition proved fragile. Many Hispanic leaders charged that they were denied an equitable share of political rewards, and they insisted that the mayor was far more interested in courting and solidifying White support than rewarding his non-White supporters (Thompson, 1996). Several Black politicians echoed the latter complaint.

Once again, the most severe conflict centered on group visibility and descriptive representation. Blacks in New York have achieved relatively greater access to political office than have other non-White groups, so they could afford to shift to "post-access" concerns for themselves and allow access concessions to others. After all, "the significantly less access [sic] that Latinos have than Blacks or Whites to political and public bureaucracy representation . . . would indicate that this would be a more salient issue to Latinos. . . . [They] seem to give greater emphasis to questions of basic group visibility, including symbolic recognition" (Falcón, 1988, 180).

Nonetheless, Latino political leaders and the Latino press charged that Dinkins' African American appointees to the 1990 city council districting commission favored Blacks over Latinos in allocating council seats. As they saw it, "although Latinos and African Americans are roughly the same proportion of the city population, the commission created twelve so-called 'winnable' seats for African American candidates but only eight Latino winnable seats" (Thompson, 1996, 77). Dinkins pointed out (plausibly) that this lopsided distribution was due largely to the geographic dispersion, low voter registration, and comparative youth of the city's Latino population. Nevertheless, the mayor's Black appointees would have been well advised to yield a few more seats to Latinos to help build reciprocity and solidify their loyalty to the coalition. Instead, "the split with Latinos revealed that parts of the Latino leadership were so displeased that they might try to break the African American/Latino alliance that helped elect Dinkins [in 1989]" (Thompson, 1996, 77).

That is just what happened in 1993, as conservative Republican candidate Rudolph Giuliani defeated Dinkins after one term. Latino voters, who had provided a critical bloc of support in Dinkins' 1989 victory, turned out in far fewer numbers in 1993, and almost one-half shifted their allegiance to Giuliani (Mollenkopf, 1994). Their demobilization and defection, along with the loss of some liberal White supporters, helped to produce Dinkins' defeat.

Mayor Giuliani has subsequently proved adept at preserving his new coalition by addressing, if only symbolically, issues of great interest to the city's new residents such as immigration reform. He has also appointed Hispanics to his administration (including, ironically, Herman Badillo, selected to run for city comptroller on Giuliani's ticket). He has simultaneously pursued fiscal and social policies that have had a disproportionately adverse impact on the poor—the predominantly Black, Hispanic, and other non-White populations. Room remains, therefore, for New York's liberal and/or non-White leaders to fashion alliances to pursue a progressive agenda.

But several changes must occur for such an alliance to hope to succeed. African American political leaders must speak out on issues such as immigration, deportation, bilingual education, and access to welfare services that particularly concern the new non-White residents of the city.[18] Coalitions must be carefully focused on discrete economic and social interests that concern all of these groups—such as expanded economic opportunity, improvements in public education, and better relations with the police—rather than on the single, short-term goal of winning elections. All groups must work hard to avoid the zero-sum competition that arises in debates over who faces the most discrimination, who should win the most offices, or who deserves the most government aid. Poor and working class New Yorkers of all backgrounds share interests and values; if leaders can keep the focus on these and assume a few personal and political risks, a coalition with greater stability could emerge. But that outcome is far from certain.

Multiracial Political Dynamics in Los Angeles

In other cities with high levels of immigration such as Los Angeles and Chicago, African American political elites face the same challenges. Circumstances and contexts differ, however. In Los Angeles, Latinos (predominantly Mexican Americans) outnumber Blacks by almost three to one.[19] The proportion of Asian Americans is small but rapidly growing, and Asian Americans are making significant political inroads into old coalitions. In Chicago, Blacks still outnumber Hispanics (mostly Mexicans, Dominicans, and other Central and South Americans) two to one, and Asian Americans are relatively unimportant politically. However, in both cities the proportions of African Americans and Whites are declining and will continue to do so at a dramatic pace. Forging coalitions with non-White immigrant-based groups is thus increasingly urgent for traditional Black and White political leaders.

Until recently, African Americans in Chicago and Los Angeles enjoyed much higher levels of political incorporation than did Blacks in New York. They also enjoyed greater success in generating alliances with other non-Whites, particularly Hispanics. In Los Angeles, former Mayor Tom Bradley, an African American, led an effective if sometimes uneasy coalition of Blacks, Latinos, Asian Americans, and liberal Whites from 1973 to 1993. Chicago's Blacks joined with Latinos and liberal Whites to elect Harold Washington, also an African American, to the office of mayor in 1983 and again in 1987.

In recent years, these political coalitions have stumbled on many of the same obstacles that have blocked alliances among people of color in New York. Blacks and Hispanics in Los Angeles have clashed over redistricting and descriptive representation; in Chicago, relations deteriorated over the same issues after Washington's death. Neighborhood-level conflicts among racial or ethnic groups have convulsed both cities. Nevertheless, previous coalitional successes offer important lessons on how to forge constructive political alliances. The Los Angeles case is arguably the most illuminating because it has been the most successful.

Consider first the successes. During the 1980 redistricting debates in the state assembly, the African American speaker, Willie Brown, wisely appointed Hispanic Assemblyman Richard Alatorre from East Los Angeles to chair the committee. After much debate, the committee selected a plan that gave the city's Hispanic constituency one assembly and two congressional seats and cost African Americans none (Skerry, 1993, 85). During the 1985 and 1986 council reapportionment debates, Mayor Bradley similarly created a Latino district and vetoed a plan that would have eliminated the city's only Asian American district (Sonenshein, 1997, 46). Finally, in 1995, African American and Latino political leaders resolved months of rancorous debate by ensuring that neither constituency would lose legislative seats through redistricting.[20] In each case, Los Angeles' Black political leaders were able to move beyond the zero-sum perspective and even to use the reapportionment decisions to build reciprocity with Asian and Latino constituencies.

However, these successes could not prevent tears in the coalitional fabric. By the late 1980s, Hispanic and Asian American political leaders had begun to chafe at their subordinate position in the Bradley coalition. Hispanics in particular vacillated between remaining a part of the multiracial Bradley coalition and seeking to "go it alone" by relying on their own growing numbers in the general population (Sonenshein, 1997, 60). Organizing Latinos into an independent, unified political bloc is no easy task in light of their nationality, citizenship, and socioeconomic differences.[21] But for many Latino political leaders, the prospect of remaining junior partners in a multiracial coalition led by Blacks or Whites is even less palatable.

This strategic uncertainty makes for an unpredictable Latino constituency perhaps increasingly prone to conflict with other groups. In the 1993 mayoral election, Latinos split their votes between the two candidates—one of whom was the clear heir to the progressive, multiracial Bradley dynasty—more than did either Blacks or Asian Americans (Sonenshein, 1993). Partly as a consequence, a conservative White-led coalition won.

The rest of the Bradley coalition largely held together in the 1993 election. Michael Woo, an Asian American city council member, won decisively among liberal Whites and attained almost 70 percent of Asian American and 86 percent of African American votes (although turnout among Blacks was somewhat depressed compared with the Bradley years). Woo's showing is all the more impressive because it came only one year after the South Central civil unrest between Asian Americans and Blacks. African American support for Woo contrasts starkly with the refusal of New York's Black political leaders to support Herman Badillo in his 1985 mayoral bid.[22] After the close election in 1993, Mayor Richard Riordan won reelection decisively in 1997; it remains to be seen whether Bradley's progressive, multiracial coalition can revive enough to defeat Riordan's coalition of moderates and conservatives.[23]

Paralleling successes and failures in the politics of redistricting and voting have been a set of alliances and conflicts revolving around substantive policy concerns. Coalition members share real interests; poor and working class Angelenos have all been affected by structural phenomena such as the movement of jobs to the suburbs and overseas, a repressive police force, and discriminatory practices of banks and realtors (Sonenshein, 1993; Davis, 1990). Middle class Angelenos are concerned about racial and ethnic discrimination, both for its own sake and because discriminatory practices inhibit the shared goal of economic development. These common interests were crucial in creating and maintaining the Bradley coalition over many years and elections.

New Yorkers also share problems and goals but have been able to coalesce only intermittently. What is different about Los Angeles? The key point, especially in comparison with New York and Chicago, is that a history of compromise on policy issues of mutual concern—which began more or less accidentally—has made the next compromise somewhat easier to create. In the late 1960s, all of the eventual coalition members were shut out from policymaking influence and political incorporation by the conservative and aggressively racial regime of Mayor Sam Yorty. Yorty was "a relentless foe of minorities and progressives, [often] using racist appeals to defeat . . . challenges" to his regime (Sonenshein, 1997, 44). That situation provided the impetus for African Americans, liberal Whites, and to a lesser extent Asian Americans and Latinos to unite around their mutual interests in political incorporation and antidiscrimination.[24]

Once the coalition took root, its own prior existence helped to keep it going. To assert that longevity is a critical dimension of most successful governing coalitions is more than tautological; historical memory, practice in negotiation, personal loyalties, a habit of reciprocity, and trust among leaders are all linchpins in the maintenance of political coalitions (Stone, 1989; Hinckley, 1981). The interests of the various coalition partners evolved over time, but leaders were able to keep them linked. Middle class African Americans and liberal Whites enjoyed a greater share of the rewards of incorporation than others. Nevertheless, the alliance was sustained for 20 years largely because the groups avoided zero-sum conflicts and focused on sites of interest convergence wherever they could be found—thus, the well-founded reputation that "Black and [Hispanic] elected officials enjoy extremely good relations" (Skerry, 1993, 84-85). Even the damage done to Korean businesses during the South Central civil unrest precipitated a new wave of dialogue between Black and Asian leaders (Regalado, 1994).

Michael Woo's 1993 campaign showed the legacy of this search for convergence. His policy platform was highly congenial to the interests of poor and working class Blacks, and he included traditional antidiscrimination planks of great concern to middle class Blacks and liberal Whites. He prominently opposed the city's controversial police chief Darryl Gates and worked tirelessly to bring about rapprochement between African Americans and Korean Americans in the aftermath of the South Central disaster. Woo "deserves major credit for brokering some agreements between these highly opposed groups. . . . [He] helped push through city hall funding for the conversion of some [Korean-owned] liquor stores to laundromats." In fact, he "nearly recreated a successful version of the Bradley coalition in very rough times" (Sonenshein, 1993, 302; Park, 1996, 161-162).

But Woo did not succeed. History does not always proceed in a straight line, and time can exacerbate tensions as well as provide resources for overcoming them. Even before the 1992 unrest, the coalition was in danger of dissolving, largely because key coalition members' interests and ideologies were diverging. After two decades, middle class Whites began to object to Mayor Bradley's aggressive pro-growth policies and stances on crime and police accountability. Poor and working class Blacks and Hispanics also became increasingly frustrated with a pro-development agenda from which very few benefits trickled down to them.

However, those disaffected constituents were split among themselves over immigration and were polarizing by class, and they could not unite either within or outside the old Bradley coalition. Relations between African Americans and immigrants became especially tense, playing out in neighborhood conflicts over jobs,[25] housing,[26] and immigrant entrepreneurial activity (Johnson and Oliver, 1989; Johnson et al., 1996). For example, in the wake of the 1992 disturbance, a few African American community organizers called for building contractors to replace Latino laborers with Blacks (Sonenshein, 1993, 298; Skerry, 1993). This substitution of zero-sum proposals for efforts to find common solutions to the common problem of underemployment provides little encouragement to those seeking a new progressive coalition.

If the Bradley coalition is not yet in complete disarray, its future is doubtful. It will take an unlikely mix of interests, ideology, and political entrepreneurialism to put it back together. Despite the growth of a new array of multiracial progressive organizations, "the Establishment Coalition and its policies have come to dominate the agenda of the city" (Park, 1996, 159).

CONCLUSIONS

Los Angeles holds important lessons for African Americans in other cities who seek to make common cause with people of color and liberal Whites. The Bradley coalition mobilized around two unifying interests with deep ideological resonance: antidiscrimination reform and political inclusion. Antiracist political reforms carried unimpeachable moral force and ringing social relevance, and political incorporation was an urgent goal for a variety of Angelenos. In addition, the policy focus on economic development provided opportunities for mutual gains and diminished the impact of direct competition—for a while. Today, political actors must identify equally compelling sites of convergence to build new political capital and more complex coalitions. However, the sites have shifted, and strategies must be updated.

As the survey data show, antidiscrimination goals are no longer the most stable arena for making common cause across racial and ethnic groups. Affirmative action and business set-asides are weighed down with symbolic meaning, some of which is negative to potential allies (Hochschild, 1998). In addition, the groups disagree on the degree to which they and others suffer from discrimination and therefore disagree on the urgency of measures to end it.

The pursuit of inclusion among decisionmakers may be equally unpromising as an arena for building alliances unless Blacks can refrain from guarding their political gains against encroachment. Both the survey data and the experience in New York suggest how difficult it will be for African Americans to set aside their (arguably correct) conviction of uniquely harmful circumstances to make room for new immigrants.

At this writing, conservatives have shown more skill in finding an alternative unifying formulation than have liberals. "In the Establishment Coalition, the aggressive recruitment and the inclusion of racial minorities can be seen as the defining difference between the conservative coalitions forged by Riordan and the previous conservative coalitions in Los Angeles. This might be precisely why Riordan's coalition will prove to be more successful and durable than its predecessors" (Park, 1996, 165). We see no reason to modify this comment much for New York, Chicago, Philadelphia, or elsewhere.

Nevertheless, most Blacks share common interests and values with many Hispanics, some Asian Americans, and some Whites that could provide the basis for new coalitions of the left. For one, political incorporation remains incomplete; the history of Los Angeles shows that it is possible to redistrict in a way that does not tear a progressive coalition apart, and the survey data show at least some concern on the part of each group for the political status of the others. In addition, many Blacks remain poor, and their interests coincide with those of many non-White immigrants and poor

Whites. Further, for once, the survey data reinforce the more analytic argument about interests because they show considerable agreement among people of color on the need for redistributive policies. Therefore, the traditional grounds for liberal interracial alliances have not disappeared, even if they have not shown much vigor recently.

If economic interests or other shared goals are to be the basis of new progressive coalitions, our evidence indicates that at least four conditions must obtain:

- Where possible, racial issues should not be the center of discussion and action. Instead, the focus should be on shared substantive policy and political goals, such as jobs in the primary sector, better schooling, nonbrutal crime control, neighborhood development, immigrant incorporation, and decent housing.

- When attention to race is deemed desirable or essential, everything possible should be done to avoid zero-sum conflicts over processes (such as redistricting or the selection of candidates) and outcomes (such as affirmative action or the funding of particular programs).

- African Americans need to pay more attention to civil rights issues of concern to immigrants, such as welfare rights, deportation, language, and immigration restrictions. They also need to recognize that other groups have the same intense desire for descriptive representation that they themselves have evinced.

- Latinos, Asian Americans, and sympathetic Whites, in return, need to accept that Blacks' history of enslavement and their continued suffering from poverty and racial discrimination are qualitatively different from the history of all voluntary immigrant groups and perhaps require distinct treatment as a consequence.

We are not calling for African Americans to suppress concerns about racial issues. Nor should they abandon their pursuit of remedies for discrimination, especially for poor Blacks who have few resources of their own with which to fight any issue. We are arguing that a focus on ending racial discrimination is not the best staging ground for seeking alliances with other people of color or potentially sympathetic Whites. Instead, African Americans would do well to consider that engaging other groups in support of antidiscrimination goals will most likely occur in the pursuit of policy goals that are not ostensibly about race.

Consider, for instance, African Americans' concerns about the potentially adverse impact of recent welfare reform policies on poor Black communities. These concerns resemble immigrants' anxieties about the broadly harmful effects of California's Proposition 187 on all immigrants, not just on illegal entrants to the United States.[27] Similarly, some provisions of the 1996 welfare reforms directly targeted poor and/or undocumented immigrants, and the new policy as a whole has left the poorest Hispanics in the same dangerous situation as the poorest Blacks.[28] Thus, immigrant advocacy groups might see as much racial or ethnic bias in the new welfare law as do Black advocacy groups (Lieberman, 1998). Shared anxieties about bias in the provision of public services are a good site for generating shared demands to reduce discrimination—but only by first emphasizing the mutual desire to maintain social services and supports for the poor of every race.

A similar case can be made for the issue of police accountability. African Americans have complained of police brutality and harassment for decades; immigrants from Latin America and the Caribbean have recently joined them. The cases in New York involving the torture of Abner Louima, a Haitian immigrant, and the killing of Amadou Diallo, a newcomer from Guinea, are highly dramatic, but not the only incidents generating this concern. How to control crime without violating individuals' rights is an issue that could bring together people of various racial and ethnic groups, including Whites, in support of antidiscrimination measures. But, as with welfare, the initial policy focus should not be race, but a shared interest in the appropriate delivery of a crucial public service in central cities.

Improving public education, ensuring health care, finding homes for children who lack stable families, and providing jobs once the economy slows are issues that have an obvious racial dimension, but they need not be approached through a framework of fighting racial discrimination. African American leaders should find ways to bring others into a coalition that focuses on the problems rather than on the identities of the coalition members so that they do not have to choose between fighting bias and finding allies.

Analytically, we are proposing that politicians and policy actors seek to create the first of our three models of diversity—that is, to promote interactive pluralism rather than group separation or Black exceptionalism. Pluralism need not, and probably should not, imply colorblindness or un-rooted individualism, as it often has in the past. It does imply that groups will come together around particular issues and perhaps separate into new groupings for other issues. The key point is that the content of issue disputes, not ethnicity or race, will determine the coalitional patterns.

All of these prescriptions are easier said than done, and historically they have proved almost impossible to sustain for long periods. Nevertheless, we retain some optimism that, despite history, it is possible to develop class-based coalitions around particular policy issues because American society is developing along several unprecedented lines. One is the growth of a Black middle class that is moving away from poorer Blacks physically and politi-cally. That phenomenon has produced declining intraracial solidarity on issues of economic redistribution, but greater intraracial solidarity on issues of discrimination and bias. Whether the growing African American middle class will be swayed more by its increasing economic conservatism or its increasing racial nationalism—or both or neither—is a question for coalition builders of the left and the right to ponder. In analytic terms, Black excep-tionalism seems to be growing culturally and politically, while declining economically and socially (Hochschild, forthcoming).

A second new phenomenon is the growing Latino population that is neither "White" nor "Black" by conventional understandings and that therefore can act as an intermediary between the two traditional antagonists. That population is becoming politically important as more Latinos become naturalized citizens and begin to engage in conventional politics.[29] It is also becoming more internally diverse, as some Latinos join the middle class and others emigrate from desperately poor communities in Mexico and Central or South America into the poorest ranks of U.S. cities. Most Latinos seek to become upwardly mobile joiners of mainstream society (Saad, 1995), but some see their group as an oppressed racial minority. Some reject conventional means to, if not conventional goals of, success, while other "Latino politicians are becoming uncomfortable with old-style minority politics" (Rodriguez, 1999). How that complexity will translate into mobilization into left or right coalitions remains uncertain.[30]

Asian Americans show some of the same political mobilization and ideological diversity as Latinos.[31] They are, on balance, more like Whites in their economic trajectory and political views, but their commitment to descriptive political representation and anxiety about racial bias make them potential members of at least some progressive coalitions. They are the most libertarian of the four groups, which makes them sometimes available for mobilization on the left (e.g., for the retention of the right to abortions) and sometimes on the right (e.g., for opposition to government regulation of business). Thus, in terms of this analysis, groups may not be moving toward political or economic separation, but they retain distinctive profiles that must be considered in any effort to create alliances.

Perhaps even the White population is becoming more internally varied; the 1997 Joint Center surveys show greater disparity across age groups than across races on many controversial policy issues. Some Whites, too, suffer when jobs leave the city, schools deteriorate, and neighborhoods crumble. They have, of course, less need to enhance descriptive representation, but Whites sometimes support non-White candidates and elected officials (Hajnal, 1999; Carsey, 1995), and they have been staunch members of progressive coalitions when their interests are sufficiently guarded and their ideological commitments engaged.

The possibilities are ripe for multiracial coalition building across races, ethnicities, classes, and locations. However, African American political leaders will fully awaken to this potential only with some reorientation of Black political discourse. They must eschew the standard biracial formulation that has traditionally marked Black politics in American cities and that has predisposed Blacks to ally primarily, if not exclusively, with liberal Whites. Other groups in the electorate can no longer be ignored. Nor can the fact that there are other bases for coalition building besides antiracism and inclusion. If progressives do not take heed, conservatives will continue to do so.

NOTES

1. Because of space limitations in this volume, we did not expand the discussion to consider ideologically based racial and ethnic coalitions in Congress and among interest or advocacy groups. The very short version of those stories is that the coalitions work surprisingly well in the U.S. House of Representatives, despite very difficult moments, and work rather poorly among advocacy groups.

2. By comparison, in 1989 the median family income for Whites was $37,600; for Blacks, $22,400; for Latinos, $25,000; and for all Asian Americans combined, $41,000 (Lien, 1998, Tables 1-1, 1-2).

3. As Bobo and Smith (1994), Kinder and Sanders (1996), and Gilens (1999) show, policy issues that are not ostensibly about race are often racially inflected in public discourse and in citizens' responses to survey questions. That phenomenon was evident in the survey questions that yielded the strongest racial divisions, such as the desirability of cutting welfare. Whether an issue is given a racial inflection, or whether an issue that is commonly thought of in racial terms can be made to seem more racially neutral, is a central concern for anyone seeking to build coalitions across races and ethnic groups. Racial connotations are at least somewhat malleable, and much political contestation in the foreseeable future will presumably revolve around whether welfare, crime control, public education, and so on are "really" about Blacks and Latinos or "really" about families and neighborhoods. We discuss this crucial issue in the "Conclusions" of the chapter.

4. We say "roughly speaking" because Whites were more concerned about health care and care for the elderly than about gang violence, and Latinos were more concerned about child abuse than about crime (U.S. Department of Justice, 1997, 115). In addition, more careful probing or qualitative interviews would probably reveal racial inflections in how various groups perceive these issues, which would expose at least some points of deep disagreement.

5. These results apparently contradict findings in other analyses, such as those of Kinder and Sanders (1996, 30) and Tate (1994, 29-39). In part, the differences simply reflect house effects of the surveys, which is to say, variations in results across different survey organizations that no one knows how to explain. In addition, both studies focus on surveys conducted about a decade before the ones that we cite in the text; it is possible that attitudinal differences between Blacks and Whites have softened since the mid-1980s. Both studies also rely heavily on American National Election Studies surveys in which the Black sample sizes are sometimes quite small and Latinos and Asian Americans are not identified separately. Even so, some of the results resemble the patterns we describe: Blacks are consistently more liberal than Whites, but on some issues there is essentially no difference in policy views across the races. Sometimes there is greater disparity between issues that are most and least favored than between Blacks' and Whites' views on the issues within that cluster.

6. This interpretation probably does not fit White respondents (unless we were to engage in a deep Freudian analysis of attraction to the disfavored other). We interpret Whites' sense of commonality with Blacks as an identification with other Americans rather than with foreigners or immigrants, an interpretation that is supported by survey data on immigration issues that we report below.

7. Perhaps Blacks concur with Patterson's (1989) enunciation of the "homeostatic principle" of racial domination or Bell's (1992) similar conviction that American racism is permanent and essentially unchanging.

8. On all of these issues, well-off and well-educated African Americans diverge more sharply from the modal White view than do poor and poorly educated African Americans (Hochschild, 1995; Joint Center, 1997a; Gallup Organization, 1997).

9. New immigrants may not interpret racially inflected encounters as African Americans typically would, so their subsequent political response (or lack thereof) may seem weak to American eyes. For example, Waters (1996) describes the discordant reactions of Afro-Caribbean immigrants and African Americans in New York to an incident in which a young Black immigrant was attacked by a mob of White teenagers. African American leaders were more inclined to politicize the incident and were much more attuned to the racial overtones of the attack than were immigrant leaders.

10. For example, Whites, Blacks, and Latinos all agree—but Asian Americans do not— that Asian Americans are "getting more economic power than is good for Southern California" (*Los Angeles Times* Poll, 1993b, Ques. 45).

11. However, Asian Americans are no more immune to self-interest than are other groups. A survey of southern Californians pointed out that there are almost three times as many Asian Americans in California's universities than would be warranted by racial proportionality among state residents. Respondents were then asked if they preferred an admissions policy that would mirror the state's racial makeup, or if "more [Asian Americans] should be admitted to college than others . . . if [they] are better qualified." Three-fourths of Asian respondents supported "merit" as specified in this question, compared with 6 in 10 Whites and roughly 4 in 10 Latinos and African Americans (Lien, 1997, Table 4).

12. One more illustration from a national sample and perhaps the best survey: on a four-item index of views of immigrants, Hispanics averaged 63 percent favorability; Anglos, 42.7 percent; and African Americans, only 34.7 percent. There were too few Asian Americans to tabulate (General Social Survey, 1996, Ques. 960A-D, Hochschild tabulations).

13. The proportion of voting-age non-White immigrants is growing steadily. In New York, for example, there are 1.5 million post-1965 immigrants eligible for naturalization. Most are from Asia, Latin America, and the Caribbean. Many of these immigrants (or their children) will become voters and thus will be critical elements in any urban coalition in the foreseeable future.

14. Non-Hispanic Whites make up 43 percent of New York City's population; Blacks, 25 percent; Hispanics, 24 percent; and Asian and others, the remaining 8 percent.

15. Asian American groups have been much less visible in New York City politics and have been slow to mobilize. Several Asian American candidates did, however, launch campaigns in recent rounds of city council elections.

16. This point is debatable; if employers prefer to hire immigrants rather than African Americans, employment niche patterns result from employer discrimination, rather than group self-sorting (Kirschenman and Neckerman, 1991; Lee, 1998).

17. However, economic inequality *within* the Black population has increased, as has "the social and political distance between the Black middle class and the Black poor" (Mollenkopf, 1994, 68). Similarly, Afro-Caribbeans, Koreans, and Colombians have fared much better than native-born Blacks, Dominicans, and Puerto Ricans.

18. Congressman Charles Rangel is a notable exception to the Black silence on these issues. See Jones-Correa (1998) on the political concerns of the new immigrants and on the lack of efforts to integrate them into political organizations.

19. Latinos now make up almost 40 percent of Los Angeles' population and outnumber all other groups. The Asian American population has more than doubled in the past 20 years and currently constitutes 10 percent of the population. After peaking at 17 percent some years ago, the African American population now hovers around 14 percent; the White population, at 48 percent of the population in 1980, constitutes just over one-third.

20. Reuel Rogers' conversation (July 15, 1997) with James H. Johnson, who served as a consultant to the reapportionment debates.

21. Although Hispanics make up 40 percent of the Los Angeles population, they are only 11 percent of registered voters. (Whites and Blacks account, respectively, for 65 and 15 percent of the city's registered voters.) The disparity is due mostly to the comparative youth and low naturalization and voter registration rates of the city's Latino residents. Hence, Latino leaders who hope to create an independent political bloc must undertake a massive mobilization effort focused on both naturalization and voter registration and turnout.

22. Several leading African American politicians, such as Congresswoman Maxine Waters and former primary candidate J. Stanley Sanders, did not endorse Woo. But he won the backing of other key Black political figures, and the city's Black leadership did not express any concerted resistance to his candidacy.

23. Park (1996) provides a useful discussion of the details of Los Angeles politics over the past few years, expressing even less optimism than we do about the resurgence of a coalition of the left.

24. The 1983 alliance among Blacks, Hispanics, and liberal Whites in Chicago was forged around similar sites of convergence. This coalition never took institutional root; rather, it was held together by Mayor Harold Washington's charisma and strong leadership. When Washington died suddenly in 1987, the alliance disintegrated almost immediately. Black political leaders became riven by factionalism among reformers, party loyalists, and racial nationalists. The latter drew a disproportionate amount of public attention and quickly alienated the White liberals and Latinos who had been subsidiary but crucial partners in Washington's coalition. Both groups shifted their allegiance to Mayor Richard Daley, Jr.'s conservative coalition, which has dominated Chicago politics since 1989. Mayor Daley now enjoys strong support from all of the city's racial and ethnic groups, including African Americans.

25. As Los Angeles' "branch-plant economy toward which working class Blacks and Chicanos had always looked for decent jobs collapsed," the two groups increasingly must compete for what remains. Even those Blacks "willing to compete for . . . menial service jobs find themselves in a losing competition with new immigrants" (Davis, 1990, 304-305).

26. Formerly all-Black neighborhoods have undergone uneasy transition as large numbers of Hispanics have moved in and Asian immigrants have opened fledgling family businesses.

27. Thus, Hispanics acted to become naturalized citizens, to register, and to vote after Proposition 187. California's Hispanics are now much more likely to vote Democratic than are Hispanics in Texas and Florida, even though they had been moving in the

direction of the Republican Party in the early 1990s (Tobar, 1998; *The Public Perspective,* 1999).

28. "As the welfare rolls continue to plunge, White recipients are leaving the system much faster than Black and Hispanic recipients, pushing the minority share of the caseload to the highest level on record. . . . The disproportionately large exodus of Whites has altered the racial balance in a program long rife with racial conflict and stereotypes. . . . The legacy of those stereotypes makes the discussion of race and welfare an unusually sensitive one" (deParle, 1998, A1; see also Swarns, 1998).

29. A few representative quotations after the 1998 elections: "The backlash from the passage of Propositions 187 and 209 in California has made Latinos the state's most powerful voting bloc" (*Migration News,* 1998). "With the mid-term elections over, Republicans and Democrats are now plotting their strategies to enlist the nation's fastest growing minority in their bid to win the White House in 2000" (*Politico,* 1998, 1). "In the last election, Hispanics were the swing vote in several key races, including those in Texas, California, Florida, New York, Arizona, Nevada, and California" (*Parade Magazine,* 1999).

30. The most systematic analysis of the political implications of a growing number of Hispanic voters finds that political and (especially) socioeconomic gains for African Americans are positively correlated with gains for Hispanics; that is, increases for one group are often concomitant with the other, and both gains come at the expense of Whites (McClain and Tauber, 1998). If that pattern persists, it permits greater optimism about coalitions among people of color, but less optimism about coalitions between Blacks and Whites or between Latinos and Whites.

31. "Voter turnout among Asian Americans reached an all-time high in the last election. . . . Their most lasting contribution may be their unique ability to transcend traditional ethnic fault lines; indeed, the political maturation of Asian Americans may signal a new era in racial politics" (Rodriguez, 1998, 21, 22).

REFERENCES

Aguirre, B.E., et al. 1989. "Discrimination and the Assimilation and Ethnic Competition Perspectives." *Social Science Quarterly* 70(3):594-606.

Bailey, T., and R. Waldinger. 1991. "The Changing Ethnic/Racial Division of Labor." In *Dual City: The Restructuring of New York.* Ed. J. Mollenkopf and M. Castells. New York: Russell Sage Foundation, 43-78.

Baldassare, M., Ed. 1994. *The Los Angeles Riots: Lessons for the Urban Future.* Boulder, Col.: Westview Press.

Bell, D. 1992. *Race, Racism, and American Law.* Boston: Little, Brown and Company.

Bobo, L.D. 2000. "Race, Interests, and Beliefs about Affirmative Action." In *Racialized Politics: The Debate about Racism in America.* Ed. D. Sears, J. Sidanius, and L.D. Bobo. Chicago: University of Chicago Press.

Bobo, L.D., and V. Hutchings. 1994. "Race, the Sense of Group Position, and Immigration Politics." Paper presented at the annual meeting of the American Political Science Association, New York.

Bobo, L.D., and R.A. Smith. 1994. "Antipoverty Policy, Affirmative Action, and Racial Attitudes." In *Confronting Poverty: Prescriptions for Change.* Ed. S. Danziger, G. Sandefur, and D. Weinberg. New York: Russell Sage Foundation and Harvard University Press, 365-395.

Brackman, H., and S. Erie. 1995. "Beyond 'Politics by Other Means'?: Empowerment Strategies for Los Angeles' Asian Pacific Community." In *The Bubbling Cauldron: Race,*

Ethnicity, and the Urban Crisis. Ed. M.P. Smith and J. Feagin. Minneapolis: University of Minnesota Press.

Browning, R., et al. 1990. "Minority Mobilization in Ten Cities: Failures and Successes." In *Racial Politics in American Cities.* 1st ed. Ed. R.P. Browning, D.R. Marshall, and D.H. Tabb. New York: Longman, 8-30.

Burns, N., et al. 1998. "Active Intersection: Gender, Race or Ethnicity, and Participation." Paper presented at the annual meeting of the Midwest Political Science Association, Chicago.

Campbell, A., and C. Wong. 1998. "'Racial Threat' and Direct Democracy: Contextual Effects in Two California Initiatives." Paper presented at the annual meeting of the Midwest Political Science Association, Chicago.

Carsey, T. 1995. "The Contextual Effects of Race on White Voter Behavior." *Journal of Politics* 57(1):221-228.

Chen, L., and Y. Espiritu. 1989. "Korean Businesses in Black and Hispanic Neighborhoods: A Study of Intergroup Relations." *Sociological Review* 32:521-534.

Citrin, J. 1996. "The Angry White Male Is a Straw Man." *Public Affairs Report* (University of California, Berkeley) 1:10-13.

Citrin, J., et al. 1997a. "Ethnic Context, Group Conflict, and Racial Attitudes: California Voters on Affirmative Action and Immigration." Paper presented at the annual meeting of the American Political Science Association, Washington, D.C.

———. 1997b. "Public Opinion Toward Immigration Reform: The Role of Economic Motivations." *Journal of Politics* 59(3):858-861.

Davis, M. 1990. *City of Quartz: Excavating the Future in Los Angeles.* London: Verso.

———. 1998. *Ecology of Fear: Los Angeles and the Imagination of Disaster.* New York: Metropolitan Books.

Dawson, M.C. 1994. *Behind the Mule: Race and Class in African-American Politics.* Princeton, N.J.: Princeton University Press.

de la Garza, R., et al. 1992. *Latino Voices: Mexican, Puerto Rican, and Cuban Perspectives.* Boulder, Col.: Westview Press.

deParle, J. 1998. "Shrinking Welfare Rolls Leave Record High Share of Minorities." *New York Times,* A1, A12.

Espenshade, T., and K. Hempstead. 1996. "Contemporary American Attitudes Toward U.S. Immigration." *International Migration Review* 30(2):535-570.

Falcón, A. 1988. "Black and Latino Politics in New York City." In *Latinos and the Political System.* Ed. F.C. Garcia. Notre Dame, Ind.: University of Notre Dame Press.

———. 1995. "Puerto Ricans and the Politics of Racial Identity." In *Racial and Ethnic Identity: Psychological Development and Creative Expression.* Ed. H. Harris, H. Blue, and E. Griffith. New York: Routledge.

Fetzer, J. 1995. "The Causes of Immigration-Related Attitudes in the United States." Unpublished paper. Yale University, Political Science Department.

Frey, W.H., and R. Farley. 1996. "Latino, Asian, and Black Segregation in U.S. Metropolitan Areas: Are Multiethnic Metros Different?" *Demography* 33(1):35-50.

Frey, W.H., and E. Fielding. 1995. "Changing Urban Populations: Regional Restructuring, Racial Polarization, and Poverty Concentration." *Cityscapes: A Journal of Policy Development and Research* 1:1-65.

Gallup Organization. 1997. *The Gallup Poll Social Audit on Black/White Relations in the United States.* Princeton, N.J.: Gallup Organization.

Gans, H. 1999. "The Possibility of a New Racial Hierarchy in the Twenty-First-Century United States." In *The Cultural Territories of Race: Black and White Boundaries.* Ed. M. Lamont. Chicago: University of Chicago Press, 371-390.

Garcia, F.C., et al. 1996. "Ethnicity and Politics: Evidence from the Latino National Political Survey." *Hispanic Journal of Behavioral Sciences* 18:91-103.

General Social Survey. 1994. J. Davis and T. Smith, principal investigators. Chicago: National Opinion Research Corporation.

———. 1996. J. Davis and T. Smith, principal investigators. Chicago: National Opinion Research Corporation.

Gilens, M. 1999. *Why Americans Hate Welfare.* Chicago: University of Chicago Press.

Gooding-Williams, R., Ed. 1993. *Reading Rodney King/Reading Urban Uprising.* New York: Routledge.

Grenier, G., and A. Stepick, Eds. 1992. *Miami Now! Immigration, Ethnicity, and Social Change.* Gainesville: University Press of Florida.

Hajnal, Z. 1999. "White Residents, Black Incumbents, and a Declining Racial Divide." Unpublished paper. University of Chicago, Political Science Department.

Hamilton, D.C., and C.V. Hamilton. 1997. *The Dual Agenda: Race and Social Welfare Policies of Civil Rights Organizations.* New York: Columbia University Press.

Hinckley, B. 1981. *Coalitions and Politics.* New York: Harcourt Brace Jovanovich.

Hochschild, J.L. 1995. *Facing Up to the American Dream: Race, Class, and the Soul of the Nation.* Princeton, N.J.: Princeton University Press.

———. 1998. "Affirmative Action as Culture War." In *The Cultural Territories of Race: White and Black Boundaries.* Ed. M. Lamont. Chicago: University of Chicago Press, 343-368.

———. Forthcoming. *Rethinking Pluralism in an Age of Identity Politics.* Notre Dame, Ind.: University of Notre Dame Press.

Hogan, D., and D. Featherman. 1978. "Racial Stratification and Socioeconomic Change in the American North and South." *American Journal of Sociology* 83(1):100-126.

Holmes, S. 1998. "Immigration Is Fueling Cities' Strong Growth, Data Show." *New York Times,* A10.

Institute of Public Policy. 1997. *The Emerging Latino Middle Class.* Los Angeles: Pepperdine University.

Jennings, J. 1992. *The Politics of Black Empowerment: The Transformation of Black Activism in Urban America.* Detroit: Wayne State University Press.

Johnson, J.H., and M. Oliver. 1989. "Inter-ethnic Minority Conflict in Urban America: The Effects of Economic and Social Dislocations." *Urban Geography* 10:449-463.

Johnson, J.H., et al. 1996. "Immigration Reform and the Browning of America: Tensions, Conflict, and Community Instability." Paper presented at the conference on "America Becoming/Becoming American." Social Science Research Council Committee on International Migration, Sanibel Island, Fla.

Joint Center for Political and Economic Studies. 1996. *1996 National Opinion Poll—Social Attitudes.* Washington, D.C.: Joint Center for Political and Economic Studies.

———. 1997a. *1997 National Opinion Poll—Politics.* Washington, D.C.: Joint Center for Political and Economic Studies.

———. 1997b. *1997 National Opinion Poll—Children's Issues.* Washington, D.C.: Joint Center for Political and Economic Studies.

Jones-Correa, M. 1998. *Between Two Nations: The Political Predicament of Latinos in New York City.* Ithaca, N.Y.: Cornell University Press.

Jones-Correa, M., and D. Leal. 1996. "Becoming 'Hispanic': Secondary Panethnic Identification Among Latin American-Origin Populations in the United States." *Hispanic Journal of Behavioral Sciences* 18(2):214-254.

Kaus, M. 1992. *The End of Equality.* New York: Basic Books.

Kinder, D., and L. Sanders. 1996. *Divided by Color: Racial Politics and Democratic Ideals.* Chicago: University of Chicago Press.

Kirschenman, J., and K. Neckerman. 1991. "'We'd Love to Hire Them, But. . . ': The Meaning of Race for Employers." In *The Urban Underclass.* 2nd ed. Ed. C. Jencks and P.E. Peterson. Washington, D.C.: Brookings Institution, 203-232.

Klineberg, S. 1996. *Houston's Ethnic Communities.* Houston: Rice University.

Lee, J. 1998. "Cultural Brokers: Race-Based Hiring in Inner-City Neighborhoods." *American Behavioral Scientist* 41(7):927-937.

Lieberman, R. 1998. *Shifting the Color Line: Race and the American Welfare State.* Cambridge, Mass.: Harvard University Press.

Lien, P.-t. 1997. "Does Under-Participation Matter? An Examination of Policy Opinions Among Asian Americans." *Asian American Policy Review* 7:38-54.

———. 1998. *Asian Americans and Political Participation: A Book Proposal.* Philadelphia: Temple University Press.

Los Angeles Times. 1993a. Poll no. 306, "Los Angeles Mayor's Race, Schools, and Immigration."

———. 1993b. Poll no. 319, "Orange County Immigration and Race Relations."

———. 1994. Times Poll, "A Look at the Electorate." November 10, B2.

———. 1996. "Elections '96: State Propositions: A Snapshot of Voters." A29.

———. 1997. Study no. 395, "City of Los Angeles Survey. Fifth Anniversary of the Rodney King Riots." April.

———. 1998. Survey no. 413, "Profile of the Electorate." June 2.

Louis Harris and Associates. 1990. *The Reebok-Northeastern Study of Youth Attitudes on Racism.* New York: Louis Harris and Associates.

Mason, J. 1997. "Voters Keep Affirmative Action Program Alive." *Houston Chronicle,* A1ff.

McClain, P.D., and S.C. Tauber. 1998. "Black and Latino Socioeconomic and Political Competition: Has a Decade Made a Difference?" *American Politics Quarterly* 26(2):237-252.

Migration News. 1994. "Proposition 187 Approved in California." 1(11), December. Available from http://www.migration.ucdavis.edu

———. 1998. "Elections, Population, Education." 5(12), December. Available from http://www.migration.ucdavis.edu

Miles, J. 1992. "Blacks vs. Browns: The Struggles for the Bottom Rung." *Atlantic Monthly* 270(4) (October):41-64.

Mollenkopf, J.H. 1994. *A Phoenix in the Ashes: The Rise and Fall of the Koch Coalition in New York City Politics.* Princeton, N.J.: Princeton University Press.

———. 1995. "Urban Political Conflicts: The Case of New York." Paper presented at the conference on "America Becoming/Becoming American." Social Science Research Council Committee on International Migration, Sanibel Island, Fla.

———. 1997. "New York: The Great Anomaly." In *Racial Politics in American Cities.* 2d ed. Ed. R.P. Browning, D.R. Marshall, and D.H. Tabb. New York: Longman, 97-115.

Moss, M., et al. 1997. *Immigration Is Transforming New York City.* New York: New York University, Taub Urban Research Center.

National Conference of Christians and Jews. 1994. *Taking America's Pulse: The Full Report of the National Conference Survey on Inter-Group Relations.* New York: Louis Harris and Associates.

Ness, C., and A. Nakao. 1996. "Opponents File Suit to Block Prop. 209; Voters Back Ban on Affirmative Action by 55-45 Percent." *San Francisco Examiner,* A1ff.

Onishi, N. 1996. "Affirmative Action: Choosing Sides." *New York Times, Education Life,* 26-35.

Parade Magazine. 1999. "Power at the Polls," 7.

Parent, T.W., and P. Stekler. 1985. "The Political Implications for Economic Stratification in the Black Community." *Western Political Quarterly* 38(4):521-538.

Park, E. 1996. "Our L.A.? Korean Americans in Los Angeles After the Civil Unrest." In *Rethinking Los Angeles.* Ed. M. Dear, H.E. Schockman, and G. Hise. Thousand Oaks, Cal.: Sage, 153-168.

Patterson, O. 1989. "Toward a Study of Black America." *Dissent* (Fall):476-486.

Pinderhughes, D. 1997. "An Examination of Chicago Politics for Evidence of Political Incorporation and Representation." In *Racial Politics in American Cities.* 2d ed. Ed. R.P. Browning, D.R. Marshall, and D.H. Tabb. New York: Longman, 117-135.

Politico. 1998. "Democrat and Republican Parties Look to Latino Vote in 2000." Available from politico1@aol.com or from http://www.latnn.com/news/politico/index.html

Portes, A., and A. Stepick. 1993. *City on the Edge: The Transformation of Miami.* Berkeley: University of California Press.

Post-Modernity Project. 1996. *The State of Disunion.* Vol. 2, Summary Tables. Ivy, Va.: Medias Research Educational Foundation.

Princeton Survey Research Associates. 1997. "Immigration." *The Polling Report* (August 11):7.

The Public Perspective. 1999. "America at the Polls—1999." 11(1).

Reed, A. 1999. *Stirrings in the Jug: Black Politics in the Post-Segregation Era.* Minneapolis: University of Minnesota Press.

Regalado, J.A. 1994. "Community Coalition-Building." In *The Los Angeles Riots: Lessons for the Urban Future.* Ed. M. Baldassare. Boulder, Col.: Westview Press, 205-235.

Rodriguez, G. 1998. "Minority Leader." *New Republic* 219(16)(October 19):21-24.

———. 1999. "From Minority to Mainstream, Latinos Find Their Voice." *Washington Post,* B1, B4.

Rodriguez, N. 1996. "U.S. Immigration and Intergroup Relations in the Late Twentieth Century: African Americans and Latinos." *Social Justice* 23(3):111-124.

Saad, L. 1995. "The Immigration Story: As Immigrants Tell It." *The Public Perspective* 6(5) (August/September):9.

Schuck, P. 1993. "The New Immigration and the Old Civil Rights." *The American Prospect* 15 (Fall):102-111.

Schuman, H., et al. 1997. *Racial Attitudes in America: Trends and Interpretations.* Cambridge, Mass.: Harvard University Press.

Skerry, P. 1993. *Mexican Americans: The Ambivalent Minority.* New York: Free Press.

Sleeper, J. 1993. "The End of the Rainbow? America's Changing Urban Politics." *New Republic.*

———. 1997. *Liberal Racism.* New York: Viking.

Smith, J.P., and B. Edmonston. 1997. *The New Americans: Economic, Demographic, and Fiscal Effects of Immigration.* Washington, D.C.: National Academy Press.

Sonenshein, R.J. 1993. *Politics in Black and White: Race and Power in Los Angeles.* Princeton, N.J.: Princeton University Press.

———. 1996. "The Battle Over Liquor Stores in South Central Los Angeles: The Management of Interminority Conflict." *Urban Affairs Review* 31:710-737.

———. 1997. "The Prospects for Multiracial Coalitions: Lessons from America's Three Largest Cities." In *Racial Politics in American Cities.* 2d ed. Ed. R.P. Browning, D.R. Marshall, and D.H. Tabb. New York: Longman, 41-63.

Stone, C. 1989. *Regime Politics: Governing Atlanta, 1948-1988.* Lawrence: University Press of Kansas.

Swarns, R. 1998. "Hispanic Mothers Lagging as Others Leave Welfare." *New York Times,* A1, B8.

Tate, K. 1994. *From Protest to Politics: The New Black Voters in American Elections.* Cambridge, Mass.: Harvard University Press.

Thompson, J.P. 1996. "The Election and Governance of David Dinkins as Mayor of New York." In *Race, Politics, and Governance in the United States.* Ed. H. Perry. Gainesville: University Press of Florida.

Tobar, H. 1998. "In Contests Big and Small, Latinos Take Historic Leap," *Los Angeles Times,* November 5, A1ff.

Tolbert, C., and R. Hero. 1996. "Race/Ethnicity and Direct Democracy: An Analysis of California's Illegal Immigration Initiative." *Journal of Politics* 58(3):806-818.

Uhlaner, C. 1991. "Perceived Discrimination and Prejudice and the Coalition Prospects of Blacks, Latinos, and Asian Americans." In *Racial and Ethnic Politics in California.* Ed. B. Jackson and M. Preston. Berkeley: IGS Press, 339-371.

U.S. Bureau of the Census. 1998a. *Statistical Abstract of the United States, 1998.* Washington, D.C.: U.S. Government Printing Office (GPO).

————. 1998b. *Money Income in the United States, 1997.* Washington, D.C.: GPO.

U.S. Department of Justice. 1996. *Sourcebook of Criminal Justice Statistics 1995.* Washington, D.C.: GPO.

————. 1997. *Sourcebook of Criminal Justice Statistics 1996.* Washington, D.C.: GPO.

Vidanage, S., and D. Sears. 1995. "The Foundations of Public Opinion Toward Immigration Policy: Group Conflict or Symbolic Politics?" Paper presented at the annual meeting of the Midwest Political Science Association, Chicago.

Waldinger, R. 1996. *Still the Promised City? Afro-Americans and New Immigrants in Postindustrial New York.* Cambridge, Mass.: Harvard University Press.

Washington Post et al. 1995. "The Four Americas: Government and Social Policy Through the Eyes of America's Multi-racial and Multi-ethnic Society." Washington, D.C.

Waters, M. 1996. "Ethnic and Racial Groups in the USA: Conflict and Cooperation." In *Ethnicity and Power in the Contemporary World.* Ed. K. Rupesinghe and V. Tishkov. London: U.N. University.

Welch, S., and M. Combs. 1987. "Intra-Racial Differences in Attitudes of Blacks." *Phylon* 46(2):91-97.

Wilson, W.J. 1999. *The Bridge Over the Racial Divide: Rising Inequality and Coalition Politics.* Berkeley: University of California Press.

Wyly, E. 1997. *Social Trends and the State of the Nation's Cities.* New Brunswick, N.J.: Rutgers University, Center for Urban Policy Research.

Yankelovich Partners, Inc. 1995. *Time,* C.N.N., Yankelovich Partners Poll. University of Connecticut, Roper Center.

Zubrinsky, C., and L.D. Bobo. 1996. "Prismatic Metropolis: Race and Residential Segregation in the City of the Angels." *Social Science Research* 25:335-374.

Zukin, C. 1997. *Taking New Jersey's Pulse.* New Brunswick, N.J.: Rutgers University, Bloustein School of Planning and Public Policy.

Chapter 4

Languishing in Inequality: Racial Disparities in Wealth and Earnings in the New Millennium

by William A. Darity, Jr.

Cary C. Boshamer Professor of Economics and Sociology,
University of North Carolina, Chapel Hill,
and Research Professor of Public Policy, Duke University

and Samuel L. Myers, Jr.

Roy Wilkins Professor of Human Relations and Social Justice,
Humphrey Institute of Public Affairs, University of Minnesota

THE PROBLEM OF RACIAL INEQUALITY

Major studies of Black economic progress in the United States have been undertaken at regular intervals and commonly address two questions: How much progress has occurred? What are the sources of advance and retreat? The most prominent of these studies were conducted by Charles S. Johnson (1930) in the 1920s, Gunnar Myrdal (1944) in the 1940s, and Gerald D. Jaynes and Robin M. Williams, Jr. (1989), in the 1980s.

The norm in social science research is to treat Whites collectively as the reference group for evaluating African American racial progress. The White population is generally not disaggregated by ethnicity or ancestry, although wide variations occur.[1] Comparisons are made between the two groups in relative earnings, income, weeks worked, unemployment rates, and so forth—outcomes linked to the labor market. Considerably less attention is given to comparisons of wealth, net worth, and asset ownership—outcomes with a much weaker link to labor market experiences.[2] Black economic progress is then gauged by how close the profile of Black accomplishment converges toward that of Whites.

Implicit in the studies of African American progress is the idealization of a particular concept of racial economic equality as a goal—equality of economic results. From the perspective that seems to inform the studies, the "race problem" in the United States would be solved if the Black population exactly mimicked the pattern of stratification in the White population. If 10 percent of White Americans are poor, only 10 percent of African Americans should be poor, rather than the current 35 percent to 40 percent. If 30 percent of Whites hold professional-managerial positions, 30 percent of Blacks should have comparable positions, instead of 16 percent. Further, Blacks should possess a share of the general wealth in the United States similar to the Black share of the U.S. population. Blacks should own a share of Fortune 500 companies that matches the Black share of the population, rather than less than 0.5 percent.

The ideal of racial economic parity based upon equal economic results leads to an examination of the occupational and income profile of Black America. Again, in the context of the studies noted above, if the profile were the same as that of White America, the U.S. race problem could be declared at an end. Blacks would have achieved representational parity with Whites in the sphere of labor market activities.

Juxtaposed against the retrospective concept of equality of economic results is a prospective concept of racial equality—equal opportunity. The principle of equal opportunity dictates that the chance to compete for society's prizes should be independent of an individual's ascriptive characteristics. Ability and motivation alone should determine the distribution of preferred positions and status in a community. Equal opportunity espouses the meritocratic ideal as the foundation of the good society. The allocation of society's rewards is to be governed strictly by an individual's worth and performance, calibrated by commonly understood and, presumably, fixed standards.

Racial equality in the sense of equal opportunity necessarily permits unequal economic results as a possibility, but it promotes an ostensibly fair environment for generating the outcomes. Under an equal opportunity regime, the distribution of population across hierarchical ranks should be solely a matter of merit—not based on nepotism, racial or ethnic preference, or the capricious choice of successors by those in power. As a guidepost for social organization, equality of opportunity aims to produce a deserving elite.

Because the ideal of equality of opportunity does not guarantee equality of results, attaining the alternative ideal—racially equal results—may require an environment with compensatory racial privilege. An environment of equal opportunity may not generate equal outcomes for many reasons: cultural differences among races; differences in culturally reinforced aptitudes and abilities among races; or, more likely, the persistent effects of historical discrimination against the group with inferior status. Even if society could, overnight, miraculously be purged of discrimination as a factor affecting the distribution of rewards, past discrimination would continue to affect the competitive capacity of individuals who are from ascriptively differentiated groups (Loury, 1996; Ruhm, 1988). Historical discrimination that excluded members of a particular ethnic or racial group from desirable options or resources they might otherwise have obtained could adversely affect their descendants' ability to engage in today's equal opportunity wars.

CHAPTER OVERVIEW

This chapter confronts three aspects of racial inequality. The first is the contention that there may no longer be a problem to remedy. This claim denies the necessity of affirmative action or race-based remedies. We present data on the earnings of Black and White family heads to show that the alleged improvements in the relative position of African Americans during the first

Clinton administration were more of a statistical anomaly than part of a sustained convergence in earnings. Moreover, the slight positive slope in the ratio of Black to White family earnings predicts that equality is many generations away.

The second aspect is the problem of the widening gap between the top and the bottom of the African American income distribution. We explore the possible impact on the racial earnings gap of the migration of higher earning Blacks out of the central cities to the suburbs. With the majority of urban Blacks living in central cities, where the racial earnings gap is presumably widening, rather than in the noncentral-city areas, where the gap is theoretically narrowing, the outmigration of middle income Blacks would be expected to produce a greater racial earnings gap. From this perspective, intraracial inequality would also result because of the growing earnings gap between Blacks in central cities and Blacks outside central cities. This aspect of the problem has prompted several analysts to reject race-based remedies such as affirmative action for Blacks as a group and to embrace means-tested remedies to assist all of the poor, including Blacks.

However, we demonstrate that the flight of the Black middle class from central-city areas has not produced economic parity with Whites. Indeed, relatively few higher income Black families have left central cities for noncentral-city areas. We also conclude that Black middle class migration has not produced a widening of the earnings gap between central-city Blacks and noncentral-city Blacks; instead, the gap has narrowed.

The third aspect relates to the problem of inequality in wealth. We contend that even if earnings inequality were equalized today, the pattern of wealth inequality that has persisted in the United States would prevent the temporarily adjusted earnings parity from being sustained. Racial wealth inequality is primarily the result of unequal inheritances that transmit generations-old disparities in asset ownership from one generation to the next. Although some portion of wealth inequality can be explained by differences in savings or in current incomes, these factors do not account for a substantial part of the gap. Moreover, the racial disparity in measured net worth is so large and deeply rooted in current institutional arrangements that it would be almost impossible to eradicate by remedies to earnings inequalities.

We conclude by arguing that wealth redistribution remains a legitimate solution to the problem of racial economic inequality. Policy discussions in the 21st century must be directed toward refining the remedy of a racial wealth redistribution, articulating its boundaries and identifying an implementation strategy.

THE LEGACY OF THE 1970s AND 1980s

In the 1970s, several economists noted evidence of remarkable economic gains achieved by Blacks collectively in the postwar era, especially after the 1950s. They claimed that a rupture had occurred in the social and economic conditions of African Americans between the pre- and post-Civil

Rights era. Some even suggested that equality, in the "equal results" sense, would be attainable in the not too distant future; Blacks and Whites would soon converge in economic status.

The expectation that American society was on a trajectory toward racial parity was ideologically satisfying to those with somewhat uncritical, mainstream views of the opportunity structure of the United States. The "American Dream" would be possible for all, even the descendants of enslaved Africans. At last the discrepancy between American beliefs and American racial practices would evaporate. Myrdal's famous dilemma would be resolved.

The Economic Convergence Theory

The evidence used to support the convergence hypothesis was drawn from aggregate data on relative earnings and incomes of Blacks and Whites. The mean income ratio for Black and White males rose from 55 percent for all workers in 1950 to 66 percent in 1975 (Smith and Welch, 1977, 1978). The mean income ratio for Black and White females increased from 61 percent in 1950 to 95 percent in 1975, close to parity (Smith, 1978). This upward trend was extrapolated forward in time to assess the prospect of closing the gap altogether. The debate then turned to attempts to explain the change in the economic status of Blacks. What accounted for the improvement?

Two major competing hypotheses were advanced. The first was the position taken by James P. Smith of the RAND Corporation and Finis Welch of the University of California at Los Angeles. They argued that the improved quantity and quality of African American education, combined with the South to North and rural to urban migration of Blacks from the 1940s through the 1960s, led to a decline in the average productivity differential between Blacks and Whites. This, in turn, produced a decline in the earnings gap. At the core of the Smith and Welch (1977, 1978) view was the decisive role given to human capital differences (which they associated largely with formal schooling) in explaining average racial wage differences. The human capital gap was closing as Black schooling improved, ostensibly due to the rising quality of southern schools attended by Blacks as well as to the superior schools in the regions to which Blacks had migrated.

Smith and Welch argued that there was a "vintage effect": younger cohorts of Blacks had educational attainments more similar to comparably aged Whites and thus had more similar human capital endowments and labor market experiences than did older Black-White cohorts. The earnings gap for younger Blacks, then, would be expected to be narrower than the earnings gap for older Blacks. Smith (1978, 1) concluded, "Blacks are becoming less distinguishable from Whites in at least one relevant index of performance—market earnings." The underlying reason, according to Smith and Welch, was the closing of the Black-White gap in human capital acquisition.[3]

Smith and Welch's Panglossian vision of African American economic progress downplayed any significant role for discrimination in labor markets as the source of racial economic inequality. In their estimation, discrimination had been an important factor in producing historical disparity in schooling opportunities for Black and White youths. They viewed this disparity as constituting a type of pre-market or extra-market discrimination; they perceived the labor market as generally processing all individuals with reasonable fairness (or market fairness) based upon the individual's productivity-linked characteristics. Therefore, according to Smith and Welch, as the historical differential in schooling opportunities apparently declined, so did the fundamental basis for earnings inequality.[4]

Their perspective led to the conclusion that the labor market generally afforded equal opportunity. As the pre-market environment came to provide equal opportunity as well, Smith and Welch's analysis suggested that equal results would be the outcome. For Smith and Welch, no necessary inconsistency existed between equal opportunity and equal results as articulated aims of racial equality. Furthermore, there was no need for any special programmatic intervention for Blacks, except to continue to ensure that educational opportunities for Blacks moved toward matching those for Whites. The labor market worked and needed no correctives such as affirmative action or antidiscrimination measures.[5]

An alternative explanation was given by Harvard economist Richard B. Freeman (1973a, 1973b, 1981). He argued that the trend toward economic convergence was attributable to a decline in labor market discrimination engineered by government antidiscrimination enforcement measures. In short, Freeman also took the position that equal opportunity would lead to equal results, but for equal opportunity to prevail, government intervention in employment markets would be required.

Although disagreeing on the causes, Freeman and Smith-Welch agreed on the "fact" of a positive trajectory for African American economic progress in the 1960s and 1970s. But there were dissenters who argued that the evidence used to make the case for convergence was misleading at best (Darity and Myers, 1980a, 1980b, 1980c).

Skepticism About the Convergence Theory

The initial basis for dissent was our discovery that the data on which Smith-Welch and Freeman based their findings did not account for zero earners—individuals continuously unemployed or out of the labor force during the year. The African American experience of long-duration joblessness is much higher than the White experience. Consequently, earnings and income ratios calculated exclusively from data on working people will be biased by the selection effect. The bias unduly raises the Black-White earnings ratios.

For males, Black labor force dropouts are disproportionately from the lower end of the income spectrum, while White dropouts are disproportionately from the higher end (Myers, 1989).[6] When the earnings time series is corrected to account for males with no income in a given year, the change in non-White to White relative earnings vanishes during the decade 1967-77.

Indeed, the Black-White earnings ratio for males was slightly lower in 1977 (55 percent) than in 1967 (57 percent) after the correction (Darity, 1980). In 1990, the Black-White male earnings ratio for full-time year-round workers was 70 percent, but for all males with or without earnings, it was only 60 percent (U.S. Bureau of the Census, 1991, Table 11, 57).

For females, the Smith-Welch and Freeman Black-White earnings and income ratios were biased by the dramatic growth of White women in the labor force after the 1950s. Black women had long had high labor force participation rates (Darity, 1980). The time series data from 1953 through 1977, unadjusted for zero income recipients among females, give the impression that the earnings ratio of Black to White females soared remarkably, from 55 percent in 1955 to 94 percent in 1975. When the data are adjusted to account for females with no income in a given year, the ratio flattens significantly. The ratio was 84 percent as early as 1953 and never dipped below 70 percent between 1954 and 1977, when it reached 94 percent. In 1990, the Black-White female earnings ratio for full-time year-round workers was 90 percent; for all women with or without earnings, it was a slightly lower 87 percent (U.S. Bureau of the Census, 1991, Table 11, 57). Both time series indicate evidence of a decline. If we extrapolate on the basis of current trends, the future will be characterized by divergence, not convergence.

Per capita income ratios certainly did not show evidence of dramatic economic progress for African Americans during the 1970s and the 1980s. In two studies, Cotton (1989, 1990) demonstrated that the per capita racial income ratio remained steady in the 55 percent to 56 percent range between 1963 and 1975. Indeed, relative per capita income, as a criterion for progress, presents a decidedly pessimistic picture. Vedder, Gallaway, and Klingaman (1990) estimated that the ratio of Black to White per capita income was 59 percent in 1980. Darity, Guilkey, and Winfrey (1996) estimated that it was virtually the same in 1980 and 1990.

Cotton (1990) also examined the tenuous labor market status of large numbers of Black males. Between 1970 and 1985, blue collar employment decreased among Black men, mainly in the operatives category, while white collar employment increased, primarily in the sales category. Paradoxically, in 1985, the shift involved movement from occupations with average earnings of $16,220 to jobs with lower earnings of $14,114.

For White men, a similar shift had dissimilar economic effects. The change from blue collar to white collar employment increased the average salary of a White male in 1985 from $18,526 as an operative to $25,292 for a job in sales. Moreover, the Black-White earnings ratio in blue collar occupations overall was 79 percent in that year, but only 67 percent in White collar occupations (Cotton, 1990).

An additional basis for skepticism about the convergence hypothesis is that data on African American family incomes have never displayed the same pattern of gap closure as data on individual earnings or incomes. Between the mid-1960s and 1980, the Black-White family income ratio stayed in a rather narrow range of between 61 percent and 64 percent. During the 1982 recession, the ratio dipped below 60 percent. In 1990, the mean Black-

---

TABLE 4-1

Wage and Salary Incomes,
Family Heads,* 1976-85

	1976	1985
Whites	$23,704	$24,660
Blacks	$15,012	$14,654
B/W ratio of family earnings	0.63	0.59

* Data for family heads with positive earnings are expressed in 1984 US$.

Source: Authors' computations from Current Population Survey tapes.

White family income ratio was 62 percent, and the median Black-White family income ratio was only 58 percent (U.S. Bureau of the Census, 1991, Table 10, 56).

From 1976 to 1985, the real earnings of heads of Black families declined, increasing Black family poverty, whereas the real earnings of White family heads increased. Black family heads with positive wage and salary incomes experienced an earnings decrease from $15,012 in 1976 to $14,654 in 1985, an absolute loss of $358 (see Table 4-1). White family heads with positive wage and salary incomes had an almost $1,000 increase in earnings during the period, from $23,704 to $24,660. The result was to leave Black families relatively worse off as the ratio of Black-White family earnings fell from 63 percent in 1976 to 59 percent in 1985. Thus, despite the evidence that racial earnings gaps among individual workers seemed to continue to narrow, the gap widened among family heads.

CLAIMS OF PROGRESS DURING THE FIRST CLINTON ADMINISTRATION

Given the mixed, but largely negative evidence of Black economic progress during the Reagan-Bush era, it is not surprising that the next administration would view any sign of improvement as proof of the Democratic Party's successful economic policies. One of the most heralded and surprising statistical artifacts during President Bill Clinton's first administration was the alleged dramatic income gains among Black families. After a period of stagnation and, at best, no growth in Black incomes, a spurt apparently occurred in the relative economic well-being of Black families. Although analysts still do not quite know how or why this happened, possible explanations include:

- the reduction in welfare rolls and the move of Black family heads into the labor force;

- the rise in earnings from Black self-employment;

- the increase in earnings among the highest Black wage workers;

- the statistical methodology of the Current Population Survey (CPS).

The first explanation suggests that an increase occurred in the proportion of African American family heads who had positive wage and salary incomes. The CPS figures reveal that the percentage of Black family heads with positive wage and salary incomes increased slightly—from 67.7 percent in 1989 to 69.1 percent in 1996. But the CPS figures also show that the share of positive earners among Black family heads dipped from 68 percent in 1991 to 65 percent in 1993, precisely the opposite direction predicted by the welfare retrenchment explanation. To be sure, the proportion of positive earners among Black family heads began to rise again in 1994. Nevertheless, the 1993 figure was lower than it was in 1989, hardly compelling evidence that reduced welfare rolls caused the spurt in Blacks' earnings.

According to the second explanation, self-employment earnings among Black entrepreneurs contributed to the increase in overall Black earnings. Figure 4-1 combines data on positive earners with data on self-employment and shows that a peak in Black self-employment earnings in fact occurred in 1995. But that peak of 3.8 percent represented merely a minuscule rise from a low of 3.3 percent in 1993 over the 1989-96 interval. It is doubtful that this change can explain the rise in Black earnings touted by the Clinton administration.

Finally, it can be argued that the spurt in Black incomes during the 1990s can be attributed to changes in the CPS statistical methodology used to construct the income series. This possibility can be rejected on at least one count. Typically, when the top-coded income increases, there is a temporary and artificial jump in earnings. Over the years, the top-coded income has indeed increased; in 1976, for example, it was $50,000, and in 1995, it was $199,988. However, these changes cannot explain the growth in Black relative earnings in the 1990s because the top code was the same in 1989 as it was in 1995.

Comparison of Earnings Among Family Heads

Further examination of data on family heads shows that the income gains reported for African Americans in Clinton's first administration may well be an anomaly. From 1989 to 1991, there was no more than one-tenth of a percentage point movement up or down in the ratio of Black to White earnings of family heads (see Figure 4-2). But after a decline of almost 2 percentage points from 1991 to 1993—the middle of the recession—earnings increased by more than 6 percentage points from 1993 to 1995. This was one of the most dramatic gains in Black relative earnings among family heads in 25 years.

FIGURE 4-1

Percentage of Black Family Heads with Positive Wage and Salary Earnings and Self-Employment Earnings, 1989-96

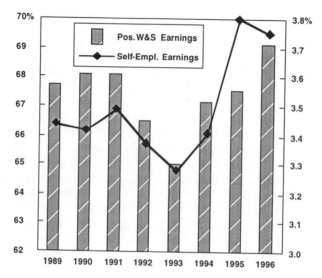

Source: Authors' computations from Current Population Surveys, March Supplements.

How much of the apparent improvement in the relative status of Black family heads from the end of the 1980s until 1995 can be explained by the growing inclusion of Hispanics in the White designation? Figure 4-2 shows that the effects were just as pronounced whether the ratios were computed for Blacks and Whites or for Blacks and White non-Hispanics. Obviously, the ratio was lower when the comparison was between Black and White non-Hispanics because White non-Hispanic earnings are higher than White earnings, but the trend was identical.

The measure chosen for family heads in Figure 4-2 (and in Figures 4-1 and 4-3) is heads of all families who reside in a household, including primary families and related subfamilies. Thus, if three generations of families live under one roof, three different heads will be identified in the sample. When the definition of family head is restricted to the head of the primary family, and thus to the householder in the sample, the ratio of Black to White earnings increases (because lower earners in Black households are excluded). The racial earnings ratio rises whether the comparison is between Blacks and Whites or between Black non-Hispanics and White non-Hispanics. Yet, regardless of how the family head is defined and how race and ethnicity are accounted for, the resulting trends remain the same: a dip in the Black-White earnings ratios during the recession, a sharp rise after the recession, and a

FIGURE 4-2

Black-White Earnings Ratios and Black-Non-Hispanic White Earnings Ratios, Family Heads, 1989-96

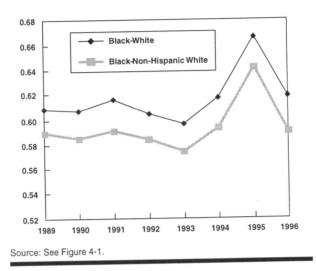

Source: See Figure 4-1.

decrease in 1996 to levels that were the same as or lower than the ratios at the beginning of the decade. With the exception of the steep earnings increases from 1993 to 1995, the overall pattern during the decade was relatively flat.

Nonetheless, the claims of progress rest upon the conspicuous growth in incomes of African American family heads during the first Clinton administration. A look at a longer period, however, reveals that the gains of the mid-1990s merely returned the earnings of Black family heads to their 1975 level. Moreover, the drop in earnings in 1996 reversed the short-lived but impressive increases made in the post-recession years of the Clinton administration. We can only speculate whether the brief gains were the result of a robust economy and whether the decrease in 1996 was precipitated by growing hostility toward affirmative action and retrenchment in the face of opposition to race-based remedies to discrimination. It is also impossible to know whether the downturn in 1996 is a predictor of worsening conditions or was merely a temporary fluctuation. It is certain, however, that the long-term pattern of earnings among Black family heads does not approach convergence with White family heads.

We estimated a simple linear regression, plotting the ratio of earnings of Black to White family heads against time to determine, "At what year will the ratio be equal to one?" An extrapolation of the rate of progress from 1970 to 1996 shows that the ratio of Black to White earnings among family heads

FIGURE 4-3

Black-White Earnings Ratios, Family Heads, 1970-96

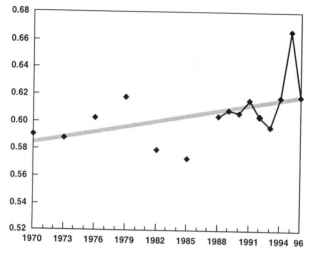

Note: The fitted equation is: $y = 0.0013x + 0.5829$ ($R^2 = 0.2627$). When $x = 320$, $y = 0.9989$.

Source: See Figure 4-1.

will not converge for almost 300 years (or almost 13 generations). Precisely along the linear trend line fitted for the 26-year period displayed in Figure 4-3, it will take until 2296 for the Black-White earnings gap to vanish, given recent trends.

THE BLACK MIDDLE CLASS FLIGHT HYPOTHESIS

A prominent explanation for the persistent and, at times, widening racial earnings gap is related to Black middle class flight from the inner cities to the suburbs. What is the possible impact of the migration of higher earning Blacks on the resulting earnings gap between Blacks and Whites? To answer this question, we looked at trend data from the 1970s through the 1980s. The argument is that potential interracial and intraracial inequalities could result from selective Black flight from the inner city.

According to the hypothesis, the outmigration of middle class Blacks should produce a widening of the racial earnings gap in the inner city and a narrowing of the gap outside the central city. With the vast majority of urban Blacks disproportionately concentrated in central cities, where the racial earnings gap is presumably increasing, rather than in noncentral-city areas, where the gap is theoretically decreasing, the net impact should be a widening of the earnings gap. Intraracial inequality should also occur because of the growing spread in incomes between Blacks living in central cities and Blacks living outside central cities.

However, as discussed below, virtually nothing in the raw data links the outmigration of higher income central-city Blacks to the increase in racial income inequality. From 1970 to 1988, there was little widening of the racial earnings gap in central cities and little narrowing of the gap between central-city residents and noncentral-city residents. The lack of support for the Black middle class flight hypothesis arises in part from the fact that, nationally at least, relatively few higher income Black families left inner cities for outside inner-city areas. Although some unique urban areas in the North such as Chicago followed this trend, the rest of the nation did not. Furthermore, the overall impact of the Black middle class movement out of central cities has been to reduce the earnings gaps among Blacks because lower income Blacks historically have resided in noncentral-city areas.

The "Social Isolation" Theory

William Julius Wilson (1987) revitalized the concept of "social isolation," whereby the plight of inner-city Blacks and other members of an "urban underclass" is inextricably linked to their isolation from mainstream values, support systems, and opportunities. According to the theory, the specific factor contributing to social isolation in the 1980s and 1990s was the migration of middle class African Americans out of the inner city. Not only did they flee to greener pastures in the suburbs, it is argued, but they also took with them the churches, clubs, organizations, and other institutional structures that underlie an achievement-oriented value system. Without these institutions, the underclass is left with negative role models, festering poverty, and despair.

The social isolation hypothesis has implications for interracial economic inequality. As noted, logically the flight of the Black middle class should contribute to a wider racial earnings gap in central cities and to a narrower gap outside central cities, assuming that middle class Whites do not leave the inner cities at rates greater than those of middle class Blacks. Evidence on the gentrification of many downtowns and the influx of affluent, although often childless families and single person households to these areas supports this assumption.

The theory also has implications for intraracial economic inequality. Black middle class outmigration would be expected to increase the income gap between Blacks who leave central cities and Blacks who stay. According to this reasoning, the lowest earners among the middle class could not afford the luxury of leaving the inner city; thus, the average income level of those who stayed would be lowered and the income level of those who moved would be raised.

Does the evidence support these predictions? We computed the ratio of Black to White incomes for male-headed and female-headed families in and outside central cities from 1970 through 1988 (Darity et al., 1994). Outside central cities, the racial earnings gap narrowed among male-headed families, with the Black-White ratio rising from 57 percent in 1970 to 74 percent in 1988. This increase clearly indicates decreasing racial disparity in the earnings of male family heads and is consistent with the assumptions of the social isolation theory.

Nonetheless, within central cities, little widening of the racial earnings gap occurred among male-headed families, despite the implications of the hypothesis. The Black-White earnings ratio of male family heads living in inner cities was only a few percentage points lower in 1988 than in 1970, although a perceptible dip in the ratio occurred in 1985 (meaning that the earnings gap widened in that year). Moreover, in 1988, the Black-White earnings ratio of male family heads in central cities was almost equal to that of male family heads outside central cities. These findings hardly provide robust evidence of a widening racial income gap between inner-city residents and suburban residents.

An examination of the earnings of female-headed families found even less support for the social isolation hypothesis. Although the Black-White earnings ratio of female family heads was lower outside than inside central cities, little apparent change occurred during the 1970-88 period. There was, however, a large increase in the Black-White earnings ratio of noncentral-city female family heads from 1970 to 1973. No obvious worsening occurred in the relative degree of income inequality facing inner-city Black female family heads.

There was also virtually no change in the inner-city-suburban gap among female-headed Black families from 1970 to 1988 (again, except for the relative improvement in the position of noncentral-city family heads between 1970-73). Nor was there much change in the position of female-headed White families when the earnings of those living outside central cities were compared with the earnings of those living in central cities.

The greatest changes occurred among Black families headed by men, and these changes provide almost the only support from economic data for the social isolation theory. The ratio of earnings of Black male family heads residing in central cities declined relative to that of comparable Blacks residing outside central cities. This decrease would be consistent with a widening of the intraracial earnings gap if those living outside central cities earned more than central-city residents.

But there was no divergence; instead, there was convergence. Surprisingly, African American male-headed families outside central cities in the 1970s had lower wage and salary incomes than comparable Blacks in central cities. Rising Black incomes in the suburbs and falling Black incomes in the central cities reduced the disparity between the two. The numbers behind the ratios tell the story.

In 1970, the average wage and salary earnings of a Black male family head living outside a central city were $11,497; the earnings of a Black male family head living in a central city were $15,493. By 1988, however, the earnings of the former were $14,089 and of the latter, $13,931. Thus, central-city Black male family heads earned less, on average, in 1988 than they did in 1970, but the opposite was the case for comparable Blacks in noncentral-city areas. The overall impact was to create near parity between the two groups. It is difficult to conclude, then, that the flight of middle class Blacks caused a widening in the earnings gap between Blacks in central cities and those outside them. By the end of the 1980s, there was little difference between the earnings of family heads in the two locations.

In short, the alleged effects of the highly publicized Black middle class flight phenomenon do not hold up under close scrutiny. This conclusion has two caveats. First, relatively few Black family heads with earnings above the mean for the Standard Metropolitan Statistical Area (SMSA) left central cities for noncentral cities. Second, we were unable to distinguish between movement to suburban areas and movement to other noninner-city areas.

Within a given year, relatively few heads of families with higher-than-average earnings move from the central city to any noncentral-city area. The percentages range from less than 1 percent of all family heads to almost 3 percent, with the lowest proportion observed in recession years among female-headed families. There are few differences between races by family type.

We computed the ratio of earnings of middle class family heads with incomes greater than 1.5 times the mean for the SMSA who moved out of central cities against the mean earnings of those who remained from 1970 to 1988 (Darity et al., 1994). These higher income inner-city movers can be termed "high-flight" people. Among male-headed families, the ratio remained virtually unchanged. Among female-headed families, the ratio declined from the early 1970s to the early 1980s, but flattened thereafter.

Education, Mobility, Occupation, and Location Factors

Education, mobility, occupation, and location factors could have intertwined to contribute to the result alluded to in the middle class flight thesis. For example, perhaps the source of change is not Black middle class flight, but divergent educational attainment among different family structures. Significant differences exist in the educational credentials of Black male and female family heads and nonheads of families. Evidence shows substantial gains in educational completion among Black female nonheads of families between 1976 and 1985, but a decline in educational completion of Black males, particularly zero earners. Black male family heads experienced improvements in educational attainment during that decade, but Black female family heads had less education than male heads or female nonheads of families. In addition, families headed by females—with less education—were concentrated in central-city areas; families headed by males—with more education—were concentrated in noncentral-city areas. Thus, a possible linkage to location arises from the relationship between education and family structure.

Another interpretation of the middle class flight hypothesis is that perhaps male-headed families disproportionately left the inner city, resulting in major locational differences in the structure of African American families. A shift in the location of Black families headed by men did indeed occur. In 1970, 57 percent of male-headed Black families lived in central-city areas; in 1988, the proportion had fallen to 46 percent, so that the majority of male-headed Black families were living in noncentral cities. But this shift did not automatically translate into higher poverty and lower incomes and thus wider intraracial inequality, in part because nontrivial numbers of Black middle class two parent families continued to reside in central cities. Social pathology and distress within the Black community cannot be blamed primarily on the alleged flight of the Black middle class.

The percentage of families headed by women varies considerably between Blacks and Whites in mobility, occupation, and location. We computed the incidence of female family heads living in and outside central cities by occupation of the family head and by residential mobility from 1970 to 1991 (Darity et al., 1994). The mobility measure, high flight, captures the concept of middle class flight inherent in Wilson's (1987) analysis of social isolation and an urban underclass. The measure is computed to be a dichotomous variable equal to one if the family head had income in excess of 1.5 times the mean for the SMSA and lived in the central city in the previous year but moved out during the current year. Few people satisfied this criterion.[7]

Nonetheless, it is instructive to note that the proportion of African American families headed by women who met this criterion far exceeded the share of female-headed White families. No more than 2 percent of White families that were high-flight were also female-headed during any one year from 1970 to 1991. However, the incidence of female-headed families escalated among Black high flight families, jumping from less than 1 percent in the earlier years to more than 20 percent in 1991.

These racial differences are apparent in other indicators as well. For example, female-headed families among central-city Whites increased from 12 percent to 18 percent over the two decades; for Blacks, the number exploded from 30 percent to 51 percent. The percentage of families headed by females was lower among noncentral-city families, but the disparity was greater among Whites. In 1991, only 12 percent of noncentral-city White families were headed by females, about one-third less than the percentage among central-city Whites. But among Black noncentral-city families, 41 percent were headed by women, a share only about one-fifth smaller than that of central-city Blacks.

As noted, occupational disparities factor into racial differences in family structure. During the period studied, there was a large gap in female-headed families between Whites who held managerial jobs and those who held sales and clerical jobs. White family heads with sales and clerical jobs rather than managerial jobs were twice as likely to be female. The difference was much smaller between Black family heads in the two occupational categories, with those holding sales and clerical jobs only one-fifth as likely to be female.

Earnings Histories

There are further differences in family structure based on earnings histories. From 1970 to 1991, families generally tended to be headed by females if the head had no positive wage and salary earnings in the past year. However, if the head previously held a managerial job, the family was less likely to be headed by a female even among nonearners. Moreover, in 1991, the gap in female-headed families was larger among African Americans than among Whites. Among Black families, 42 percent had female heads when the head held a managerial job and had positive earnings. Only 1 percent of Black families had female heads when the head's last occupation was manager and had no wage and salary income in the past year. In contrast, 11 percent of White families with heads who were managers and who had positive incomes in the past year were headed by females. For White families whose heads were managers, but who had no wage and salary income in the past year, 7 percent were headed by females. In other words, earnings and nonearnings status mattered little in determining whether White families were headed by females who were managers; it mattered a great deal for Blacks.

The incidence of female-headed families is not restricted to inner-city African Americans nor to those at the bottom of the occupational ladder. High proportions of families headed by females live outside central-city areas, at least among Blacks. These include heads who are managers and sales and clerical workers as well as some with comparatively higher incomes who have left the inner city. There are no significant numbers of female-headed Black families when the head is a nonearning professional. While nontrivial numbers of Whites can afford the luxury of maintaining a home on rents, dividends, interest, and possibly public as well as private transfers, Blacks cannot. Even when the head of the family is a professional Black woman, she more often than not must be at work, which explains the virtual absence of female-headed families among nonearners in this category.

In summary, there is little evidence to support the hypothesized linkage between the rise in racial earnings inequality among family heads and the flight of the Black middle class from the central city.

- There is only negligible outmigration of middle class Blacks in any given year.

- There are narrowing racial differentials in family structure by education, mobility, occupation, and location.

- Paradoxically, the Black middle class that leaves has contributed to the *narrowing* of the earnings gap among Black central-city and noncentral-city residents.

WEALTH, ASSETS, AND RACIAL INEQUALITY

The largest component of measured net worth among American households is the home. Home ownership accounted for 41 percent of net worth in 1984 and for 44 percent in 1993 (see Figure 4-4). Interest-earning assets (interest-earning checking and savings accounts, money market deposit

FIGURE 4-4

**Distribution of Measured Net Worth in Home Ownership
and Interest-Earning Assets, Various Years**

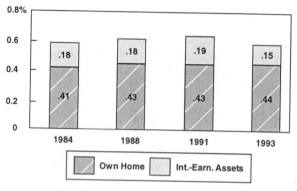

Source: U.S. Bureau of the Census (1993).

accounts, and certificates of deposit) were the second largest component of net worth. The share of measured net worth held in these assets was 18 percent in 1984 and 15 percent in 1993.[8] Housing and interest-bearing assets accounted for a stable three-fifths of net worth among U.S. households.

Black measured net worth falls considerably short of White net worth for two reasons. First, Blacks have far lower asset holdings than Whites in interest-earning accounts at financial institutions. Few Blacks, for example, own interest-bearing checking accounts, and their savings accumulations are much lower than those of Whites. In 1991, 14 percent of all Black household heads had interest-earning checking accounts compared with 41 percent of White households. In that year, the median value of interest-earning assets at financial institutions for Blacks was $933; for Whites, it was $4,081 (Eller and Fraser, 1995).

The second, more important reason for the disparity in net worth is the combination of lower home ownership rates and lower median housing values for African Americans who own homes compared with White home owners. Blacks are far less likely to own their own homes than Whites, and when they do, the value of their homes net of mortgages is substantially less than the value of White homes. In 1991, 45 percent of Black households owned their homes compared with 68 percent of White households. The median value of equity in the home was $26,992 for Blacks and $44,477 for Whites (Eller and Fraser, 1995).

As a consequence of the two factors, White net worth is considerably higher than Black net worth. In 1991, median Black net worth was $4,844 (in 1993 dollars) and in 1993, $4,418. In contrast, median White net worth was $47,075 in 1991 and $45,740 in 1993. Thus, White median net worth was 9.7

to 10.4 times larger, respectively, than Black median net worth in those years (see Figure 4-5).

Oliver and Shapiro (1995) have demonstrated a number of ways that the racial wealth gap perpetuates Black-White economic disparity. Access to wealth expands an individual's higher education options, an individual's flexibility in adjusting to major emergencies, and an individual's potential to enter self-employment. According to Fairlie (1999, 103), "Racial differences in asset levels provide an important contribution to the Black-White gap in the entry rate into self-employment." Access to wealth also affects people's ability to leave an inheritance to their children, which in turn increases the latter's options. In fact, as discussed below, the major source of wealth today is inheritance (Blau and Graham, 1990).

Of course, average White incomes are higher than average Black incomes, which accounts in part for Blacks' lower measured net worth. Lower incomes limit Blacks' savings account balances, affect their access to interest-bearing checking accounts that often require large minimum balances, and reduce their investments in interest-bearing accounts. Lower incomes also prevent Blacks from purchasing homes and diminish the value of their housing when they are home owners.

White net worth exceeds Black net worth even within each household income quintile. In the highest monthly income quintile, pegged at $4,636 per month in 1993, White median net worth was $123,350, whereas Black median net worth was $45,023. This 2.75 advantage enjoyed by Whites over Blacks at the top of the income distribution represented an escalation of the wealth gap in a short time span. In 1991, at the top income quintile, White median net worth was $128,298, 2.25 times larger than the Black median net worth of $56,922 (see Figure 4-5). In the bottom quintile in 1993, median net worth among White households with monthly incomes below $1,071 was

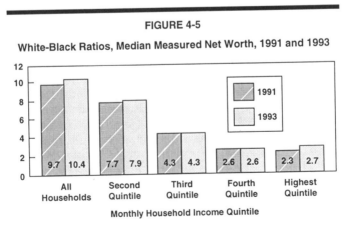

FIGURE 4-5

White-Black Ratios, Median Measured Net Worth, 1991 and 1993

Monthly Household Income Quintile

Source: U.S. Bureau of the Census (1993).

$7,605, but only $250 among Black households. White median net worth at the very bottom of the income distribution was thus 30 times larger than Black net worth. There is one direct explanation for these wide gaps in net worth: racial differences in home ownership.

The Legacy of Unequal Home Ownership by Race

Ample evidence exists of the substantial racial disparities in home ownership and housing equity. These gaps have the potential to block the equalization of wealth in American society. Conventional explanations for credit, financial, and home ownership inequalities focus on the low incomes and poor financial skills of minorities. Myers and Chung (1996) examined a unique data set of preretirement-age householders to test the hypothesis that poor financial skills, low incomes, and other sociodemographic factors are at the root of racial inequalities in housing. As others have found, financial variables are not the primary reason for racial disparities in housing equity (VanderHart, 1994) or in home ownership. Despite the proliferation of lender-initiated programs designed to enhance Blacks' ability to navigate local mortgage markets, the empirical evidence does not support the view that Blacks' lack of knowledge causes their poor performance.

However, racial differences in expected housing equity (discussed below) can be explained only to a limited degree by racial inequalities in home ownership and its determinants. Although there are sizable Black-White income disparities that lead to lower Black home ownership rates, they account for merely about one-fourth of the gap in expected housing equity. Moreover, evidence suggests that, in addition to income, most of the gap is due to location and wealth factors (Long and Caudill, 1992). Thus, wealth inequalities in the past translate cumulatively across generations into current wealth disparities, even though the original acts of discrimination and seg-regation that led to the initial disparities are distant and invisible. Put simply, long after legalized discrimination and segregation ceased, their intergenera-tional impacts persist.

To reach this conclusion, Myers and Chung (1996) estimated a model of expected home equity, a measure that is the product of the probability of home ownership and the value of a home less the mortgage or debt. The model was estimated for preretirement-age household heads to rid the analysis of life-cycle investment effects. Myers and Chung calculated the independent contribution of a series of variables to the racial gap in expected housing equity by computing what the Black expected housing equity would be if Blacks had the same financial, demographic, and geographic advantages as Whites.

About 27 percent of the racial difference in expected housing equity was caused by income differences. Overall, the model explained little more than 40 percent of the gap. Myers and Chung concluded that, although many variables differ substantially between Black and White householders, few have much impact on overall housing inequality, except family income. Endowing Blacks with advantages enjoyed by Whites will not alter the expected housing equity differential to a great degree. Instead, the 60 percent "unexplained" or "discriminatory" factors still play a critical role in curtailing movement toward racial equality in housing.

The legacy of unequal home ownership by race has immediate implications for continuing racial and ethnic inequality. In 1970, almost 48 percent of all private wealth in the United States was embodied in residential structures. (The other components of private wealth include nonresidential equipment and structures.) A total of $8.1 trillion (in constant 1987 dollars) of private gross stocks of wealth were recorded in 1970, with residential structures accounting for $3.8 trillion. This amount exceeded the $3.0 trillion of government equipment and structures, including federal, state, and local holdings. By 1991, the share of private wealth in residential structures had fallen to about 44 percent, although the total value (in constant 1987 dollars) had risen to $6.9 trillion. Figure 4-6 shows the steep decline in the share of private wealth in residential housing from the 1970s until the 1980s.

What is the practical implication of this decline, given that housing still accounts for a substantial share of private wealth? The answer is that the dramatic housing inflation of the 1970s allowed the comparatively few who were able to purchase property during this unique era to cash in on immediate gains, permitting investment in assets such as mutual funds, stocks, and bonds. The appreciation of these residential assets also enabled the owners to finance the higher education of their children, to provide start-up funds for small businesses, and to subsidize the first home purchases of their offspring.

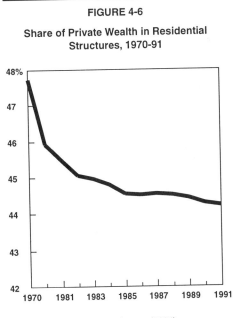

FIGURE 4-6

Share of Private Wealth in Residential Structures, 1970-91

Source: U.S. Bureau of the Census (1994).

The intergenerational impact of the 1970s' housing stock appreciation continues to have repercussions for economic inequality in the 21st century.

Blau and Graham (1990) found that the wealth of young African American families (heads of households age 24 to 34) is, on average, 18 percent of the wealth of young White families. They also found that Black families tend to hold less of that wealth in net liquid assets and net business assets and more of it as equity in houses and automobiles. According to Wolff (1992), throughout the 1980s, the mean net worth of all Black families averaged only 23 percent that of White families, and Black family median net worth was only 9 percent of comparable Whites' net worth. (His data were based on the 1983 Survey of Consumer Finances and the 1984 and 1988 Survey of Income and Program Participation.) He attributed the marked difference to "the large number of Black families with zero net worth" (855-856).

The Effects of Historical Deprivations

According to Blau and Graham (1990), the gap in net worth is not due to racial differences in savings rates or in rates of return earned on comparable assets.[9] The racial disparity in net worth is linked most decisively to a gap in access to the major source of wealth in American society—inheritance. African American parents and grandparents of earlier generations simply had less wealth to pass on to their descendants because of the historical limitations that confronted them. Previous eras of lack of access to credit, a barrier to ownership of farms and homes, have converged to lead to the present unequal distribution of wealth. Intergenerational transfers of household wealth can be made only if there is family wealth to transfer. To the extent that Blacks themselves were property and then systematically denied opportunities to accumulate property after emancipation, their wealth was severely truncated.[10]

For example, it is widely noted that native Black Americans tend to have lower rates of self-employment than many other ethnic groups. Data from the General Social Survey for 1983 to 1987 indicate that fewer than 5 percent of Americans of primarily African ancestry were self-employed compared with 25 percent of Jewish Americans and 12 percent of Americans of English, German, or Asian ancestry. Moreover, self-employed Blacks earned less than each of the White ethnic groups in the survey: $5,000 less than Italian Americans; about $6,000 less than Irish Americans; $10,000 less than Polish Americans; and more than $20,000 less than Jewish Americans (Butler and Herring, 1991, 84-85, 90).

Why is this the case? Despite commonplace anecdotal data about cultural differences in attitudes toward entrepreneurship and regulatory barriers that disproportionately inhibit minority business participation, three factors are critical in explaining the self-employment gap:

- differences in educational backgrounds, particularly regarding professional credentials (a factor of growing importance in an era of small business activity geared increasingly toward providing professional services);

- differences in social learning opportunities; and

- most important, differences in wealth.[11]

The social learning hypothesis posits that exposure to the self-employment activity of a relative, especially a father, raises the likelihood that individuals themselves will be self-employed. However, racial differences in wealth make it less likely that Blacks, compared with Whites, have had a self-employed relative. Such differences also lower the range of educational options.

The effects of historical deprivations are cumulative. Persistent economic deprivations in the past—borne of exclusion, seizure of property, and containment—reduce the average level of wealth in a population. Lower levels of wealth adversely affect not only attainable levels of education and participation in small business activity for past generations, but also access to quality housing and the amenities associated with living in comfortable communities with good schools for the current generation. Furthermore, in the context of self-employment activity, lower levels of wealth affect the conditions for entry into the business environment. Access to bank loans, for example, is greatly reduced if the potential applicant does not have sizable equity capital (Bates, 1991, 35). A well-known complaint of aspiring African American businesspeople is that they are trapped in a Catch-22 situation. Without adequate financial capital they cannot get their enterprise off to a proper start. Without equity capital they cannot get debt capital. Without either they cannot have adequate operating capital.

To compound matters, there is strong evidence of discriminatory lending to Blacks by commercial banks. Ando (1988) examined the rate of bank acceptances of short-term loan applications of owners of established small businesses in the early 1980s. She found that the acceptance rate was much lower for Blacks than for Hispanics, Whites, and Asians; in fact, the rate was highest for Asians and virtually identical for Whites and Hispanics. After controlling for various indicators of possible risk differentials, Ando's conclusions were the same: Black owners of companies were significantly less likely than other minority business owners to have their loan applications accepted.

In 1990, 46 million families received property income. Almost 42 million of them were White. For the 2.8 million African Americans who received any interest, dividends, rents, royalties, or income from trusts or estates, most property income came from interest. Even among Black families with incomes above $100,000, very little income was derived from dividends or rents.

REMEDIES FOR RACIAL ECONOMIC INEQUALITY

Public policies designed to reduce or eradicate racial economic inequality appear to have lost their moral, political, and intellectual standing in the past two decades. Policies such as affirmative action, racial preferences, and set-asides are increasingly viewed by many as unnecessary and unfair. However, the philosophical basis for opposition to such policies ignores the sustained power of White privilege.

Current public policies advanced as alternatives to affirmative action are rooted in a conceptual framework that points to the cultural and human capital deficiencies of Blacks and other non-Whites compared with Whites. These deficiencies include lower educational attainment, lower labor force attachment, higher rates of female-headed families, and poorer skills that leave minority group members concentrated in occupations and industries that pay low wages. Conspicuously absent in recent discussions of what to do about the widening economic gap between White and non-White families is the role of discrimination and the continued barriers to advancement based on race. Also absent, until recently, has been a serious discussion about remedies to inequalities in wealth.

Race-Based and Nonrace-Based Remedies

There are two broad categories of remedies for racial inequality: race-based and nonrace-based. Despite an apparent attachment to the ideal of equal opportunity, Americans in general are opposed to continuing direct efforts to achieve equality of opportunity through race-based measures. The targets of their opposition include affirmative action, set-asides, quotas, and preferential scoring. The alternative, nonrace-based remedies, encompasses various forms of assistance, generally means-tested programs for low income people. These efforts also include assistance to businesses and other institutions if their activities are designed to aid those at the bottom, which may have the impact of disproportionately benefiting African Americans. Other examples are education vouchers, income transfers, and grants for entrepreneurial development.

Race-based and nonrace-based remedies attack the problems of intraracial and interracial inequalities in different ways. The race-based strategy ostensibly focuses on results. It attempts to reduce inequality by using the observed racial gap as the direct yardstick for assessing the degree of movement toward equality. The nonrace-based effort aims to create equality of opportunity among a class of people, without regard to race, who are willing to contract with the state. The class may include small White businesses as well as small Black businesses. An entrepreneurial training program, for example, might disproportionately benefit Blacks, but it would not be reserved exclusively for them.

The Problems with Nonrace-Based Remedies

The central objection to solving racial inequality through nonrace-based remedies—especially those that attack current market inequalities—is that they do little to redress the historical inequities in wealth that are transmitted from one generation to the next. For example, the problem of current racially unequal business ownership might be addressed by directing capital and resources to Black inner-city areas. However, the small number of African American beneficiaries could be overwhelmed by the large number of White and other non-White entrepreneurs who, because of previous experience and opportunities to acquire businesses, would hasten to take advantage of the program.

Even if the program were restricted to "disadvantaged" businesses or to potential entrepreneurs who have never owned businesses, it would fail to deal with the historical inequality in wealth. The rush to participate by White firms would not only deplete the program's resources and overwhelm it with bureaucratic overlays, but would also largely defeat the main purpose of rectifying racial inequality. While programs for disadvantaged businesses can be justified on many grounds, there is little to commend them as non-race-based remedies for racial inequality.

Economic research in the area of education vouchers is in its infancy, and solid and convincing empirical results are few. Hoxby's (1994) research contends that incentives such as vouchers that favor private schools actually assist public schools by creating additional competition. Her research, while plausible, does not address the question of whether African American students as a group will necessarily benefit from vouchers if private schools replicate the tracking and pattern of failure that many minority students face in inner-city and suburban public schools (Myers, 1997).

More important in understanding the weakness of education vouchers as a remedy for racial inequality is the reality that far more White children than Black children will take advantage of this benefit simply because more White children will be eligible. Despite the infatuation of many policymakers with equating the terms "poor" and "Black," the stark truth is that the vast majority of the poor are White. The primary beneficiaries of a voucher targeted to the poor will thus be the majority children whom public schools have historically succeeded in advancing. However, if the voucher were restricted to poor Blacks (or minorities), the voucher would no longer be race-neutral.

In sum, despite substantial political opposition to race-based remedies for racial economic inequality, nonrace-based remedies do not qualify as appropriate alternatives. They will be more costly, will be less effective, and will do little to address the underlying causes of inequality.

Theoretical and Empirical Disputes Over Affirmative Action

One aspect of the current assaults on affirmative action comes from Black conservatives. Boston University economist Glenn C. Loury argues that affirmative action does not help the group most deserving of and needing help, the truly disadvantaged. According to Loury (1996, 51), "The policy advances under the cover of providing assistance to disadvantaged persons when in fact, by its very nature, its ability to assist poor Blacks is severely limited." The opposition to race-based remedies stems from the belief that affirmative action based on race alone provides adverse incentives for racial minority groups as a whole. Loury states:

Affirmative action also introduces uncertainty into the process by which individuals make inferences about their own abilities. . . . Racial preferences undermine the ability of Black people to be confident that they are as good as their achievements would suggest. . . . Preferential treatment also leads to patronization [setting of lower standards for Blacks than for Whites] because of the belief that Blacks are not as capable as Whites. . . . The use of different criteria reduces the incentives Blacks have for developing needed skills (54-56).

Loury's logic requires a determined attachment to unbridled individualism. If only individual Blacks could unleash their energies to fulfill their natural potential, the problem of racial inequality would diminish. The sole barrier admitted in this analytical model is the barrier arising from lack of opportunity. That is why Loury argues for continuation of affirmative action for the truly disadvantaged, but not for Blacks as a group. This perspective leaves unaddressed the question of whether group membership alone serves as a barrier to advancement in a world structured by racism. If racial group membership persists as an explicit and impervious barrier to equality of opportunity, why even in the absence of affirmative action will patronization or inherent beliefs about Black inferiority disappear? Further, as long as such beliefs persist, and given the individualistic logic of Loury's model, why will incentives to invest in the development of skills be any different than they are in the presence of affirmative action? Assume, as Loury does, that the primary worry of successful Black students or employees is what White people think about them. Why then are Blacks more worried when they benefit from redress for prior wrongs than they are when they must confront racism blindly, not knowing whether they are competent and detested or competent and accepted?

Beyond the theoretical dispute over affirmative action is the empirical issue of whether dramatic, sustained economic gains persisted as a result of affirmative action. Those who point to data on individual earnings growth bypass an important venue for exploring the relative position of Blacks within a more meaningful context—the family. The data presented above confirm that the alleged advances of the Black middle class and Black family heads resulting from affirmative action were short-lived at best. The continuing distress faced by Blacks as a group and the continuing inequality between the earnings of Black and White family heads suggest the need for alternative remedies to achieve equality.

Wealth Redistribution Remedies

If inequalities in current economic prospects are rooted in historical inequalities, e.g., home ownership and wealth, a case can be made for redistributing wealth to eliminate racial economic inequality. One controversial form of wealth redistribution is reparations, which can be defined as compensatory payment for an acknowledged grievous social injustice to a group. The social injustices inflicted upon African Americans include the historical experiences of slavery, the legally sanctioned "apartheid" or Jim

Crow practices, and ongoing discrimination. These three facets constitute the particular pattern of injustice affecting Blacks and have led some to advocate a scheme of reparations as restitution for those wrongs (see, e.g., America, 1990).

Considerably less dramatic redistributive measures than substantial reparations have been proposed by Sherraden (1991) and Stegman (1999). Their proposals seek to build asset accumulation among low income Americans by providing government matching funds in Individual Development Accounts for savings set aside by the poor from their wages. Of course, the plans presume that low income Americans will have sufficient employment opportunities to generate savings from earnings. More important, the proposals use income rather than race as the criterion for government assistance in building wealth. Thus, they do not address the historically produced and pervasive Black wealth disadvantage that crosses lines of socioeconomic status.

In the late 1980s, Haveman (1988) proposed a Youth Capital Account plan. The scheme would award each American youth $20,000 upon his or her 18th birthday as a foundation for equity development. A universal plan unlike the means-tested Sherraden and Stegman proposals, it would do even less to redress racial wealth disparity, particularly if it is not presumed that there are sharp diminishing returns to the accumulation of wealth.

No compensation has ever been paid to relatives or descendants of the slaves who died during the drive to the African coast from the interior of the continent, during the Middle Passage, or during the "seasoning" period in the New World. Nor has any compensation been paid to those who worked from sunup to sundown under a regime of forced labor for more than 200 years. The end of slavery in the United States came with war, and when the war ended, four million largely illiterate ex-slaves were thrust into a ravaged, economically battered region. No effort was made for restitution, nor were any significant attempts made to invest in the ex-slaves except for the modest, short-lived activities of the Freedman's Bureau and the brief actions of the ex-slaves in southern state legislatures (DuBois, 1935).

The collapse of slavery and the demise of reconstruction gave way to a formal American system of apartheid in the southern United States that lasted roughly from 1873 to 1960, directly affecting the lives of four generations of African Americans beyond slavery. Thereafter, the Civil Rights revolution launched a series of legislative initiatives that dismantled the formal structure of American apartheid. These initiatives included the adoption of federal antidiscrimination and affirmative action legislation (Anderson, 1994).

Affirmative action and related civil rights efforts have reduced the most visible aspects of racial segregation in schools and the workforce. The benefits to African Americans, to other racial minority group members, and even to Whites as a group are noteworthy. Nevertheless, anti-Black discrimination is still powerfully operative, particularly in dictating access to occupations and earnings (see the papers in Fix and Struyk, 1992; Darity, Guilkey, and Winfrey, 1996). Ongoing discrimination is a persistent obstacle to racial equality.

There is little dispute that markets today are different than they were before the Civil Rights initiatives. Nevertheless, large racial gaps in earnings and wealth remain, rooted in part in the legacy of slavery and segregation. Most apparent in inequalities in wealth, the gaps have persisted from generation to generation because of the role of inheritance in transmitting wealth. While better education, better schools, and better jobs through affirmative efforts can assist racial minority group members in narrowing current market inequalities, much more is needed to eradicate the legacy of prior inequalities.

Reparations Coupled with Vigorous Antidiscrimination Enforcement

The current attacks on affirmative action create a unique window of opportunity for examining alternative remedies. The assaults must be met with a focused and renewed emphasis on finding an alternative. That alternative could be reparations. Even vociferous opponents of affirmative action such as Krauthammer (1991) now seem to endorse reparations as a substitute for affirmative action. We also argue that there is no substitute for continued, vigorous enforcement of existing antidiscrimination statutes. Without a government-backed, publicly supported antidiscrimination mechanism, direct redistribution of $1 trillion to African Americans would not suffice to eliminate racial economic inequality for all time. While antidiscrimination enforcement efforts are essential to prevent further erosion of Blacks' economic position, it is doubtful that they alone are sufficient to assure equality.

But would direct redistribution of wealth along with antidiscrimination enforcement be enough to bring about racial equality? How would a redistribution scheme affect the large numbers of incarcerated African Americans; the many poorly trained, unskilled young Black adults; and the young Black males who have dropped out of the labor force, turning to illegal activities for their livelihood?

Enterprise and Entrepreneurship

The answer may lie in enterprise and entrepreneurship. There is a long tradition in the United States of attempting to translate the enterprising skills of the poor and the criminal talents of inner-city youths into productive entrepreneurial activity. However, traditional training programs have focused on preparing Black youths for industrial and manufacturing jobs when blue collar jobs have been disappearing and crime has become more and more attractive. This has meant that many young Blacks have been all too frequently destined for lives of crime, drugs, and ultimately imprisonment, or joblessness, unemployment, and ultimately economic dependency. The strategy advocated here is deceptively simple: train young disadvantaged Blacks to be managers and entrepreneurs, not low skilled workers.

In a wealth redistribution scheme, the poorest Blacks could become entrepreneurs, home owners, and small business owners. Black youths could apply entrepreneurial skills learned in the booming, lucrative drug market to legal, viable economic activities with high long-term returns. The phenomenal talents of young street hustlers could be redirected so that they could produce and sell, for example, food and clothing products in the Black community. Mothers once on welfare could receive training in accounting, tax law, finance, and bookkeeping so that they could run their own businesses.

Enhancing the involvement of the poorest African Americans in enterprise and entrepreneurship is one way to assure that they are the beneficiaries of strategies designed to redistribute wealth, such as reparations. The poor will thus not be disadvantaged once again if wealth redistribution through reparations occurs.

The neoconservative appeal to the power of the marketplace and to self-help strategies for solving the problems of poverty and race remains limited. Self-help, market-oriented policies are useless if discrimination continues and if unequal wealth persists from generation to generation. Direct redistribution of wealth remains one of the key policies with any potential for reducing racial economic inequality. Nonetheless, a "subpolicy" of entrepreneurship and self-help embraced by many conservatives emerges as a practical vehicle for utilizing the redistributed wealth to assure that the gains benefit Blacks at the bottom of the economic ladder.

In the final analysis, in considering the direction of public policies to reduce racial inequality, a twin dilemma will have to be faced:

- On the one hand, conventional human capital policies that are non-race-based do not necessarily address the problems of those completely outside the productive spheres of the economy, in part because of racially discriminatory barriers that still exist structurally in the economy.

- On the other hand, race-based strategies have lost considerable support from the majority of Americans.

It is possible, of course, to target human capital programs toward racial minorities, but this course no longer appears to be politically feasible. It is also possible that a focus on direct transfers to the poor, who are disproportionately minority, could narrow racial gaps more in the future than the negligible narrowing that occurred in the past. However, the expenditures needed to bring about these transfers may be substantial and politically unsupported. We restate this dilemma as one of finding remedies or strategies that hold hope for making Blacks and other disadvantaged minorities better off without making Whites worse off. The challenge for policymakers will be to confront the empirical evidence showing that racial inequality is likely to remain quite large in American society even in the best of circumstances and to recognize that conventional policies may do little to narrow that inequality.

NOTES

1. For exceptions to this pattern, see Farley (May 1990) and Darity, Guilkey, and Winfrey (1995, 1996). It is even more unusual for researchers to disaggregate the Black population by ancestry or domestic versus foreign origin; however, the 1990 census indicates that no more than 2 percent of the U.S. Black population were foreign-born anyway. Moreover, the most substantive study of this type, a comparison of labor market experiences of native Blacks and immigrant Blacks undertaken by Woodbury (1991), shows no significant difference in the treatment of each group. For given observable characteristics, both groups of Blacks face comparable disadvantages.

2. Exceptions to this pattern include Blau and Graham (1990), Oliver and Shapiro (1995), Chiteji and Stafford (1998), and Shapiro and Wolff (forthcoming).

3. Smith and Welch have continued to maintain the same position in more recent work for the same reasons. See Smith and Welch (1989) and Welch and Smith (1989).

4. This is much the same viewpoint adopted by Margo (1990) in his book *Race and Schooling in the South, 1880-1950: An Economic History*, which relies heavily on Smith and Welch's research. The companion perspective is represented by the Thernstroms (1997) in *America in Black and White: One Nation, Indivisible.* They argue that all of the remaining disparity in Black and White earnings can be explained by a cognitive skills gap between the races that is due, in turn, to remaining racial differences in the quality of schooling.

5. Welch has been a prominent expert witness in defense of businesses confronted with discrimination suits. For an example of the nature of the arguments he uses in his testimony, see Welch (1989). It is of interest to note that Welch observed at the close of his essay, "A number of recent studies have shown that the longer-run gain in relative earnings of Black men can be attributed to three primary sources: rising levels of school completion, emigration from the rural South, and increasing value of additional schooling" rather than affirmative action (187). The "recent studies" that he referred to are his work with Smith.

6. For a related analysis, see Butler and Heckman (1977). They also argued that the labor force dropout effect artificially raised Black-White earnings and income ratios, but they attributed the higher Black labor force dropout rate to the work disincentive effects of the American social welfare system. Why those effects—to the extent that they exist— would have a different racial impact is not clear. We take up this issue in depth below.

7. The percentages for heads of families in 1970 and 1988, respectively, were: Black males, 1.72 percent and 0.83 percent; Black females, 0.20 percent and 0.37 percent; White males, 2.74 percent and 0.58 percent; and White females, 0.16 percent and 0.10 percent. These are very low proportions.

8. See Eller and Fraser (1995), Table A, "Ownership Rates, Median Value of Asset Holdings, and the Distribution of Measured Net Worth by Asset Type: 1993, 1991, 1988, and 1984."

9. Indeed, several studies on consumption behavior have shown that at any given level of income, Blacks, on average, have a lower propensity to consume and a higher propensity to save than Whites. See Friedman (1957), Alexis (1971), and Hamermesh (1982). Only Galenson's (1972) study found no racial differences in savings rates.

10. For a comprehensive statement of this argument, see Swinton (1992); also see Higgs (1980).

11. Relevant studies include those of Bates (1991) as well as Butler and Herring (1991). It is notable here that recent immigrant populations who have high rates of self-employment typically have high rates of advanced educational credentials. The case of Korean immigrants is of signal importance in this regard. See Steinberg (1981).

REFERENCES

Alexis, M. 1971. "Some Negro-White Differences in Consumption." In *The Black Consumer*. Ed. G. Joyce and N.A.P. Govoni. New York: Random House, 257-274.

America, R.F. Ed. 1990. *The Wealth of Races: The Present Value of Benefits from Past Injustices.* Westport, Ct.: Greenwood Press.

Anderson, B.E. 1994. "Affirmative Action Policy Under Executive Order 11246." In *Civil Rights and Race Relations in the Post Reagan-Bush Era*. Ed. S.L. Myers, Jr. Westport, Ct.: Greenwood Publishing Group, Inc.

Ando, F. 1988. *An Analysis of Access to Bank Credit*. Los Angeles: UCLA Center for Afro-American Studies.

Bates, T. 1991. "Discrimination and the Capacity of New Jersey Area Minority and Women-Owned Businesses." Working Paper, New School for Social Research, Graduate School of Management and Urban Policy, August.

Blau, F.D., and J.W. Graham. 1990. "Black/White Differences in Wealth and Asset Composition." *Quarterly Journal of Economics* (May):321-339.

Butler, J.S., and C. Herring. 1991. "Ethnicity and Entrepreneurship in America." *Sociological Perspectives* 34(1).

Butler, R., and J. Heckman. 1977. "The Government's Impact on the Labor Market Status of Black Americans: A Critical Review." In *Equal Rights and Industrial Relations*. Ed. L.J. Hausman et al. Madison, Wis.: Industrial Relations Research Association, 235-281.

Chiteji, N., and F. Stafford. 1998. "Portfolio Choices of Parents and Their Children as Young Adults: Asset Accumulation by African American Families." *American Economic Review* 89(2)(May):377-380.

Cotton, J. 1989. "Opening the Gap: The Decline in Black Economic Indicators in the 1980s." *Social Science Quarterly* 70(4) (December):803-819.

———. 1990. "Recent Changes in the Structure and Value of African-American Male Occupations." *Trotter Institute Review* 4(3) (Fall):6-11.

Darity, W.A., Jr. 1980. "Illusions of Black Economic Progress." *Review of Black Political Economy* 10(2) (Winter):154-168.

Darity, W.A., Jr., D. Guilkey, and W. Winfrey. 1995. "Ethnicity, Race and Earnings." *Economic Letters* 47(3-4) (March):401-408.

———. 1996. "Explaining the Differences in Economic Performance Among Racial and Ethnic Groups in the USA: The Data Examined." *American Journal of Economics and Sociology* 55 (October 4):411-426.

Darity, W.A., Jr., and S.L. Myers, Jr. 1980a. "Black Economic Progress: A Case Against the Dramatic Improvement Hypothesis." In *Discussion Paper #613-80*. Institute for Research on Poverty.

———. 1980b. "Changes in Black-White Income Inequality, 1969-1978: A Decade of Progress?" *Review of Black Political Economy* 10(4) (Summer):355-379.

———. 1980c. "The Vintage Effect and the Illusion of Black Progress." *Urban League Review* 5(1):54-65.

Darity, W.A., Jr., S.L. Myers, Jr., E.D. Carson, and W. Sabol. 1994. *The Black Underclass: Critical Essays on Race and Unwantedness*. New York: Garland Publishing.

DuBois, W.E.B. 1935. *Black Reconstruction in America, 1860-1880.* 1st ed. New York: Harcourt, Brace.

Eller, T.J., and W. Fraser. 1995. *Asset Ownership of Household, 1993.* Current Population Reports, P70, House Economic Studies, No. 47 Washington, D.C.: U.S. Government Printing Office (GPO).

Fairlie, R.W. 1999. "The Absence of the African-American Owned Business: An Analysis of the Dynamics of Self-Employment." *Journal of Labor Economics* 17(1):80-107.

Farley, R. 1990. "Blacks, Hispanics, and White Ethnic Groups: Are Blacks Uniquely Disadvantaged?" *American Economic Review: Papers and Proceedings* 80(2) (May):237-241.

Fix, M., and R.J. Struyk, Eds. 1992. *Clear and Convincing Evidence: Measurement of Discrimination in America.* Washington, D.C.: Urban Institute Press.

Freeman, R.B. 1973a. "Changes in the Labor Market for Black Americans, 1948-1972." *Brookings Papers on Economic Activity.*

———. 1973b. "Decline of Labor Market Discrimination and Economic Analysis." *American Economic Review* (May):280-286.

———. 1981. "Black Economic Progress After 1964: Who Has Gained and Why?" In *Studies in Labor Markets.* Ed. S. Rosen. Cambridge, Mass.: National Bureau of Economic Research, 247-294.

Friedman, M. 1957. *A Theory of the Consumption Function.* Princeton, N.J.: Princeton University Press.

Galenson, M. 1972. "Do Blacks Save More?" *American Economic Review* 12(1) (March):211-216.

Hamermesh, D. 1982. "Social Insurance and Consumption." *American Economic Review* 72(1) (March):101-113.

Haveman, R. 1988. *Starting Even: An Equal Opportunity Program to Combat the Nation's New Poverty.* New York: Simon and Schuster.

Higgs, R. 1980. *Competition and Coercion: Blacks in the American Economy, 1865-1914.* Chicago: University of Chicago Press.

Hoxby, C.M. 1994. "Do Private Schools Provide Competition for Public Schools?" NBER Working Paper No. 4978. Cambridge, Mass.: National Bureau of Economic Research.

Jaynes, G.D., and R.M. Williams, Jr. 1989. *A Common Destiny: Blacks and American Society.* Washington, D.C.: National Research Council.

Johnson, C.S. 1930. *The Negro in American Civilization: A Study of Negro Life and Race Relations in the Light of Social Research.* New York: Henry Holt.

Krauthammer, C. 1991. "Reparations for Black Americans." *Time,* December 31, 18.

Long, J.E., and S.B. Caudill. 1992. "Racial Differences in Home Ownership and Housing Wealth, 1970-1986." *Economic Inquiry* 30(1) (January):83:100.

Loury, G.C. 1996. "Performing Without a Net." In *The Affirmative Action Debate.* Ed. G. Curry. Reading, Mass.: Addison-Wesley Publishing Co., Inc.

Margo, R.A. 1990. *Race and Schooling in the South, 1880-1950: An Economic History.* Chicago, Ill.: University of Chicago Press.

Myers, S.L., Jr. 1989. "How Voluntary Is Black Unemployment and Labor Force Withdrawal?" In *The Question of Discrimination: Racial Inequality in the U.S. Labor Market.* Ed. S. Shulman and W.A. Darity, Jr. Middletown, Ct.: Wesleyan University Press.

——. 1997. "Analysis of the 1996 Minnesota Basic Standards Test Data." Working Paper, Humphrey Institute of Public Affairs, University of Minnesota, March.

Myers, S:L., Jr., and C. Chung. 1996. "Racial Differences in Home Ownership and Home Equity Among Preretirement-Aged Households." *The Gerontologist* 36(3):350-360.

Myrdal, G. 1944. *An American Dilemma: The Negro Problem and Modern Democracy.* New York: Harper and Row.

Oliver, M., and T. Shapiro. 1995. *Black Wealth/White Wealth: A New Perspective on Racial Inequality.* New York: Routledge.

Ruhm, C.J. 1988. "When 'Equal Opportunity' Is Not Enough: Training Costs and Inter-generational Inequality." *Journal of Human Resources* 23(2) (Spring):155-172.

Shapiro, T., and E. Wolff, Eds. Forthcoming. *The Benefits and Mechanisms for Spreading Asset Ownership.* Cheltenham, U.K.: Edward Elgar Publishers.

Sherraden, M. 1991. *Assets and the Poor: A New American Welfare Policy.* Armonk, N.Y.: M.E. Sharpe.

Smith, J.P. 1978. "The Convergence to Racial Equality in Women's Wages." In *RAND Paper Series P-6026* (January).

——. 1978. "The Improving Status of Black Americans." In *RAND Paper Series P-6055,* 1.

Smith, J.P., and F. Welch. 1977. "Black-White Male Wage Ratios: 1960-1970." *American Economic Review* 67 (March).

——. 1978. *Race Differences in Earnings: A Survey and New Evidence.* Santa Monica, Cal.: RAND Corporation (March).

——. 1989. "Black Economic Progress After Myrdal." *Journal of Economic Literature* 27 (June):519-564.

Stegman, M.A. 1999. *Savings for the Poor: The Hidden Benefits of Electronic Banking.* Washington, D.C.: Brookings Institution Press.

Steinberg, S. 1981. *The Ethnic Myth: Race, Ethnicity and Class in America.* Boston: Beacon Press.

Swinton, D.H. 1992. "The Economic Status of African Americans: Limited Ownership and Persistent Inequality." In *The State of Black America 1992.* New York: National Urban League, Inc.

Thernstrom, A., and S. Thernstrom. 1997. *America in Black and White: One Nation, Indivis-ible.* New York: Simon and Schuster.

U.S. Bureau of the Census. 1991. *The Black Population in the United States.* Current Population Reports. Washington, D.C.: GPO.

——. 1993. *Asset Ownership of Households: 1993.* Current Population Reports, P70-47. Washington, D.C.: GPO.

——. 1994. *Statistical Abstract of the United States, 1994.* Washington, D.C.: GPO.

VanderHart, P.G. 1994. "An Empirical Analysis of the Housing Decisions of Older Homeowners." *Journal of the American Real Estate and Urban Economics Association* 22(2) (Summer):205-233.

Vedder, R., L. Gallaway, and D. Klingaman. 1990. "Black Exploitation and White Benefits: The Civil War Income Revolution." In *The Wealth of Races: The Present Value of Benefits from Past Injustices.* Ed. R.F. America. Westport, Ct.: Greenwood Press.

Welch, F. 1989. "Affirmative Action and Discrimination." In *The Question of Discrimina-tion: Racial Inequality in the U.S. Labor Market.* Ed. S. Shulman and W.A. Darity, Jr. Middletown, Ct.: Wesleyan University Press, 153-189.

Welch, F., and J.P. Smith. 1989. *Closing the Gap: Forty Years of Economic Progress for Blacks*. R-3330-DOL. Santa Monica, Cal.: RAND Corporation.

Wilson, W.J. 1987. *The Truly Disadvantaged: The Inner City, the Underclass and Public Policy*. Chicago: University of Chicago Press.

Wolff, E.N. 1992. "Changing Inequality of Wealth." *American Economic Review: Papers and Proceedings* 92(2) (May).

Woodbury, S. 1991. "Earnings of Black Immigrants: Implications for Racial Discrimination." In *New Approaches to Economic and Social Analyses of Discrimination*. Ed. R. Cornwall and P. Wunnava. New York: Praeger.

Chapter 5

Large Gains, Recent Reversals, and Continuing Inequality in Education for African Americans

by Michael T. Nettles
Professor of Education, University of Michigan

and Gary Orfield
Professor of Education and Social Policy, Harvard University

INTRODUCTION

The second half of the 20th century ushered in unprecedented break-throughs for African Americans in elementary, secondary, and higher education. Their success in school has been mainly a story of a growing demand for education, a massive rise in educational attainment, and measurable gains in achievement levels. These successes, however, have been accompanied by some enormous disappointments.

Prior to World War II, Blacks were still primarily a rural southern population relying upon rigidly segregated and inferior schools in some of the poorest and least educated areas in the nation. High school graduation was uncommon. Almost all Black teachers and principals were concentrated in Black schools, and virtually no Black officials were heads of school districts. At that time, it would have been extremely optimistic to forecast the remarkable achievements that African Americans would later make in education. But by the late 1980s, Black administrators were supervising many of the nation's largest school districts, and the Black-White gap in achievement scores had declined (Nettles and Perna, 1997b). By 1994, the Black on-time high school graduation rate had reached 80 percent, and almost 50 percent of Black high school graduates had entered colleges and universities immediately after graduating from high school. Furthermore, a Black-led social movement helped destroy the "apartheid" education system of the South, making the heartland of discrimination the nation's least segregated region.

The other side of the equation, however, is rather grim. The escape of African Americans from segregation and discrimination in the South and their migration to the metropolitan industrial centers in the North were accompanied by severe problems: social crises stemming from the consolidation of urban ghettos; deep poverty for almost one-half of the nation's Black children; and an enormous increase in the number of Black children growing up in often overburdened single parent families. Even as African Americans reduced the racial gap in graduation rates, they experienced dramatic declines in real earnings as the labor market changed and the value of that credential rapidly decayed. The large city school systems that were powerhouses of American education in the first half of the century have become centers of educational failure. Further, the U.S. Supreme Court, the genuine hope of Blacks who were shut out of politics in the South of the 1950s, is now the bastion of civil rights resistance, giving clear signals supporting a backward movement on several key education rights.

The Black population is better educated today, and Black students and teachers can be found in an array of settings. Nevertheless, after major gains in the 1970s and early 1980s, the racial gaps in achievement widened yet again in the early 1990s. Large gaps remain in indicators such as standardized test scores, representation of students and teachers in critical curricula, and enrollment in the nation's most selective schools, colleges, and universities. For Blacks, there has also been an increase in the high school dropout rate, a college access crisis, and a chronic shortage of college students preparing to become teachers and of college graduates receiving doctoral degrees.

Migration, economic change, law, politics, and education reform have all contributed to the considerable progress made by African Americans in education, as well as to the deep disappointments. This chapter describes the trends in both directions and explores some of the important factors related to the present educational circumstance of Blacks in the United States. It then suggests policies needed to improve conditions in the 21st century.

EARLIER TRENDS AND EFFECTS OF ANTIDISCRIMINATION LEGISLATION

Much of the 20th century was a period of huge Black migration—from rural areas and small towns in the South where poverty was the norm to cities in the North that offered better jobs; from states with weak education systems to states with better schools. In 1950, 38 percent of Blacks still lived in rural areas, and 68 percent lived in states with segregationist laws (U.S. Bureau of the Census, 1950). The 10 states spending the least on schools were all in the rural South.[1] The Black middle class was minuscule, precarious, and limited to a few occupations, mostly within the Black community. In the first half of the century, most of the Black migration was from the South to the North, but after 1975, it reversed direction. Today, 56 percent of the Black population reside in the South compared with 51 percent in 1975 (Nettles and Perna, 1997b).

From the Civil War to the 1950s, Blacks struggled simply to obtain the fundamentals of education, such as decent school buildings, a regular school year, fair pay for teachers, and financing and recognition by accrediting associations for segregated Black colleges and universities. Much of this struggle involved efforts to gain concessions from overtly racist White leaders by powerless people without an economic and political base who were not even allowed to register and vote in much of the South. Black reformers, often led by the National Association for the Advancement of Colored People (NAACP), faced seemingly impossible odds as they turned to the courts that had upheld segregationist laws for more than half a century. After World War II, public revulsion against Germany's racist dictatorship, President Harry S. Truman's human rights report (1979), and increasing Black political power in northern cities led the Truman and Eisenhower administrations to ask the Supreme Court to render the South's system of Black education unconstitutional.

The federal government became a major force in education reform and in civil rights enforcement. But as it entered the battle, it did not operate any major public school program nor fund any higher education institution; therefore, it had no authority to bring lawsuits or enforce civil rights. In the remarkable period from 1954 to 1972, the Supreme Court declared the entire southern system of imposed educational separation unconstitutional, and Congress passed the first major Civil Rights Act. This act outlawed discrimination in all school districts, colleges, and universities receiving federal aid. Class action lawsuits challenged the racially dual systems of public higher education just as the *Brown* v. *Board of Education of Topeka* (1954) case did for elementary and secondary schools. The federal agenda had a strong central focus on equalizing education for those who had been excluded from school or had attended inferior schools because of their race. An unprecedented exercise of federal power crushed the segregationist laws of the South and vastly increased the Black electorate in those states.

At the same time, the huge migration from rural areas in the South continued, with Blacks moving into America's industrial heartland. Suburbanization was taking hold, and baby boomers were entering school and going on to college. Unemployment was low, real incomes were rapidly increasing, and poverty rates were falling. Racial attitudes appeared to be more open to change. The conditions for racial progress were more favorable than they had been in decades.

The revolutionary changes brought by the federal government's major programs of preschool education, compensatory education, and college scholarships were readily apparent in the 17 mandatory segregation states. Millions of Black students were able to attend interracial schools, colleges, and universities that received funds aimed at closing the racial gap in education and improving race relations. The 1960s also saw the government's first efforts to significantly reduce poverty since the New Deal, with education being fundamental to many of the new programs.

Beginning with the 1964 Economic Opportunity Act and the 1965 Elementary and Secondary Education Act, the federal government launched a national compensatory education program, Title I. This program became the cornerstone of the federal contribution to public education and has served millions of African American students in high poverty schools. Other programs in President Lyndon Johnson's War on Poverty provided preschool education (Operation Head Start), special outreach (Upward Bound), help for those having trouble in public schools (Job Corps), and financial assistance to make college, graduate, and professional education affordable for low income students.

Antidiscrimination legislation had a variety of effects. Many jobs opened up that were previously closed to Blacks, such as teaching positions in schools, colleges, and universities. Teacher tests and other requirements, however, made it more difficult for Black students from weak schools to become teachers and professors. On the other hand, new job opportunities in other fields made teaching jobs much less desirable. The number of Black college students studying education plummeted as the number studying business administration and other areas soared, a situation that continues today.

The expansion of the Black middle class both reflected educational attainment and produced intensified demands for education. In 1950, before *Brown* v. *Board of Education of Topeka,* only about one-fifth of adult African Americans graduated from high school. But by 1994, the majority of Black Americans were at least high school graduates, approaching the level of White students if General Educational Development (GED, or high school equivalency) degrees are included. College attendance and graduation also dramatically increased, with almost one-half of Black high school graduates going on to college. By 1994, African Americans represented 10 percent of college and university enrollment. Further, almost 50 percent of African Americans who entered college graduated within six years, representing more than 7 percent of the nation's college graduates each year from 1988 to 1996 (Nettles and Perna, 1997c). Despite educational, economic, and social changes that raised graduation requirements, moved jobs and resources away from the central city, and intensified other problems, the schools managed to make progress.

Ever since achievement test statistics were first collected in the United States, there have been large racial and ethnic gaps in achievement levels. Yet no other impoverished, isolated group has as low achievement scores as African Americans. Nevertheless, from the 1960s through the early 1980s, there was a modest decline in the Black-White gap in achievement. The shift was particularly notable because a rapidly rising proportion of African Americans were staying in school, so that later tests included many students who would probably have dropped out in the past. African American scores rose on the National Assessment of Educational Progress (NAEP), which measures a national sample of students on consistent tests over the years. Test gains were especially evident in the early grades. In addition, average American College Test (ACT) scores and Scholastic Aptitude Test (SAT) scores for Blacks increased somewhat, notwithstanding the larger numbers taking the tests. However, progress in reducing the gaps on the NAEP tests and on the college admissions tests ended by the early 1990s (NAEP, 1997).

THE STATE OF AFRICAN AMERICAN EDUCATION

The mix of education policies and economic opportunities present in the 1960s and early 1970s enabled Blacks to make major gains in education in the 1970s and early 1980s. The opposite occurred in the late 1980s and 1990s.

Preschool Experience and Risk Factors Affecting Achievement

Education no longer begins in kindergarten. The large increase in the number of working mothers with young children during the past three decades resulted in an equally large increase in formal preschool attendance.

The traditional parental role is being displaced by outside preschool providers, even though the United States is the only Western country without a general public day care system. During the War on Poverty, the federal government moved to upgrade the quality of preschool opportunities for poor children by creating Operation Head Start. Today, however, the unequal availability and uneven quality of day care have increased the skill deficiencies that children in low income families already experience and have widened the gap between low and high socioeconomic status people.

There have been no significant gaps in Black participation in preschool mainly because of the substantial Black enrollment in the Head Start programs. Between 1970 and 1994, as the participation of mothers in the workforce expanded, the number of three- and four-year-olds enrolled in preschool approximately doubled. In 1995, although large overall national differences by income existed (particularly among families with three-year-olds), 40 percent of both Black and White three-year-olds attended preschool; among four-year-olds, 66 percent of Black and 60 percent of White children went to preschool.

The skills of prekindergarten children differ substantially by race, family structure, income, and the number of parents present in the home. In 1994, White four-year-olds were 25 percent more likely than African American children to know their colors, 33 percent more likely to know their letters, and 17 percent more likely to be able to write their names. Preschoolers from families with higher incomes scored better on letters and colors. Children with two parents at home scored better on all skills. Data from the National Longitudinal Survey of Youth show that average vocabulary scores on the Peabody Picture Vocabulary Test are lower for African American preschoolers than for White preschoolers (Nettles and Perna, 1997b). These simple measures reflect a broader set of differences in vocabulary and experiences that tend to cause problems for Black students from the beginning of their formal school experience.

The strongest influence on a child's level of educational attainment is the family. A number of risk factors are connected with African American family life that work against the educational success of Black children. These include developmental disabilities before birth; being born to a teenage mother, to a high school dropout, into a single parent family, and/or into poverty; and serious untreated health problems. Additional risk factors include moving frequently because of lack of a stable place to live; living in a community of concentrated economic failure and poverty; growing up with few role models of educational success; and attending school in a dangerous community where many good teachers refuse to teach. Although some resilient students persist and succeed in the face of multiple risk factors, there are strong statistical relationships that lower achievement.

The poverty rate for children under age 18 declined sharply in the 1960s and remained relatively stable in the 1970s. In 1980, however, it rose above 20 percent for the first time in a generation and remained high—20.5 percent in 1996. In that year, among Black children under age 18, 40 percent were living below the poverty level. In 1994, 65 percent of Black families with children under age 18 were headed by a single parent (up from 32 percent in 1970), and 68 percent of Black children were born to unmarried women (Nettles and Perna, 1997b).

There are powerful relationships between parents' level of income and education and their children's educational success. Impoverished children face many disadvantages, including poor nutrition and health care, exposure to noisy and unstimulating environments, and lack of good child care if their parents work. In the 1990s, Black children were more than twice as likely as White children to have low birth weights (13 percent compared with 6 percent), a strong predictor of developmental problems (U.S. Bureau of the Census, 1997). Data from the National Household Education Survey for 1992 show that fewer African American than White preschoolers daily eat breakfast (87 percent compared with 94 percent) or a hot meal (83 percent compared with 90 percent) (Nettles and Perna, 1997b). Children with a single parent have less contact with that parent, and the contact they have is not as verbally rich as in dual parent families. A smaller percentage of African American parents of preschoolers than White parents regularly read to their children. Impoverished adults struggling to make ends meet may have emotional and substance abuse problems that affect their children. In 1992, about 16 percent of the mothers of African American preschoolers, compared with only 4 percent of the mothers of White preschoolers, were looking for employment (Nettles and Perna, 1997b). Also, in 1992, about 20 percent of the mothers of African American preschoolers did not complete high school compared with 8 percent of the mothers of White preschoolers.

Virtually all children attend elementary school, but the schools have differing resources and burdens, teachers with varying levels of qualifications, and differing tracking systems. In these areas as well as those noted above, African American children face more limited opportunities than White children.

Isolation by Race and Poverty in Public Schools

Isolation by race and poverty in schools greatly diminished in the desegregation era of 1964 to 1972. It began, however, to increase in the late 1980s and accelerated after the Supreme Court authorized resegregation of schools in its 1991 Dowell decision (*Board of Education of Oklahoma City* v. *Dowell*, 1991).

African American students attend urban schools in much larger proportions than other groups because of residential segregation. In 1993-94, the 10 largest central-city school districts in the United States enrolled 17.8 percent of all African American students, but only 1.7 percent of the nation's White students (Nettles and Perna, 1997b). The economic, political, and educational crises of large U.S. cities therefore have serious consequences for Black students.

In addition, Blacks are much more likely than Whites to be in segregated schools that have high concentrations of poverty (Nettles and Perna, 1997b). In fact, many of the problems attributed to African American education are related more to poverty concentrations in schools, to social crises, and to shrinking tax resources in communities than to their race.[2] Yet poverty and race are highly interrelated at the school level, and few White schools of concentrated poverty exist. School characteristics associated with poverty and isolation are thus often ascribed to race and to the inadequacies of the minority faculties and administrators who frequently serve central-city schools. This syndrome of "blaming the victim" became much more common after release in 1983 of the Reagan administration's report, *A Nation at Risk*. The education reform agenda then turned from issues of equity to issues of raising standards while ignoring social context (U.S. National Commission, 1983).

In the 1994-95 school year, 34 percent of African American students were in intensely segregated schools that had more than nine-tenths African American and Latino students. These schools were 16 times more likely than segregated White schools to experience concentrated poverty (defined as more than one-half the students receiving free lunches) (Orfield and Miller, 1998; Orfield and Eaton, 1996).[3] Another 34 percent of African American students were in schools that had fewer than one-half Whites and that tended to have much higher poverty levels than White schools. The relationship between segregation by race and segregation by poverty in public schools is exceptionally strong. The correlation between the percentage of Black and Latino enrollments and the percentage of students receiving free lunches was an extremely high 72 percent in 1994-95.

Sixty-one percent of U.S. schools had less than 20 percent Black and Latino students in the early 1990s, whereas 80 percent of the schools that were concentrated in big cities had 80-100 percent Black and Latino students. Ninety-five percent of the schools with 90-100 percent White and Asian students had less than 50 percent low income students. But among schools that were 90-100 percent African American and/or Latino, 89 percent were predominantly poor, and only 3 percent had less than 25 percent poor children. These schools represent different worlds of educational opportunity that are powerfully related to racial segregation (Orfield and Eaton, 1996).

Educational Achievement

School-level achievement scores nationally and in many states consistently show that high poverty schools have much lower levels of educational performance on virtually all outcomes. Low achievement levels are not entirely caused by the school; as discussed, family background is a powerful influence.

High poverty schools, however, are unequal in many critical areas that affect educational outcomes, and school poverty level is strongly related to average student achievement level. Concentrated poverty schools have to deal with family and health crises and security issues more often than do low poverty or middle income schools. They must devote considerable time and resources to children who do not speak standard English, who are seriously disturbed, who lack educational materials in their homes, and who are poorly prepared for school. High poverty schools tend to attract less qualified teachers and to hold the ones they attract for shorter periods of time than other schools. They often have to invest heavily in remediation but less than adequately in advanced and gifted classes and in materials for these classes. High poverty schools also have very low levels of competition, regardless of the students' interests and abilities, as well as low levels of peer group support for educational achievement. The community, schools and colleges at the next level of education, and potential employers tend to have a negative view of concentrated poverty schools. In states that have implemented high stakes testing, denying graduation or flunking students, high poverty schools generally have the highest rates of sanctions. The educational problems of these schools are highlighted whenever achievement statistics are reported in the press.

The relationship between poverty and educational achievement, however, is neither inexorable nor without exceptions. Some districts have one or several high poverty schools that perform well above the norm. Students with similar family backgrounds may perform at different levels of achievement, and virtually every school has talented students and teachers. Nevertheless, the overall relationship is powerful.

In 1992, a study of Title I reported that this large federal intervention had no visible effect on educational outcomes and that Title I students attending concentrated poverty schools had weak achievement records even when they received special services. Since the reauthorization of Chapter 1 in 1994, however, students in low poverty schools have made noticeable reading and mathematics achievement gains (U.S. Department of Education, 1999).

Title I centers on elementary education in basic skills, and it reaches large numbers of African American children. The fundamental focus of education reform at all levels of government has been on the early years. It is far from clear why Black students make the most progress in academic achievement in those years. Almost all African American kindergarten students are reported by their parents to look forward to school (98 percent), to like their teacher (93 percent), and to say positive things about school (96 percent). In addition, data from the National Longitudinal Survey of Youth show that African American preschoolers and White preschoolers have comparable scores, on average, on tests of motor and social development and verbal memory (Nettles and Perna, 1997b).

Measuring Academic Achievement

The United States did not have a valid and consistent measure of academic achievement until the initiation of the National Assessment of Educational Progress. The NAEP data are available from 1969 for science, 1971 for reading, 1973 for mathematics, and 1984 for writing. There are no nationally representative achievement data covering the periods before the migration from the rural South, the Civil Rights movement, and the War on

Poverty. Data on the earlier periods can be derived only by assessing trends in tests given to large numbers of students across the nation but without a sufficient representative sample of Blacks. The Iowa Test of the ACT and the California Achievement Test, the most widely used school tests, were given by school districts year after year, and the large declines in the scores probably reflected real changes in the population. The majority of colleges and universities require either the SAT or the ACT for admission, and consequently these two are taken by two-thirds of the nation's students. However, they provide measures of the achievement scores of only the college-bound population; students who do not plan to apply to college are rarely included. The SAT and the ACT, therefore, provide limited information about changes in overall achievement. Nevertheless, some interesting trends can be observed. SAT and ACT college entrance scores for African Americans rose in the 1970s and early 1980s, and the achievement gaps between White scores narrowed somewhat among the populations applying to college. As discussed, the data for the higher grades reflected the experience of a rapidly growing share of the Black school age population.

The Black proportion of ACT test takers declined from 9 percent in 1987 to 8 percent in 1995. During the same period, the percentage of Black SAT test takers increased from 9 percent to 11 percent. The average verbal score rose by 6 points and the math score by 11 points, both larger increases than White gains. More recent data, however, show that the gaps between Black and White scores remain large and are no longer shrinking. African Americans score about 92 points below their White counterparts on the SAT's verbal section and about 100 points lower on the quantitative section (College Entrance Examination Board, 1996). Black scores are at the bottom of all racial/ethnic groups year after year, and the gaps are not decreasing.

A study by Daniel Koretz (1992) of the Rand Corporation explored long-term education achievement trends by examining the year-by-year, grade-by-grade trends in the Iowa Test scores for the nation. Koretz concluded that the greatest decline in the racial gap occurred for students who entered school at the peak of reform in the late 1960s. That decade had seen extraordinary economic growth, large increases in desegregated education and compensatory education programs, and major Black migration to U.S. cities. Some early NAEP reports show that the greatest Black gains were in the South where those changes had been the most dramatic.

In 1960, only 20.1 percent of the Black population over age 25 were high school graduates. That proportion rose to 31.4 percent in 1970, to 42.5 percent in 1980 (equal to the White level in 1960), and to 66.2 percent in 1990. However, high school graduation rates for African Americans plateaued during the 1980s, while the rates for Whites continued to rise. About 78 percent of African Americans completed high school on time in the early 1980s and early 1990s compared with 87 percent and 91 percent of Whites, respectively (Nettles and Perna, 1997c).

During the period of expansion in the proportion of Blacks enrolled in high school, there was also an explosion of testing based on the recommendations in *A Nation at Risk*. The growing population of test takers might have been projected to generate lower average test scores for Blacks. Even if test scores had merely remained constant during that period, there would have been real gains because of the expanded size of the test-taking population. Thus, indicators of rising test scores should be viewed as an underestimate of the true increases over the long term. Because the gains were made under conditions of weakening family structure and growing poverty for African American children, they are all the more significant.

The NAEP data, which are much more representative of the population than the ACT or SAT data, show a substantial decline in the racial achievement gap in elementary schools through the late 1980s, but a widening again in the 1990s. For example, from 1984 to 1988, the average math score for fourth graders climbed 11 points for Blacks and 8 points for Latinos; during 1990-96, however, because the average White score rose 12 points, the racial gap actually increased. In grade 12, the average math score increased 10 points for Whites, 12 points for Blacks, and 11 points for Latinos, leaving the large gaps virtually unchanged during a period of intense focus on math achievement (Reese et al., 1997). Black and Latino seniors' performance in math was about the same as that of White eighth graders. The 1994 NAEP reading assessments demonstrated a significant decrease in the scores of both Blacks and Latinos in elementary school and a substantial decline in the scores of all three groups in high school. Because Black and Latino reading scores dropped more rapidly than White scores, the gaps widened. The senior-year reading scores of Black and Latino students were close to the eighth grade scores of Whites. Further, there were large disparities by race at all grade levels in science achievement (NAEP, 1997).

The recent test score trends offer little reason to expect that the racial gaps in achievement at the end of high school will narrow or disappear. This assessment comes after more than a decade of emphasis on test performance, expanded course requirements, and increased testing under the Reagan administration's "excellence" reform proposals that were subsequently adopted in 47 states. In fact, many states now require a specified level of test performance to graduate (a standard adopted by some southern states 25 years earlier). These requirements have had a modest effect on scores, principally reflected in a slight increase in science and math offset by a significant decline in reading. After 30 years of compensatory education and a generation of standards-based reforms, the data show that it is extremely difficult to substantially increase achievement scores; that scores are strongly linked to family background; and that the government's education reforms have not been powerful enough or appropriately targeted to alter achievement levels among various racial and ethnic groups in the United States.

High School Dropouts: Less Success Than Meets the Eye

Much has been written in the popular press about the decline in Black high school dropouts and the virtual end of the Black-White gap in high school completion. Yet neither claim is accurate, based on a careful examination of the evidence. As Table 5-1 demonstrates, the percentage of Blacks

TABLE 5-1

High School Graduation Rates for 18-24 Year-Olds, 1988-96
(%)

	1988	1990	1992	1994	1996	Change
Total	80.3	80.6	81.2	78.8	76.4	− 2.9
Black	76.1	77.9	75.9	75.2	73.0	− 3.1

Note: The Current Population Survey data (1988-96) on which these numbers are based exclude inmates of correctional and medical facilities as well as members of the armed services. Given the significant proportion of young Black males in correctional facilities and the typically low education level of inmates, the data doubtless overstate the Black high school completion rate.

Source: U.S. Department of Education (1996a), 26.

graduating from high school remained stable between 1988 and 1996. The gap between the completion rates of Blacks and Whites also stayed much the same.

There were still dramatic differences in high school completion by family income levels, with 96.9 percent of young people from the upper one-fifth of the income distribution completing high school compared with 74.5 percent of those from the lowest one-fifth. In other words, the noncompletion rate was 3.1 percent for high income students, but 25.5 percent for low income students.

No substantial changes occurred between 1990 and 1995 in equalizing college enrollment and graduation among Black and White high school students, and the gaps remained large. In 1995, 12 percent fewer Black high school graduates than Whites enrolled in college.

High Aspirations Require Academic Effort

The aspirations of African American youths for higher education are at their highest level ever, as is the representation of Blacks in all levels of postsecondary education. The National Educational Longitudinal Study (NELS) of 1988 eighth graders revealed that the proportion of high school sophomores in 1990 expecting to eventually receive a Ph.D. or other advanced degree was 33 percent for students overall, but 36 percent for African Americans. From 1980 to 1990, the percentage of Black high school sophomores who anticipated graduating from college with at least a bachelor's degree rose from 35 percent to 70 percent (Nettles and Perna, 1997c).

There has also been a substantial increase in the proportion of African American and other students enrolled in academic courses in high school, an important prerequisite for access to academic degree programs in postsecondary education. Overall, the proportion of students in an academic track increased from 43 percent in 1980 to 66 percent in 1990. During that period, the percentage of Black students in academic programs increased from 38 percent to 59 percent, still 11 percentage points below the proportion of Black sophomores who expected to graduate from college (Nettles and Perna, 1997c).

Students who intend to earn a bachelor's degree must take rigorous courses in high school, yet it is clear that far too many African Americans do not. As discussed below, there is a considerable Black-White gap in academic tracking. High aspirations and expectations, while desirable, are by themselves not enough to enable students to go on to colleges and universities; academic effort and achievement in high school combined with access to high quality curricula are also necessary.

Gaps in Academic Tracking, in Critical Curricula, and in Qualified Teachers

The data in Table 5-2 reveal that considerably more White high school seniors than Black seniors are enrolled in the academic track in their schools and take the key "gateway" courses that prepare them for college admission and success in college. The causes of the inequality in academic tracking are actively debated, yet it is not known how much is due to lack of appropriate courses and qualified teachers, inadequate counseling, low parental education level or involvement in their children's education, negative peer group pressures, or other influences. It is clear, however, that concentration in an academic course of study is vital preparation for college success and that Black students infrequently select the proper courses.

The problem affects not only central-city and low income Black children; studies of suburban districts such as Evanston, Illinois, Cambridge, Massachusetts, and Shaker Heights, Ohio, also reveal different patterns of course-taking by race. Middle class and professional Black parents often confront the issue of school placement of their children in lower track courses. Given the overall gap in educational attainment by race, counselors

---

TABLE 5-2

Percentage of High School Seniors Enrolled in Academic Track Compared to Other Programs, 1980 and 1992

(%)

Race/Gap	College Prep Program		General Program		Vocational Program	
	1980	1992	1980	1992	1980	1992
White	39.8	49.9	37.1	38.7	23.1	11.4
Black	35.2	40.2	33.0	42.8	31.7	17.0
Gap	− 4.6	− 9.7	− 4.1	+ 4.1	+ 8.6	+ 5.6

Source: U.S. Department of Education (1995), 19.

and others may make racially stereotypical assumptions about the appropriate placement of students.

The gap in the academic track is serious, but even more serious are the gaps in the nature of the courses taken and in the teaching and level of the same courses. Critical courses in science and math taught by teachers with credentials in the area that they are teaching tend to be much more prevalent in middle class schools than in high poverty schools. In the 1993-94 school year, for example, 57.3 percent of teachers in schools with 1-10 percent minority students had their main teaching assignments in the fields of their college major or graduate degree; however, only 47 percent of accredited teachers taught in their fields in schools that were more than one-half minority. In 1992, Black high school graduates were less than one-half as likely as Whites to have taken three years of high school math courses. Compared with 22.6 percent of Whites and 38.2 percent of Asians, only 15.5 percent of Blacks had completed three years of basic high school laboratory sciences. Data from the Schools Staffing Survey show that public schools with a majority of African American students have more teacher vacancies than schools with few African American students. Furthermore, teachers assigned to predominantly minority schools were significantly more likely to leave the school within a year in 1995, 1996, and 1997 (Nettles and Perna, 1997b).

The same course generally covers less material and is less effective when taught in a class dominated by students lacking the prerequisite skills for mastering the material. As noted, two-thirds of Black students attend majority non-White schools with high poverty levels, and average minority and low income students are far behind White and middle class students in achievement levels. Teachers in such schools face the choice of failing large numbers of students, and thereby losing sufficient enrollment to maintain their courses and their jobs, or of passing students whose performance is inadequate. Courses in urban and concentrated poverty schools are often taught at a slower pace than suburban middle class courses, and teachers in those schools expect lower performance to attain grades.

Peer group gaps must also be considered. The problems in high poverty urban schools may be intensified by attitudes among the school's dominant social groups that marginalize academically oriented students and give prestige to nonacademically oriented students. Children who are better prepared for school may be hindered in learning not only if they are placed in settings without other prepared children, but also if they are in social settings that do not support academic achievement (Fordham and Ogbu, 1986).

Higher Education

Major breakthroughs have occurred in the participation, distribution, and performance of African Americans in higher education in the past two and one-half decades. Adequate information and facts on Blacks in the U.S. higher education system have only been available since 1976 when the

Department of Education began collecting data by race on enrollments and degrees awarded. That period—which began more than a decade after the Civil Rights Act and Johnson's War on Poverty launched massive financial aid programs—witnessed an explosion of access to higher education. Blacks, like Whites, attended college at a higher rate than ever before, and they began to exercise their option to attend predominantly White colleges and universities. The shift of the majority of African American enrollment from Black to White colleges and universities is one of the most dramatic sea changes in U.S. higher education in the past 25 years.

Shift in Black Enrollment to White Colleges

In the immediate post-World War II era, the majority of African Americans attended the historically Black colleges and universities (HBCUs) in the South, with only a few enrolled in the predominantly White universities in the North. Mingle (1976) estimated that 90 percent of African American college students attended Black colleges in the early 1950s. In 1976, 35 percent of African Americans obtained their bachelor's degrees from HBCUs, but by 1996, that proportion had declined to 28 percent. In 1977, approximately 45 percent of Black doctoral degree recipients received their baccalaureate degrees from HBCUs compared with about 24 percent today (Nettles and Perna, 1997a). Seventy-two percent of African Americans now receive their baccalaureate degrees from the nation's predominately White universities, most of which continue to struggle with this still new diversity. In courts of both law and public opinion, White institutions are fending off challenges to affirmative action policies that have helped increase Black enrollment in the most selective colleges and universities (discussed below).

Among African American undergraduates enrolled in colleges and universities nationwide (two- and four-year schools combined), the proportion attending HBCUs declined from 19 percent in Fall 1976 to 16 percent in Fall 1994. The number of Blacks attending HBCUs, however, grew at all levels during this period. Thus, the decline in representation is attributable to an overall increase in Black enrollment at other higher education institutions nationwide rather than to an enrollment decrease at HBCUs. Between 1976 and 1994, African American undergraduate enrollment at HBCUs rose by about 20 percent (from 175,411 to 210,876) compared with a 74 percent increase in White undergraduates at HBCUs (from 16,565 to 28,878). Black students have clearly expanded their undergraduate representation at non-HBCUs at a greater rate than they have at HBCUs, whereas White undergraduates have expanded their representation at HBCUs at five times the rate that they increased in enrollment overall—74 percent compared with 15 percent.

Enrollments and Degrees Awarded

Although the African American rate of participation in higher education increased during the past two and one-half decades, it has not yet reached the rates of Whites and Asians. Each year from 1976 to 1994, approximately 66 percent of the nation's high school graduates entered some form of postsecondary education within a year of completing high school, but only 49 percent of African American high school graduates went on to college (Nettles and Perna, 1997a).

Table 5-3 shows that in 1994, the college undergraduate enrollment of African American students was 10 percent. While this is the highest level of Black participation achieved during the period surveyed (1976-94), it is still below the 14 percent that African Americans represent in the traditional college age population. African American enrollments have grown at every level of postsecondary education, with the greatest increases at the first-professional degree level. In 1976, almost 5 percent of the Black college-age population were enrolled in first-professional schools, and that proportion increased to 7 percent in 1994.

African Americans have also made substantial gains in all college degrees awarded except for the master's degree. From 1976 to 1994, the number of Blacks receiving associate's degrees rose 37 percent compared with 23 percent for Whites, and those receiving bachelor's degrees increased 40 percent versus 14 percent for Whites. The number of Blacks awarded doctoral degrees grew 7 percent compared with an almost 3 percent decrease for Whites. First-professional degrees for African Americans climbed an impressive 71 percent during the period, whereas the increase was less than 1 percent for Whites.

Financial Aid

Financial aid has been a significant factor in the increased access of Black Americans to postsecondary education and academic success. In Fall 1992, 66 percent of Black undergraduates received financial aid at four-year not-for-profit colleges and universities compared with 49 percent of Whites. At less than four-year for-profit institutions, 83 percent of African American and 72 percent of White undergraduates were given financial aid. Among undergraduates at public two-year and less than two-year institutions, 34 percent of African Americans and 28 percent of Whites were the recipients of financial aid (Nettles and Perna, 1997c). More financial aid may be required for Blacks to expand their enrollment in higher education institutions and to eliminate the Black-White gap in postsecondary enrollment rates.

A positive relationship exists between financial need and performance on college admissions tests and between financial aid and college degree completion. Thus, an examination of financial aid is useful in determining the prospects of African American students in entering highly selective colleges and universities. As with the general population, high income African Americans, on average, have higher admission test scores than low income Blacks. In 1997, however, a larger percentage of Black SAT test takers (52 percent) were from families with incomes below $30,000 than Asian (37 percent) and White (16 percent) examinees. Only 7 percent of Black 1997 SAT examinees were from families with annual incomes above $80,000 compared with 19 percent of Asians and 25 percent of Whites. Among ACT test takers

TABLE 5-3

Percentage of Fall Enrollment at U.S. Colleges and Universities by Race and Gender, Selected Years, 1976-94

(Numbers In Thousands)

Year	Level	Total			White, Not Hispanic			African American, Not Hispanic			Hispanic			Asian American/ Pacific Islander			American Indian/ Alaskan Native			Nonresident Alien		
		Total	Male	Female	Total	Male	Female	Total	Male	Female	Total	Male	Female	Total	Male	Female	Total	Male	Female	Total	Male	Female
1976	Total Enroll.	100.0 / 10,985.6	52.7 / 5,794.4	47.3 / 5,191.2	82.6 / 9,076.1	43.8 / 4,813.7	38.8 / 4,262.4	9.4 / 1,033.0	4.3 / 469.9	5.1 / 563.1	3.5 / 383.8	1.9 / 209.7	1.6 / 174.1	1.8 / 197.8	1.0 / 108.4	0.8 / 89.4	0.7 / 76.1	0.4 / 38.5	0.3 / 37.6	2.0 / 218.7	1.4 / 154.1	0.6 / 64.6
	Undergraduate	100.0 / 9,419.0	52.0 / 4,896.9	48.0 / 4,522.1	82.2 / 7,740.5	43.0 / 4,052.2	39.2 / 3,688.3	10.0 / 943.4	4.6 / 430.7	5.4 / 512.7	3.7 / 352.9	2.0 / 191.7	1.7 / 161.2	1.8 / 169.3	1.0 / 91.1	0.8 / 78.2	0.8 / 69.7	0.4 / 34.8	0.4 / 34.9	1.5 / 143.2	1.0 / 96.4	0.5 / 46.8
	Grad.	100.0 / 1,322.5	53.5 / 707.9	46.5 / 614.6	84.3 / 1,115.6	44.5 / 589.1	39.8 / 526.5	5.9 / 78.5	2.4 / 32.0	3.5 / 46.5	2.0 / 26.4	1.1 / 14.6	0.9 / 11.8	1.9 / 24.5	1.1 / 14.4	0.8 / 10.1	0.4 / 5.1	0.2 / 2.7	0.2 / 2.4	5.5 / 72.4	4.2 / 55.1	1.3 / 17.3
	First-Prof.	100.0 / 244.0	77.7 / 189.6	22.3 / 54.4	90.1 / 220.0	70.6 / 172.4	19.5 / 47.6	4.5 / 11.1	2.9 / 7.2	1.6 / 3.9	1.8 / 4.5	1.4 / 3.5	0.4 / 1.0	1.7 / 4.0	1.2 / 2.9	0.5 / 1.1	0.5 / 1.3	0.4 / 1.1	0.1 / 0.2	1.3 / 3.0	1.1 / 2.5	0.2 / 0.5
1980	Total Enroll.	100.0 / 12,086.8	48.5 / 5,868.1	51.5 / 6,218.7	81.4 / 9,833.0	39.5 / 4,772.9	41.9 / 5,060.1	9.2 / 1,106.7	3.8 / 463.7	5.3 / 643.0	3.9 / 471.7	1.9 / 231.6	2.0 / 240.1	2.4 / 286.5	1.3 / 151.3	1.1 / 135.2	0.7 / 83.9	0.3 / 37.8	0.4 / 46.1	2.5 / 305.0	1.7 / 210.8	0.8 / 94.2
	Undergraduate	100.0 / 10,469.1	47.7 / 4,997.4	52.3 / 5,471.7	81.0 / 8,480.7	38.7 / 4,054.9	42.3 / 4,425.8	9.7 / 1,018.8	4.1 / 428.2	5.6 / 590.6	4.1 / 433.0	2.0 / 211.2	2.1 / 221.8	2.3 / 248.7	1.2 / 128.5	1.1 / 120.2	0.7 / 77.9	.3 / 34.8	0.4 / 43.1	2.0 / 209.9	1.3 / 139.8	0.7 / 70.1
	Grad.	100.0 / 1,340.9	50.1 / 672.2	49.9 / 668.7	82.4 / 1,104.7	40.2 / 538.5	42.2 / 566.2	5.6 / 75.1	2.1 / 28.2	3.5 / 46.9	2.4 / 32.1	1.2 / 15.7	1.2 / 16.4	2.4 / 31.6	1.4 / 18.6	1.0 / 13.0	0.4 / 5.2	0.2 / 2.5	0.2 / 2.7	6.9 / 92.2	5.1 / 68.7	1.8 / 23.5
	First-Prof.	100.0 / 276.9	71.7 / 198.5	28.3 / 78.4	89.4 / 247.6	64.8 / 179.5	24.6 / 68.1	4.7 / 12.9	2.7 / 7.4	2.0 / 5.5	2.4 / 6.5	1.7 / 4.6	0.7 / 1.9	2.2 / 6.1	1.5 / 4.1	0.7 / 2.0	0.3 / 0.8	0.2 / 0.5	0.1 / 0.3	1.0 / 2.9	0.8 / 2.3	0.2 / 0.6
1984	Total Enroll.	100.0 / 12,233	47.9 / 5,858.3	52.1 / 6,374.7	80.2 / 9,814.6	38.3 / 4,689.9	41.9 / 5,124.7	8.8 / 1,075.8	3.6 / 436.8	5.2 / 639.0	4.4 / 535.0	2.1 / 253.8	2.3 / 281.2	3.2 / 389.5	1.7 / 210.0	1.5 / 179.5	0.7 / 83.5	0.3 / 37.4	0.4 / 46.1	2.8 / 334.5	1.9 / 230.4	0.9 / 104.1
	Undergraduate	100.0 / 10,610.8	47.1 / 5,002.4	52.9 / 5,608.4	79.9 / 8,484.0	37.7 / 4,005.1	42.2 / 4,478.9	9.4 / 995.0	3.8 / 404.8	5.6 / 590.2	4.7 / 495.2	2.2 / 233.9	2.5 / 261.3	3.2 / 343.1	1.7 / 181.7	1.5 / 161.4	0.7 / 77.8	0.3 / 34.6	0.4 / 43.2	2.0 / 215.8	1.3 / 142.3	0.7 / 73.5
	Grad	100.0 / 1,343.7	49.9 / 671.1	50.1 / 672.6	80.9 / 1,087.3	38.8 / 521.3	42.1 / 566.0	5.1 / 67.4	1.9 / 24.9	3.2 / 42.5	2.4 / 31.8	1.1 / 14.7	1.3 / 17.1	2.8 / 37.1	1.7 / 22.4	1.1 / 14.7	0.4 / 4.8	0.2 / 2.2	0.2 / 2.6	8.6 / 115.3	6.4 / 85.6	2.2 / 29.7
	First-Prof.	100.0 / 278.5	66.4 / 184.9	33.6 / 93.6	87.4 / 243.4	58.7 / 163.6	28.7 / 79.8	4.8 / 13.4	2.5 / 7.1	2.3 / 6.3	2.9 / 8.0	1.9 / 5.2	1.0 / 2.8	3.4 / 9.4	2.1 / 5.9	1.3 / 3.5	0.3 / 1.0	0.2 / 0.6	0.1 / 0.4	1.2 / 3.4	0.9 / 2.5	0.3 / 0.9

(continued)

TABLE 5-3 continued

Year	Level	Total	Male	Female	White, Not Hispanic Total	White Male	White Female	African American, Not Hispanic Total	AfrAm Male	AfrAm Female	Hispanic Total	Hispanic Male	Hispanic Female	Asian American/ Pacific Islander Total	Asian Male	Asian Female	American Indian/ Alaskan Native Total	AmInd Male	AmInd Female	Nonresident Alien Total	NRA Male	NRA Female
1990	Total Enroll.	100.0 / 13,818.6	45.5 / 6,283.9	54.5 / 7,534.7	77.6 / 10,722.5	35.2 / 4,861.0	42.4 / 5,861.5	9.0 / 1,247.0	3.5 / 484.7	5.5 / 762.3	5.7 / 782.4	2.6 / 353.9	3.1 / 428.5	4.1 / 572.4	2.1 / 294.9	2.0 / 277.5	0.7 / 102.8	0.3 / 43.1	0.4 / 59.7	2.9 / 391.5	1.8 / 246.3	1.1 / 145.2
	Undergraduate	100.0 / 11,959.1	45.0 / 5,379.8	55.0 / 6,579.3	77.5 / 9,272.6	35.0 / 4,184.4	42.5 / 5,088.2	9.5 / 1,147.2	3.7 / 448	5.8 / 699.2	6.0 / 724.5	2.7 / 326.9	3.3 / 397.6	4.2 / 500.5	2.1 / 254.5	2.1 / 246.0	0.8 / 95.4	0.3 / 39.9	0.5 / 55.5	1.9 / 218.7	1.1 / 126.1	0.8 / 92.6
	Grad.	100.0 / 1,586.2	46.5 / 737.4	53.5 / 848.8	77.5 / 1,228.3	34.0 / 538.8	43.5 / 689.5	5.2 / 83.9	1.8 / 29.3	3.4 / 54.6	3.0 / 47.2	1.3 / 20.6	1.7 / 26.6	3.4 / 53.3	1.9 / 29.7	1.5 / 23.6	0.4 / 6.2	0.2 / 2.6	0.2 / 3.6	10.5 / 167.3	7.3 / 116.4	3.2 / 50.9
	First-Prof.	100.0 / 273.4	61.0 / 166.8	39.0 / 106.6	81.0 / 221.5	50.4 / 137.8	30.6 / 83.7	5.8 / 15.9	2.7 / 7.4	3.1 / 8.5	3.9 / 10.7	2.3 / 6.4	1.6 / 4.3	6.9 / 18.7	4.0 / 10.8	2.9 / 7.9	0.4 / 1.1	0.2 / 0.6	0.2 / 0.5	2.0 / 5.4	1.4 / 3.8	0.6 / 1.6
1994	Total Enroll.	100.0 / 14,278.8	44.6 / 6,371.9	55.4 / 7,906.9	72.9 / 10,415.7	32.5 / 4,645.5	40.4 / 5,770.2	10.1 / 1,448.2	3.8 / 549.6	6.3 / 898.6	7.4 / 1,056.6	3.3 / 469.0	4.1 / 587.6	5.4 / 773.9	2.7 / 384.8	2.7 / 389.1	0.9 / 127.8	0.4 / 53.2	0.5 / 74.6	3.2 / 456.5	1.9 / 269.7	1.3 / 186.8
	Undergraduate	100.0 / 12,262.6	44.2 / 5,422.1	55.8 / 6,840.5	72.6 / 8,904.8	32.3 / 3,957.9	40.3 / 4,946.9	10.7 / 1,317.0	4.1 / 502.8	6.6 / 814.2	7.9 / 979.3	3.5 / 434.5	4.4 / 544.8	5.5 / 673.7	2.7 / 331.2	2.8 / 342.5	1.0 / 117.8	0.4 / 48.9	0.6 / 68.9	2.2 / 269.9	1.2 / 146.8	1.0 / 123.1
	Grad.	100.0 / 1,721.4	45.1 / 775.8	54.9 / 945.6	74.7 / 1,286.8	32.0 / 551.4	42.7 / 735.4	6.4 / 110.7	2.2 / 37.7	4.2 / 73.0	3.7 / 63.9	1.6 / 27.0	2.1 / 36.9	4.2 / 72.6	2.2 / 38.3	2.0 / 34.3	0.5 / 8.1	0.2 / 3.3	0.3 / 4.8	10.5 / 179.5	6.9 / 118.1	3.6 / 61.4
	First-Prof.	100.0 / 294.8	59.0 / 174.0	41.0 / 120.8	76.0 / 224.2	46.2 / 136.2	29.8 / 88.0	7.0 / 20.6	3.1 / 9.1	3.9 / 11.5	4.6 / 13.4	2.6 / 7.5	2.0 / 5.9	9.4 / 27.6	5.2 / 15.3	4.2 / 12.3	0.6 / 1.8	0.3 / 1.0	0.3 / 0.8	2.4 / 7.1	1.6 / 4.8	0.8 / 2.3

Source: U.S. Department of Education (1990, 1994).

in the same year, 55 percent of African Americans came from families that had incomes below $30,000 compared with 34 percent of Asians and 21 percent of Whites. Just 4 percent of African American ACT examinees were from families with annual incomes above $80,000 compared with 13 percent of Asians and 15 percent of Whites (Nettles and Perna, 1997a).

In 1996, 40 percent of African Americans who received financial aid achieved a bachelor's degree within five years compared with 22 percent who received no financial aid. Of the Black students who were awarded aid, 30 percent dropped out compared with 46 percent who did not receive aid. These data suggest that financial aid is a key factor in African American retention and graduation rates in higher education.

Grade Point Average and Years Needed to Complete Degrees

Although access to higher education has increased for African Americans, considerable progress is needed in improving their performance. Almost 61 percent of Black men and 51 percent of Black women receiving their bachelor's degrees in 1992-93 had grade point averages below 3.0 compared with only 35 percent of White men and 22 percent of White women (see Table 5-4).

Table 5-5 illustrates that Black students continue to take longer to complete their undergraduate degrees than White students. Regardless of age at initial college entry, fewer African American men than African American women, White men, and White women complete their degrees in four years. Among those who were age 18 in the 1992-93 academic year, 22 percent of Black men—but 35 percent of White men, 37 percent of Black women, and 46 percent of White women—earned their degrees in four years. Among all bachelor's degree recipients, 32 percent of African Americans required more than six years to obtain their degrees compared with 25 percent of Whites. Yet when only 18-year-olds entering college are considered, the proportion of Blacks and Whites who required at least six years to complete their degrees are about the same (22 percent versus 20 percent).

Academic Field Distribution

Another important part of the African American higher education story is the academic field distribution. In 1994, a higher percentage of Black bachelor's degree recipients than their White counterparts earned degrees in business management and administration (24 percent versus 20 percent), protective services (4 percent versus 2 percent), and public administration and services (3 percent versus 1 percent). A smaller share of Black women than White women received bachelor's degrees in education (9 percent versus 15 percent). A smaller proportion of African American men than White men obtained their bachelor's degrees in engineering or engineering technology (9 percent versus 12 percent).

Almost one-half of all master's degrees nationwide were awarded in two fields in 1994: education (26 percent) and business (24 percent). Compared with the distribution of master's degrees awarded by all colleges and

TABLE 5-4

Percentage of Cumulative Grade Point Average of 1992-93 Bachelor's Degree Recipients by Race and Gender

(Weighted Sample Size in Parentheses)

Grade	White, Not Hispanic			African American, Not Hispanic			Hispanic			Other		
	Total	Male	Female	Total	Male	Female	Total	Male	Female	Total	Male	Female
Total*** +++ ~~~	100.0 (1,102,071)	100.0 (499,431)	100.0 (602,640)	100.0 (66,577)	100.0 (22,819)	100.0 (43,758)	100.0 (52,702)	100.0 (23,391)	100.0 (29,311)	100.0 (48,561)	100.0 (22,333)	100.0 (26,228)
Less than 3.0	30.0 (330,905)	36.5 (182,208)	24.7 (148,697)	54.3 (36,153)	60.8 (13,874)	50.9 (22,279)	38.2 (20,128)	45.7 (10,691)	32.2 (9,437)	29.1 (14,140)	28.6 (6,391)	29.5 (7,749)
3.00 to 3.49	42.0 (462,847)	42.0 (209,567)	42.0 (253,280)	34.4 (22,929)	26.2 (5,977)	38.7 (16,952)	41.8 (22,018)	38.9 (9,097)	44.1 (12,921)	47.7 (23,179)	46.4 (10,367)	48.8 (12,812)
3.50 and above	28.0 (308,319)	21.6 (107,656)	33.3 (200,663)	11.3 (7,495)	13.0 (2,968)	10.3 (4,527)	20.0 (10,556)	15.4 (3,603)	23.7 (6,953)	23.2 (11,242)	25.0 (5,575)	21.6 (5,667)

Notes: *** Test of statistical significance compares African Americans with Whites. *** p < .001, ** p < .01, * p < 0.5.

+++ Test of statistical significance compares White men with White women. +++ p < .001, ++ p < .01, + p < .0.

~~~ Test of statistical significance compares African American men with African American women. ~~~ p < .001, ~~ p < .01 ~ p < .05.

Tests of statistical significance calculated using adjusted sample weight to control for influence of large sample sizes.

Sample includes U.S. citizens only.

"Other" includes American Indian/Alaskan Native, and nonresident alien.

Source: U.S. Department of Education (1996b).

New Directions

TABLE 5-5

Years from College Entry to Bachelor's Degree Attainment Among 1992-93 Degree Recipients by Race and Gender (%)
(Weighted Sample Size In Parentheses)

Years	Total	Male	Female	White, Not Hispanic			African American, Not Hispanic			Hispanic			Other		
				Total	Male	Female	Total	Male	Female	Total	Male	Female	Total	Male	Female
All students															
Total*** +++ ---	100.0 (1,064,330)	100.0 (481,330)	100.0 (583,000)	100.0 (902,110)	100.0 (414,116)	100.0 (487,994)	100.0 (64,133)	100.0 (21,589)	100.0 (42,544)	100.0 (50,758)	100.0 (22,901)	100.0 (27,857)	100.0 (47,325)	100.0 (22,722)	100.0 (24,603)
4 years	35.5 (377,793)	30.7 (147,940)	39.4 (229,853)	36.9 (332,836)	31.9 (132,110)	41.1 (200,726)	25.4 (16,283)	17.3 (3,736)	29.5 (12,547)	22.0 (11,167)	17.0 (3,886)	26.1 (7,281)	37.0 (17,505)	36.1 (8,207)	37.8 (9,298)
4 to 5 years	27.7 (295,173)	29.8 (143,476)	26.0 (151,697)	27.5 (248,416)	29.8 (123,604)	25.6 (124,812)	28.2 (18,107)	26.6 (5,742)	29.1 (12,365)	29.8 (15,134)	29.2 (6,690)	30.3 (8,444)	28.6 (13,516)	32.7 (7,440)	24.7 (6,076)
5 to 6 years	11.0 (116,884)	13.4 (64,556)	9.0 (52,328)	10.5 (94,509)	12.8 (53,171)	8.5 (41,338)	14.7 (9,455)	22.6 (4,875)	10.8 (4,580)	13.1 (6,658)	15.3 (3,499)	11.3 (3,159)	13.2 (6,260)	13.2 (3,010)	13.2 (3,250)
More than 6 years	25.8 (274,480)	26.0 (125,358)	25.6 (149,122)	25.1 (226,349)	25.4 (105,231)	24.8 (121,118)	31.6 (20,288)	33.5 (7,236)	30.7 (13,052)	35.1 (17,799)	38.5 (8,826)	32.2 (8,973)	21.2 (10,044)	17.9 (4,065)	24.3 (5,979)
Students who were 18 at college entry															
Total*** +++ ---	100.0 (740,505)	100.0 (335,524)	100.0 (404,981)	100.0 (644,739)	100.0 (298,264)	100.0 (346,475)	100.0 (38,087)	100.0 (11,940)	100.0 (26,147)	100.0 (29,080)	100.0 (11,984)	100.0 (17,096)	100.0 (28,599)	100.0 (13,336)	100.0 (15,263)
4 years	39.8 (294,715)	34.3 (115,246)	44.3 (179,469)	40.9 (263,493)	35.4 (105,462)	45.6 (158,031)	32.4 (12,355)	22.1 (2,639)	37.2 (9,716)	27.2 (7,904)	20.6 (2,466)	31.8 (5,438)	38.3 (10,963)	35.1 (4,679)	41.2 (6,284)
4 to 5 years	29.5 (218,528)	31.9 (107,116)	27.5 (111,412)	29.2 (188,154)	31.4 (93,674)	27.3 (94,480)	29.6 (11,260)	34.4 (4,104)	27.4 (7,156)	34.8 (10,111)	36.9 (4,418)	33.3 (5,693)	31.5 (9,003)	36.9 (4,920)	26.8 (4,083)
5 to 6 years	10.6 (78,421)	12.9 (43,194)	8.7 (35,227)	10.1 (65,225)	12.4 (36,967)	8.2 (28,258)	16.4 (6,262)	23.7 (2,830)	13.1 (3,432)	10.5 (3,043)	11.6 (1,385)	9.7 (1,658)	13.6 (3,891)	15.1 (2,012)	12.3 (1,879)
More than 6 years	20.1 (148,841)	20.9 (69,968)	19.5 (78,873)	19.8 (127,867)	20.8 (62,161)	19.0 (65,706)	21.6 (8,210)	19.8 (2,367)	22.3 (5,843)	27.6 (8,022)	31.0 (3,715)	25.2 (4,307)	16.6 (4,742)	12.9 (1,725)	19.8 (3,017)

Notes: *** Test of statistical significance compares African Americans with Whites. *** p < .001, ** p < .01, * p < .05.

+++ Test of statistical significance compares White men with White women. +++ p < .001, ++ p < .01, + p < .05.

--- Test of statistical significance compares African American men with African American women. --- p < .001, -- p < .01, - p < .05

Tests of statistical significance calculated using adjusted sample weight to control for influence of large sample sizes

Sample includes U.S. citizens only.

"Other" includes American Indian/Alaskan Native, and nonresident alien

Source: U.S. Department of Education (1996b)

universities, a greater share of master's degrees at HBCUs were in education (41 percent versus 26 percent) and a smaller share in business management and administration (15 percent versus 24 percent). Among male master's degree recipients, more African Americans than Whites received degrees in education (21 percent versus 16 percent), and fewer African Americans than Whites obtained degrees in engineering (7 percent versus 11 percent). Among women, a higher share of African Americans than Whites were awarded degrees in public administration and services (13 percent versus 7 percent).

Sixteen percent of doctoral degree recipients at all colleges and universities in 1994 were awarded degrees in education compared with 46 percent of African American doctoral recipients. Among recipients of the same sex, the proportion of Blacks obtaining doctoral degrees in education was about twice that of Whites (48 percent of Black women compared with 27 percent of White women and 25 percent of Black men compared with 14 percent of White men). The percentage of Blacks receiving doctorates in theology or religious studies was about twice that of Whites, 14 percent of African American men compared with 6 percent of White men and 3 percent of African American women compared with 1 percent of White women. Among doctoral recipients, a smaller share of Blacks than Whites received doctorates in the following fields: physical sciences (3 percent and 9 percent, respectively), biological or life sciences (5 percent and 10 percent, respectively), and engineering (4 percent and 8 percent, respectively).

Affirmative Action

The progress made by African Americans in enrolling in higher education and in attaining degrees can be attributed in part to affirmative action policies. Because of affirmative action, colleges and universities have been able to take extraordinary steps to admit underrepresented minorities and to award financial assistance as an inducement to enroll. Such policies and practices are now in jeopardy as legal and political actions are being taken to dismantle them. The effects are already visible. In Texas, for example, the case of *Hopwood* v. *State of Texas* (1996) yielded a court decision to eliminate the use of different criteria for admitting students of various races. Consequently, the African American applicant pool and the number of African Americans enrolling in and attending the law school declined dramatically. The same outcome occurred in California after passage of Proposition 209. Given the enormous challenges that African Americans face in school, their far greater poverty status, and their limited prospects for improving academic achievement under present conditions, extraordinary measures will be needed to prevent the abatement of progress.

THE PERPETUATION OF INEQUALITY

There is a fierce debate over the causes of and cures for the inequality that African American students experience in U.S. schools. It is clear that

Black children are much more likely to be in families, neighborhoods, and schools that are unequal in many critical ways to those of their White contemporaries. Black experiences are much more similar to the experiences of other deeply impoverished and poorly educated minority communities—Native Americans, Latinos from Puerto Rico and Mexico, and refugees from Southeast Asia, particularly those from the poorly educated rural areas of Cambodia, Laos, and Vietnam.

The syndrome of inequality includes the much lower level of parental education of Blacks than Whites (although the level has increased substantially during the past 50 years), the much higher levels of personal poverty, and the much greater exposure to concentrated poverty (and isolation from the middle class). The inequality syndrome also includes weaker preparation in the preschool skills of Blacks than Whites, their more serious developmental and health and nutrition problems, and their greater instability of residence and of school enrollment. Many more African American students than White students attend big central-city schools and those in declining sectors of suburbia where segregated Black communities have been forming for the past three decades. These contextual inequalities are reflected in schools containing poorly prepared students and teachers working outside their field and leaving their positions after a short time. The schools that are best organized to create and support upward movement in education are in the most educated and affluent White communities; the schools that are supposed to create equal opportunity for Blacks are systematically unequal.

CONCLUSIONS

The basic cures for the education problems of African Americans advocated by policy debates and lawsuits have been overwhelmingly limited to schools, colleges, and universities, even though many of the roots of the problems are outside these formal settings. A central debate reflects the dialogue ongoing for a century in the African American community: one side advocates ending the system of racial (and poverty) isolation through desegregation and related policies; the other side recommends building up the community and its institutions through local control and affirmation of Black culture and community leadership. Given the persistent social segregation of America's residential communities and schools and the movement of many African Americans into racially diverse communities, colleges, and universities, these are no longer competing goals. In the 21st century, the solutions for African Americans will be found by pursuing social, educational, economic, and cultural prosperity in both worlds.

The idea of choice as a solution to ending racial isolation grew out of the desegregation battles of the 1960s and 1970s. Since the early 1980s, there have been additional debates about the extent to which raising academic requirements and testing and/or creating market-based competitive schools using vouchers and charters could address the inequalities in schools. As charter schools evolve and private school choice emerges, these may become, in the short term, part of the solution for African American access to high quality elementary and secondary education. But policy leaders will have to ensure that such avenues do not lead to deterioration of local communities by removing resources that are used to sustain them.

Some important bases for thinking about other challenges and policy options, however, are apparent in recent trends. There is a strong aspiration for education and a remarkable rise in educational attainment among African Americans even in the face of severe negative social and economic realities. Supportive government policies, particularly broad reform agendas that move beyond schools and concentrate on barriers within schools, appear to be linked to nonincremental gains. The data suggest a strong trend toward convergence of educational attainment that has not been held since 1990. The standards-based reforms beginning in 1983 have not been associated with a significant narrowing of gaps and may be connected to widening disparities. Educational opportunities remain systematically unequal in many critical respects, particularly for students being educated in schools of concentrated poverty. If education is to be the key to more equitable opportunity in society and the economy, a great deal of work is still to be done.

At the preschool level, government policies such as those that instituted Head Start need to be modernized to focus more attention on education standards. Head Start and comparable preschool programs for the poor should have the highest quality educators who are trained in reading, vocabulary, math, and other subject areas to adequately prepare youngsters for school. This challenge must be addressed in the public policy arena early in the first decade of the 21st century.

As discussed, choice and vouchers may provide only a short-term solution to some of the education problems at the elementary and secondary levels. Unless more Black teachers emerge from the nation's colleges and universities, African American and other students in the nation's schools will rarely experience learning from Black teachers. Perhaps the most severe challenges at the elementary and secondary levels are finding teachers adequately trained in the subjects they teach and administrators with enough belief in the abilities of their faculty and students to encourage them to pursue rigorous curricula. These are the main ingredients that will result in higher test scores and greater access to higher education for African Americans.

African Americans need a renewed commitment by the nation to freedom, equality, social justice, and economic prosperity early in the 21st century. The focus of policy action should be to improve access to high quality preschools, to improve the quality of elementary and secondary schools, to better prepare high school students for academic success in college, and to obtain higher levels of financial aid for college attendance and persistence. America must also continue to work to overcome ongoing discrimination and isolation; to provide the needed teachers, curriculum, and connections to students wherever they are; and to create full access for Black students to the full range of educational opportunities throughout society.

NOTES

1. See, for example, the discussion of the relationship of disadvantaged school status and educational opportunity in Peng and Hill (1995) and in Oakes, Ormseth, and Campbell (1990).

2. A study of 1992 test scores in Greater Cleveland showed that district poverty-level differences "explained as much as 39 percent of the differences in school district passing rates" on the state proficiency test (*Cleveland Plain Dealer,* 1995).

3. Asian students, who are having far greater success in U.S. schools, attend schools that have only about one-fourth African American and Latino students, and they are far less likely to be in high poverty schools (*Asian Students and Multiethnic Desegregation,* 1994).

REFERENCES

Asian Students and Multiethnic Desegregation. 1994. Harvard Project on School Desegregation, October.

Board of Education of Oklahoma City v. *Dowell.* 1991. 498 U.S. 237.
Brown v. *Board of Education of Topeka.* 1954. 347 U.S. 483.

Cleveland Plain Dealer. 1995. 8 October, 3-C.
College Entrance Examination Board and Educational Testing Service. 1996. *Profile of SAT Program Test Takers, College Bound Seniors, National Report.* New York.

Economic Opportunity Act. 1964. Public Law No. 89-452, 78 Stat. 408.
Elementary and Secondary Education Act. 1965. Public Law No. 89-750, 79, Stat. 27.

Fordham, S., and J.U. Ogbu. 1986. "Black Students' School Success: Coping with the Burden of 'Acting White'." *Urban Review* 18(3):176-206.

Hopwood v. *State of Texas.* 1996. 78 F. 3d 932 (5th Cir.), reh'g denied, 84 F. 3d 720 (5th Cir.), cert. denied, 116 S. Ct. 2580.

Koretz, D. 1992. "What Happened to Test Scores and Why?" *Educational Measurement: Issues and Practice* 11(4):7-11.

Mingle, J.R. 1976. "Faculty and Departmental Response to Increased Black Student Enrollment: Individual and Contextual Predictors." Unpublished dissertation, University of Michigan, Ann Arbor.

NAEP (National Assessment of Educational Progress). 1997. *NAEP 1996 Trends in Academic Progress.* Washington, D.C.: National Center for Education Statistics. ERIC Document Reproduction Service No. ED.
Nettles, M.T., and L.W. Perna. 1997a. *The African American Education Data Book: Preschool Through High School Education.* Vol. I. Fairfax, Va.: Frederick D. Patterson Research Institute.
———. 1997b. *The African American Education Data Book: Preschool Through High School Education.* Vol. II. Fairfax, Va.: Frederick D. Patterson Research Institute.
———. 1997c. *The African American Education Data Book: Transition from School to College and School to Work.* Vol. III. Fairfax, Va.: Frederick D. Patterson Research Institute.

Oakes, J., R. Ormseth, and P. Campbell. 1990. *Multiplying Inequalities: The Effects of Race, Social Class, and Tracking on Opportunities to Learn Mathematics and Science.* Santa Monica, Cal.: Rand Corporation.

Orfield, G., and S.E. Eaton. 1996. *Dismantling Desegregation: The Quiet Reversal of Brown v. Board of Education.* New York: New Press.

Orfield, G., and E. Miller, Eds. 1998. *Chilling Admissions: The Affirmative Action Crises and the Search for Alternatives.* Cambridge, Mass.: Harvard Education Publishing Group.

Peng, S.S., and S.T. Hill. 1995. *Understanding Racial/Ethnic Differences in Secondary School Science and Mathematics Achievement.* Washington, D.C.: U.S. Department of Education, 51.

Reese, C.M., K.E. Miller, J. Mazzeo, and J.A. Dossey. 1997. *NAEP 1996 Mathematics Report Card for the Nation and the States.* Available from http://nces.ed.gov/nationsreportcard/96report/97488.html. February.

Truman, H.S. 1979. *The Truman Administration, Its Principles and Practice.* Westport, Ct.: Greenwood Press.

U.S. Bureau of the Census. 1950. *1950 Census Data.* Washington, D.C.: U.S. Government Printing Office (GPO).
———. 1961. *Statistical Abstract of the United States, 1961.* Washington, D.C.: GPO, 30-31, 104.
———. 1997. Current Population Survey: 1959-1997. Available from http://www.census.gov/hhes/income/histinc/index.html

U.S. Department of Education. 1990, 1994. National Center for Education Statistics. *Integrated Postsecondary Education Data System, "Enrollment" Survey for 1990 and 1994.* Washington, D.C.: GPO.
———. 1995. National Center for Education Statistics. *Trends Among High School Seniors, 1972-1992.* Washington, D.C.: GPO.
———. 1996a. National Center for Education Statistics. *Dropout Rates in the United States: High School Completion Rates.* Available from http://nces.ed.gov/pubs98/dropout/ch06t13a.html
———. 1996b. National Center for Education Statistics. *Baccalaureate and Beyond Longitudinal Study 1993/94, First Follow-up* (Report No. NCES-96-149). Washington, D.C.: NCES.
———. 1999. National Assessment of Chapter 1 Independent Review Panel (United States). *Promising Results, Continuing Challenges: Final Report of the National Assessment of Title I* (May). Available from http://www.ed.gov/offices/OUS/eval/hlights.html

U.S. National Commission on Excellence in Education. 1983. *A Nation at Risk: The Imperative for Educational Reform. A Report to the Nation and the Secretary of Education, United States Department of Education.* Washington, D.C.: GPO. ERIC Document Reproduction Service No. ED.

Chapter 6

African Americans and Health Policy: Strategies for a Multiethnic Society

by Thomas A. LaVeist

Associate Professor of Health and Public Policy,
Associate Professor of Sociology,
School of Hygiene and Public Health,
Johns Hopkins University

INTRODUCTION

The health status of a people manifests the underlying social conditions in which they live. Nowhere can this be observed more clearly than for America's Black population. African Americans are sicker during their lifetimes and younger when they die than any racial or ethnic group in America (U.S. Department of Health and Human Services, 1985; LaVeist, Wallace, and Howard, 1995). They are targeted for the consumption of products that diminish the health of individuals and communities (LaVeist and Wallace, 2000; Dawkins, Ferrell, and Johnson, 1979; Cummings, Giovino, and Mendicino, 1987; Bullard, 1983). They reap fewer benefits from advances in medical knowledge than other groups (Wenneker and Epstein, 1989; Whittle, Good, and Lofgren, 1993), even though they have borne a greater burden of medical experimentation (Savitt, 1982; Gamble, 1993; Thomas and Quinn, 1993).

There is no consensus as to the causes of the persistent health deficits of African Americans. Some have argued that poor Black health is the result of biological differences between racial groups (Wilson and Grim, 1991; Reed, 1969; Ruston and Bogart, 1989). However, the evidence of true biological differences between African Americans and other racial groups is extremely limited (LaVeist, 1994; Cooper, 1986; Curtin, 1992; Littlefield et al., 1982; Livingstone et al., 1962). In contrast, there is abundant evidence of social inequalities between Blacks and other racial groups that may account for racial disparities in health (LaVeist, 1989, 1992, 1993; Horton, 1992; Feagin, 1991; Boozer, Krueger, and Wolkon, 1992; Maxwell, 1994; Kirschenman and Neckerman, 1991).

Because of persistent racial segregation, African Americans and Whites live in essentially separate worlds (LaVeist, 1989, 1993; Massey, 1990). These separate worlds—demarcated by the American color line—contribute to the poor African American health profile. Hitherto, the discussion of racial differences in health have involved Caucasians and African Americans. Given the projected changes in America's racial and ethnic landscape in the 21st century, the discussion must broaden. However, just as living in a racially segregated America has produced negative health consequences for African Americans, so too will the coming shift to a multiethnic America.

This chapter examines African Americans' health status and the health policy issues that are likely to affect Black health as America becomes increasingly ethnically diverse. The chapter is divided into two sections. The first describes the state of health of African Americans and discusses the underlying factors that produce their generally poor health profile. The second section examines health and social policies as they affect African Americans in a diversifying nation.

THE HEALTH STATUS OF AFRICAN AMERICANS

Reliable data on the health status of White Americans have been available since the beginning of the 20th century, but similar data for African Americans have been available only since the 1940s, and national data for other ethnic groups only since the early 1980s. Examination of the data reveals two general long-term trends for Black Americans: first, there has been a steady decline in morbidity and mortality throughout the 20th century; and second, there has been persistent, substantial racial disparity, with Whites at an advantage compared with African Americans. The death rate for African Americans is more than 1.5 times that of White Americans. Table 6-1 shows the leading causes of death for Blacks and Whites in 1994. With the exception of suicide (the Black rate per 100,000 population was 6.6

TABLE 6-1

Racial Differences in the 10 Leading Causes of Death, 1994

Black		Rank	White	
Cause of Death[1]	Rate[2]		Cause of Death[1]	Rate[2]
Heart disease	251.0	1	Heart disease	163.6
Cancer	167.8	2	Cancer	125.2
Stroke	44.2	3	Stroke	24.5
HIV	41.4	4	Accidents	29.9
Accidents	36.7	5	Pulmonary disease	21.5
Homicide	30.6	6	Pneumonia	12.2
Diabetes	28.8	7	Diabetes	12.0
Pneumonia	17.8	8	Suicide	11.6
Pulmonary disease	17.8	9	Liver disease	7.3
Perinatal conditions	13.2	10	HIV	7.2

1. Cause of death based on the Ninth Revision, International Classification of Diseases, 1975.
2. Age-adjusted rates per 100,000 U.S. standard population.

Source: U.S. Department of Health and Human Services (1998).

compared with the White rate of 11.6) and pulmonary disease (the Black rate was 17.8 compared with the White rate of 21.5), African Americans have a higher age-adjusted mortality rate for all major causes of death.

Although heart disease, cancer, and stroke are the leading causes of death for both Blacks and Whites, Blacks die at a faster rate from each cause. In 1994, homicide was the 6th leading cause of death for African Americans, but it did not rank in the top 10 causes for Whites. Human Immunodeficiency Virus Infection (HIV) was the 4th leading cause of death for Blacks, but the 10th cause of death among Whites. Perinatal conditions are another cause of death that substantially affects African Americans. It was the 10th leading cause of death for Blacks in 1994, but it was not among the 10 leading causes of death for Whites. In addition, Black infants die at more than twice the rate of White infants.

The true impact of a cause of death can be demonstrated by computing years of potential life lost before age 65 (YPLL-65). YPLL indicates the average number of years of life lost per 1,000 persons, assuming that each individual would otherwise live to age 65. It is an important indicator of the effect of a cause of death on a population because it takes into account the age distribution of the cause of death. Because causes of death that afflict younger people contribute a greater number of potential years of life lost, YPLL-65 is helpful in demonstrating the primary contributors to race differences in life expectancy and reflects the societal impact of lost potential.

Table 6-2 shows years of potential life lost before age 65 for Black and White males and females in 1992. The table demonstrates that Black men had the highest number of YPLL-65 at 102.3 years per 1,000 persons. White men had the next highest number (50.1), followed by Black women (48.6) and White women (24). Both Black men and women had more than twice the number of YPLL-65 than their White counterparts. In addition to substantial racial differences in YPLL-65, there are gender differences, with Black and White men having YPLL-65 double that of their female counterparts.

Among Black men, homicide is the greatest contributor to lost potential, and YPLL-65 caused by accidents is also high. Homicide and accidents produce such a high number of years of life lost because deaths by these causes tend to occur at young ages. For example, in 1992, 71 percent of all Black male homicide victims were under age 35, with more than one-third (34.6 percent) between the ages of 15 and 24. This is in stark contrast to the leading cause of death, heart disease—only 2.7 percent of deaths from heart disease among African American males occurred before age 35 in 1992. However, age differences in the distribution of causes of death alone cannot account for the substantial racial differences in YPLL-65.

The racial and gender disparities in YPLL-65 are dramatically apparent in Figure 6-1. In 1992, homicide accounted for 24.2 YPLL-65 per 1,000 Black men, about eight times as many years as for White men and more than five times as many years as for Black women. Cerebrovascular disease (stroke) YPLL-65 for Black men and women is also higher than for Whites. In 1992, the Black male stroke mortality rate was one and one-half times the rate for White men and women. Further, the Black female rate was almost as high as

TABLE 6-2

Years of Potential Life Lost (YPLL) per 1,000 Persons Before Age 65 by Race and Gender and Black/White Ratio for Six Leading Causes of Death, 1992

Cause of Death	White Males	Black Males	B/W Ratio	White Females	Black Females	B/W Ratio
Total[1]	50.1	102.3	2.04	24.0	48.6	2.02
Heart disease	9.1	21.9	2.41	3.0	9.6	3.20
Cancer	7.7	9.7	1.26	7.2	8.7	1.21
Stroke	0.9	2.4	2.67	0.7	1.9	2.71
Homicide	3.2	24.2	7.56	0.9	4.5	5.00
Accidents	12.2	15.0	1.23	4.1	5.4	1.32
HIV	5.4	15.5	2.89	0.5	4.2	8.40

1. Total YPLL for all causes of death.

Source: National Center for Health Statistics (1998).

the Black male rate. The Black male HIV mortality rate was almost three times more than the White male rate. The differences in HIV mortality among females were even more striking, with the rate for Black females more than eight times the rate for White females.

Health Costs of Color

Disparities in morbidity and mortality between Whites and African Americans can be viewed as the added burden of living in America as a Black

FIGURE 6-1

**YPLL per 1,000 Persons Before Age 65 by Race and Gender
for Six Leading Causes of Death, 1992**

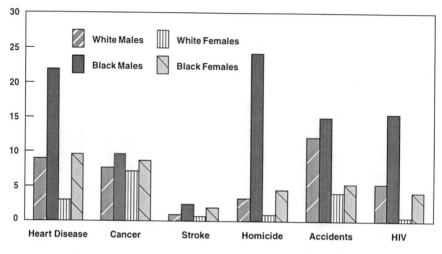

Source: National Center for Health Statistics (1998).

person expressed in terms of life and death. This added burden can be empirically expressed by calculating excess deaths. Excess death refers to the difference between the actual number of African American deaths and the expected number of deaths if the Black mortality rate were equal to the White rate.

Table 6-3 presents excess deaths per 1,000 people for the leading causes of death for African Americans. In 1996, 36.2 percent of all deaths among African Americans were excess deaths. Heart disease is the greatest contributor to excess mortality among African Americans, accounting for 28.2 percent of all excess deaths in 1996. Cancer accounted for 13.7 percent and HIV for 11 percent of all excess deaths among Blacks. The table also shows that in addition to the overall mortality cost of being African American, the consequences vary by cause of death. For homicide, for example, there is a staggering 79.8 percent additional cost of being Black; for HIV, the additional cost is 60 percent.

African American Health in a Broader Context

Comparisons of African American and White American health status are abundant, and they consistently demonstrate that Blacks have a substantial health deficit compared with Whites. However, this deficit is not often examined in a broader international context. One notable exception is W.E.B.

TABLE 6-3

Excess Deaths for African Americans, 1996

Cause of Death	Excess Deaths[1]	% of Deaths That Are Excess	% of Total
Total	103,900	36.2	–
Heart disease	29,291	37.3	28.2
Cancer	14,276	23.6	13.7
Stroke	6,602	35.7	6.4
Homicide	8,613	79.8	8.3
Accidents	2,279	17.9	2.2
HIV	11,461	60.0	11.0

1. The number of excess deaths per 1,000 persons.

Sources: U.S. Department of Health and Human Services (1998); and U.S. Bureau of the Census (1998).

DuBois's (1899) classic study of the Philadelphia Black population of the late 1800s, *The Philadelphia Negro*. In the study, DuBois observed that, "Compared with modern nations, the death rate of Philadelphia Negroes is high, but not exceptionally so." His analysis showed that the mortality rate of African American men and women in Philadelphia in 1890 was lower than that in Hungary and slightly higher than the rates in Austria and Italy.

Table 6-4 expands DuBois's study by comparing life expectancy at birth for Black Americans with life expectancy at birth for a larger group of industrialized nations in 1996. This analysis shows that the White American life expectancy at birth of 76.8 years is comparable to other Western countries. However, the Black American life expectancy of 70.3 years is closer to some developing countries. Black males could expect to live an average of 66 years in 1996, 8 years less than the average lifespan of White males.

Sociopolitical Forces and Race Differences in Health

Since early in the 20th century, researchers have observed an association between the standard of living and morbidity and mortality (Newsholme, 1910; Ogburn and Thomas, 1922). In the seminal work on this subject, *Mirage of Health* (1959), Dubose credited general improvements in the standard of living, economic development, and improved sanitation for the substantial decline in mortality rates during the first half of the 20th century. Numerous studies have supported this contention (McKinlay and McKinlay, 1977; Pampel and Pillai, 1986; McKeown, 1976; Rydell, 1976). Since Illich's (1975) elaboration, this theory of mortality decline has become the dominant

TABLE 6-4

**International Comparisons of Expectations of
Life at Birth, 1996**

Rank[1]	Country	Expectation of Life at Birth (Years)
1	United States—White Female	**79.6**
2	Canada	79.1
3	Spain	78.3
4	Japan	78.1
5	Sweden	78.1
6	Israel	78.0
7	Netherlands	77.7
8	Switzerland	77.6
9	United States—White (Total)	**76.8**
10	United States—Total	**76.0**
11	Portugal	75.3
12	Cuba	75.1
13	Chile	74.5
14	United States—Black Female	**74.2**
15	United States—White Male	**73.8**
16	Colombia	72.8
17	Croatia	72.8
18	Poland	72.1
19	Venezuela	72.1
20	Turkey	71.9
21	Ecuador	71.1
22	Bulgaria	71.0
23	United States—Black (Total)	**70.3**
24	United States—Black Male	**66.1**
25	South Africa	59.5
26	Nigeria	54.3

1. Rank of selected countries.

Source: U.S. Bureau of the Census (1996).

perspective in medical sociology and public health (Conrad and Kern, 1986, 7-9).

The theory holds that social factors have been primarily responsible for reducing mortality rates. As noted above, the factors include societal transitions in economic conditions, urbanization, improved sanitation, lower fertility rates, and improved social status of women. Modernization led to greater urbanization, which promoted access to quality housing (Rydell, 1976). Higher incomes and a better standard of living led to better nutrition and to sanitary conditions that were more conducive to good health. Modernization also led to fertility decline and thus to an older maternal age at birth (Knodel and Hermalin, 1984). A more highly educated population led to attitudinal and lifestyle changes that promoted good health (Showstack, Budetti, and Minkler, 1984).

Social factors have also been shown to contribute to racial differences in health status. In a previous study (LaVeist, 1990), I demonstrated that relatively modest reductions in poverty rates could translate into meaningful improvements in the racial disparity in post-neonatal mortality. In 1996, a special issue of the journal *Ethnicity and Disease* was devoted to the relationship between race and health. Studies have demonstrated a link between race and blood pressure (Kreiger, 1990; James et al., 1984), mental health (Neighbors et al., 1996), and general physical health status (Jackson et al., 1996; Broman, 1996). In an earlier analysis (LaVeist, 1992), I showed that higher levels of Black political empowerment in a city were associated with a smaller racial disparity in infant mortality. Racial differences in social conditions are a major contributor to racial disparities in mortality and morbidity. As a group, African Americans have significantly greater exposure than Whites to social factors that place them at greater risk for negative health outcomes. This is due, in part, to the substantial racial residential segregation that continues to be a feature of American society.

Throughout the 20th century, African Americans have been engaged in a philosophical debate between opposing visions of the appropriate response to second-class social status. The choice has been either to seek integration with Whites or to adapt to segregation. Although integration seems to have been the nation's consensus, the reality of the American racial landscape is in stark contrast to this ideal. To quote the often cited Kerner Commission Report, "Two societies—one Black, one White, separate and unequal" (U.S. National Advisory Commission on Civil Disorders, 1968). The United States continues to be a highly racially segregated society.

Table 6-5 shows that in 1996 the U.S. infant mortality rate ranked 16th internationally. However, when the U.S. Black-White disparity is viewed in an international context, the rate for White Americans improved to 8th, while the rate for African Americans dropped to 25th. If America has indeed become two societies, then White American society is comparable to other industrialized nations, whereas Black American society is similar to developing nations.

The health consequences of a racially segregated America have been outlined elsewhere (LaVeist, 1993, 1992, 1989). A study of the effect of racial residential segregation on race differences in infant mortality in U.S. cities found that the Black infant mortality rate was higher and the White rate lower in highly segregated cities (LaVeist, 1989). Although the empirical link between segregation and mortality is relatively straightforward, the specific mechanisms that connect these variables are less direct. Previous studies have demonstrated a greater prevalence of negative social conditions in many highly segregated African American urban communities. These studies have shown that such communities are highly toxic environments (Bullard, 1983; U.S. General Accounting Office, 1983) that are not well served by basic city services (Schneider and Logan, 1982, 1985) and that lack adequate medical services (Law, 1985). A recent study also demonstrates an excessive

TABLE 6-5

International Comparisons of Infant Mortality Rates, 1996

Rank[1]	Country	Rate[2]
1	Japan	4.4
2	Sweden	4.5
3	Finland	4.9
4	Netherlands	4.9
5	Hong Kong	5.1
6	Australia	5.5
7	Germany	6.0
8	**United States—White (Total)**	**6.0**
9	Canada	6.1
10	Austria	6.2
11	France	6.2
12	Spain	6.3
13	United Kingdom	6.4
14	Belgium	6.4
15	Italy	6.9
16	**United States—Total**	**7.2**
17	Greece	7.4
18	Portugal	7.6
19	Czech Republic	8.4
20	Israel	8.5
21	Cuba	9.0
22	Hungary	12.3
23	Poland	12.4
24	Chile	13.6
25	**United States—Black (Total)**	**14.2**

1. Rank of selected countries.
2. Number of deaths of children under one year of age per 1,000 live births in a calendar year.

Source: U.S. Bureau of the Census (1996).

availability of alcohol in greatly segregated cities (LaVeist and Wallace, 2000). Thus, racial segregation is an indication of the magnitude of the differences in material conditions in which African Americans and Whites live in the same city. A wide racial divide in exposure to these conditions measured by racial segregation is manifested in racial differences in health outcomes.

If racial differences in exposure to negative social forces are primarily responsible for the comparatively poor health profile of African Americans, how will the likely changes in social conditions that will accompany the increasing ethnic diversity of the United States affect African American health? This question is discussed next.

AFRICAN AMERICANS AND HEALTH
AND SOCIAL POLICIES

Just as racial segregation has had a substantial impact on African American health in a dual race society, the shift to a multiethnic America will also create health consequences for Blacks. Racism is a long-standing component of American culture. Middle class African Americans are leaving central cities, and Hispanics and Asians are moving in. Interethnic racism will likely increase if this pattern continues and if community leaders do not act to bring about peaceful coexistence. For example, the perception that Hispanic illegal immigrants are causing an overwhelming burden on the public medical care system has led to policies that deny medical services to noncitizens. This approach may be tempting to some African Americans who may feel that competition from Hispanics will erode gains made over decades of struggle. However, such a policy would be unwise. Not even the most extreme racial segregation can prevent infectious diseases from crossing racial lines, threatening the health of all.

The flight of capital from urban industrial centers to offshore and suburban service and technical destinations has led to joblessness in central cities. Given the U.S. employer-based health insurance system, joblessness has resulted in increases in the number of uninsured people and a greater burden on local governments to provide for the medically indigent. With the diminishing tax base in central cities caused by the outmigration of the middle class, the burden of providing health and social services in urban areas will be even more daunting.

The cities could become the political battleground for African Americans and Hispanics, but the political power of the Black middle class will be further diluted if Blacks continue to abandon the cities for the suburbs where they make up a smaller portion of the voting population. This outmigration will decrease Black political power and diminish the ability of African Americans to influence health and social policy.

Strategies for a Diversifying Nation

In addressing health policies for African Americans in the coming decades, three points must be considered. First, African Americans are not monolithic. What is important for one segment of the population may not be important for another. For example, one-third of African Americans live below the poverty level (Pamuk et al., 1998). An alternative way of presenting the same information is to state that the overwhelming majority of African Americans live *above* the poverty line. However, because government activity in health policy primarily addresses lower income groups, it is this population that is generally targeted in addressing African Americans and health policy. But because African Americans are diverse, and consequently have diverse interests, health policy that is advantageous for one segment of the Black population could be of little interest or even injurious (if only in theory) to another.

Second, technically good public policy differs from politically feasible public policy. There has been much discussion of so-called universal programs versus targeted programs (Skocpol, 1991; Greenstein, 1991). Universal programs provide a benefit to all citizens, whereas targeted programs are designed to benefit a specific group in need of the benefit. On the one hand, universal policies are more politically viable because they are perceived to be fair and to have a larger constituency—anyone can benefit from them. On the other hand, targeted programs are more efficient because they focus limited resources on those who have a demonstrated need. In the current political climate, the trend in policy and politics is movement away from race-specific and other targeted public policies. Even programs designed to help the poor seem to be looked upon less favorably than in past decades.

Third, not all public policy that is beneficial to health is strictly "health policy." Health policy typically refers to the organization, financing, and availability of medical care services. But issues covered by this traditional definition are unlikely to eliminate racial disparities in health status. The issues preponderantly responsible for racial health disparities require a broader conceptualization of health policy that includes exposure to hazards in the physical environment and macroeconomic factors.

During a recent lecture on the health of African Americans, I was asked by a member of the audience the essential bottom-line question: If I could do just one thing to improve the health of African Americans, what would it be? I responded that I would give every African American a job with health benefits. I could have said that I would move every African American into good quality, crime-free housing. While these are not classical health policy solutions, it seems likely that if every African American had a job with health benefits, he or she would act like anyone else in that position and move into quality housing. While some improvements in health might be noticeable immediately, such as a lower homicide rate, most improvements in health would take decades to become evident. Nevertheless, a job with benefits would probably improve the health status of African Americans more than any "health policy" solution under the traditional definition.

Social and Political Policies

The social forces that have made it necessary for African Americans to choose between segregation and integration are still present. However, while African Americans continue to ponder the integration/segregation question, the emerging social realities of the coming century will necessitate consideration of a previously unthinkable fact: African Americans may have to compete for the most prominent position on the nation's racial/ethnic agenda when Hispanics become the largest minority group in the United States. Heretofore, Blacks held almost monopolistic control over that position. In such a climate, the question looming largest for African Americans will be whether to pursue ethnic confrontation or to seek coalition with Hispanics and other ethnic groups composing the emerging American minority majority. Either approach has its prospects and problems.

The prospects for coalition lie in the shared interests of African Americans, Hispanics, and other racial/ethnic groups. Many of the negative social forces that have affected African American health status will likely impact other minority populations as well.

While there are many points of common interest among African, Asian, and Hispanic Americans, the points of divergence are contentious. The points of divergence primarily concern political and economic control of the cities and older suburbs. As the focus of health policy spending shifts from the national to the state level, competition among ethnic groups for scarce local resources in the public medical sector will increase. For example, if state funds are spent on indigent care in Baltimore, Maryland (a majority African American jurisdiction), funds will not be available for the growing Central American community in Montgomery County, Maryland. Such political clashes are already unfolding within the unique parameters of local politics throughout the nation. These clashes will make the development of a coordinated national agenda for minority solidarity difficult, but not impossible.

While the task of national multiethnic coalition building is daunting, there is some potential for success. The potential does not lie in Black Americans attempting to create permanent partnerships that will inevitably lead to untenable compromises. Rather, the potential lies in Black Americans partnering with other ethnic groups when common interests exist, while continuing to act independently when their own interests demand it. Among the many common interests of American ethnic minorities concerning health policy are access and availability of health services (Keith and LaVeist, 1996), occupational accidents and injuries (Robinson, 1984), urban exposure to environmental toxins (Bullard, 1983), and prison health (Kaplan and Busner, 1992; Snider, Budetti, and Minkler, 1989; Haycock, 1989). A series of studies of health care issues affecting Hispanics and African Americans conducted by the Joint Center for Political and Economic Studies and the Johns Hopkins School of Public Health outlined these common health policy concerns (Lillie-Blanton, Leigh, and Alfaro-Correa, 1996).

Federal Policies

Several recent federal policies have run counter to the interests of many African Americans. In 1983, the report of the Greenspan Commission (National Commission on Social Security Reform, 1983), appointed by President Ronald Reagan, led to several important changes in Social Security. Among the changes were the taxation of Social Security benefits, the coverage of federal employees, and the increase in retirement age. The new retirement age of 67 began a 30-year phase-in period in 1997. In 2027, people born after 1959 will not be eligible to receive full Social Security benefits until age 67. There are also proposals to further increase the retirement age to 73, but Congress has not yet acted on these.

The increase in retirement age will have a detrimental impact on African Americans, particularly males. Average life expectancy at birth for Black men reached 65 years first in 1982 and, after declining for several years, again in 1992. This is in sharp contrast to White males and Black and White females, whose life expectancy reached 65 in 1942, 1958, and 1933, respectively. Given the average annual rate of change for Black male life expectancy between 1982 and 1989 and assuming a linear trajectory, Black male life expectancy will not reach age 67 until 2047, 20 years after the new retirement age has been fully implemented. It is important that policymakers resist future attempts to increase the retirement age without analysis demonstrating that an increase would not continue to have disproportionate adverse consequences for African Americans or any ethnic group.

One of the provisions of the 1996 welfare reform (PL 104-193) was the uncoupling of the Medicaid program from Aid to Families with Dependent Children (AFDC has now been eliminated). It is possible (although not probable) that this uncoupling may benefit African American males. Before the passage of welfare reform, it was almost impossible for anyone to qualify for Medicaid without receiving AFDC. Because males were infrequently eligible for AFDC, there was no government program to provide health insurance for men too old to receive Medicaid as a dependent and too young to receive Medicare. This group, which includes males roughly between the ages of 18 and 65, was ineligible for publicly funded health insurance while suffering high unemployment rates. Consequently, this segment of the African American population was the group most likely to be uninsured and to have excessive morbidity and mortality rates. The potential benefit, however, will probably not materialize because most states are likely to institute policies to raise the threshold for Medicaid eligibility, effectively reducing the Medicaid population to levels below pre-1996 enrollment levels.

Over the past few decades, African Americans have become a larger proportion of the high utilizers of health care (Berk and Monheit, 1992). This most likely reflects improved access to health care and the fact that African Americans generally enter the health care system at later points in the disease process when treatment is more expensive. Consequently, African Americans make up a larger proportion of Medicare and Medicaid expenditures. Thus, politicians who represent African American constituencies must be diligent in protecting their interests in these programs in terms of health care expenditures and tax policies designed to provide relief for individuals with high health care expenses.

Although the Clinton administration was unsuccessful in establishing universal health care coverage, it is imperative that this effort not be abandoned. This is the single most important health policy issue facing African Americans, and it must receive a proportionate amount of attention from African American policymakers.

State and Local Government Policies

Before the 1930s, health and social welfare was primarily the domain of the states. But after the New Deal, the federal government played an expanded role in the regulation and administration of health care. However, in recent years, the federal government has reduced its involvement in providing for the general welfare of the public so that, increasingly, the states are again formulating health and social policy. The block granting of social service programs will likely lead to overall reductions in benefits and further concentrate health policy activity at the state level of government where African Americans have been least influential.

Other trends in health policy will also have an impact on African Americans. States are increasingly developing managed care programs within their Medicaid and Medicare programs. This trend is particularly relevant for African Americans because of their disproportionate level of dependence on these programs. Managed care, while often presented as a system of delivering health care, is primarily a system for controlling medical care costs. In some areas, African American physicians report difficulty in becoming part of managed care organization networks. Under managed care, patients have reduced choices in selecting a health care provider and thus less access to African American physicians. This issue should be followed as managed care programs increase. However, well-carried-out managed care has potential benefits. The case management approach could lead to better access and utilization of preventive services among the poor. The use of preventive services could, in the long term, lead to the earlier diagnosis of some chronic conditions that could, in turn, reduce African American mortality rates.

Health Policy Research

As the focus of health policy shifts to state governments, it is imperative that the scientific community be involved in influencing policy. There is also the need to monitor policy and evaluate its effectiveness. What are the sociocultural barriers to utilization of health services for African Americans? What will be the effect of continued managed care on low income African Americans and on Black health care providers? What subtle forms of discrimination remain in health care settings, and what can be done about them? Health researchers are uniquely qualified to answer these essential questions.

As this chapter has demonstrated, African Americans suffer a higher rate of morbidity and mortality from a wide variety of causes. It is now common for studies to include African Americans in the study population (Jones, LaVeist, and Lillie-Blanton, 1991). These studies usually attempt to "control" for variation caused by racial differences or to describe the magnitude of the racial divide in health status. However, it is still uncommon for studies to attempt to explain why such inequalities exist. There is need for a paradigm shift from descriptive to explanatory studies of the disparities in health by race. The eventual elimination of racial differences in health status is the most compelling issue facing health researchers.

REFERENCES

Berk, N.I.L., and A.C. Monheit. 1992. "The Concentration of Health Expenditures: An Update." *Health Affairs* (Winter):145-149.

Boozer, M.A., A.B. Krueger, and S. Wolkon. 1992. "Race and School Quality Since *Brown v. Board of Education.*" *Brookings Papers on Economic Activity*:269-338.

Broman, C. 1996. "The Health Consequences of Racial Discrimination: A Study of African Americans." *Ethnicity and Disease* 6(1, 2):148-154.

Bullard, R.D. 1983. "Solid Waste Sites and the Black Houston Community." *Sociological Inquiry* 53(2/3):273-288.

Conrad, P., and R. Kern. 1986. *The Sociology of Health and Illness: Critical Perspectives.* New York: St. Martin's Press.

Cooper, R. 1986. "The Biological Concept of Race and Its Application to Public Health and Epidemiology." *Journal of Health Politics, Policy and Law* 1(11):97-116.

Cummings, K.M., G. Giovino, and A. Mendicino. 1987. "Cigarette Advertising and Black-White Differences in Brand Preference." *Public Health Reports* 102(6):699-704.

Curtin, P.D. 1992. "The Slavery Hypothesis for Hypertension Among African Americans: The Historical Evidence." *American Journal of Public Health* 82(12):1681-1686.

Dawkins, N.V., W.C. Farrell, and J.H. Johnson, Jr. 1979. "Spatial Patterns of Alcohol Outlets in the Washington, D.C. Black Community." *Proceedings of the Pennsylvania Academy of Sciences* 53(l):89-97.

DuBois, W.E.B. 1899. *The Philadelphia Negro: A Social Study.* Philadelphia: University of Pennsylvania Press (1996).

Dubose, R. 1959. *Mirage of Health.* New York: Harper and Row.

Ethnicity and Disease. 1996. Special issue on racism 6(1, 2).

Feagin, J.R. 1991. "The Continuing Significance of Race: Anti-Black Discrimination in Public Places." *American Sociological Review* 56:101-116.

Gamble, V.N. 1993. "A Legacy of Distrust: African Americans and Medical Research." *American Journal of Preventive Medicine* 9(6):35-38.

Greenstein, R. 1991. "Universal and Targeted Approaches to Relieving Poverty: An Alternative View." In *The Underclass.* Ed. C. Jencks and P.E. Peterson. Washington, D.C.: Brookings Institution.

Haycock, J. 1989. "Race and Suicide in Jails and Prisons." *Journal of the National Medical Association* 81(4):405-411.

Horton, H.D. 1992. "Race and Wealth: A Demographic Analysis of Black Home Ownership." *Sociological Inquiry* 62(4):480-489.

Illich, I. 1975. *Medical Nemesis: The Exploration of Health.* London: Chalder & Boyars.

Jackson, J.S., et al. 1996. "Racism and the Physical and Mental Health Status of African Americans: A Thirteen-Year National Panel Study." *Ethnicity and Disease* 6(1, 2):132-147.

James, S.A., A.Z. LaCroix, D.G. Kleinbaum, and D.S. Strogatz. 1984. "John Henryism and Blood Pressure Differences Among Black Men. The Role of Occupational Stressors." *Journal of Behavioral Medicine* 7:278.

Jones, C.P., T.A. LaVeist, and M. Lillie-Blanton. 1991. "'Race in the Epidemiologic Literature: An Examination of the *American Journal of Epidemiology, 1921-1990.*" *American Journal of Epidemiology* 134:1079-1084.

Kaplan, S.L., and J. Busner. 1992. "A Note on Racial Bias in the Admission of Children and Adolescents to State Mental Health Facilities Versus Correctional Facilities in New York." *American Journal of Psychiatry* 149(6):768-772.

Keith, V.M., and T.A. LaVeist. 1996. "Social, Economic and Health Determinants of the Use of Health Care Services by Whites, African Americans and Mexican Americans." In *Achieving Equitable Access: Studies of Health Care Issues Affecting Hispanics and African Americans.* Ed. M. Lillie-Blanton, W.A. Leigh, and A.I. Alfaro-Correa. Washington, D.C.: Joint Center for Political and Economic Studies, 27-54.

Kirschenman, J., and K.M. Neckerman. 1991. "'We'd Love to Hire Them, But . . .': The Meaning of Race for Employers." In *The Urban Underclass.* Ed. C. Jencks and P.E. Peterson. Washington, D.C.: Brookings Institution, 203-232.

Knodel, J., and A. Hermalin. 1984. "Effects of Birth Rank, Maternal Age, Birth Interval, and Sibship Size on Infant and Child Mortality: Evidence from 18th and 19th Century Reproductive Histories." *American Journal of Public Health* 74:1098-1106.

Krieger, N. 1990. "Racial and Gender Discrimination: Risk Factors for High Blood Pressure?" *Social Science and Medicine* 30(12):1273-1281.

LaVeist, T.A. 1989. "Linking Residential Segregation with the Infant Mortality Race Disparity in U.S. Cities." *Sociology and Social Research* 73(2):90-94.

———. 1990. "Simulating the Effects of Poverty on the Race Disparity in Postneonatal Mortality." *Journal of Public Health Policy* 11:463-473.

———. 1992. "The Political Empowerment and Health Status of African Americans: Mapping a New Territory." *American Journal of Sociology* 97(4):1080-1095.

———. 1993. "Segregation, Poverty and Empowerment: Health Consequences for African Americans." *Milbank Quarterly* 71(1):41-64.

———. 1994. "Beyond Dummy Variables and Sample Selection: What Health Services Researchers Ought to Know about Race as a Variable." *Health Services Research* 29(1):1-16.

———. 1996. "Why We Should Continue to Study Race . . . But Do a Better Job." *Ethnicity and Disease* 6(1, 2):21-29.

LaVeist, T.A., and J.M. Wallace. 2000. "Health Risk and Inequitable Distribution of Liquor Stores in African American Neighborhoods." *Social Science and Medicine* 51(4):613-617.

LaVeist, T.A., J.M. Wallace, and D.L. Howard. 1995. "The Color Line and the Health of African Americans." *Humbolt Journal of Social Relations* 21(1):119-137.

Law, R. 1985. "Public Policy and Health-Care Delivery: A Practitioner's Perspective." *The Review of Black Political Economy* 14:217-225.

Lillie-Blanton, M., W.A. Leigh, and A.I. Alfaro-Correa. 1996. *Achieving Equitable Access: Studies of Health Care Issues Affecting Hispanics and African Americans.* Washington, D.C.: Joint Center for Political and Economic Studies.

Littlefield, A., et al. 1982. "Redefining Race: The Potential Demise of a Concept." *Current Anthropology* 23:641-647.

Livingstone, F.B., et al. 1962. "On the Non-Existence of Human Races." *Current Anthropology* 3: 279-281.

Massey, D.S. 1990. "American Apartheid: Segregation and the Making of the Underclass." *American Journal of Sociology* 96:329-357.

Maxwell, N.L. 1994. "The Effect of Black-White Wage Differences on the Quantity and Quality of Education." *Industrial and Labor Relations Review* 47:249-264.

McKeown, T. 1976. *The Modern Rise of Population.* London: Edward Arnold.

McKinlay, J., and S. McKinlay. 1977. "The Questionable Contribution of Medical Measures to the Decline of Mortality in the United States in the Twentieth Century." *Milbank Quarterly* 55:405-428.

National Center for Health Statistics. 1996. *Vital Statistics of the United States, 1992,* Vol. II, "Mortality Part A." Washington, D.C.: Public Health Services.

———. 1998. *Vital Statistics of the United States, 1998,* Vol. II, "Mortality Part A." Washington, D.C.: Public Health Services.

National Commission on Social Security Reform. 1983. *Report of National Commission on Social Security Reform.* Washington, D.C.: U.S. Government Printing Office (GPO).

Neighbors, H.W., J.S. Jackson, C. Broman, and E. Thompson. 1996. "Racism and the Mental Health of African Americans: The Role of Self and System Blame." *Ethnicity and Disease* 6(1, 2):167-175.

Newsholme, A. 1910. *39th Annual Report of the Local Government Board* (London, England). Report Cd 5312.

Ogbum, W., and D. Thomas. 1922. "The Influence of the Business Cycle on Certain Social Conditions." *Journal of the American Statistical Association* 18:324-340.

Pampel, F.C., and V.K. Pillai. 1986. "Patterns and Determinants of Infant Mortality in Developed Nations, 1950-1975." *Demography* 23:525-542.

Pamuk, E., et al. 1998. *Socioeconomic Status and Health Chartbook, United States.* Hyattsville, Md.: National Center for Health Statistics.

Reed, T.E. 1969. "Caucasian Genes in American Negroes." *Science* 165:767.

Robinson, J.C. 1984. "Racial Inequality and the Probability of Occupation-Related Injury or Illness." *Milbank Quarterly* 62(4):567-590.

Ruston, J.P., and A.F. Bogart. 1989. "Population Differences in Susceptibility to AIDS: An Evolutionary Analysis." *Social Science and Medicine* 28(12):1211-1220.

Rydell, L.H. 1976. "Trends in Infant Mortality: Medical Advances or Socio-Economic Changes?" *Acia Sociologica* 19:147-168.

Savitt, T. 1982. "The Use of Blacks for Medical Experimentation and Demonstration in the Old South." *Journal of Southern History* 48(3):331-348.

Schneider, M., and J.R. Logan. 1982. "Suburban Racial Segregation and Black Access to Local Public Resources." *Social Science Quarterly* 63:762-770.

———. 1985. "Suburban Municipalities: The Changing System of Intergovernmental Relations in the Mid-1970s." *Urban Affairs* 21:87-105.

Showstack, J.A., P.P. Budetti, and D. Minkler. 1984. "Factors Associated with Birth Weight: An Exploration of the Roles of Prenatal Care and Length of Gestation." *American Journal of Pubic Health* 74:1003-1008.

Skocpol, T. 1991. "Targeting Within Universalism: Politically Viable Politics to Combat Poverty in the United States." In *The Underclass.* Ed. C. Jencks and P.E. Peterson. Washington, D.C.: Brookings Institution.

Snider, D.E., L. Salinas, and G.D. Kelly. 1989. "Tuberculosis: An Increasing Problem Among Minorities in the United States." *Public Health Reports* 104(6):646-53.

Thomas, S.B., and S.C. Quinn. 1993. "The Burdens of Race and History on Black Americans' Attitudes Toward Needle Exchange Policy to Prevent HIV Disease." *Journal of Public Health Policy*:320-347.

U.S. Bureau of the Census. 1996. *Statistical Abstract of the United States: 1996.* 116th ed. Washington, D.C.: GPO.

———. 1998. *Statistical Abstract of the United States: 1998.* 118th ed. Washington, D.C.: GPO.

U.S. Department of Health and Human Services. 1985. *Report of the Secretary's Task Force on Black and Minority Health,* Vol. 1. "Executive Summary." Washington, D.C.: GPO.

———. 1998. "Deaths. Final Data for 1996." *National Vital Statistics Report,* 47(9). Hyattsville, Md.: National Center for Health Statistics.

U.S. General Accounting Office. 1983. *Citing of Hazardous Waste Landfills and Their Correlation with the Racial and Economic Status of Surrounding Communities.* Washington, D.C.: GAO.

U.S. National Advisory Commission on Civil Disorders. 1968. *Report of the National Advisory Commission on Civil Disorders.* Washington, D.C.: GPO.

Wenneker, M.B., and A.M. Epstein. 1989. "Racial Inequalities in the Use of Procedures for Patients with Ischemic Heart Disease in Massachusetts." *Journal of the American Medical Association* 261(2):253-257.

Whittle, J., J. Conigilaro, C.B. Good, and P.P. Lofgren. 1993. "Racial Differences in the Use of Invasive Cardiovascular Procedures in the Department of Veterans Affairs Medical System." *New England Journal of Medicine* 329(9):621-627.

Wilson, T.W., and C.E. Grim. 1991. "The Biohistory of Slavery and Blood Pressure Differences in Blacks Today: A Hypothesis." *Hypertension* 17:122-128.

Chapter 7

Considerations in the Development of Family Policy for African Americans

by M. Belinda Tucker

Professor of Psychiatry and Biobehavioral Sciences,
University of California, Los Angeles

INTRODUCTION

This chapter examines African American* families in a sociocultural and environmental context, exploring structural changes over time and perspectives on causation and policy. First, it summarizes major African American family trends since the 1960s, drawing heavily from the many available reviews on the topic. Next, it discusses the major conceptual models that have attempted to account for the trends and briefly examines consequent tests of those theories when they exist. Third, the chapter explores the conceptualization of the "problem" in discourse concerning African American families: Is there consensus, as observed in both scholarly and lay writing, about what features of some African American families constitute either problem or crisis, necessitating intervention? Finally, it examines the extent to which the empirical literature has offered particular strategies for social policy and discusses the kinds of issues that policy formulations should address. The discussion is anchored within the broader context of family change in Western societies generally, the increasing heterogeneity of the Black population, and more global reconceptualizations of family.

Underlying this presentation is the fundamental recognition that society's ideas about marriage and family are essentially culture- and tradition-bound. Although the family as a form of social organization is virtually universal, anthropological texts note the difficulty of constructing a single definition of family because of its remarkable heterogeneity across and within societies (Oswalt, 1986; Stephens, 1963). As Harris (1988, 327) concluded, "One of the most important facts about human domestic arrangements is that no single pattern can be shown to be more 'natural' than any other." Therefore, notions of "correctness" and "appropriateness" in the United States may have a greater basis in sociocultural and religious belief systems than in empirical derivation. Under these terms, public debate takes on an emotional tenor that rivals the abortion controversy. Recent discourse on the academic treatment of family reflects fundamental differences in values related to marriage and childbearing behavior and to domestic organi-

---

* The term "African American" refers to people of African descent who were born and raised in the United States. "Black" describes those of African descent more generally, such as Caribbean Americans and African immigrants.

zation more generally (e.g., Cherlin, 1993, 1997; Glenn, 1997a, 1997b; Popenoe, 1993; Scanzoni, 1997; Skolnick, 1997; Stacey, 1993). Such conflict is perhaps to be expected as the present-day reality of significant family policy reform has raised the stakes in family research considerably.

The culture-bound nature of conceptualizations of family becomes especially salient with respect to the increased diversification of the African-descended population in the United States. The 1990 census counted nearly one million people of West Indian ancestry, almost one-half million from sub-Saharan Africa, and 650,000 Black Hispanics (U.S. Bureau of the Census, 1990). Because these are surely undercounts (and because Blacks from other areas around the globe are not included), it can be assumed that at least 8 percent of the "Black" population as defined by the census is not African American. The diversity of family life that these cultural influences represent must be recognized. Further, the increased income and educational distribution of the African American population (as described elsewhere in this volume) is reflected in family formation values and behavior.

Although I draw on writings from various disciplines, I primarily employ social psychological and sociological perspectives to assess the contributions of empirical literature to understanding family change and difference within the population of those of African descent in the United States. In this discussion, I also refer to new data collected in my program of research that addresses African American family formation behavior, family organization, and attitudes and beliefs related to these issues in a community context. The most recent phase of this research is a national study of 21 cities with populations over 100,000 that incorporates both individual and community-level variables in an attempt to determine predictors and correlates of family formation behavior (Tucker and Mitchell-Kernan, 1997). The community context is conceptualized in terms of the demographic and economic features of American cities that may influence family formation behaviors and attitudes.

AFRICAN AMERICAN FAMILY TRENDS SINCE THE 1960s

A number of scholars have described and analyzed recent trends in African American family structure and household organization (e.g., Bennett, Bloom, and Craig, 1989, 1992; Cherlin, 1981; Epenshade, 1985; Hernandez, 1993; Hill, 1993; Mare and Winship, 1991; Rodgers and Thornton, 1985; Tucker and Mitchell-Kernan, 1995b; U.S. Bureau of the Census, 1992; Wilson, 1987). These assessments consistently reveal that family formation behavior among African Americans over the past 40 years has undergone dramatic change in some respects. Yet conclusions about the nature, magnitude, and meaning of the trends vary, reflecting differences in temporal boundaries, comparative intent, and ideological orientation.

First, the extent and nature of the changes are very much a function of the period examined. Although this volume focuses on events since the 1960s, analyses of certain aspects of family status in the United States that use the 1950s as a base will clearly produce conclusions that differ substantially from those that take a broader historical perspective. As a number of authors have pointed out (Cherlin, 1981; Oppenheimer, Blossfeld, and Wackerow, 1995; Tucker and Mitchell-Kernan, 1995b), the 1950s through the early 1960s was a fairly aberrant period in terms of marital behavior for the nation as a whole. Early marriage was normative, and marital prevalence was exceptionally high; therefore, an understanding of trends in these areas requires a longer period of observation. By the same token, the changes in African American family formation during the past 40 years are especially striking when viewed in the context of its remarkable stability over previous generations. Commenting on that resilience prior to the 1960s, noted historian John Hope Franklin (1997, 8) observed, "The strong family tradition among Blacks thus survived the slave system, then legal segregation, discrimination, and enforced poverty."

Second, behavioral trends that are evident society-wide, across ethnic and racial groups, must be distinguished from those that seem to be peculiar to African Americans or to certain subpopulations of Blacks. Furthermore, it is important to determine whether African Americans are simply "ahead of the curve" with respect to some family formation patterns—that is, exhibiting behaviors that reflect later societal trends—or are truly unique regardless of the genesis of the behavior. One example of the former is the tendency toward greater levels of nonmarital birth evident in the African American population as a whole. During the mid-1970s, after Moynihan (1967) wrote his controversial report, *The Negro Family: The Case for National Action,* approximately one out of every four births among Blacks was to an unmarried couple. Today, one-fourth of all births in the United States are nonmarital.

Third, it is important to distinguish whether and under what conditions a comparative framework is meaningful. That is, a number of the analyses of family formation trends adopt an analytical focus based on explicit comparisons of African American and White family formation behavior. There are certainly situations and conditions that demand such comparisons to reveal inequities that can be addressed with appropriate public policy. One example is the low birth weights of Black infants compared with White newborns. However, whether marriage and childbearing behavior falls into such a category is open for discussion. Historian Stevenson (1995, 1996) and a University of Pennsylvania-based group of historical sociologists (McDaniel, 1994; McDaniel and Morgan, 1996; Morgan et al., 1993) have recently argued that African American family formation behavior has always been distinctive. This is due to a combination of factors, including retentions from the West African cultures of origin for American Blacks, social adaptation to the harsh conditions of slavery and its aftermath, and lingering economic and social disadvantages. This line of research suggests that, even during periods when African American marriage and childbearing behavior appeared to be more similar to that of Euro-Americans, specific aspects of family organization differed considerably.

Finally, it is apparent that descriptions of societal trends often reflect the political context in which they are viewed. Distinctive sets of assessments, interpretations, and remedies are associated with liberal versus conservative political perspectives. The issue of the impact of family type on children has been particularly prone to such ideological standoffs.

With these issues in mind, this chapter will review changes in African American family formation behavior in the areas that have been a key focus of policy debates: marriage behavior; household organization; childbearing behavior; and children's living arrangements. Marriage behavior is the first topic to be examined because shifts in this area appear to be driving many of the changes in the other aspects of family organization. In each case, comparable data on Whites are also presented and, when available, on Hispanic origin and Asian/Pacific Islander origin groups as well. (There are too few data on Native American populations to include them in this discussion.) However, because Whites are the most populous and the most privileged racial group, they are the primary reference group for the majority of the discussion. It should be noted that the data presented from non-census years is derived from the Current Population Survey, which provides population estimates based on sample surveys.

Marital Behavior

As shown in Table 7-1, during the period 1960-98, the overall proportion of Black men and women who were married steadily decreased, falling by 32 percent among men and 39 percent among women. Declines also characterized marital behavior generally in the United States during this period; the proportion currently married among Whites decreased by 13 percent for men and 14 percent for women. Although figures for Hispanic origin and Asian/Pacific Islander populations are not available for the full period examined, more than one-half of women and men in both groups were married in 1998. Some group variations are due to differences in the age structures of the populations. Whites are substantially older as a group than all other U.S. ethnic populations, which accounts in part for their greater tendency to be married. In 1998, the median age was 37.9 for non-Hispanic Whites, 30.2 years for Blacks, 31.2 for Asian/Pacific Islanders, and 26.6 for Hispanics (U.S. Bureau of the Census, 1998a).

The patterns of change observed in Table 7-1 reflect several trends among Blacks and Whites: greater marital delay; a greater tendency for some to never marry; and higher divorce rates. First marriages have occurred increasingly later in the general population for both men and women, reaching record highs in the mid-1990s. In 1998, the median age at first marriage was 25.0 for women and 26.7 for men; in 1970, the comparable ages were 23.2 and 20.8 (U.S. Bureau of the Census, 1999a). The increase has been even greater for Black women, rising from the median age of 21.3 in 1970 to 26.0 in 1988 (the most recent estimate available). Yet when a longer historical span is considered, it is clear that marital timing has been highly variable over the years. Figure 7-1 shows that in 1940, Blacks were more likely than Whites to marry prior to age 24 and that the most dramatic change in early marital behavior became evident in the 1980 census.

TABLE 7-1

Marital Status of Persons 15 Years and Older by Gender, Race, and
Hispanic Origin for Available Years, 1960-98
(%)

			Males		
Race	Total[a]	Married	Never Married	Widowed	Divorced
Black					
1960	6,143	60.9	32.4	4.8	2.0
1970	6,936	56.9	35.6	4.4	3.1
1980	8,292	48.9	41.1	3.7	6.3
1990	9,948	44.1	43.4	3.4	8.1
1998	11,283	41.4	46.0	3.4	9.2
Asian/ Pacific Islander					
1997	3,703	56.6	37.7	1.5	4.3
Hispanic					
1998	10,944	52.9	39.3	1.2	5.9
White					
1960	54,130	70.3	24.5	3.4	1.8
1970	62,868	68.0	27.2	2.7	2.1
1980	71,887	65.0	28.1	2.3	4.7
1990	78,908	62.8	28.0	2.4	6.8
1998	85,219	60.2	29.1	2.5	8.3
1998[b]	74,703	61.1	27.6	2.6	8.6

(continued)

Table 7-2 shows a more detailed breakdown of marital behavior by age in 1998. Although marriage is unlikely before the age of 24 among Blacks, Hispanics, and Whites, 75 percent of Black women age 40-44 and almost 90 percent of those age 55-64 have been married. Marriage is still normative for older Black men, with almost 70 percent of those in their early 40s and 85 percent of those age 45-54 having been married at least once. Indeed, as recently as 1980, almost 80 percent of both Black men and women age 30-34 had been married (U.S. Bureau of the Census, 1985). Oppenheimer, Blossfeld, and Wackerow (1995) note that it is difficult to distinguish the likelihood of never marrying from delay in younger years, but that as individuals reach their 40s without marrying, the possibility that they will never marry becomes increasingly likely. This suggests that growing numbers of African Americans, particularly women, will never marry.

Table 7-2 indicates that Hispanic marital patterns may also be undergoing change. Although differences in how Hispanics are defined from

TABLE 7-1 continued
(%)

Race	Total[a]	Married	Never Married	Widowed	Divorced
			Females		
Black					
1960	6,747	59.8	21.6	14.3	4.3
1970	8,108	54.1	27.7	13.8	4.4
1980	10,108	44.6	33.6	13.0	8.7
1990	11,966	40.2	36.9	11.6	11.2
1998	13,715	36.3	41.5	10.0	12.2
Asian/ Pacific Islander					
1997	3,876	60.1	28.4	7.2	4.4
Hispanic					
1998	10,485	56.4	29.3	5.9	8.4
White					
1960	57,860	66.6	18.7	12.3	2.5
1970	68,888	62.8	21.3	12.4	3.4
1980	77,882	60.7	21.0	11.9	6.4
1990	84,508	59.1	20.6	11.6	8.6
1998	89,489	57.5	21.9	10.4	10.2
1998[b]	79,502	57.5	21.1	11.0	10.4

a. Numbers in thousands.
b. Non-Hispanic Whites only.

Source: U.S. Bureau of the Census (1997, 1999c).

census to census and the absence of earlier data of any kind make it difficult to examine their marital trends, younger male Hispanics are now as likely to remain unmarried as White males. After the age of 30, Hispanic women are more likely to have never been married than White women, but less so than Black women.

The substantial role of divorce in the decline of marriage is evident in Figure 7-2. The divorce ratio (the number of divorces per 1,000 married persons) of both Blacks and Whites has more than quadrupled since 1960. The period of greatest change was the decade 1970-80 when divorce more than doubled. Over the entire 1960-90 period, however, Black divorce ratios have consistently been approximately double the ratios of Whites.

This focus on broad racial comparisons obscures the diversity in marital behavior of Blacks from other countries and cultures. As shown in Table 7-3,

FIGURE 7-1

Percentage Married by Age 20-24 by Race, 1940-90

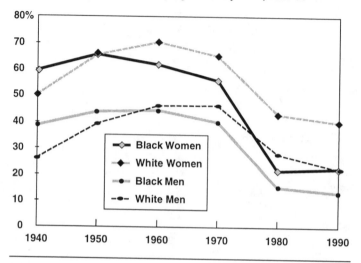

Source: U.S. Bureau of the Census (1953, 1966, 1971, 1975a, 1975b, 1991).

there is considerable variation in both marital and divorce behavior as a function of ancestry. For example, those from the Dutch West Indies and Nigeria have a greater tendency to marry, and Dutch West Indians and Cape Verdeans are more likely to divorce. (Note that these ancestry categories are not exclusively Black and likely contain people with other racial identities.)

Childbearing Behavior

Overall birthrates of Black women in general (without respect to marital status) have declined substantially over the past three and one-half decades, from 31.9 in 1960 to 18.2 in 1995 (National Center for Education Statistics, 1997). (The 1960 figures are somewhat distorted by the presence of other non-White racial groups, but the category is predominantly Black.) In fact, the 1995 birthrate for Black women as a group differs little from that of other U.S. racial groups: 16.6 for American Indians; 17.3 for Asian/Pacific Islanders; and 14.2 for Whites (National Center for Education Statistics, 1997). Further, in 1996, births among African American teenagers reached the lowest point ever recorded—54.7 births per 1,000 women (Ventura, Curtin, and Matthews, 1998).

Despite these trends, childbearing is the most controversial family policy issue, owing to the greatly increased tendency for single women in the United States to bear children. Birthrates among unmarried American women in general have increased for all age cohorts between 15 and 44, but

TABLE 7-2

Marital Status of Persons 18 Years and Older by Gender, Age, Race, and Hispanic Origin, 1998
(%)

Age	Total[1]	Never Married	Males Married, Spouse Present	Married, Spouse Absent	Widowed	Divorced
Black						
Total 18+	10,297	40.9	39.7	5.6	3.7	10.1
18 to 19	536	97.0	0.2	1.6	–	1.2
20 to 24	1,183	91.9	7.0	1.2	–	–
25 to 29	1,177	64.4	30.0	2.7	–	2.9
30 to 34	1,212	43.2	41.0	6.3	0.3	9.3
35 to 39	1,306	39.7	43.9	7.5	0.2	8.7
40 to 44	1,211	32.3	46.2	6.5	0.7	14.2
45 to 54	1,636	15.5	56.7	7.2	2.1	18.6
55 to 64	968	10.8	53.7	12.4	7.3	15.9
65+	1,068	5.5	53.4	3.5	24.7	13.0
Hispanic						
Total 18+	10,082	34.8	50.1	7.4	1.3	6.4
18 to 19	573	95.4	3.7	0.9	–	–
20 to 24	1,455	76.4	18.3	4.9	–	0.4
25 to 29	1,510	49.4	42.1	6.5	0.1	1.9
30 to 34	1,408	27.4	58.9	8.0	–	5.6
35 to 39	1,329	26.8	55.5	8.2	0.6	8.9
40 to 44	1,025	12.7	66.9	7.9	0.2	12.3
45 to 54	1,322	12.0	65.2	10.6	0.5	11.7
55 to 64	768	5.7	71.6	10.3	2.3	10.1
65+	681	4.5	67.0	6.7	14.0	7.8
Non-Hispanic White						
Total 18+	70,693	23.5	62.1	2.5	2.8	9.1
18 to 19	2,568	97.7	1.5	0.6	–	0.1
20 to 24	5,824	82.9	13.7	1.2	–	2.2
25 to 29	6,275	47.4	44.8	2.6	0.1	5.1
30 to 34	6,890	26.8	62.1	2.7	0.2	8.1
35 to 39	8,156	18.0	66.6	3.7	0.3	11.4
40 to 44	8,049	13.9	68.9	3.4	0.5	13.4
45 to 54	13,009	8.1	74.4	2.9	0.8	13.8
55 to 64	8,519	4.8	79.4	2.2	2.0	11.6
65+	11,403	3.7	74.7	2.0	14.1	5.5

(continued)

TABLE 7-2 continued
(%)

Age	Total[1]	Never Married	Females Married, Spouse Present	Married, Spouse Absent	Widowed	Divorced
Black						
Total 18+	12,793	37.3	31.0	8.0	10.7	13.1
18 to 19	615	97.8	1.7	0.5	–	–
20 to 24	1,380	85.1	12.1	1.7	0.2	1.0
25 to 29	1,425	59.4	29.4	7.1	0.1	3.9
30 to 34	1,485	47.2	35.0	8.9	0.7	8.1
35 to 39	1,545	34.3	35.0	12.4	2.4	15.9
40 to 44	1,437	25.4	42.2	10.4	3.1	19.0
45 to 54	2,028	15.2	41.2	10.9	6.2	26.5
55 to 64	1,255	10.8	37.1	9.1	21.0	21.9
65+	1,623	6.9	24.3	5.0	54.4	9.2
Hispanic						
Total 18+	9,753	24.3	52.8	7.5	6.3	9.1
18 to 19	555	86.6	10.9	2.3	–	0.3
20 to 24	1,209	60.7	31.6	5.4	0.4	1.9
25 to 29	1,285	32.9	57.7	5.3	0.6	3.5
30 to 34	1,284	19.5	63.8	8.2	0.9	7.5
35 to 39	1,166	13.2	65.5	8.4	1.4	11.5
40 to 44	1,075	8.4	65.1	10.6	1.6	14.2
45 to 54	1,377	8.1	61.6	10.0	5.5	14.7
55 to 64	865	8.7	56.2	9.2	10.6	15.4
65+	937	5.5	37.0	5.7	41.7	10.1
Non-Hispanic White						
Total 18+	75,675	17.1	57.6	2.7	11.6	10.9
18 to 19	2,459	95.0	4.2	0.6	–	0.1
20 to 24	5,807	68.5	25.9	2.3	0.1	3.1
25 to 29	6,332	34.8	55.1	3.3	0.4	6.5
30 to 34	7,015	16.8	68.7	3.9	0.4	10.2
35 to 39	8,162	10.7	71.4	3.8	1.0	13.0
40 to 44	7,979	7.5	71.7	3.6	1.2	15.9
45 to 54	13,289	5.9	70.0	3.0	3.4	17.6
55 to 64	9,040	3.5	68.6	1.9	12.4	13.7
65+	15,592	4.5	42.6	1.6	44.6	6.7

1. Numbers in thousands.

Source: U.S. Bureau of the Census (1999d).

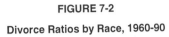

FIGURE 7-2

Divorce Ratios by Race, 1960-90

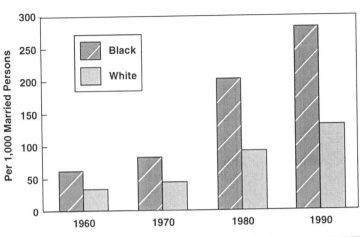

Note: Divorce ratio is the number of divorces per 1,000 married persons.

Source: Farley (1995).

most substantially among those between 15 and 24 (see Table 7-4). The birthrate for the youngest cohort of women has essentially tripled since 1960. In 1995, the overall birthrate for unmarried women was highest among Hispanics, 95.0, compared with 75.9 for Blacks and 28.2 for non-Hispanic Whites (Ventura et al., 1997, Table C). The National Center for Education Statistics (1997) notes that this is due especially to the greater prevalence of nonmarital births among Latinos age 20 and over who are more likely to be in cohabiting relationships. This pattern is particularly prominent in Puerto Rico, which again demonstrates the problem of using broad group-based data to explore these issues.

Since the 1960s, the birthrate among Black single women has declined in most age cohorts. There is fluctuation across years, and the greatest declines were evident between 1970 and 1980. After age 19, unmarried birthrates for Hispanic women in 1995 were substantially greater than those observed for any age cohort of African American women. In all White age cohorts, there has been a steady increase in the birthrates for unmarried women, with the most substantial increase occurring during the 1980-90 decade when most rates essentially doubled. Yet these figures do not tell the full story because Hispanic and White figures cannot be distinguished in years prior to 1994. However, even the 1995 non-Hispanic White age group rates are substantially higher than the 1980 figures for both White and Hispanic women. Historian Ruggles (1997) observes that the magnitude of the differential in Black and White nonmarital births has narrowed consid-

TABLE 7-3

Marital Status of Persons 15 Years and Older by Selected Ancestry, 1990 Census
(%)

Ancestry	Total[1]	Married	Never Married	Widowed	Divorced
British West Indian	30,794	49.4	38.5	4.4	7.7
Dutch West Indian	27,618	65.6	16.9	6.1	11.5
Guyanese	61,164	55.0	34.4	3.6	6.9
Haitian	206,324	51.7	37.8	3.2	7.3
Cape Verdean	34,763	46.2	37.6	5.6	10.6
Ethiopian	26,911	46.2	45.5	2.0	6.3
Nigerian	61,929	59.5	29.9	2.5	8.1

1. Numbers in thousands.

Source: U.S. Bureau of the Census (1998e). "Selected Characteristics for Persons of British West Indian Ancestry: 1990"; "Selected Characteristics for Persons of Cape Verdean Ancestry: 1990"; "Selected Characteristics for Persons of Dutch West Indian Ancestry: 1990"; "Selected Characteristics for Persons of Ethiopian Ancestry: 1990"; "Selected Characteristics for Persons of Guyanese Ancestry: 1990"; "Selected Characteristics for Persons of Haitian Ancestry: 1990"; "Selected Characteristics for Persons of Nigerian Ancestry: 1990."

erably over the past 40 years. In the 1940s and 1950s, the unmarried fertility ratio for non-Whites was 10 times the White ratio, and by 1990, the magnitude of difference was only 2.6.

Discussions of birthrates rarely focus on men, the coproducers of these trends. Table 7-5 shows that birthrates for Black men fell substantially between 1990 and 1995 and at nearly double the extent of decline for White men (17.4 percent and 9.9 percent, respectively). The birthrate among U.S. men overall in 1980, 1990, and 1995 is highest among those in their late 20s, as was the case with Black men in 1980. Now, however, birthrates are highest among Black men in their early 20s, at a level almost triple that of teenagers. Males (1992) has noted that many of the fathers in teen mother situations are adults rather than fellow teens, which raises the question of exploitation in those relationships.

Household Organization

Change in household organization has occurred along with change in marital patterns. In particular, Black married couple households have

TABLE 7-4

Birthrates for Unmarried Women by Race, Age, and Hispanic Origin for Available Years, 1960-95 (Rates per 1,000 Unmarried Women in Specified Group)

	Total 15-19	15-17	18-19	20-24	25-29	30-34	35-39	40-44
Black								
1960[a]	98.3	–	–	166.5	171.8	104.0	–	–
1970	96.9	77.9	136.4	131.5	100.9	71.8	32.9	10.4
1980	87.9	68.8	118.2	112.3	81.4	46.7	19.0	5.5
1990	106.0	78.8	143.7	144.8	105.3	61.5	25.5	5.1
1995	92.8	68.6	131.2	127.7	84.8	54.3	25.6	6.0
White								
1960	9.2	–	–	18.2	18.2	10.8	–	–
1970	10.9	7.5	17.6	22.5	21.1	14.2	7.6	2.0
1980	16.5	12.0	24.1	25.1	21.5	14.1	7.1	1.8
1990	30.6	20.4	44.9	48.2	43.0	29.9	14.5	3.2
1995	35.5	23.6	55.4	58.0	48.7	34.2	16.9	4.2
Hispanic								
1995	78.7	56.3	117.9	148.9	133.8	89.2	43.4	12.2
Non-Hispanic White								
1995	27.7	17.6	44.5	43.8	34.9	25.3	13.0	3.2

a. Includes Blacks and other races.

Sources: National Center for Education Statistics (1997); Ventura et al. (1997).

TABLE 7-5

Birthrates by Age and Race of Father for Available Years, 1980-95

	15-54[a]	15-19[b]	20-24	25-29	Age of Father 30-34	35-39	40-44	45-49	50-54	55+
All Races										
1980[c]	57.0	18.8	92.0	123.1	91.0	42.8	17.1	6.1	2.2	0.3
1990	58.4	23.5	88.0	116.4	97.8	53.0	21.0	7.5	2.8	0.4
1995	52.0	24.3	86.0	107.2	93.3	51.0	20.3	7.1	2.6	0.3
Black										
1980[c]	83.0	40.1	145.3	152.8	109.6	62.0	31.2	13.6	5.9	1.1
1990	84.9	55.2	158.2	144.9	103.2	60.4	31.1	15.0	7.1	1.4
1995	70.1	50.5	140.5	126.6	89.6	52.6	25.7	12.1	5.6	1.1
White										
1980[c]	3.4	15.4	84.9	119.4	87.8	39.7	15.0	5.1	1.8	0.3
1990	54.6	18.1	78.3	113.2	96.1	50.9	19.2	6.5	2.2	0.3
1995	49.2	19.7	78.5	105.7	92.9	49.6	19.0	6.3	2.2	0.2

a. Rates are computed by relating total births, regardless of age of father, to men age 15-54.
b. Rates are computed by relating births of fathers under 20 years of age to men age 15-19.
c. Based on 100 percent of births in selected states and on a 50 percent sample of births in all other states.

Source: Ventura et al. (1997).

TABLE 7-6

Percentage Distribution of Household Type by Race and Hispanic Origin, 1998
(%)

	Blacks	Whites	Non-Hispanic Whites	Hispanics	Asian/ Pacific
Total households (in thousands)	12,474	86,106	77,936	8,590	3,125
Married couples	31.5	55.8	55.7	55.9	62.3
with children	16.5	25.4		36.3	–
without children	15.0	30.4		19.6	–
avg. no. of children	1.9	1.9	–	2.2	–
Other families	36.0	13.3	12.1	25.1	13.9
with children	20.6	5.7		13.1	–
without children	10.9	3.9		5.7	–
avg. no. of children	1.8	1.7	–	2.1	–
People living alone	28.9	25.5	26.7	14.4	–
Other nonfamily households	3.7	5.4	5.5	4.6	23.8[a]

a. Includes people living alone.

Source: U.S. Bureau of the Census (1999b), Table 16; (1999e).

sharply declined, with a corresponding increase in households headed by females with no male present. The decline was first evident in 1960, and by 1998, less than one-third (32 percent) of Black households were headed by a wife-husband couple (U.S. Bureau of the Census, 1999c). Table 7-6 shows the current range of household types for Blacks, Whites, non-Hispanic Whites, Hispanics, and Asian/Pacific Island Americans. Blacks, Whites, and non-Hispanic Whites are now equally likely to live alone and are more likely to do so than Hispanics or Asian/Pacific Islander groups. Black family formation has moved closer to the White pattern in this area. In 1970, less than 2 percent of Black households contained a single adult compared with 15 percent of Whites (U.S. Bureau of the Census, 1970).

Sudarkasa (1997) argues that the change in Black family organization over the past 40 years that has had the greatest impact on African American communities is the increased disaggregation of households, which incorporates the decline of both two parent and multigenerational households, as well as the increase in single person households, particularly among the elderly. African American families remain somewhat larger than those of Whites, but smaller than Hispanic families (U.S. Bureau of the Census, 1998a). In 1998, the average size of Black married couple families was 3.6 compared with 4.1 for Hispanics and 3.2 for Whites, and the average size of

Black female householder families was 3.3 compared with 3.5 for Hispanics and 2.9 for Whites (U.S. Bureau of the Census, 1998a). The much lower size of White female households is due in large part to the preponderance of elderly White women who live alone.

Children's Living Arrangements

Table 7-7 illustrates that, overall, the living arrangements of children under age 18 in the United States have changed considerably since 1960,

TABLE 7-7

Living Arrangements of Children Under 18 Years by Race and Hispanic Origin for Available Years, 1960-98

(%)

	Total with Children Under 18 Yrs.[a]	Living with ...				
		Two Parents	Mother Only	Father Only	Other Relatives	Nonrelatives
Black						
1960[b]	8,650	67.0	19.9	2.0	9.5	1.5
1970	9,422	58.5	29.5	2.3	8.7	1.0
1980	9,375	42.2	44.0	2.0	10.7	1.3
1990	10,018	37.7	51.2	3.5	6.5	1.0
1998	11,414	36.2	51.1	3.7	7.4	1.5
Hispanic						
1960	–	–	–	–	–	–
1970[c]	4,006	77.7	–	–	–	–
1980	5,459	75.4	19.6	1.5	3.4	0.1
1990	7,174	66.8	27.1	2.9	2.5	0.8
1998	10,863	63.6	26.8	4.4	3.5	1.6
White						
1960	55,077	90.9	6.1	1.0	1.4	0.5
1970	58,791	89.5	7.8	0.9	1.2	0.6
1980	52,242	82.7	13.5	1.6	1.7	0.5
1990	51,390	79.0	16.2	3.0	1.4	0.4
1998	56,124	74.0	18.2	4.6	2.1	1.1

a. Numbers in thousands.
b. 1960 Black includes all non-White.
c. 1970 Hispanic is persons of Spanish origin.

Source: U.S. Bureau of the Census (1999d). "Living Arrangements of Black Children under 18 Years Old: 1960 to Present"; "Living Arrangements of Hispanic Children under 18 Years Old: 1960 to Present"; and "Living Arrangements of White Children under 18 Years Old: 1960 to Present."

particularly among African Americans. In 1960, two-thirds of Black children lived with both parents, whereas in 1998, only about one-third lived with a mother and a father. One-half of Black children now live with their mothers without a father present. Similar though less dramatic changes are evident for Hispanic and White children: less than two-thirds of Hispanic children and three-fourths of White children currently live in two parent households, compared with 78 percent and 90 percent, respectively, in 1970. One out of five White children live with a mother only. The shift from two parent to single mother childrearing occurred predominantly in the 1970-80 decade. Since 1990, however, the proportion of mother-only households has remained steady among Blacks. The slight decline in the proportion of Black children in two parent households since 1990 seems to be offset by the slight rise in the proportion of children living with other relatives or in other nonparental situations.

These statistics, however, do not tell the full story of who lives with and is involved in rearing children. Even within two parent homes, the composition of relationships has changed in recent decades. Among African American two parent families, the proportion of children in stepparent households increased from 23 percent in 1980 to 31 percent in 1990 (U.S. Bureau of the Census, 1992). Children in homes without two parents may still live with a nonparental male or with other relatives, including grandparents. The March 1996 Current Population Survey data show that 13 percent of Black children lived in households maintained by their grandparents compared with 7 percent for Hispanics and 4 percent for Whites (U.S. Bureau of the Census, 1998). (These figures do not include children who lived in homes that included grandparents but were maintained by someone else.) Almost one-third of Black children in mother-only homes were living with other adult relatives as well (U.S. Bureau of the Census, 1998). One-half of children who lived with neither parent were living with a grandparent. Although African American households have always been more likely to include extended family members, there has been an increase in the number of grandparents, particularly grandmothers, who have primary care of children. The U.S. Bureau of the Census (1998d) found through multivariate analysis that grandmother-grandchild households (without parents) were significantly more likely to be Black, in the South, in central cities, and poor.

This trend is society-wide, however. Overall, the proportion of children in the United States living in the home of their grandparents has almost doubled during the past 25 years, increasing from 3 percent in 1970 to 5.5 percent in 1997 (U.S. Bureau of the Census, 1998d). The work of Wilson (1984) and Flaherty, Facteau, and Garver (1987) has been particularly instructive in elucidating the critical role of African American grandparents in care-giving, instruction, and management. Burton (1985), Burton and Dilworth-Anderson (1991), and Minkler and Roe (1993) note that the context of grandparent involvement has changed, with both younger entry into grandparenthood and more parental incapacitation (e.g., through drug addiction or institutionalization), which places greater stress on providers.

TABLE 7-8

**Proportion of Families with Children Under 18 Years of Age Below
Poverty Level by Race, Family Type, and Hispanic Origin, 1997
(%)**

Race	All Families with Children	Married Couple Families	Male Householder, No Wife Present	Female Householder, No Husband Present
Black	30.5	9.0	25.6	46.9
Hispanic	30.4	21.0	30.5	54.2
White	13.0	6.7	17.5	37.6

Source: U.S. Bureau of the Census (1998b).

This shift in children's living arrangements has been accompanied by a substantial increase in the proportion of Black children living below the official poverty level. In the 1960s, when two-thirds of all African American children were impoverished, society seemed to be conquering the incredibly pervasive poverty of children. By 1970, that figure had dropped to 35 percent, where it remained through 1990. By 1995, however, the proportion of Black children living below the poverty level had increased to 43 percent compared with 17 percent of White children. Table 7-8 shows the differences in poverty levels by family type in 1997. Although 9 percent of Black two parent families with children were impoverished, 47 percent of Black single mother families had incomes below the poverty level. Of married couple families, Hispanics had the highest level of impoverishment, and 54 percent of Hispanic female householder families with children were impoverished.

Family Type and Income

As Chapter 4, "Languishing in Inequality: Racial Disparities in Wealth and Earnings in the New Millennium," in this volume details, Black-White family income ratios generally declined over the period 1967 to 1990. Family type is strongly associated with income. Although the income pattern is the same for all races (i.e., two parent households are in the best economic circumstances, and single women are the worst off), Black families with children earned considerably less than White and Asian/Pacific Islander families. In fact, Asian/Pacific Islander families with female householders now earn one-third more than White families in similar circumstances. However, among Blacks, both two parent families and those headed by women currently have higher incomes than similar Hispanic families.

As shown in Table 7-9, among Blacks, married couple families had incomes that came closest to White income levels. The problem here is that

TABLE 7-9

Median Family Income by Type, Race, and Hispanic Origin with Income Ratios, for Available Years, 1967-97 (1997 $)

Married Couple Families

	White	Black	B/W Ratio	Hispanic	H/W Ratio	Asian/Pacific	AP/W Ratio
1967	$38,153	$25,883	.68	—	—	—	—
1970	41,672	30,375	.73	—	—	—	—
1980	45,831	36,260	.79	$33,857	.74	—	—
1990	49,527	41,487	.84	34,379	.69	$56,791	1.15
1997	52,098	45,372	.87	33,914	.65	55,864	1.07

Female Householder, No Husband Present

	White	Black	B/W Ratio	Hispanic	H/W Ratio	Asian/Pacific	AP/W Ratio
1967	$21,572	$13,331	.62	—	—	—	—
1970	22,361	13,897	.62	—	—	—	—
1980	23,223	14,480	.62	$13,712	.59	—	—
1990	23,980	14,890	.62	14,630	.61	$27,738	1.16
1997	22,999	16,879	.73	14,994	.65	30,303	1.32

Male Householder, No Wife Present (in 1996 $ for Black and White Only)

	White	Black	B/W Ratio	Hispanic	H/W Ratio	Asian/Pacific	AP/W Ratio
1967	$32,511	$20,007	.62	—	—	—	—
1970	37,012	26,236	.71	—	—	—	—
1980	36,529	24,488	.67	$25,941	.71	—	—
1990	37,540	26,892	.72	27,930	.74	—	—
1997	34,802	25,654	.74	25,541	.73	—	—

Source: U.S. Bureau of the Census (1998c).

African American two parent families are decreasing as a proportion of total families. This group is therefore more select than in previous times and is likely to reflect the greater tendency of professional Black women and men (compared with lower income groups) to marry and remain married. In addition, the Black-White income ratio for male householders without wives increased by 20 percent between 1967 and 1997, but this was due in part to a substantial drop in the income of White male householders without wives. In contrast, during this period, the Black-White income ratios for single female households remained virtually stagnant until the late 1990s. Table 7-9 also demonstrates the growing income inequity between African American family types. For example, the median income of Black females maintaining households alone between 1967 and 1997 increased by 27 percent, while the median income of Black married couple families grew by 75 percent.

Table 7-10 shows the number of wage earners reported by household type and race for 1997. For both Black and White married couple households, approximately two-thirds relied on two or more salaries. Because the gap in the median incomes of Black husbands and wives is substantially less than

TABLE 7-10

Household Type by Percentage with Number of Earners by Race, 1997

Family Type

Number of Earners	Total	Married Couple	Female Householder, No Spouse	Male Householder No Spouse
Black				
Total[1]	8,455	3,851	3,947	657
No earners	16.6%	10.0%	24.2%	9.1%
One earner	38.1	22.0	50.5	57.6
Two earners	35.6	53.8	19.5	25.0
Three or more earners	9.8	14.1	5.7	8.2
Non-Hispanic White				
Total[1]	52,625	43,276	6,875	2,475
No earners	14.2%	14.3%	14.9%	9.7%
One earner	26.3	20.4	54.4	50.2
Two earners	21.3	51.1	24.5	32.6
Three or more earners	31.5	14.1	6.2	7.6

1. Numbers in thousands.

Source: U.S. Bureau of the Census (1998a).

the income difference in White couples, Black two parent families are more dependent on wives' incomes. The table also shows that three-fourths of single Black female-headed homes contained at least one earner and that more than one-fourth lived in households with two or more earners. Indeed, there is only a 10 percentage point difference between Black and White female-headed households with no earners. These data indicate that the stereotypical characterization of households headed by African American women as primarily welfare dependent is erroneous and fundamentally mythic.

Other Trends

Additional changes have occurred in African American marital behavior. Many of the trends discussed above are examined with the implicit assumption that Black families and households consist entirely of Blacks. Although marriage in the United States still overwhelmingly occurs within racial groups, the number of interracial and interethnic marriages has gradually climbed over the past 40 years. The number of marriages involving Blacks and other races has increased more than sixfold since 1960—from 58,000 couples to 373,000 couples in 1998 (U.S. Bureau of the Census, 1999c). Although the number of interracial marriages involving Black men is currently twice the number involving Black women, the rate of increase in interracial marriages has grown substantially for Black women since 1993, resulting in a doubling of Black female-White male marriages between 1993 and 1995. The implication of this growing phenomenon for Black family formation patterns is unknown. However, the greater tendency of Black men to date and marry women of other races may be a factor in the lower marriage rate of Black women (Tucker and Mitchell-Kernan, 1999).

As noted earlier, for American society in general, definitions of family have become more inclusive. Although the discussion here has focused heavily on married couple and single parent families (the focus of most policy debates), the range of family configurations now routinely encountered has expanded considerably. Billingsley (1968, 1992) produced classic accounts of the complexity of African American family forms. However, with growing awareness and acceptance of same-gender relationships and various combinations of family figures, current notions of family organization have evolved even further. Families with two male parents, two female parents, or combinations of biological and nonbiological parentage with same-gender relationships must be considered in addressing the needs of African American families as a whole.

The context for the African American behavioral trends that have been examined in this chapter has changed as the rest of the U.S. population has begun to approximate African American patterns. This is particularly the case for female labor force participation. In 1965, White women were much less likely than Black women to be employed—34 percent versus 42 percent, respectively, of women over 17 years of age (U.S. Bureau of the Census, 1979, Table 45). In 1997, labor force participation rates of White and Black women were almost comparable at 60 percent versus 64 percent, respectively (U.S. Bureau of Labor Statistics, 1997, Table A-2). The same is true for married couple employment. In 1970, both the wife and the husband held jobs in 51 percent of Black couples compared with 38 percent of White couples (U.S. Bureau of the Census, 1970). By 1990, dual employment characterized 53 percent of Black and 49 percent of White married couples (U.S. Bureau of the Census, 1992). There is also convergence in single person living arrangements. In 1970, less than 2 percent of Blacks lived alone compared with 15 percent of Whites (U.S. Bureau of the Census, 1970); in 1997, the percentage of households containing people who lived alone had reached about 25 percent for both Blacks and Whites (U.S. Bureau of the Census, 1999b).

In sum, there has been a change in the construction of family and in the living arrangements of African Americans as a whole, particularly regarding marital and childbearing behavior. The economic inequities associated with different family forms have greatly worsened over the past 30 years. Without making judgments about the kinds of family arrangements that society or any part of it deems superior and worthy of support and encouragement, it is clear from this review that there has been a recent, rapid decline in the economic well-being of African American children. A large proportion of African American families are impoverished, and those with children are in the worst of circumstances. Furthermore, African American women are shouldering a much greater share of the burden of household maintenance and the raising of children than they did previously.

UNDERSTANDING CHANGE AND DIFFERENCE

How should these shifts in African American family formation and organization be interpreted? To what forces or conditions should they be attributed? A marked distinction exists between theorizing about family formation changes that are society-wide and those that are more specific to African Americans. The broader conceptualizations center on two categories of conditions as causative: the shift among Americans to a more individualistic orientation in which the needs of others are not prioritized (e.g., Rossi, 1987) and converging global economic trends. It has been suggested that the drive in capitalist systems to depress wages creates the need for more salaried employees within households, thereby placing more pressure on husbands and wives and leaving less time for parents to meet the needs of children (Hochschild, 1995; Schor, 1991). At the same time, as women's economic opportunities have expanded and their income potential has risen relative to men's, their economic dependence on men has declined (Bianchi, 1995). These forces decrease the incentive to marry and destabilize existing marriages. Although logical on its face, there seems to be little empirical support for the "female economic independence" theory (Oppenheimer, Blossfeld, and Wackerow, 1995), and women with greater economic potential appear to be more likely to marry. However, Wetzel (1995) reverses this causal ordering, arguing that it is because of delayed marriage and the growing risk of divorce that women have an increased incentive to earn money.

Recent discussions about the origins of current trends in African American family formation, while related in some respects to the larger societal arguments, center on a different set of themes. Features of the debate bear a striking resemblance to the earlier controversy sparked by the writings of sociologist E. Franklin Frazier (1957) and anthropologist Melville Herskovits (1970) that took place before the evolution of current trends. Although it is the dramatic change in the family formation of White Americans that has instigated the current family values debate, it is the perceived distinction between the behavior of Blacks and Whites that is motivating family policy reform (a point that I will address at greater length later). Indeed, the concerns of Frazier and Herskovits specifically centered on how African American families differed from White families. Frazier viewed the differences as a consequence of the harsh, destructive experience of slavery, while Herskovits regarded many of the distinctive features of Black family structure as West African cultural retentions. Of course, today's discourse is not so dichotomized, and gendered perspectives have at least informed the debate, although an analysis of family change that recognizes and truly integrates the functions of race, class, and gender is yet to be offered.

The following sections briefly describe the more dominant among current perspectives on change, placing particular emphasis on those that have been used to justify shifts in social policy. The theories are categorized according to the hypothesized primary cause of family change. Six dominant types are identified: circumstantial economic; circumstantial demographic; circumstantial structural; sociohistorical/cultural; failed social policy; and attitudinal shifts. Importantly, theories with diametrically opposed interpretations and remedies can be of fundamentally the same type.

Circumstantial Economic

One argument is associated most directly with sociologist William Julius Wilson (1987, 1996), but also offered in a different, related form by economists William Darity and Samuel Myers (1986/87, 1995). It holds that African Americans are less likely to marry or stay married because the increasing economic marginality of Black males has made them less attractive as potential husbands; Black males, in turn, are less interested in becoming husbands because they are constrained in their ability to perform the provider role in marriage. Although used primarily to explain the social consequences of the disintegrating economic base of inner cities, the theory has been tested by others in connection with the decline of marriage among African Americans generally.

Some research has shown that the economic viability of African American men is related to their marital behavior (Testa and Krogh, 1995; Tucker and Taylor, 1989) and that provider-role concerns affect marital success for Black men (Hatchett, Veroff, and Douvan, 1995). However, other studies suggest that declines in the pool of economically viable men only partially explain African American marital patterns over the past 40 years (e.g., Ellwood and Rodda, 1991; Mare and Winship, 1991; Wood, 1995). It should be noted that an economic effect on marriage has not been observed among Mexican Americans (Oropesa, Lichter, and Anderson, 1994). Wilson now argues that the long-term impact of a decaying inner-city economy has been the transformation of norms supporting husband-wife families and the weakening of social sanctions against nonmarital births (Wilson, 1996; Early, 1996). This suggests that joblessness has both direct and indirect effects on family formation behavior that standard empirical assessments cannot directly observe. That is, the statistical relationship (or lack thereof) between joblessness and marriage rates addresses neither the evolution of alternative value systems resulting from economic disadvantage nor the dimensions of community experience that support or sanction particular behaviors.

There is other evidence that attempts to test for the impact of joblessness by examining only direct effects are faulty. Sampson (1995) analyzed census data for 171 cities and found that high levels of male unavailability (due to unemployment and low gender ratios) led to greater family disruption, which in turn led to higher rates of violence. More recently, medical researchers at the University of California found evidence suggesting that the level of joblessness in a community is directly related to gang activities (*Los Angeles Times,* October 28, 1997).

Circumstantial Demographic

Guttentag and Secord (1983) offered the provocative view that the decline in African American gender ratios that began in the 1920s played a major role in current Black marital and childbearing behavior. This decline is rooted in higher Black male mortality that is now exacerbated by the extraordinary levels of incarceration of young Black men (Mauer and Huling, 1995), an issue that is addressed at length in Chapter 9 of this volume, "Race, Crime, and Punishment: Old Controversies and New Challenges." From a sociohistorical perspective, Guttentag and Secord (1983) argue that imbalanced gender ratios throughout time have had major societal consequences. Male shortages have led to higher rates of "singlehood," divorce, nonmarital births, adultery, and transient relationships; less commitment among men to relationships; lower societal value on marriage and the family; and a rise in feminism. Although this argument has been viewed with considerable skepticism, it is closely related to the demographic notion of "marriage squeeze" first introduced two decades earlier to describe the decrease in the availability of marriage partners for female, mainly White, members of the baby boom generation (Glick, Heer, and Beresford, 1963). According to this view, the delays in marriage and lower marriage rates that began in the late 1960s were due to the shortage of partners for women that resulted from the gradual increase in birthrates after World War II coupled with the tendency of women to marry slightly older men. Baby boom women were therefore seeking husbands from older, smaller cohorts.

Epenshade (1985) argued that because Black marital decline has been recent, but the gender ratio has been declining since 1920, the phenomena cannot be related. Yet a number of researchers have found support for particular aspects of Guttentag's and Secord's (1983) speculations. In fact, Sampson (1995) observed that the gender ratio was a much stronger predictor of family formation than the male employment rate. Similarly, using the National Survey of Black Americans data set, Keicolt and Fossett (1995) found that the gender ratio affected the likelihood that Black women would have ever been married and that ever-married Black women would be separated or divorced. Furthermore, an aggregate level analysis of Louisiana cities and counties demonstrated that the gender ratio had strong positive effects on the percentage of Black women who were married with spouse present, the rate of marital births per 1,000 Black women age 20-29, the percentage of husband-wife families, and the percentage of children living in husband-wife families. Keicolt and Fossett also observed that the incidence of fewer men relative to women living in a location was associated with an increase in nonmarital births. Similarly, South (1996), using National Longitudinal Survey data, found that marriage among Black women was accelerated by increased percentages of employed men in the local marriage pool, although he also observed that, paradoxically, greater percentages of males in the respondent's high school increased nonmarital birth.

The predictions of marriage based on the male availability perspective and the male marriageability view can be precisely the opposite for higher income African American men. Such men are numerically scarce, which would discourage them from marrying (because they are in demand and can play the field), but they are also the most marriageable (in economic terms). Findings from the 21-city survey indicate that economic concerns and availability concerns can be influential in family formation behavior and attitudes (James, 1997).

The decreased availability of Black men due to high levels of criminal justice system involvement raises other issues of family welfare and maintenance. That is, the absence of potential partners for heterosexual women is but one aspect of the impact of the increased criminalization of Black men (and, increasingly, Black women) on the broader community. In addition to the stress of dealing with the criminal justice process (financially, legally, and so forth), families often lose a key economic provider, a source of socioemotional support, and a father figure. This obviously places a strain on existing relationships. Lidell (1998) examined the mental health correlates and adaptive behavior of African American women whose husbands or nonmarital partners were imprisoned. She found high levels of stress among the women as indicated by a range of physical symptoms, as well as practical difficulties such as transportation, financial problems, and dealing with the reactions of children to their father's absence.

Circumstantial Structural

It has become popular in political circles to attribute increased poverty and welfare dependence among African American children to the structural changes brought about by marital decline. That is, the increased "feminization of poverty" is said to stem largely from the fact that because women make much lower salaries than men, when they decide to "go it alone," their households, especially children, suffer accordingly. Perhaps due to its simplicity and the implicit suggestion that such women are largely responsible for their plight (by eschewing marriage), the argument has informed the conservative welfare reform movement, e.g., the Personal Responsibility Act (Republican National Committee, 1994).

However, the available evidence strongly contradicts this view. Hernandez (1993) demonstrates that very little of the economic decline in African American households headed by single women is due to changes in household structure. He shows that if the proportion of children living in mother-only families in 1959 had the same poverty rates as children living in two parent homes in 1988, poverty rates would have been only 24 percent to 30 percent less at the earlier date. But because many of the absent fathers would certainly not have been able to make financial contributions to households sufficient to lift their families out of poverty, the actual proportion accounted for by structural changes would be even lower. A similar conclusion about race-specific economic inequality is reached in the Economic Report of the President (Council of Economic Advisers, 1998). By adjusting income and poverty rates for changes in family structure since 1967, the report shows that only 20 percent of the difference in Black-White income and poverty levels is due to an increase in the proportion of families headed by women alone.

Sandefur's and Mosley's (1997) review of the literature on family structure and children's well-being reaches a somewhat different conclusion. They argue that divorced and single parent households have less access to certain economic, parental, and community resources because of the accommodations required by lone parenting. These include less access to fathers' incomes (because of the low level of compliance with child support orders), the detachment of many nonresidential fathers from children, and the increased time demands on the custodial parent. They also assert that two parent families have better access to community resources, such as day care centers, better schools, and parks, due in large part to higher salaries. Again, I question whether access to many of these resources would be improved by the presence of an impoverished father. However, those findings suggest that higher income Black families benefit in certain ways when marriages are maintained.

Another problem with the structural argument is highlighted by Burton's (1998) elaborate study of poor adolescent mothers. Examining both familial and neighborhood contexts over a period of five years, she documented the fluidity among households and neighborhoods that exists in such circumstances. Notions of family were not limited to blood or marital ties or to residential status; a fictive aunt who lived across the street might be as much a part of a family home as actual residents. Moreover, the young women and their families in Burton's study were highly transient, moving within a fairly small city among different neighborhoods and to different household constellations. The empirical snapshots that make up much of the work on this subject do not begin to fully recognize the actual construction and maintenance of Black families and their support systems.

Sociohistorical/Cultural

Recently, some historians and historical sociologists have revisited the question of African American family structure and function during slavery and at the turn of the century. Stevenson (1995, 1996) has been particularly instrumental in presenting a revisionist perspective on family life during slavery. She has critiqued prevailing historical treatments of Black family structure (e.g., Gutman, 1976) that emphasized similarities between European and African American family forms. On the basis of her analysis of plantation records from Virginia, she argues that the slavery experience created and fostered critical differences between African American and White families that have persisted and that have led to current racial differences in family formation behavior. She writes:

> The basic premise asserted here is that the Black family under slavery differed profoundly from that of European Americans structurally and in the ways in which family members functioned as contributors, administrators, and recipients of family resources. The slave family was not a static, imitative institution that necessarily favored one form of family organization over another. Rather, it was a diverse phenomenon, sometimes assuming several forms even among the slaves of one community. Moreover, this diversity cannot in itself be equated with a weak or flawed institution, although some variety certainly was part of the African American response to the difficulties of slave life. It also was a response to the slave's cultural difference. Far from having a negative impact, the diversity of slave marriage and family norms, as a measure of the slave family's enormous adaptive potential, allowed the slave and the slave family to survive (29).

Historical sociologists have found some support for this perspective. In a series of studies, McDaniel and Morgan and their associates (McDaniel, 1994; McDaniel and Morgan, 1996; Morgan et al., 1993) used census data to conduct comparative examinations of living arrangements of African Americans and Whites just after the turn of the 20th century. They observed significant racial differences in a number of respects. For example, although both African Americans and European Americans were likely to violate the norm of mother-child coresidence when crises developed, African American mothers were more likely to live separately from their children even when a crisis situation did not exist. They argued that the differences stem from cultural continuities of West African and European traditions. Although the sociohistorical view provides a foundation for certain forms of African American family organization, it does not explain the recent dramatic shift.

There is contemporary evidence that conceptualizations of family organization in African American communities accommodate a greater variety of forms than those presented as being characteristic of middle class Whites, including the incorporation of nonblood and extraresidential ties (e.g., Billingsley, 1968, 1992; Shimkin, Shimkin, and Frate, 1978; Wilson et al., 1995). This flexibility also extends to child residence, as others "take in" children to deal with crises and needs. Generally, these findings and observations are viewed as evidence of the adaptive function of more flexible kin structures in the face of severe economic hardship and racial discrimination.

Failed Social Policy

According to scholars from very different philosophical positions, federal social policy of the 1960s and 1970s created conditions that have destabilized and otherwise threatened African American families. Jewell (1988) argued that the social and economic policies initiated by President John F. Kennedy and expanded by President Lyndon B. Johnson were well-intended and created to combat chronic poverty and racial discrimination. Among the well-known programs developed during this era were Aid to Families with Dependent Children (AFDC), Comprehensive Employment Training Act, Job Corps, Medicaid, and Work Incentive Programs. Jewell contended that these programs were not designed to remove the social barriers that prevented African American families from moving into mainstream American society and, further, that there were no mechanisms in place to assess and correct the shortcomings of these initiatives. Jewell also contended that the programs fostered a dependency that supplanted the functions of traditional institutions, including two parent families, extended families, Black-owned businesses, and Black-controlled educational institutions. Because it appeared, erroneously, that the roadblocks to progress had been removed (via affirmative action and other strategies), the blame for lack of progress shifted to the individual, rather than to society. This set the stage for the conservative trend in social policy that followed.

Murray (1984) also blamed liberal social policy, but from an entirely different standpoint. He argued in his now-familiar critique of the U.S. welfare system, *Losing Ground*, that the social programs of the 1960s and 1970s did more harm than good to the poor by removing incentives to work and to marry. That is, receiving welfare benefits became more attractive than working in low paying jobs, and the availability of AFDC payments reduced or eliminated reliance on fathers for support, thereby discouraging marriage. Murray's views have been critiqued by many (e.g., Prager, 1988; Rury, 1986), yet his arguments and ideas have clearly informed efforts to transform the nature of government assistance to families, e.g., Contract with America (Republican National Committee, 1994).

Here again, however, the preponderance of the evidence does not support this view. It has often been pointed out that the rise in nonmarital births and mother-only families took place at precisely the time when real AFDC payments were decreasing, which makes implausible the assertion that welfare availability encouraged single parenting (Darity and Myers, 1995). Hernandez (1993) showed that the increase in the absolute value of welfare programs after 1959 resulted in an increase of only 1-2 percentage points in both the proportion of children living in mother-only families and in the overall child poverty rate by 1988.

Attitudinal Shifts

Still other theorists argue that changing family formation behavior reflects significant shifts in societal views of the institution of marriage and gender roles. With respect to the first, there has been some question about whether marriage is still highly valued in U.S. society generally and by African Americans in particular. Thornton (1989) reviewed results from a number of major data sets from the late 1950s to the middle 1980s and found a substantial weakening over the period in the "normative imperative" to marry, to remain married, to have children, to be faithful to one's spouse, and to differentiate male and female roles. However, he found no significant shifts in the desire to marry eventually or the desire to remain single or childless, with more than 90 percent of respondents typically expecting to marry. These studies as a whole indicate that Americans in general and African Americans in particular have become increasingly more accepting of singlehood, divorce, and nonmarital birth (e.g., Thornton and Freedman, 1982), but that valuation of marriage remains high, extending even to the near universal desire to marry.

Table 7-11 displays data from the Tucker and Mitchell-Kernan 21-city survey relevant to this point. Multiple classification analyses show no ethnic differences in the value placed on marriage whether there is control for age, education, and income. Furthermore, there are no ethnic differences in the desire to marry some day or in the expectation of marrying. Most notably, there is no difference between African Americans and Whites in the value placed on having children when married. Both groups believe rather strongly that one should be married when bearing children. Mexican Americans place even greater emphasis on marital births.

These findings show that the expressed values of African Americans regarding aspects of family formation appear to be no different than those held by other Americans, especially when demographic differences are controlled. In addition, although African American parents are perceived to be somewhat less disapproving of nonmarital births than the other groups, the respondents in all three ethnic groups strongly believe that both their mothers and fathers would disapprove.

Bell-Kaplan's (1997) ethnographic work on Black teenage mothers in a low income community is illuminating on this point. Indeed, her rich account of the complex forces that surround the girls' decisions and behaviors clearly shows that families neither sanctioned nor condoned the pregnancies and that mothers made their disappointment in their daughters' actions obvious. As Bell-Kaplan observes, the girls' pregnancies broke "several important and long-standing cultural norms greatly valued by adult Black mothers" (69). Although the immediate motivation for pregnancy in her study was a sense of isolation and being unloved (so they "created" a relationship), the larger cause was the absence of resources (e.g., adequate education) to support alternative choices. The mothers' strong negative reaction to the pregnancies was also a response to new demands on limited financial and personal resources.

TABLE 7-11

Family Formation Values by Race/Ethnicity, Controlling for Age, Income, and Education, Results from 21-City Survey

Importance of marriage (1-10 scale)

	n	mean	eta	mean adjusted for covariates	beta
African Americans	1,366	7.84		7.85	
Mexican Americans	224	8.33		8.30	
White Americans	1,792	7.72	.07	7.72	.06

Importance for "you personally" to get married some day? (1-10 scale)
(never married only)

	n	mean	eta	mean adjusted for covariates	beta
African Americans	510	7.11		7.11	
Mexican Americans	55	7.03	7.06		
White Americans	525	7.11	.02	6.96	.01

Would like to get married some day (1-10 agreement)
(never married only)

	n	mean	eta	mean adjusted for covariates	beta
African Americans	510	7.60		7.62	
Mexican Americans	55	7.99		7.74	
White Americans	525	7.83	.04	7.83	.04

Expectation of marrying (1-10)
(singles only)

	n	mean	eta	mean adjusted for covariates	beta
African Americans	829	6.47		6.52	
Mexican Americans	95	7.33		7.11	
White Americans	850	6.58	.06	6.56	.04

Importance of being married when having children
(1-10 scale)

	n	mean	eta	mean adjusted for covariates	beta
African Americans	1,370	8.21		8.22	
Mexican Americans	226	8.56		8.60	
White Americans	1,794	8.22	.03	8.21	.03

(continued)

TABLE 7-11 continued

Importance of an adequate income for a successful marriage
(1-10)

	n	mean	eta	mean adjusted for covariates	beta
African Americans	1,375	8.57		8.50	
Mexican Americans	225	7.96		7.78	
White Americans	1,795	7.53	.26	7.60	.22

Perceived maternal approval of nonmarital birth
(1-10)

	n	mean	eta	mean adjusted for covariates	beta
African Americans	1,341	4.48		4.43	
Mexican Americans	221	4.29		4.10	
White Americans	1,761	3.82	.10	3.89	.08

Perceived paternal approval of nonmarital birth
(1-10)

	n	mean	eta	mean adjusted for covariates	beta
African Americans	1,235	4.33		4.31	
Mexican Americans	206	3.97		3.83	
White Americans	1,673	3.70	.10	3.73	.10

Source: Tucker and Mitchell-Kernan, in press.

Strong racial differences on one attitudinal dimension have been found that may provide clues to some of the behavioral patterns. African American respondents viewed having adequate finances as much more critical to the success of marriage than did either Mexican American or White respondents. We found precisely the same pattern in 1989 in a similar survey of southern Californians (Tucker and Mitchell-Kernan, 1995b). These findings (supported by our other results on economic context) suggest that African Americans are cognizant of and particularly sensitive to the influence of economic hardship on Black marriages—so much so that a reluctance to enter into marriage and face economic and emotional risk has developed. Perhaps because of this, the opposition to nonmarital birth, although still quite strong, is no longer as extreme in African American communities as it once was.

There has also been greater discussion of the part played by changing gender role expectations in family formation behavior. A number of feminist writers have criticized both the Wilson male marriageability hypothesis as well as the "welfare dependency" theorists for assuming either implicitly or explicitly that "restoring" male headship to homes is the key to building strong families (e.g., Baca Zinn and Eitzen, 1992; Blum and Deussen, 1996; Crenshaw, 1989). Phenomenological investigation has shown that some poor and working class African American women share a notion of community-based independence that emphasizes kin-based support networks and long-term partnerships with men, but not necessarily marriage (Blum and Deussen, 1996; Stack, 1974). Indeed, Stack's classic ethnography of a low income African American community showed that marriage could be disruptive to fragile kin-based social economies.

Analysis of our 21-city data shows interesting trends in the conceptualization of the male role in families (Taylor, Tucker, and Mitchell-Kernan, in press). We found greater investment by African Americans and Mexican Americans than Whites (and by women compared to men) in male responsibility for economic provision, despite strong support for the work role of women. This finding is ironic given the lesser likelihood that men of color would have the financial means to support families, and it reflects the greater economic needs of Black and Latino women.

Subramanian, Tucker, and Mitchell-Kernan (under review), and Tucker and Mitchell-Kernan (under review) address other aspects of the same issue. The first paper suggests that men have begun to prioritize finding an economically viable mate, due perhaps to the increased economic pressures on families to have two workers. The second paper finds that increased reliance on dual incomes, coupled with economic insecurities (i.e., gender-specific community unemployment levels) are reshaping gender role expectations within relationships. Among African American men and women, predictors of marital/relationship happiness and commitment include satisfaction with a partner's economic contributions, as well as community-level economic indicators. For example, Black men's relationship well-being was shaped by Black female unemployment levels, which were more predictive than their own income. The paper interprets this finding as an indication that economic uncertainty or the perception of economic risk (as conveyed by community-level unemployment) may be even more damaging to African American relationships than economic status. The findings on the salience of financial concerns in marriage further support this notion. The high divorce rate of African Americans could be both a consequence of and a contributor to economic concerns. That is, as financial problems are seen as a factor in marital dissolution, that perception discourages others from making the effort.

Summary

Perspectives on the source of changing patterns of African American family formation are highly divergent; clearly, no one factor can explain the complex phenomenon of rapidly changing African American marital behavior. Yet, some theories have broader empirical support than others. There is convincing work attesting to the long-standing structural differences between African American and Euro-American families, which are likely to be both adaptive and cultural (e.g., the reliance on extended family systems). Also, the critical role of economic factors seems well-established, even if the precise process by which this occurs remains unspecified. Further, there is evidence that marriage market forces do constrain African American women's family formation choices. Despite the continued high value placed on marriage and marital childbearing, it is clear that tolerance for a greater range of family lifestyles has increased.

WHAT IS THE PROBLEM?

It is likely that some consensus can be achieved about the areas of family formation in which change has been most conspicuous. However, it is more difficult to reach concurrence on the aspects of change that are considered to be problematic. To construct remedies for even one of the least controversial issues—that of the increasing impoverishment of Black children—requires making certain value-laden judgments. Several of the more dominant theories about changing families contain the either tacit or explicit assumption that a working husband would address many of the difficulties of poor women and children. Earlier in this chapter, I discussed the problems associated with such a premise from an economic standpoint. (Although I am reminded here of Barbara Ehrenreich's (1986) tongue-in-cheek assertion that because of the economic limitations of poor Black men, impoverished Black women would have to be married to three such men—simultaneously—to achieve an average family income.) However, a belief in the curative function of marriage for poor women and children persists and has led to troubling legislative initiatives. In 1998, Arizona Representative Mark Anderson sponsored a state bill that would have appropriated $2 million for a pilot program aimed at welfare recipients "interested in pursuing a career track in home management." The proposed program would have included teaching women to understand the "economic and personal benefits of marriage" (*Arizona Daily Star*, February 2, 1998). Labeled the "how-to-get-a-husband program" by opponents, the bill was defeated, but Anderson vowed to revive it.

Although the empirical evidence indicates that very little of the increase in child poverty has been due to the greater prevalence of mother-children only households, the literature is less definitive on the association between household structure and the socioemotional well-being of children. This question is at the core of the current family studies' controversy. Amato and Booth (1997) report results demonstrating that family conflict and divorce have long-term negative social and psychological effects on children. Yet, Ahrons and Rodgers (1987) found that research as a whole reveals that the majority of children of divorced families appear to adjust within the normal range. According to Hernandez's (1993) review of the broader literature, there is evidence that children from single parent homes are more likely to "be exposed to parental stress, exhibit behavioral problems, receive or need professional psychological help, perform poorly in school, and experience health problems" (57). There is consensus, however, that highly conflictual relationships are more damaging to children than is single parenthood.

Research on this question is plagued by methodological limitations, including the fact that many studies were not designed to disentangle the effects on children of economic deprivation versus being raised by one parent. The studies also tended to focus more on divorce than on other forms of single parenthood. Moreover, true assessments of the difference between life with a specific mother and father compared to life with only one parent are impossible to carry out, so one can never determine whether life with the absent parent would have been better. Finally, single parenthood has become a loaded, almost pejorative term that in reality covers a range of very different living arrangements. In such situations, the availability of and proximity of other adults who can contribute to childrearing may vary substantially. Whether other family members or "family-like" friends and acquaintances live next door or across the street may be critical factors to consider when assessing children's environments.

These studies also do not simulate the decisionmaking process of parents, mothers in particular. It is important to note that nonmarital child-bearing is now overwhelmingly adult behavior. The proportion of births to girls under age 18, which should be considered a distinctive phenomenon, is declining. Adult women who choose to bear children are often making decisions that are rational from their perspective, given their options. As discussed, heterosexual African American women have a narrower range of partnering options than their White counterparts: there are fewer African American men to choose from, and those available have fewer economic resources. At the same time, African American men have more mating options given the larger number of Black women and the greater inclination among Black men to date and marry women of other ethnic groups. Poor heterosexual women face additional constraints on partnering because the men available to them have even less incentive to marry given provider role demands. The 21-city survey noted above shows that, although the value placed on marriage as an institution is not affected by income levels, poorer men are significantly less likely to feel that getting married is important to them "personally" (Taylor, Tucker, and Mitchell-Kernan, in press).

This line of thought emphasizes the barriers to relationship formation for Black women, but presumes that marriage or a long-term relationship is the goal. There may be costs associated with such commitments. With record numbers of young African American men imprisoned, on parole, or on probation (Mauer and Huling, 1995) and epidemic levels of drug addiction, the legal bond of marriage with someone experiencing such difficulties may be an emotional and financial risk. Coontz and Franklin (1997) also point out that because homicide is the leading cause of death among Black males age 15 to 24, "many won't live long enough to be father figures." Burton (1998) reports that many of the young men in her study do not expect to reach the age of 25. These facts discourage long-term commitments.

The "American family" with its attendant problems is now the center-piece of a broader sociopolitical agenda, which is evident by the ongoing alignment of family researchers via membership in organizations designed to influence public policy. A number of social scientists have become known for their advocacy of marriage (e.g., Glenn, 1997a, 1997b, 1998; Popenoe, 1996; Waite, 1996). Some are affiliated with the Council on Families, which is sponsored by the Institute for American Values—a self-described "think tank" dedicated to examining the "status and future of the family" (Institute for American Values, 1999) and viewed by many as politically conservative. The Council on Families, designed to influence policy, has released two highly controversial reports in recent years, including *Marriage in America: A Report to the Nation* in 1995 and *Closed Hearts, Closed Minds: The Textbook Story of Marriage* (Glenn, 1997a). The latter condemned college-level marriage and family life textbooks, citing their content as both cause and result of the weakening of marriage in society. Partly in response to these developments, the more politically moderate to liberal Council on Contemporary Families (CCF) was formed in 1997. Its stated mission is "to reframe the current ideology about 'family values' and to promote political agendas that value all forms of contemporary families" (Council on Contemporary Families, 1997). The CCF seeks to infuse the current discussion of family with a greater appreciation of the diversity of family forms and values.

In the context of this debate, the nature of problem designation and remedy establishes the broader social agenda. If one accepts the view that marriage improves individuals and families, then one set of remedies would be directed toward encouraging marriage and providing supports for existing relationships. Another set would focus more specifically on the employment prospects of men, including education and training. The alternative view, which takes issue with the notion that marriage is the solution to a range of social ills, would focus on remedies that address the limited economic opportunities for poor women and poor men. Addressing this problem would require an entirely different set of resources and would include challenging the current system of public education, providing enhanced job training opportunities, and improving salary structure (e.g., raising the minimum wage). This specification of the problem would have to include an emphasis on the care of children, including improving prenatal health and providing affordable child care.

A separate issue that is often enmeshed in the family structure debate is the role of fathers in raising children. No one would argue against encouraging greater participation of fathers in the lives of their children. Jackson (1993) studied Black, single, employed but low income mothers with three- to four-year-old children and found that greater role strain and depression were associated with having no postsecondary education and having a male child. She interprets this finding as an indication that raising boys is particularly stressful for women with multiple roles and fewer educational resources. The special risks for African American boys generally and especially those in impoverished communities are well-known. These findings suggest that it may be difficult for some overburdened mothers to provide guidance in the successful negotiation of the demands of masculinity in such settings. The involvement of successful male role models could help address this need. Father-daughter relationships are also critical, and although the subject has been little studied, there is evidence that this relationship is key in a daughter's development of healthy relationships with men in adulthood (Cochran, 1997).

Another view identifies the problem as a dysfunctional value system that has presumably developed in chronically depressed communities. It is suggested that when jobs are scarce, when large proportions of the population are welfare dependent, and when most households are without male heads, a value system develops that is incompatible with traditional avenues of success (e.g., work ethic). Wilson (1996) views the reshaping of community values as a casualty of the disappearance of jobs from inner cities. Yet there is recent evidence that the attitudes of impoverished African Americans toward employment, family, and welfare are not distinct from those of the nonpoor (Jones and Luo, in press). Still, most job training programs (including those developed to address the imperatives of welfare reform) emphasize instilling or reinforcing values and behaviors thought to be consistent with workplace demands.

Although rates of birth among African American teens have decreased significantly in recent decades, some view early childbearing as a core problem in African American family formation. However, several new studies question the notion that early childbearing impairs the life chances of poor women. In an innovative study that compares the life experiences of young African American women who bore children as teenagers versus those in similar circumstances who miscarried, Hotz, Mullin, and Sanders (1997) found that teenage childbearing did not limit the life chances of teenage mothers. In fact, teenage childbearing seemed to enhance the women's economic attainment relative to those who did not have live births. It appears that, within the context of impoverished communities, bearing children early allows women to focus on self-development later. Women of all ages could benefit from adequate family planning and reproductive health services that minimize unintended pregnancies and ensure healthier children and mothers.

Although differing frameworks and focuses have generated competing assessments of needs, the following are areas in which the situation of African Americans has substantially worsened in recent decades and which are key impediments to the well-being of African American families:

- the extraordinary levels of child impoverishment;

- the dire economic straits of families maintained by women without partners;

- the decline of living wage jobs for those without advanced degrees;

- the extraordinary levels of imprisonment and other criminal justice involvement by Black men and, increasingly, Black women;

- the need for greater involvement of fathers and other significant male figures in childrearing;

- the diminished mate availability for heterosexual African American women;

- the need for resources to help maintain existing marriages; and

- the increased grandparental responsibility for the care and raising of grandchildren.

CONSIDERATIONS FOR AFRICAN AMERICAN FAMILY POLICY

In this last section, I will discuss what I believe are necessary considerations for a new social policy regarding African American families. Specific policy recommendations are not presented, but I will outline the concerns that must be embodied in a family policy that addresses the needs of African Americans in the new millennium. In this task, the substantial efforts already made by others in the field must certainly be considered. For example, Hill, with a group of well-known family scholars, conducted a research-based assessment of the African American family at the beginning of the 1990s (Hill et al., 1993). They offered a set of "action implications" that included stimulating economic growth; achieving full employment; expanding job training, subsidized jobs, and child care; reforming AFDC and foster care; enhancing child support, education, and physical and mental health; enhancing public housing; and expanding low income housing. Wilson (1996) focused on joblessness as the core factor in the crisis of family among the urban poor and proposed a series of economic and educational reforms, including national performance standards for public schools; support for disadvantaged schools (equalization of resources); family policies that support children and reinforce the learning system (including high quality preschool and child support assurance programs); school-to-work transition programs; greater city-suburban cooperation; and increased federal support of cities. Drawing upon these reviews and others and the assessments presented earlier in this chapter, I suggest that the following are critical considerations in the development of effective family policy for African Americans.

Recognition of Diversity

With the increased diversity of Blacks in the United States, it seems clear that no single policy or set of policies can address the needs of the population as a whole. Single working mothers and fathers have different needs than do two parent families. Same-gender parents may face issues that are different from those confronting most heterosexual parents. Foreign-born Black families often struggle with problems and issues associated with the immigration process, including the separation of family members. This suggests that policy cannot be conceptualized as African American family-specific. Policy must be problem-focused.

A Holistic Approach

A number of observers have emphasized the need for family policy that is holistic and integrated rather than a set of piecemeal, disconnected efforts (e.g., Hill et al., 1993; National Task Force on African American Men and Boys, 1996). As the mosaic of attempts to address the needs of Black families becomes more complex and idiosyncratic, the need for coordination is greater than ever.

Economic Development

Despite the various ways in which policymakers, scholars, and other observers have chosen to define the problems facing African American families, a root cause of many familial difficulties is economic deprivation caused ultimately by a history of racial oppression and, more recently, by the disastrous impact on inner cities of the postindustrial global economy. Economic issues are addressed directly in Chapter 2, "Demographic, Economic, and Social Trends." Suffice it to note here that a range of recommendations has been repeatedly identified as central to improving the situation of African Americans, including the need for greater economic development in inner cities, the guarantee of a living wage, adequate training, and the elimination of discrimination in the workplace. Yet family development occurs in a larger context, and adequacy of economic resources is important, but not sufficient. Evidence citing the harmful effects of economic uncertainty suggests that job security and the expectation of employment in a given environment are also essential ingredients for healthy families.

Support for Children

Proper support for the emotional, physical, and intellectual development of all children is an essential consideration for family policy. Wilson's (1996) focus on academic preparation is essential in the current global economy that demands more highly skilled workers than ever before. An enormous number of programs currently exist to address the needs of children. For example, the Black Community Crusade for Children, sponsored by the Children's Defense Fund, offers the Freedom Schools, a program that sends trained college students to work as teachers, counselors, and role models for less advantaged children in the summer. This program provides children with meals, academic and cultural enrichment, and supervised recreation. Similar academic and social mentoring programs are being conducted by churches, community organizations, educational institutions, corporations, and others. Harnessing and evaluating such efforts, clarifying goals, and expanding successful programs should be one aim of effective family policy.

Another area of policy consideration is child care, including affordable, convenient, and safe care, as well as after-school care and homework supervision. This is particularly problematic for middle-school age children (when such care is often unavailable through traditional mechanisms at a time when children are at particular risk for engaging in inappropriate activities). Given the conflict between school schedules and most adult work shifts, many children of all races and all income levels are now left on their own after school. In some communities, after-school homework clubs are bridging the gap between school and home. Such facilities address both the needs of working parents and the academic requirements of children.

Support for Marriage

Given the exceptional rates of separation and divorce among Black Americans, family policy should address the distinctive strains on African American marriages. Although research has shown that Black marriages are especially vulnerable to economic stress, there is evidence that the cause of strain is not solely inadequate financial resources. Economic insecurity and cultural expectations about appropriate gender role behavior are also instrumental. Attempts to strengthen families should consider how to reshape cultural gender role expectations to better reflect the demands and realities of modern life.

Confronting Criminal Justice Inequities

A comprehensive family policy must also address the devastating impact on families of the increased criminal justice system involvement of African American men and women. Such policies would confront the root causes of the current situation (i.e., systemic inequities and the lack of viable alternatives for youth) as well as the immediate consequences of incarceration for individuals and family members.

Other Concerns

Although the above topics are intended to cover the basic survival needs of families, other researchers have discussed the more spiritual and socioemotional needs of the broader community. Sudarkasa (1997) emphasizes instilling and reinforcing a commitment to the "Rs"—respect, responsibility, restraint, reciprocity, reason, and reconciliation—that are West African-based principles of family life. She argues that these values sustained extended family structures over the centuries and remain useful for coping with the difficulties facing African American families today. Similarly, the National Task Force on African American Men and Boys has presented a platform for change that emphasizes core values in both the identification of problems and the generation of solutions. Included among the core concepts are civic dialogue; public kinship (the assumption of community as family); moral unity among civic, social, religious, and cultural entities; and the concept of *Polis,* which embodies the establishment and teaching of particular values, manners, morals, and etiquette needed for structuring public life in communities.

It is possible to read this chapter as just another pessimistic recitation of "ills." Although I believe that real reform requires a national commitment that may be lacking in the present political climate, I also believe that the potential for transformation from within is greater today than ever before. Despite some setbacks, people of African descent in the United States are more highly educated and have greater access to economic resources than previous generations. The Black population now includes a thriving middle class, has great philanthropic potential among the economic elite, and has numerous churches and civic organizations with the will and the financial means to effect change. These same characteristics make a galvanized and unified African American population a formidable political presence. It is time that these tools were used to bring about meaningful change in African American family life.

REFERENCES

Ahrons, C.R., and R.H. Rodgers. 1987. *Divorced Families: A Multidisciplinary Developmental View.* New York: W.W. Norton.
Amato, P.R., and A. Booth. 1997. *A Generation at Risk: Growing Up in an Era of Family Upheaval.* Cambridge, Mass.: Harvard University Press.

Baca Zinn, M., and D.S. Eitzen. 1992. *Diversity in Families.* New York: Harper and Row.
Bell-Kaplan, E. 1997. *Not Our Kind of Girl: Unraveling the Myths of Black Teenage Motherhood.* Berkeley, Cal.: University of California Press.
Bennett, N.G., D.E. Bloom, and P.H. Craig. 1989. "The Divergence of Black and White Marriage Patterns." *American Journal of Sociology* 95:692-722.
———. 1992. "American Marriage Patterns in Transition." In *The Changing American Family: Sociological and Demographic Perspectives.* Ed. S.J. South and S.E. Tolnay. Boulder, Col.: Westview.
Bianchi, S. 1995. "Changing Economic Roles of Women and Men." In *State of the Union: America in the 1990s.* Vol. 1, *Economic Trends.* Ed. R. Farley. New York: Russell Sage Foundation, 107-154.
Billingsley, A. 1968. *Black Families in White America.* Englewood Cliffs, N.J.: Prentice-Hall.
———. 1992. *Climbing Jacob's Ladder: The Enduring Legacy of African American Families.* New York: Simon and Schuster.
Blum, L.M., and T. Deussen. 1996. "Negotiating Independent Motherhood: Working-Class African American Women Talk about Marriage and Motherhood." *Gender and Society* 10:199-211.
Burton, L.M. 1998. "Setting the Cadence and Keeping Time: Neighborhood Rhythms and the Lives of Families and Teens." Paper presented to the Social and Community Psychiatry Division, Department of Psychiatry and Biobehavioral Sciences, School of Medicine, University of California, Los Angeles, April 16.
Burton, L.M., and P. Dilworth-Anderson. 1991. "The Intergenerational Roles of Black Americans." *Marriage and Family Review* 16:311-330.
Burton, L.M., and V.L. Bengtson. 1985. "Black Grandmothers: Issues of Timing and Continuity of Roles." In *Grandparenthood.* Ed. V.L. Bengtson and J.F. Robertson. Beverly Hills, Cal.: Sage, 61-77.

Cherlin, A.J. 1981. *Marriage, Divorce, Remarriage.* Cambridge, Mass.: Harvard University Press.
———. 1993. "Nostalgia as Family Policy." *Public Interest* 110:77-84.

———. 1997. "A Reply to Glenn: What's Most Important in a Family Textbook." *Family Relations* 46:209-211.

Children's Defense Fund. 1999. *The Black Community Crusade for Children.* Available from http://www.childrensdefense.org/bccc.html

Cochran, D.L. 1997. "African American Fathers: A Decade Review of the Literature." *Families in Society* (July-August):340-350.

Coontz, S., and D. Franklin. 1997. "When the Marriage Penalty Is Marriage." *New York Times* A23 (N), col. 2.

Council of Economic Advisers. 1998. *The Economic Report of the President.* Office of Management and Budget. Washington, D.C.: U.S. Government Printing Office (GPO). February 10. Available from http://www.access.gpo.gov/omb/omb004.html

Council on Contemporary Families. 1997. "Reframing the Politics of Family Values." Report of the Council on Contemporary Families: Inaugural Conference. Washington, D.C., November 14-17. Available from http://www.slip.net/~ccf/CCF_conference.html

Crenshaw, K. 1989. "Demarginalizing the Intersection of Race and Sex: A Black Feminist Critique of Antidiscrimination Doctrine, Feminist Theory and Antiracist Politics." *The University of Chicago Legal Forum 1989. Feminism in the Law: Theory, Practice and Criticism,* 139-167.

Darity, W.A., Jr., and S.L. Myers, Jr. 1986/87. "Public Policy Trends and the Fate of the Black Family." *Humboldt Journal of Social Relations* 14:134-164.

———. 1995. "Family Structure and the Marginalization of Black Men: Policy Implications." In *The Decline in Marriage Among African Americans: Causes, Consequences and Policy Implications.* Ed. M.B. Tucker and C. Mitchell-Kernan. New York: Russell Sage Foundation, 263-308.

Early, G. 1996. "William Julius Wilson: A Leading Scholar of Urban Poverty Has a Prescription for the Ghetto: Jobs." *Mother Jones* 21(5):20-26.

Ehrenreich, B. 1986. "Two, Three, Many Husbands." *Mother Jones* (July/August):8-9.

Ellwood, D.T., and D.T. Rodda. 1991. *The Hazards of Work and Marriage: The Influence of Male Employment on Marriage Rates.* Working Paper #H-90-5. Cambridge, Mass.: Malcolm Wiener Center for Social Policy, John F. Kennedy School of Government, Harvard University.

Epenshade, T.J. 1985. "Marriage Trends in America: Estimates, Implications, and Underlying Causes." *Population and Development Review* 11:193-245.

Farley, R., Ed. 1995. *State of the Union. America in the 1990s: Social Trends (The 1990 Census Research),* Vol. 2. New York: Russell Sage Foundation.

Flaherty, M.J., L. Facteau, and P. Garver. 1987. "Grandmother Functions in Multigenerational Families: An Exploratory Study of Black Adolescent Mothers and Their Infants." *Maternal Child Nursing Journal* 60:61-73.

Franklin, J.H. 1997. "African American Families: A Historical Note." In *Black Families,* 3rd ed. Ed. H.P. McAdoo. Thousand Oaks, Cal.: Sage.

Frazier, E.F. 1957. *The Negro Family in the United States.* Rev. ed. New York: Macmillan Co.

Glenn, N.D. 1997a. "A Critique of Twenty Families and Marriage and the Family Textbooks." *Family Relations* 46:197-208.

———. 1997b. "A Response to Cherlin, Scanzoni, and Skolnick: Further Discussion of Balance, Accuracy, Fairness, Coverage, and Bias in Family Textbooks." *Family Relations* 46:223-226.

———. 1998. "Closed Hearts, Closed Minds: The Textbook Story of Marriage." *Society* 35:69-79.

Glick, P.C., D.M. Heer, and J.C. Beresford. 1963. "Family Formation and Family Composition: Trends and Prospects." In *Sourcebook in Marriage and the Family*. Ed. M.B. Sussman. New York: Houghton Mifflin, 30-40.

Gutman, H. 1976. *The Black Family in Slavery and Freedom. 1750-1925*. New York: Pantheon Books.

Guttentag, M., and P.F. Secord. 1983. *Too Many Women: The Sex Ratio Question*. Beverly Hills, Cal.: Sage.

Harris, M. 1988. *Culture, People, Nature: An Introduction to General Anthropology*. 5th ed. New York: Harper and Row.

Hatchett, S., J. Veroff, and E. Douvan. 1995. "Marital Instability Among Black and White Couples in Early Marriage." In *The Decline in Marriage Among African-Americans: Causes, Consequences and Policy Implications*. Ed. M.B. Tucker and C. Mitchell-Kernan. New York: Russell Sage Foundation, 177-218.

Hernandez, D.J. 1993. *America's Children: Resources from Family, Government and the Economy*. New York: Russell Sage Foundation.

Herskovits, M. 1970. *The Myth of the Negro Past*. Boston: Beacon.

Hill, R.B., et al. 1993. *Research on African American Families: A Holistic Perspective*. Boston: William Monroe Trotter Institute, University of Massachusetts.

Hochschild, J.L. 1995. *Facing Up to the American Dream: Race, Class, and the Soul of the Nation*. Princeton, N.J.: Princeton University Press.

Hotz, V.J., C.H. Mullin, and S.G. Sanders. 1997. "Bounding Causal Effects Using Data from a Contaminated Natural Experiment: Analyzing the Effects of Teenage Childbearing." *Review of Economic Studies* 64:575-603.

Institute for American Values. 1999. Available from http://www.americanvalues.org/about_iav.html

Jackson, A.P. 1993. "Black, Single Working Mothers in Poverty: Preferences for Employment, Well-being and Perceptions of Preschool-Age Children." *Social Work* 38:1-120.

James, A.D. 1997. "A Multilevel Analysis of Nonmarital Childbearing Among Women." Paper presented at the annual meeting of the American Psychological Association, Chicago.

Jewell, K.S. 1988. *Survival of the Black Family: The Institutional Impact of U.S. Social Policy*. New York: Praeger.

Jones, R., and Y. Luo. In press. "The (Non)culture of Poverty and the Significance of Race." *Sociological Perspectives*.

Kiecolt, K.J., and M.A. Fossett. 1995. "Mate Availability and Marriage among African Americans: Aggregate- and Individual-Level Analyses." In *The Decline in Marriage Among African Americans: Causes, Consequences and Policy Implications*. Ed. M.B. Tucker and C. Mitchell-Kernan. New York: Russell Sage Foundation, 121-135.

Lidell, A. 1998. *Length of Incarceration, Perceived Discrimination and Social Support as Predictors of Psychological Distress in African American Spouses of Inmates*. Ph.D. Dissertation, California School of Professional Psychology, Los Angeles.

Males, M. 1992. "Adult Liaison in the 'Epidemic' of 'Teenage' Birth, Pregnancy, and Venereal Disease. *Journal of Sex Research* 29:525-545.

Mare, R.D., and C. Winship. 1991. "Socioeconomic Change and the Decline of Marriage for Blacks and Whites." In *The Urban Underclass*. Ed. C. Jencks and P. Peterson. Washington, D.C.: Brookings Institution, 175-202.

Mauer, M., and T. Huling. 1995. *Young Black Americans and the Criminal Justice System: Five Years Later*. Washington, D.C.: Sentencing Project.

McDaniel, A. 1994. "Historical Racial Differences in Living Arrangements of Children." *Journal of Family History* 19:57-76.

McDaniel, A., and P. Morgan. 1996. "Racial Differences in Mother-Child Coresidence in the Past." *Journal of Marriage and the Family* 58:1011-1017.

Minkler, M., and K.M. Roe. 1993. *Grandmothers as Caregivers: Raising Children of the Crack Cocaine Epidemic.* Newbury Park, Cal.: Sage.

Morgan, S.P., A. McDaniel, A.T. Miller, and S.H. Preston. 1993. "Racial Differences in Household and Family Structure at the Turn of the Century." *American Journal of Sociology* 98:799-828.

Moynihan, D.P. 1967. "The Negro Family: The Case for National Action." In *The Moynihan Report and the Politics of Controversy.* Ed. L. Rainwater and W.L. Rainwater. Cambridge, Mass.: MIT Press.

Murray, C.A. 1984. *Losing Ground: American Social Policy, 1950-1980.* New York: Basic Books.

National Center for Education Statistics. 1997. *Youth Indicators 1996. Indicator 7: Births to Unmarried Women, by Age and Race.* Available from http://nces01.ed.gov:80/pubs/yi/y9607c.html

National Task Force on African American Men and Boys. 1996. *Repairing the Breach.* Chicago: Noble Press.

Oppenheimer, V.K., H.P. Blossfeld, and A. Wackerow. 1995. "Chapter 7: United States of America." In *The New Role of Women: Family Formation in Modern Societies.* Ed. H.P. Blossfeld. Boulder, Col.: Westview Press.

Oropesa, R.S., D.T. Lichter, and R.N. Anderson. 1994. "Marriage Markets and the Paradox of Mexican American Nuptiality." *Journal of Marriage and the Family* 56:889-907.

Oswalt, W.H. 1986. *Life Cycles and Lifeways: An Introduction to Cultural Anthropology.* Palo Alto, Cal.: Mayfield Publishing.

Popenoe, D. 1993. "American Family Decline, 1960-1990: A Review and Appraisal." *Journal of Marriage and the Family* 55:527-555.

———. 1996. "A World Without Fathers." *Wilson Quarterly* 20(2):12-29.

Prager, C.A.L. 1988. "Poverty in North America: Losing Ground?" *Canadian Public Policy/Analyse de Politiques* 14:52-65.

Republican National Committee. 1994. *Contract with America: The Bold Plan by Rep. Newt Gingrich, Rep. Dick Armey, and the House Republicans to Change the Nation.* New York: Random House.

Rodgers, W.L., and A. Thornton. 1985. "Changing Patterns of First Marriage in the United States." *Demography* 22:265-279.

Rossi, A.S. 1987. "Parenthood in Transition: From Lineage to Child to Self-Orientation." In *Parenting Across the Life Span: Biosocial Dimensions.* Ed. J.B. Lancaster, J. Altmann, A.S. Rossi, and L.R. Sherrod. Hawthorne, N.Y.: Aldine Publishing Co., 31-81.

Ruggles, S. 1997. "The Effects of AFDC on American Family Structure, 1940-1990." *Journal of Family History* 22:307-326.

Rury, J.L. 1986. "The New Moral Darwinism." *Urban Education* 21:316-324.

Sampson, R. 1995. "Unemployment and Imbalanced Sex Ratios: Race-Specific Consequences for Family Structure and Crime." In *The Decline in Marriage Among African Americans: Causes, Consequences and Policy Implications.* Ed. M.B. Tucker and C. Mitchell-Kernan. New York: Russell Sage Foundation, 229-254.

Sandefur, G.D., and J. Mosley. 1997. "Family Structure, Stability, and the Well-Being of Children." In *Indicators of Children's Well-Being.* Ed. R.M. Hauser, B.V. Brown, and W.R. Prosser. New York: Russell Sage Foundation, 325-328.

Scanzoni, J. 1997. "A Reply to Glenn: Fashioning Families and Policies for the Future—Not the Past." *Family Relations* 46:213-217.

Schor, J.B. 1991. *The Overworked American: The Unexpected Decline of Leisure.* New York: Basic Books.

Shimkin, D.B., M. Shimkin, and D.A. Frate, Eds. 1978. *The Extended Family in Black Societies.* The Hague, Switzerland: Mouton.

Skolnick, A. 1997. "A Response to Glenn: The Battle of the Textbooks: Bringing in the Culture Wars." *Family Relations* 46:219-222.

South, S. 1996. "Mate Availability and the Transition to Unwed Motherhood: A Paradox of Population Structure." *Journal of Marriage and the Family* 58:265-279.

Stacey, J. 1993. "Good Riddance to 'The Family': A Response to David Popenoe." *Journal of Marriage and the Family* 55:545-547.

Stack, C. 1974. *All Our Kin: Strategies for Survival in a Black Community.* New York: Harper and Row.

Stephens, W.N. 1963. *The Family in Cross-Cultural Perspective.* New York: Holt, Rinehart and Winston.

Stevenson, B.E. 1995. "Black Family Structure in Colonial and Antebellum Virginia: Amending the Revisionist Perspective." In *The Decline in Marriage Among African Americans: Causes, Consequences and Policy Implications.* Ed. M.B. Tucker and C. Mitchell-Kernan. New York: Russell Sage Foundation.

———. 1996. *Life in Black and White: Family and Community in the Slave South.* Oxford: Oxford University Press.

Subramanian, S., M.B. Tucker, and C. Mitchell-Kernan. Under review. "Can't Buy Me Love: Economic Considerations in Mate Selection Criteria." University of California, Los Angeles.

Sudarkasa, N. 1997. "African American Families and Family Values." In *Black Families.* 3d ed. Ed. H.P. McAdoo. Thousand Oaks, Cal.: Sage.

Taylor, P.L., M.B. Tucker, and C. Mitchell-Kernan. In press. "Ethnic Variations in Perceptions of Men's Provider Role." *Psychology of Women Quarterly.*

Testa, M., and M. Krogh. 1995. "The Effect of Employment on Marriage Among Black Males in Inner-City." In *The Decline in Marriage Among African Americans: Causes, Consequences and Policy Implications.* Ed. M.B. Tucker, and C. Mitchell-Kernan. New York: Russell Sage Foundation, 59-95.

Thornton, A. 1989. "Changing Attitudes Toward Family Issues in the United States." *Journal of Marriage and the Family* 51:873-893.

Thornton, A., and D.S. Freedman. 1982. "Changing Attitudes Toward Marriage and Single Life." *Family Planning Perspectives.* 14:297-303.

Tucker, M.B., and C. Mitchell-Kernan. 1995a. "Marital Behavior and Expectations: Ethnic Comparisons of Attitudinal and Structural Correlates." In *The Decline in Marriage Among African Americans: Causes, Consequences and Policy Implications.* Ed. M.B. Tucker and C. Mitchell-Kernan. New York: Russell Sage Foundation.

———. 1995b. "Trends in African American Family Formation: A Theoretical and Statistical Overview." In *The Decline in Marriage Among African Americans: Causes, Consequences and Policy Implications.* Ed. M.B. Tucker and C. Mitchell-Kernan. New York: Russell Sage Foundation.

———. 1997. "Understanding Marital Decline Among African Americans." *African American Research Perspectives* (Winter):40-45.

———. 1999. "Mate Availability Among African Americans: Conceptual and Methodological Issues." In *Advances in Black Psychology,* Vol. 1. Ed. R.L. Jones. Richmond, Va.: Cobb and Henry.

———. Under review. "Economic Contributions to Marital/Relationship Happiness." University of California, Los Angeles.

Tucker, M.B., and R.J. Taylor. 1989. "Demographic Correlates of Relationship Status Among Black Americans." *Journal of Marriage and the Family* 51:655-665.

U.S. Bureau of Labor Statistics. 1997. Table A-2, "Employment Status of the Civilian Population by Race, Sex, Age, and Hispanic Origin." Revised June 6. Available from http://stats.bls.gov/news.release/empsit.t02.html

U.S. Bureau of the Census. 1953. *U.S. Census of the Population: 1950.* Vol. II. *Characteristics of the Population,* Part 1, *United States Summary.* Washington, D.C.: GPO.

————. 1966. *U.S. Census of the Population: 1966. Subject Reports. Marital Status.* Final Report PC(2)-4E. Washington, D.C.: GPO.

————. 1970. *U.S. Census of the Population: 1970.* Vol. 1. *Detailed Population Characteristics. United States Summary.* Washington, D.C.: GPO.

————. 1971. "Population Characteristics: Marital Status and Family Status, March, 1970." *Current Population Reports,* P20- 212. Washington, D.C.: GPO.

————. 1975a. *Historical Statistics of the United States, Colonial Times to 1970.* Bicentennial Ed., Part 1. Washington, D.C.: GPO.

————. 1975b. *Historical Statistics of the United States, Colonial Times to 1970.* Bicentennial Ed., Part 2. Washington, D.C.: GPO.

————. 1979. "The Social and Economic Status of the Black Population in the United States: An Historical View, 1790-1978." *Current Population Reports,* P23-80. Washington, D.C.: GPO.

————. 1984. *U.S. Census of the Population: 1980,* Vol. I. *Characteristics of the Population,* Chap. D, *Detailed Population Characteristics,* Part 1, *United States Summary,* Sect. A. Washington, D.C.: GPO.

————. 1985. *U.S. Census of the Population: 1980,* Vol. 2. *Subject Reports: Marital Characteristics.* PC80-2-4C. Washington, D.C.: GPO.

————. 1990. "Household and Family Characteristics: March 1990 and 1989." *Current Population Reports,* P20-447. Washington, D.C.: GPO.

————. 1991. "Marital Status and Living Arrangements: March 1990." *Current Population Reports,* P20-450. Washington, D.C.: GPO.

————. 1992. "The Black Population in the United States: March." *Current Population Reports,* P20-471. Washington, D.C.: GPO.

————. 1998a. *Resident Population of the United States: Estimates, by Sex, Race, and Hispanic Origin, with Median Age.* Published December 28. http://www.census.gov/population/estimates/nation/intfile3-1.txt

————. 1998b. "Poverty in the United States: 1997." *Current Population Reports,* P60-201. Washington, D.C.: GPO. Available from http://www.census.gov/prod/3/98pubs/p60-201.pdf

————. 1998c. *Historical Income Tables—Families.* Revised November 6. Available from http://www.census.gov/hhes/income/histinc/

————. 1998d. "Coresident Grandparents and Their Grandchildren." *Current Population Reports,* Special Studies P23-198. Available from http://www.census.gov/prod/99pubs/p23-198.pdf

————. 1998e. "Selected Characteristics for Persons of . . . Ancestry." Available from http://www.census.gov/population/socdemo/ancestry

————. 1999a. *Estimated Median Age of First Marriage, by Sex: 1890 to the Present.* Published January 7. Available from http://www.census.gov/population/socdemo/ms-la/tabms-2.txt

————. 1999b. "Household and Family Characteristics: March 1998" (Update). *Current Population Reports,* P20-515. Detailed tables. Available from http://www.census.gov:80/population/www/socdemo/hh-fam.html

————. 1999c. "Interracial Married Couples: 1960 to Present." January 7. Available from http://www.census.gov/population/socdemo/ms-la/tabms-3.txt

————. 1999d. "Marital Status and Living Arrangements: March 1998" (Update). *Current Population Reports*, P20-514. Detailed tables. Washington, D.C.: GPO. Available from http://www.census.gov/prod/99pubs/p20-514.pdf

————. 1999e. Table 4. "Selected Characteristics of Households, by Type, Region and Race of Householder: March 1998." Current Population Survey. Detailed tables, PPL-113. Available from http://www.census.gov/population/socdemo/race/api98/table04.txt

Ventura, S.J., et al. 1997. *Report of Final Natality Statistics, 1995. Monthly Vital Statistics Report,* 45(11), Supplement (June 10). Hyattsville, Md.: National Center for Health Statistics.

Ventura, S.J., S.C. Curtin, and T.J. Matthews. 1998. *Teenage Births in the United States: National and State Trends, 1990-1996.* Hyattsville, Md.: National Center for Health Statistics.

Waite, L.J. 1996. "Social Science Finds: 'Marriage Matters'." *The Responsive Community* 6(3):26-35.

Wetzel, J.R. 1995. "Labor Force, Unemployment, and Earnings." In *State of the Union: America in the 1990s.* Vol. 1, *Economic Trends.* Ed. R. Farley. New York: Russell Sage Foundation, 59-106.

Wilson, M.N. 1984. "Mothers' and Grandparents' Perceptions of Parental Behavior in Three-Generation Black Families." *Child Development* 55:1333-1339.

Wilson, M.N., et al. 1995. "African American Family Life: The Dynamics of Interactions, Relationships, and Roles." In *African American Family Life: Its Structural and Ecological Aspects.* Ed. M.N. Wilson. San Francisco: Jossey-Bass, 5-21.

Wilson, W.J. 1987. *The Truly Disadvantaged: The Inner City, the Underclass, and Public Policy.* Chicago: University of Chicago Press.

————. 1996. *When Work Disappears: The World of the New Urban Poor.* New York: Knopf.

Wood, R.G. 1995. "Marriage Rates and Marriageable Men—A Test of the Wilson Hypothesis." *Journal of Human Resources* 30:163-193.

Chapter 8

An Overview of Black American Politics and Political Participation Since the Civil Rights Movement

by Paula D. McClain
Professor of Political Science and Law, Duke University

and Joseph Stewart, Jr.
Professor of Political Science, University of New Mexico

INTRODUCTION

Nowhere are the effects of the Civil Rights movement more pronounced than in Black politics and political participation. While the Civil Rights Act of 1964 was the vehicle that began to pull down the barriers to segregation in public accommodations and employment, the Voting Rights Act of 1965 (VRA) opened the way for increased Black electoral participation and the election of Blacks to public office, particularly in the South. The simple act of voting has important symbolic and potentially important practical effects. The right to cast a ballot separates the insiders (citizens) from the outsiders (noncitizens) and the dependents (the underaged). When aggregated, votes determine who will be the nation's public policymakers, the people who allocate public resources. In short, the vote is seen as a tool for protecting other rights and achieving other goals—a means rather than an end.

Most Americans assume that all citizens have the right to vote. In fact, post-Civil War constitutional amendments banned intentional discrimination by public officials based on race or previous condition of servitude (the Fourteenth Amendment, ratified in 1868) and prohibited the denial or abridgment of the right to vote by officials at all levels of government on the basis of race, color, or previous condition of servitude (the Fifteenth Amendment, ratified in 1870). Nevertheless, the U.S. Supreme Court declared much of the legislation designed to enforce the Fifteenth Amendment unconstitutional within a few years after its passage, and Congress repealed related legislation. Thus, when federal supervision of southern elections ended in 1877, states were effectively free to disenfranchise the Black electorate, which they systematically did. Against this backdrop, the Black Civil Rights movement pressed for the right to vote as a top priority. The ballot was viewed as a tool for achieving other changes sought by the movement.

CHAPTER OVERVIEW

This chapter examines Black politics and participation since the Civil Rights movement. The first section presents an overview of that movement and of the evolution of the right to vote. The VRA and recent challenges to majority minority districts are discussed. Next, nationwide changes in the levels of Black voter registration and voting from 1964 to 1996 are explored, with particular attention to changes in registration and voting in the South. Then, data from three major surveys of Black political attitudes are used to show Black ideological and partisan identifications.

The section that follows discusses the increases in Black elected officials at all levels of government since the VRA, the effect of the 1992 redistricting on the number of Black elected officials, and the results of the 1996 and 1998 congressional elections. The Black church and its continued significant role in Black political life are then examined.

One public policy issue of considerable concern to Black Americans, violent crime, is highlighted next, and differences in social realities for Blacks and Whites in the United States are outlined. The final section looks at important political issues that continue to confront Black Americans.

THE CIVIL RIGHTS MOVEMENT AND
THE VOTING RIGHTS ACT OF 1965

With the end of federally supervised southern elections in 1877, the states were able to restructure and operate their own electoral processes. The systematic disenfranchisement of Black voters followed. Through a variety of devices, such as discriminatorily administered literacy tests, poll taxes, and White primaries, southern states passed some of the most effective discriminatory electoral legislation ever enacted. The result was that between 1896 and 1900, the number of registered Black voters in, for example, Louisiana dropped from 130,334 to 5,320. Likewise, at the end of the 20th century, only 9 percent of Mississippi's Black voting-age population were registered to vote compared with 70 percent three decades earlier (U.S. Commission on Civil Rights, 1968).

In the early part of the 20th century, some legal progress was made in attacking various methods of disenfranchisement. In 1915, the Supreme Court, in *Guinn* v. *United States*, declared the grandfather clause unconstitutional, a device that southern states had used to deny the vote to those whose grandparents were slaves, thereby allowing the states to circumvent the Fifteenth Amendment. In 1944, in *Smith* v. *Allwright*, the Supreme Court invalidated Texas's White primary as a violation of the Fifteenth Amendment. This primary had been based on the logic that the state's Democratic Party was a private organization, and thus its method of nominating candidates—the White primary—was not covered by the Fourteenth Amendment's equal protection clause. The Democratic Party was the dominant party in Texas, and the individual who won the primary was the predetermined winner in the general election. If the Democratic Party were a private organization and if only party members could vote in the primary, Black voters were effectively blocked from participation. Despite these two court victories, the day-to-day realities for Black citizens rarely changed.

The Voting Rights Act of 1965

The VRA, which was amended or extended in 1970, 1975, and 1982, was passed at least partially in response to the Black Civil Rights movement. The act, as amended:

1. prohibits "tests or devices" used in the past to disenfranchise racial minorities—for example, literacy tests, education requirements, tests of good character, racial gerrymandering, and English-only elections in jurisdictions in which a single linguistic minority constitutes more than 5 percent of the voting-age population;

2. requires that "covered" jurisdictions[1] gain federal assent for any changes in election laws or procedures to assure that such changes do not abridge the right to vote on the basis of race, color, or language minority status; and

3. makes clear that if the effect of a practice is discriminatory, it is unlawful regardless of the intent of its originator.

Legislation has been fairly effective in dealing with vote denial. Although gaps still exist in the political participation rates of Blacks and Whites, the gaps have narrowed since passage of the VRA (explored in detail in another section).

Minority Vote Dilution

More work remains in the area of vote dilution. Vote dilution involves "the impairment of the equal opportunity of minority voters to participate in the political process and to elect candidates of their choice" (McDonald and powell, 1993, 27). Drawing on Supreme Court decisions mandating that voting power must be apportioned equally based on population (the one-person, one-vote decisions), the reasoning has been extended to mandate that voters have the right to cast ballots with the potential to elect candidates of their choice. The following practices have been used at various times to dilute minority voting strength: at-large elections; racially gerrymandered districting schemes that unnecessarily fragment or concentrate minority group voters; laws that prohibit single-shot voting (i.e., voting for only one candidate when multiple offices are at stake on a ballot); discriminatory annexations or de-annexations; and the abolition of elected or appointed offices or the changing of the means of selection. These practices by themselves do not necessarily dilute, but combined with other social or historical circumstances, they may create an unequal opportunity for minority voters to elect their preferred candidates.

The determination of whether a jurisdiction is engaging in minority vote dilution requires an examination of the "totality of circumstances." The circumstances that courts examine include racial bloc voting; a history of discrimination; depressed minority socioeconomic status; a paucity of elected minority officials; the use of racial campaign appeals; the existence of formal or informal "slating" groups (groups of candidates who band together or are endorsed as a group by other organizations); and the use of devices that enhance the possibility for discrimination, such as numbered positions.

When vote dilution is found or when legislators are reapportioning or redistricting after a census, a common remedy is to draw districts in which a majority of the residents are non-White—"majority minority" districts. Both the creation of these districts and the shape of some of them are matters of continuing controversy.

Drawing Majority Minority Districts

A series of Supreme Court decisions on the appropriateness of considering race in the drawing of congressional districts, raised in the context of some oddly shaped districts, have apparently limited the ability to draw majority minority districts. The original case of this kind, *Shaw* v. *Reno* (1993), focused on a congressional district drawn in North Carolina in the round of redistricting after the 1990 census in response to pressure from the U.S. Department of Justice to recognize potential minority voting strength in certain parts of the state. The plan that was adopted created a district in the north-central part of North Carolina that linked two Black urban population concentrations with a 160-mile-long "bridge," at times no wider than the Interstate 85 right of way. The Supreme Court subjected this arrangement to strict scrutiny and ultimately struck down the district as an example of racial gerrymandering (*Shaw* v. *Hunt*, 1996). Specifically, the Court found that when a district's redrawn shape is so bizarre that it is inexplicable on grounds other than race, strict scrutiny by the Court is required. Building on and clarifying *Shaw* v. *Reno*, the Court struck down a redistricting plan in Georgia (*Miller* v. *Johnson*, 1995) that would have created three majority Black districts. It also struck down a redistricting plan in Texas (*Bush* v. *Vera*, 1996) that would have formed two majority Black and one majority Latino districts. Congressional districts in both states were required to be redrawn. In 1997, federal district courts declared the majority Black Third District in Virginia and the majority Latino Twelfth District in New York unconstitutional. These rulings suggest that in the next round of redistricting, after the census of 2000, the ability to craft new majority minority districts will be severely limited.

The controversy over majority minority districts centers on the idea of representation and its meaning. The structure of the U.S. electoral process, and who wins and loses, affects who will raise the issues and what positions will be taken. Lani Guinier, Harvard University law professor (and President Bill Clinton's failed nominee for Assistant Attorney General for Civil Rights), questions whether it is fair in a majoritarian system for a majority—50 percent plus 1 percent—in any given election to hold 100 percent of the power. Because the other 50 percent minus 1 percent are in the minority, should they be excluded from the governing body? In Guinier's view, minority refers to any numerical minority, whether racial, gender, or partisan. She also questions whether concentrating racial minorities in majority minority districts is the best approach to rectifying the exclusion of those minorities from the political process. Guinier advocates cumulative voting as one means of achieving minority representation (Guinier, 1994). Her ideas are gaining currency.

Cumulative Voting

Cumulative voting is a mechanism that benefits numerical minorities, whether they are Blacks, Latinos, Asians, Indians, women, Democrats, or Republicans. The concept is simple. Under the current process, if there are seven seats on the city council, each voter can vote for one individual in each of the seven contests. In essence, each voter has seven votes but can vote for only one candidate in each contest. In cumulative voting, each voter has seven votes and can assign them however he or she wants. The voter can give five votes to one candidate and one each to two others or can give all seven votes to one candidate. Under this method, numerical minorities could give all of their votes to a particular candidate, thus increasing their chances of electing members of their own group.

Cumulative voting was used until recently by Illinois in its legislative races. Cumulative voting systems enabled the Sisseton Sioux Indians in South Dakota to elect a representative to the local school board and Blacks in Chilton County, Alabama, to elect a Black and, for the first time, two White Republicans to the county council. In 1994, a federal judge ordered the institution of a cumulative voting system in Worcester County on Maryland's Eastern Shore to overcome the inability of Blacks to elect members to the County Board of Commissioners.

Often advocated as beneficial to minority groups, cumulative voting can also benefit Whites, who are increasingly becoming numerical minorities in many urban centers. As the composition of the electorate changes nationally and subnationally, there will be more discussion about how much access numerical minorities should have to the political system.

The Voting Rights Act has had a tremendous effect on the level of Black registration and voting. Black voters were able to exercise their newly protected franchise in states that had denied them the opportunity to vote. This changed the political landscape in a number of states. The next section examines Black registration and voting and Black political attitudes.

BLACK POLITICAL PARTICIPATION

Voting and Registration

Before the VRA, only 6.7 percent of voting-age Blacks in Mississippi were registered to vote; by 1967, 59.8 percent were registered. In the seven states originally covered by the act, Black registration is estimated to have increased from 29.3 percent in 1965 to 56.6 percent in 1971-72. Moreover,

"The Justice Department estimated that in the five years after passage, almost as many Blacks registered in Alabama, Mississippi, Georgia, Louisiana, North Carolina, and South Carolina as in the entire century before 1965" (Davidson, 1992, 21).[2]

Table 8-1 shows the 1996 registration and voting figures for the 20 states with the highest proportion of Black electorates. In these states, Blacks ranged from just under 9 percent of the electorate in Pennsylvania to a high of almost 35 percent in Mississippi. In 8 states, Blacks were at least one-fifth of the electorate.

In general, White age-eligible registration rates slightly exceed those of Blacks. There are exceptions, however, in both directions. In 1996, in 3 of the 20 states (New York, Florida, and Ohio), White registration rates outpaced Black registration rates by more than 10 percentage points. The biggest gap was in Ohio where more than two-thirds of Whites old enough to vote were

TABLE 8-1

Black and White Voting-Age Population (VAP) Registration and Voting for 20 States with Highest Black Proportion of the Electorate, 1996

State	% of Total Electorate	% of VAP Registered		% of VAP Reported Voting	
	Black	White	Black	White	Black
Mississippi	34.1	75.0	67.4	59.3	48.8
Georgia	29.6	67.8	64.6	52.3	45.6
Louisiana	29.3	74.5	71.9	62.6	60.9
South Carolina	24.9	69.7	64.3	56.6	56.2
Alabama	24.5	75.8	69.2	56.3	54.3
Maryland	23.4	65.8	70.3	54.7	56.9
Virginia	20.8	68.4	64.0	58.5	53.3
Delaware	20.5	66.6	57.9	58.2	46.0
North Carolina	18.8	70.4	65.5	56.4	48.7
Tennessee	17.9	66.3	65.7	52.8	56.0
Arkansas	16.7	64.5	65.8	52.1	50.6
New York	16.5	65.1	52.5	55.1	42.4
Illinois	15.8	67.6	71.5	55.4	60.2
Florida	13.1	63.7	53.1	52.7	40.5
New Jersey	12.9	66.0	62.7	57.1	53.8
Michigan	11.9	72.2	75.5	58.1	63.0
Texas	10.8	62.7	63.2	46.7	47.1
Ohio	10.5	70.5	56.8	60.8	47.3
Oklahoma	9.3	71.3	67.1	60.5	52.0
Pennsylvania	8.7	66.0	67.3	55.3	57.7

Source: U.S. Bureau of the Census (1998b).

registered, while just over one-half of similarly qualified Blacks were on the voting rolls. On the other hand, in 6 of the 20 states, Black registration rates exceeded those of Whites. The difference was only 0.5 percentage points in Texas and 1.3 percentage points in Pennsylvania and Arkansas, but it was 3.3, 3.9, and 4.5 percentage points in Michigan, Illinois, and Maryland, respectively.

A similar picture emerges from examining turnout. White turnout generally exceeded Black turnout in 1996—in 4 of the 20 states by more than 10 percent (see Table 8-1). Again, Ohio reported the biggest gap, with White turnout surpassing Black turnout by 13.5 percentage points. In 6 states (Maryland, Tennessee, Illinois, Michigan, Texas, and Pennsylvania), a greater proportion of the Black voting-age population reported voting than did the White population. The differences were about the same regarding registration, ranging from a 0.4 percentage point difference in Texas to a 4.9 percentage point difference in Michigan. Because "most American national elections are won by 5 percent or less," Blacks have the potential to be a significant force in determining the outcome (Williams, 1987, 101).

In assessing how well the Black community is mobilizing its resources at the polls, it is useful to examine registration and turnout together. On the positive end of the spectrum are the states in which Blacks both register and vote at rates higher than White rates. Table 8-1 demonstrates that Blacks in Maryland, Tennessee, Illinois, Michigan, Texas, and Pennsylvania maximized their electoral potential in 1996, relative to other states. A puzzling point involves the states in which Blacks register at least at the same rate as Whites, but do not exercise their right to vote at a comparable rate. The states with unfulfilled potential in 1996 included Georgia and Oklahoma. Finally, there are the doubly disadvantaged states in which low Black registration rates are compounded by low turnout rates. Delaware, New York, Florida, and Ohio were clearly in this category in 1996.

In 1996, 193.7 million Americans were eligible to vote. Blacks accounted for 11.6 percent of the total voting-age population. Table 8-2 shows national historical registration and voting data for Black and White voting-age populations from 1964 to 1996. It also illustrates the percentage of the registered voting-age population who voted in each year. In 1968, a 9.2 percentage point gap existed between Black and White voter registration rates, which narrowed to only 1.3 percentage points in 1986 (Williams, 1987). But by 1994, the gap had widened again, to 6.1 percent—64.6 percent of the White voting-age population were registered to vote compared with 58.5 percent of Black voting-age residents. Data for 1996 show that the gap narrowed slightly to 4.2 percentage points. What explains the fluctuations in the gap between White and Black voters?

Since 1964, Black registration rates have generally followed national trends, rising in the 1960s, falling in the 1970s, and increasing again in the 1980s (Williams, 1987). Black registration reached its peak of 66.3 percent in 1984 and declined steadily to 58.5 percent in 1994 (see the second column in Table 8-2). The drop in Black registration after 1984 parallels the decrease in White registration. Jesse Jackson's 1984 presidential campaign and the resultant voter registration drive apparently increased national Black voter regis-

TABLE 8-2

Black and White Voting-Age Population (VAP) Registration and Voting, and Black and White Registered Voters Voting, 1964-96

	% of VAP Registered	% of VAP Voted	% of VAP Registered Who Voted[1]
1964 (Pres. election/Johnson-Goldwater)			
White	NA	70.7	NA
Black	NA	58.5	NA
1966			
White	71.6	60.2	84.1
Black	60.2	41.7	69.3
1968 (Pres. election/Nixon-Humphrey)			
White	75.4	69.1	91.6
Black	66.2	57.6	87.0
1970			
White	69.1	56.0	81.0
Black	60.8	43.5	71.5
1972 (Pres. election/Nixon-McGovern)			
White	73.4	64.5	87.9
Black	65.5	52.1	79.5
1974			
White	63.5	46.3	72.9
Black	54.9	33.8	61.5
1976 (Pres. election/Ford-Carter)			
White	68.3	60.9	89.1
Black	58.5	48.7	83.2
1978			
White	63.8	47.3	74.1
Black	57.1	37.2	65.1
1980 (Pres. election/Carter-Reagan)			
White	68.4	60.9	89.0
Black	60.0	50.5	83.3
1982			
White	65.6	49.9	76.1
Black	59.1	43.0	72.7
1984 (Pres. election/Reagan-Mondale)			
White	69.6	61.4	88.2
Black	66.3	55.8	84.1
1986			
White	65.3	47.0	71.9
Black	64.0	43.2	67.5

(continued)

TABLE 8-2 continued

	% of VAP Registered	% of VAP Voted	% of VAP Registered Who Voted[1]
1988 (Pres. election/Bush-Dukakis)			
White	67.9	59.1	87.0
Black	64.5	51.5	79.8
1990			
White	63.8	46.7	73.2
Black	58.8	39.2	66.7
1992 (Pres. election/Bush-Clinton)			
White	70.1	63.6	90.7
Black	63.9	54.0	84.5
1994			
White	64.6	47.3	73.2
Black	58.5	37.1	63.4
1996 (Pres. election/Clinton-Dole)			
White	67.7	56.0	82.7
Black	63.5	50.6	79.7

1. % voting-age population reported voting/% voting-age population reported registered.

Source: U.S. Bureau of the Census (1998a).

tration to the peak noted above. But Jackson's 1988 run, although more success-ful in terms of primary outcomes, may not have had the same effect (Tate, 1993), as the Black registration rate dropped somewhat to 64.5 percent. In 1996, both Black and White registration rates increased, but only time can determine whether this rise will become a trend or was merely a one-election increase.

The third column in the table presents the share of those eligible to vote who voted. While the Black-White gaps in both registration and voting have fluctuated over time, the gap in actual voting is always the higher of the two. In looking just at presidential election years, in 1964, the gap between Black and White voting was 12.2 percentage points in the Lyndon Johnson-Barry Goldwater election and remained about the same in the 1972 Richard Nixon-George McGovern contest. The gap decreased, however, to 10.4 percentage points in the 1980 Jimmy Carter-Ronald Reagan race. In 1984, the gap between Black and White voting dropped significantly to 5.6 percentage points when Ronald Reagan ran for reelection against Walter Mondale, but increased to 7.6 percentage points in the 1988 race between George Bush and Michael Dukakis. In 1992, when Bush ran for reelection against Bill Clinton, the Black and White voting gap rose to 9.6 percentage points, but narrowed to 5.4 percentage points in Clinton's 1996 reelection bid against Bob Dole. The fluctuation in the Black-White voting gap has no single explanation, but depends on the differ-ential forces affecting mobilization in different communities.

The fourth column in Table 8-2 taps the rate of mobilization by reporting, by race, the percentage of those registered to vote who voted. Whites who register to vote consistently follow through, and they vote at a higher rate than Blacks. In examining the presidential election years from 1968 to 1996, the widest gap in the turnout of Black and White registered voters, 8.4 percentage points, occurred in the 1972 contest between Nixon and McGovern. In the most recent election, 1996, the gap between the turnout of White and Black registered voters was only 3 percentage points, the narrowest margin during the period. Clinton's efforts to provide more Black representation in government, despite some disappointments, and his experience in appealing to the Black electorate may have contributed to the narrowing of the gap.

Table 8-3 highlights gender differences in Black registration and voting for presidential election years 1992 and 1996 and for a midterm congressional election year, 1994. In all three years, Black women had higher registration and, with the exception of 1994, voting rates than Black men. In 1994, a slightly higher proportion of Black men than Black women who were registered to vote reported voting. The generally increased registration and voting rates of Black women may be the result of their higher levels of education and greater labor force distribution in white collar jobs than Black men; Black women also have higher turnout rates than Black men within the same occupation, income, education, and employment status group. Furthermore, survey data on group consciousness suggest that because Black women perceive discrimination based on both race and gender, this dual consciousness may foster higher registration and voting rates among Black women than racial consciousness alone stimulates in Black men (Williams, 1987).

The 1996 Presidential Election

President Clinton was elected in 1992 and 1996 with solid Black support, 84 percent and 83 percent, respectively. Overall voter turnout in 1996

TABLE 8-3

**Black Registration and Voting by Gender, 1992, 1994, and 1996
(%)**

Category	1992		1994		1996	
	Male	Female	Male	Female	Male	Female
% VAP[1]	5.1	6.3	5.1	6.3	5.3	6.4
% VAP registered	60.8	66.4	55.2	61.3	60.0	66.2
% VAP reported voting	50.8	56.7	35.7	38.3	46.6	53.9
% VAP registered who voted[2]	83.5	85.4	64.7	62.5	77.7	81.4

1. VAP = voting-age population.
2. % voting-age population reported voting/% voting-age population reported registered.

Source: U.S. Bureau of the Census (1993, 1995, 1998a).

was estimated to have been at its lowest level since 1924, and it dropped from the 1992 level of 104.4 million to 95.8 million (Bositis, 1996a). Black voter turnout, however, increased during these years, from 8 percent (8.4 million votes) of all votes cast in 1992 to 10 percent (9.6 million votes) in 1996.

As noted, Black women outvoted Black men in 1992 and 1996. Although both Black women and men overwhelmingly voted for Clinton in 1996, a larger proportion of Black women voted for him than did Black men, 89 percent and 78 percent, respectively. It is interesting that 39 percent of Black Republicans and 69 percent of Black Independents voted for Clinton as well (Bositis, 1996a).

Group Cohesion

Actual or perceived group cohesion (group solidarity) has been identified in political science research as being strongly associated with increased levels of political participation by racial and ethnic minority groups in the United States (Olsen, 1970; Verba and Nie, 1972). The more that individuals identify with other members of a group, the more they are likely to participate in politics and to coalesce around candidates and issues that they perceive as being beneficial to the group. One measure of group cohesion among racial and ethnic minorities is the degree of perceived discrimination against the individual and the individual's group. Another measure is how close an individual feels to others in the group regarding ideas and feelings about issues.

According to the 1984 National Black Election Study (NBES), 90 percent of Blacks surveyed believed that discrimination was still a problem for Blacks, with 68 percent strongly believing (Gurin, Hatchett, and Jackson, 1989, 75-81). Another data source reported that a majority of Blacks indicated they had experienced discrimination in education, housing, employment, and wages (Sigelman and Welch, 1991). The same pattern was evident in the 1988 NBES data (Tate, 1993).

In terms of closeness in feelings and ideas, 93 percent of Black respondents in the 1984 NBES reported being close to other Blacks (Gurin, Hatchett, and Jackson, 1989, 75-81), and a majority believed that what happened to the group affected them personally. As Table 8-4 illustrates, three-fourths of Blacks surveyed in the 1984 and 1988 NBES and in the 1993-94 National Black Politics Study (NBPS) believed that what happened to other Black people would shape their lives. These results are consistent with other research on the topic (Shingles, 1981; Dawson, 1994; Bobo and Gilliam, 1990; Tate, 1993).

Ideological Orientation

The media often refer to Blacks as liberal on a number of political dimensions, yet this is a naive view of the complexity of Black attitudes. Many assume that Blacks as a group are liberal because a predominant proportion of Black Americans believe that the federal government should take a more active role in reducing unemployment, providing services for

TABLE 8-4

Proportion of Blacks Perceiving that They Share
a Common Fate with Other Blacks
(%)

	1984[a]	1988	1993-94[b]
Yes	73.5 (796)[c]	77.4 (339)	77.9 (904)
No	26.5 (287)	22.6 (99)	22.1 (256)
Total	100.0 (1,083)	100.0 (438)	100.0 (1,160)

a. Preelection sample, 1984 and 1988 National Black Election Studies.
b. 1993-94 National Black Politics Study.
c. Figures in parentheses represent the number of respondents.

Source: McClain and Stewart (1999).

the poor, and improving the socioeconomic position of Blacks and other racial minorities. Survey data show, however, that a majority of Blacks also support prayer in public schools, a position that is on the conservative end of the spectrum. Are Blacks liberal or conservative? The answer is both, but the survey responses must be viewed within the context of being Black in the United States. Stereotyping Black Americans as liberal or conservative misses the complexity behind these responses.

As Table 8-5 shows, Blacks are spread across the ideological spectrum. (If one combines all Blacks who identify themselves as some degree of liberal and contrast that group with all Blacks who identify themselves as some degree of conservative, the differences are not great. There was an approximately 10 percentage point gap in favor of liberals in the 1984 and 1988 NBES, but only a roughly 4 percentage point gap in the same direction in the 1993-94 NBPS, with slightly different wording of questions.) The meaning behind these labels is unclear. Some respondents were unable to define what they meant by identifying themselves as liberal or conservative. Moreover, higher income Blacks were no more likely than lower income Blacks to label themselves as conservatives. Older Blacks, however, were far more likely than younger Blacks to call themselves liberal. Regardless of self-identified ideological labels, Blacks' policy preferences are generally fairly liberal across a variety of issues; but with the exception of capital punishment, they are relatively conservative on a range of social issues (Tate, 1993, 31-32, 38).

Partisan Identification

As each presidential election nears, the media point to the heavily Democratic orientation of the Black community, which Black voters acknow-

TABLE 8-5

Black Ideological Identification
(%)

Ideology	1984[a]		1988[a]		1993-94[b]	
Strongly liberal	21.8	(154)[c]	18.5	(63)	23.9	(241)
Not very strongly liberal	12.9	(91)	18.0	(61)	11.9	(121)
Slightly liberal	16.5	(116)	18.0	(61)	— [d]	
Moderate/leaning liberal	—		—		15.4	(155)
Moderate	7.0	(49)	1.8	(6)	2.4	(24)
Moderate/leaning conservative	—		—		22.7	(219)
Slightly conservative	16.6	(117)	22.1	(75)	—	
Not very strongly conservative	11.3	(80)	10.2	(35)	9.3	(94)
Strongly conservative	13.9	(98)	11.4	(39)	15.4	(155)
Total	100.0	(705)	100.0	(340)	100.0	(1,009)

a. Postelection sample, 1984 and 1988 National Black Election Studies.
b. 1993-94 National Black Politics Study.
c. Figures in parentheses represent the number of respondents.
d. Differences in response categories between National Black Election Studies and National Black Politics Study.

Source: McClain and Stewart (1999).

ledge. This orientation should be viewed within the historical dynamics of the relationship of Blacks to both the Republican and Democratic Parties.

The post-Civil War connection between Blacks and the Republican Party persisted into the Civil Rights movement era, albeit in weakened form. Although Blacks were a significant part of the New Deal Democratic coalition, an estimated 38 percent of the Black vote was cast for reelection of Republican President Dwight D. Eisenhower in 1956 (Gurin, Hatchett, and Jackson, 1989). The large Black vote may have been the result of Eisenhower's appointment during his first term of Supreme Court Chief Justice Earl Warren, author of the *Brown* v. *Board of Education of Topeka* (1954) desegregation decision. In his second term, however, Eisenhower was less committed to civil rights and equality, as evidenced by his reluctance to implement the 1957 Civil Rights Act and to take a strong stand on enforcing school desegregation in Little Rock, Arkansas. This reluctance played to the Democrats' advantage in the 1960 presidential election between John Kennedy and Richard Nixon, although both parties actively campaigned for the Black vote. The Black vote shifted slightly to the Democrats in that election primarily because Kennedy's call to Coretta Scott King expressing concern over the jailing of her husband, Martin Luther King, Jr., in Georgia was made before Nixon's call. The shift was solidified in 1964 when the Republican Party nominated conservative Arizona Senator Barry Goldwater as its presidential candidate. Goldwater's extreme positions and opposition to Civil Rights legislation made continued Black allegiance to the Republican Party very problematic. Black voters have remained solidly Democratic since 1964.

A 1996 survey by the Joint Center for Political and Economic Studies (Bositis, 1996b) found that 4 percent of Black Americans identified themselves as Republican, and another 4.7 percent indicated leaning toward Republican. These percentages have remained constant since the Joint Center began its surveys in 1984, with the exception of 1990 when a combined 10 percent of Blacks identified themselves as or leaning toward Republican. (The percentages in the Joint Center's survey are similar to those in the three surveys reported next in Table 8-6.)

As Table 8-6 demonstrates, 83.5 percent of Blacks surveyed in the 1984 NBES considered themselves Democrats, yet the degree of partisanship varied, with less than one-half (45.8 percent) reporting themselves as strong Democrats. In 1988, considerably more Blacks (57 percent) identified themselves as strong Democrats, but that percentage dropped to one-half (49.5 percent) in the 1993-94 NBPS. In addition, the 1984 and 1988 data point to a gender split within the Black electorate; Black women were more likely to identify strongly with the Democratic Party than were Black men, who were

TABLE 8-6

Black Partisan Identification
(%)

Partisan Identification	1984[a]		1988[a]		1993-94[b]	
Strong Democrat	45.8	(521)[c]	57.0	(260)	49.5	(597)
Weak Democrat	23.5	(267)	21.5	(98)	20.7	(249)
Independent/leaning toward Democrat	14.2	(162)	10.3	(47)	12.4	(149)
Independent	4.8	(55)	2.9	(13)	6.5	(78)
Independent/leaning toward Republican	—[d]		—		3.3	(40)
Republican—all strengths	7.8	(88)	6.3	(29)	3.7	(45)
Other/apolitical	3.8	(44)	2.0	(9)	3.9	(47)
Total	100.0	(1,137)	100.0	(456)	100.0	(1,205)

a. Preelection sample, 1984 and 1988 National Black Election Studies.
b. 1993-94 National Black Politics Study.
c. Figures in parentheses represent the number of respondents.
d. Differences in response categories between National Black Election Studies and National Black Politics Study.

Source: McClain and Stewart (1999).

more likely to identify as weak Democrat, independent leaning toward Democrat, political independent, or Republican (Tate, 1993, 64). The 1993-94 NBPS suggests, however, that the gender split may have dissipated; Black men were just as likely as Black women to identify strongly with the Democratic Party.

A generational division also exists, with older Blacks tending to be more strongly Democratic than younger Blacks. Younger Blacks between the ages of 18 and 29 are more inclined to lean toward or identify as Republican than older Blacks, but that proportion was only 13.8 percent in 1996, down from 16.3 percent in 1984 (Bositis, 1996b). In analyzing cohorts over time from 1984 to 1996, Bositis found that young Blacks do not maintain their relatively greater support for the Republican Party as they age. According to Bositis, young Blacks "try on" a Republican identity when young, but in their twenties and thirties they move closer to the Democratic Party.

After 12 years of Republican administration, Black Americans did not have favorable views of Presidents Reagan and Bush or the Republican Party (Tate, 1993), and they continue to hold unfavorable opinions of Republicans, with the exception of Colin Powell (68.1 percent favorable). In the 1996 Joint Center survey, 60.8 percent of Blacks viewed Newt Gingrich unfavorably, and 48 percent gave the 1996 Republican presidential candidate, Senator Bob Dole, an unfavorable rating (Bositis, 1996b). Although Gingrich's unfavorable rating declined slightly in 1998, it was still a substantial 58.1 percent. Moreover, while 39.7 percent of Blacks believed that the Republican-led Congress was doing an excellent or good job in 1998, a majority of 51.7 percent believed that Congress was doing a poor or fair job (Joint Center, 1998b). These unfavorable evaluations may hinder Republican Party attempts to recruit more Blacks, at least in the near future.

BLACK ELECTED OFFICIALS

The number of Black elected officials has significantly increased since ratification of the Voting Rights Act in 1965, when an estimated fewer than 500 Blacks held elected office. By 1997, 8,656 Blacks were in office at all levels of government. Of that number, 32.5 percent (2,813) were Black females, a dramatic increase since 1970, when only 160 Black women were in office (Joint Center, 1998a). The following sections examine the issue of Black elected officials at the national, state, and local levels of government.

National Government Level

In 1954, only 2 Blacks, both Democrats, served in the U.S. House of Representatives. This number increased to 5 Democrats in 1966, the first congressional election after passage of the VRA. In 1971, when the Congressional Black Caucus was formed, 13 Black Democrats were in the House, and 1 Black Republican, Edward Brooke of Massachusetts, was in the Senate. Brooke lost his seat in 1978, and until the election of Carol Moseley-Braun

(D-IL) in 1992, no other Black served in the Senate. (Moseley-Braun was the first Black Democrat and Black female to be in the Senate.) Redistricting for the 1992 elections added 13 Blacks to the House. Redistricting was the result of the Bush administration's interpretation of the VRA to create as many majority Black and Latino districts as possible. Given this interpretation, the Republican National Committee developed a strategy to "bleach" districts adjacent to concentrations of minority populations in an attempt to make them more Republican, an approach that achieved its goal with the blessing of Black and Latino elected officials. The question of whether the strategy led to an increase in the number of Republicans in the House is still being studied (Petrocik and Desposato, 1998). At the same time, the strategy created challenges to the newly configured majority minority districts, raising questions of the "fairness" of Black and Latino representation of White minorities.

In the 1996 elections, 37 Blacks were elected to the House, including 10 women, 1 Republican, and 2 Black female Democratic nonvoting delegates from the District of Columbia and the U.S. Virgin Islands. After the election, however, Representative Ron Dellums (Ninth District, California) retired in midterm after 27 years in the House, and Representative Floyd Flake (Sixteenth District, New York) resigned to return to his church responsibilities. Dellums and Flake were both replaced by Blacks in special elections—Dellums by Barbara Lee and Flake by Gregory Meeks.

Several congressional races were hotly contested in 1996, primarily because the Supreme Court invalidated the majority minority districts in Georgia and Texas. (North Carolina's districts were also invalidated, but the federal district court ruled that the state did not have to redraw its districts until the 1998 elections.) After Georgia redrew its lines, one out of the three majority Black districts remained (Representative John Lewis's Fifth District). Representatives Cynthia McKinney's Eleventh District and Sanford Bishop's Second District were redrawn. McKinney decided she would have a better chance of reelection in the Fourth District, which was approximately one-third Black, and she and the incumbent switched districts. Running as the incumbent, she won the Democratic primary with 67 percent of the vote and ran against White Republican John Mintick in the general election. The campaign was tense and full of turmoil. Mintick tried to link McKinney to Louis Farrakhan, while McKinney had to apologize for her father's anti-Semitic comments. McKinney won the race with 57.8 percent of the vote.

Bishop's reelection race in Georgia's Second District, while competitive, was not as contentious as McKinney's contest. The conservative Bishop won the Democratic primary with 59 percent of the vote, as well as the November election, garnering 53.8 percent of the vote.

Democrat Corrine Brown of Florida's Third District also ran in a reconfigured district (*Johnson et al.* v. *Mortham*, 1995). Her old district had a Black voting-age population of approximately 60 percent, compared with approximately 40 percent in the new district (McClain and Stewart, 1999). In 1994, Brown ran a spirited reelection contest against a Black Republican, winning 58 percent of the vote, and in 1996, she again faced a Black Republican, winning handily with 61.4 percent of the vote.

All of Texas's congressional districts were redrawn as a result of *Bush v. Vera* (1996), forcing the state's congressional delegation into a primary election on November 5 and into runoff races in December if a candidate did not receive a majority of the votes. The Eighteenth District represented by Sheila Jackson Lee and the Thirtieth District represented by Eddie Bernice Johnson no longer had a Black majority after redistricting, but they retained a sizable Black population base. Both Jackson Lee and Johnson won majorities on election day, 77.1 percent and 54.6 percent, respectively, thereby avoiding a runoff contest.

Another significant race in 1996 was the election of Julia M. Carson to the Tenth District in Indianapolis. The district is about 27 percent Black and heavily Democratic, but Republicans have made gains over the years. Carson ran against a moderate White Republican, and the race was a statistical dead heat as the election approached. Nevertheless, she won 52.6 percent of the vote compared with her opponent's 45.1 percent.

We caution against drawing the conclusion from these races that Blacks can win in majority White districts, particularly southern ones. Several Blacks lost in 1996 congressional contests in southern majority White districts (Bositis, 1996a). In addition, the McKinney, Bishop, Brown, Jackson Lee, and Johnson victories had the advantage of incumbency and were in primarily Democratic districts. (Bishop's district is the most conservative of the new districts.) Moreover, while Jackson Lee's and Johnson's districts were no longer majority Black, each contained a significant portion of Latinos (23 percent and 18 percent, respectively), so that the districts remained majority minority. Finally, with the exception of Bishop's district, Bill Clinton won handily in the other four congressional districts in percentages close to or exceeding the percentages of the incumbents.

The issue is one not simply of drawing majority minority districts, but of what the districts mean relative to the ability of Blacks and Latinos to be elected to office, to the continued existence of racially polarized voting, and to the use of racial appeal tactics in political campaigns (Davidson and Grofman, 1994; Grofman, Handley, and Niemi, 1992; Reeves, 1997). Controversy exists because some believe that the VRA has become an affirmative action tool to get minorities elected, thereby making representation an entitlement, that racism among Whites has decreased, and that racially polarized voting is no longer a problem (Thernstrom, 1987). According to this reasoning, if minorities are not elected in White majority districts, it is not because of racial issues; therefore, the redrawing of districts to maximize minority electoral prospects is unnecessary (Reeves, 1997). This debate will not recede in the near future. Quite the contrary, as the new round of redistricting and reapportionment after the 2000 census approaches, the questions of what is meant by representation and what it means to be represented will again move front and center.

1998 Elections[3]

The 1998 midterm elections occurred against the backdrop of the Republican-led impeachment of President Clinton, who was viewed favorably by 88.6 percent of Black Americans (Joint Center, 1998b). While some believe that the story of the 1998 elections was the Republican loss of five seats in the House of Representatives, the real story is the influence of racial minorities on the outcomes of several congressional and state-level races. If 1992 was characterized as the "Year of the Woman," 1998 was surely the "Year of Racial Minority Influence." Black voters were key players in some of the most important races in the country.

Despite momentum in the final stages of her campaign, Black Democrat Carol Moseley-Braun of Illinois lost her reelection bid for the U.S. Senate by a 47 percent to 51 percent margin. However, in the House, Louis Stokes (Eleventh District, Ohio) retired and was replaced by Black Democrat Stephanie Tubbs-Jones. All of the other Black incumbents were reelected. Melvin Watt of the Twelfth District of North Carolina was initially considered vulnerable because his district had been redrawn as a result of the Supreme Court's decision in *Shaw* v. *Hunt* (1996), which reduced the percentage of Blacks in the district. But the district remained Democratic-leaning, and Watt faced no serious opposition. There are now 37 Blacks (or 8.5 percent) in the House, excluding nonvoting delegates, and 32.4 percent are women, again excluding nonvoting delegates.

Blacks provided the key margin of victory in senatorial and gubernatorial elections in several southern states in 1998. In South Carolina, Blacks were 25 percent of the voters who went to the polls. Although U.S. Senator Ernest Hollings received only 39 percent of the White vote, he received 91 percent of the Black vote, giving him 52 percent of the total vote (see Table 8-7). Clearly, without overwhelming support from Black South Carolinians, Democrat Hollings would have lost his seat. The same factors accounted for the upset loss of incumbent South Carolina Governor David Beasley. He took 58 percent of the White vote, but only 6 percent of the Black vote, making his Democratic opponent, Jim Hodges, the winner with 53 percent of the total vote. In North Carolina, incumbent U.S. Senator Lauch Faircloth received 57 percent of the White vote, but Blacks, who were 20 percent of the voters, gave Democrat John Edwards 91 percent of their votes, resulting in his 51 percent to 47 percent victory.

The same pattern was evident in Georgia and Alabama. In Georgia, Blacks, who were 29 percent of the voters, put Democrat Roy Barnes in the governor's office. Barnes had only 37 percent of the White vote but 90 percent of the large Black vote, which provided him the necessary margin to win (see Table 8-7). Blacks in Alabama helped Democrat Donald Siegelman defeat the incumbent Republican governor. Although Siegelman received only 48 percent of the White vote, Blacks were 19 percent of the voters and gave 95 percent of their vote to him.

State Government Level

At the state level in 1997, the largest numbers of Black elected officials of all levels of government were in 11 states—Mississippi (803), Alabama (726), Louisiana (645), Georgia (579), Illinois (545), South Carolina (542),

TABLE 8-7

Black Voting and Election Outcomes in Selected 1998 State Elections
(%)

South Carolina

	% of Total Vote	Governor		Senate	
		Hodges	*Beasley*	*Hollings*	*Inglis*
White	74	40	58	39	59
Black	25	92	6	91	8
Total of vote		53	45	52	46

North Carolina

	% of Total Vote	Governor		Senate	
		–	–	*Edwards*	*Faircloth*
White	79	–	–	41	57
Black	20	–	–	91	8
Total of vote		–	–	51	47

Georgia

	% of Total Vote	Governor		Senate	
		Barnes	*Millner*	–	–
White	69	37	58	–	–
Black	29	90	8	–	–
Total of vote		53	44	–	–

Alabama

	% of Total Vote	Governor		Senate	
		Siegelman	*James*	–	–
White	79	48	51	–	–
Black	19	95	5	–	–
Total of vote		58	42	–	–

Maryland

	% of Total Vote	Governor		Senate	
		Glendening	*Sauerbrey*	–	–
White	75	45	54	–	–
Black	21	90	9	–	–
Total of vote		56	44	–	–

Source: Voter News Service, 1998.

North Carolina (506), Arkansas (484), Texas (448), Virginia (333), and Michigan (333) (Joint Center, 1998a). Except for Texas, Illinois, Arkansas, and Michigan, these states are covered at least in part by the original VRA.

While significant progress has been made since 1954 in the absolute number of Blacks elected to Congress, progress in the number of Blacks elected to statewide offices has not been as pronounced. To win a statewide campaign, Blacks must attract a large number of White votes. L. Douglas Wilder made history in 1989 when he was elected Governor of Virginia, the first Black elected to this office in the country's history. (In 1872, P.B.S. Pinchback served as the appointed Governor of Louisiana for one month when the sitting governor was impeached.) Wilder's victory was not easy. Despite being far ahead in the polls on election day, he won by only slightly more than 4,000 votes. The polls had fallen victim to "social desirability" distortion. Whites, reluctant to tell interviewers that they would not vote for a Black, found refuge in the privacy of the voting booth and narrowed Wilder's lead (Finkel, Guterbock, and Borg, 1991).

Between 1993 and 1997, the number of Blacks elected to statewide judicial and administrative office increased from 21 to 26 (Joint Center, 1998a). In 1998, Blacks were successful in several statewide races below the governor's office. In Georgia, Democrat Thurbert Baker was elected Attorney General and Democrat Michael Thurmon, Labor Commissioner, the first Blacks to hold statewide elective office. Republican Vikki Buckley was reelected Secretary of State of Colorado; Democrat H. Carl McCall was reelected Comptroller of New York; and Republican Ken Blackwell, Ohio State Treasurer, was elected Secretary of State. After the 1998 elections, the number of Blacks elected to statewide offices was approximately the same as in 1997.

Local/Urban Government Level

For Blacks, cities historically have been the centers of economic and political opportunity. Between 1910 and 1930, almost 2 million Blacks—one-tenth of the Black population in the rural South—moved to cities in the Northeast and Midwest (Judd, 1979). Migration to the northeastern states was followed by migration to selected manufacturing centers in the Midwest that continued into the post-World War II era. Many of the migrants were seeking not only increased economic opportunities, but also escape from the harsh life of segregation and racial discrimination in the South. By 1960, these trends had resulted in a concentration of Blacks in most of the nation's urban centers outside the South (Rose, 1971). Coupled with the influx of Blacks into the cities was the exit of a sizable portion of Whites from the central cities to the newer surrounding suburbs.

This population shift created a political resource base for electoral politics—plurality and majority Black cities. Blacks began to be elected as mayors of major U.S. cities in 1967 with the historic elections of Carl Stokes in Cleveland and Richard Hatcher in Gary, Indiana. Elected mayor of Los Angeles in 1973,Thomas Bradley was the first Black mayor in a city in which

Blacks did not constitute at least a plurality of the population. (Bradley put together a formidable coalition of Blacks, Latinos, Asians, and liberal Whites, primarily Jewish, that lasted 20 years.) Since those early victories, Black mayors have been elected in cities as diverse as the majority Black cities of Detroit and Atlanta and the majority White cities of Denver, Seattle, and Minneapolis. In 1998, 413 Blacks were serving as mayors of American cities, and 83 were females.

Scholars are divided on the question of whether the election of a Black mayor makes a difference in implementing policies of concern to Black city residents. Many Black mayors were elected when their cities were declining, with many in dire fiscal straits. Tax bases had shifted to the suburbs, along much of the industry. Some Black mayors faced the daunting task of rebuilding cities with few tools. Coupled with these bleak fiscal realities were equally bleak economic conditions for Black inner-city residents. Economic recession had pushed many urban Blacks further into poverty. In addition, because a Black now held the mayor's office, Black citizens had increased expectations that their lives would improve.

Some argue that those conditions made it virtually impossible for Black mayors to be successful. According to Nelson (1992), Black mayors were unable to make significant changes in the political power structure in their cities, White business communities retained the reins of power, and inner-city residents gained little from city hall. Moreover, Black mayors unwilling to play a major leadership role in furthering Black political incorporation beyond the elected office (Nelson, 1992). He points out that "effective Black political incorporation must involve the institutionalization of Black influence across broad dimensions of the policy-making process, not merely the election of Black politicians to office" (192). On the other hand, Nelson contends that, despite shortcomings, Black mayors have accomplished a great deal. Priorities of city government have changed as reflected in budget allocations; more attention has been given to the policy issues of housing, job training, and police-community relations; and Black mayors have been instrumental in opening the doors of city government purchasing and contracting to minority-owned businesses.

An important issue at this point concerns political succession—replacing a Black mayor with a Black mayor, particularly in cities with majority or plurality Black populations. While many cities have been able to maintain Black mayoral leadership over time (e.g., Atlanta, Detroit, and Newark), others have not. After Harold Washington's death in 1987, Chicago's mayoralty returned to White hands in the next regular election cycle with the election of Richard Daley. When Tom Bradley of Los Angeles retired in 1993, his successor was a White Republican, Richard Riordan. David Dinkins of New York lost his reelection bid in 1993 to a conservative White Republican, Rudolph Giuliani. W. Wilson Goode of Philadelphia, elected in 1983, served two troubled four-year terms before being replaced by a White Democrat, Edward Rendell. Succession is related to the accumulation and institutionalization of political power. The ability of Blacks to accumulate and wield political power is directly related to winning, maintaining, and expanding elected and appointed political positions. The question of succession will be at the forefront of discussions of Black urban electoral power in the future.

Interminority and Coalition Competition in Urban Politics

Urban politics in the 1990s increasingly became multiracial events with Whites, Blacks, Latinos, and Asians as participants. This was in contrast to the overwhelming Black-White dynamic that characterized urban politics in the 1960s and 1970s. Competition among groups for political outcomes has been a focus of much of urban politics research. Although Chapter 3 in this volume, "Race Relations in a Diversifying Nation," examines interminority group relations in detail, it is important to highlight here the presence of interminority stress in urban politics.

Much of the study of interminority group interactions begins with the assumption that shared racial minority group status generates a natural potential for political coalitions. The reasoning is that similarities in the status of politically marginalized groups create mutual respect and shared political goals and ideals, leading to the formation of political coalitions in the pursuit of mutual political outcomes. Indeed, many studies demonstrate the existence of multiracial political coalitions in numerous metropolitan areas—a "rainbow coalition" approach (Saito, 1993; Sonenshein, 1990, 1993; Henry, 1980; Henry and Muñoz, 1991; Browning, Marshall, and Tabb, 1984, 1990; Stewart, 1993; Regalado, 1994). Simultaneously, other works find little basis upon which to build coalitions and identify competition as the emerging pattern (Mollenkopf, 1990; Bobo and Hutchings, 1996; Bobo et al., 1994; Oliver and Johnson, 1984; Johnson and Oliver, 1989; Johnson et al., 1992; Meier and Stewart, 1990; Falcón, 1988; Warren, Corbett, and Stack, 1986, 1990; See, 1986-87; Freer, 1994; Cohen, 1982; Tedin and Murray, 1994; Dyer, Vedlitz, and Worchel, 1989). Still others find elements of both patterns (McClain and Karnig, 1990; McClain, 1993; McClain and Tauber, 1994, 1995, 1998; McClain, 1996; McClain and Stewart, 1999; Jennings, 1992).

There are numerous examples of coalitions between Blacks and Latinos, particularly Mexican Americans. Alliances of 30 years ago, particularly at the height of the social movement of the 1960s, were based on a shared concern for civil rights, civil liberties, and poverty issues (Estrada, Garcia, and Marcias, 1981). Research on Los Angeles and other California cities provides rich illustrations of Black, Latino, and sometimes Asian coalition building (see, e.g., Browning, Marshall, and Tabb, 1984; Henry and Muñoz, 1991; Sonenshein, 1990, 1993; Saito, 1993). During the immigration debates in the late 1980s, Asians and Latinos coalesced to oppose the Simpson-Mazzoli immigration bill (Espiritu, 1992). Blacks, Latinos, and Asians recently came together in California in unsuccessful attempts to defeat both Proposition 187, denying benefits to illegal aliens, in 1994, and Proposition 209, banning affirmative action in state government, including educational institutions, in 1996.

Nevertheless, research suggests that support for biracial and multiracial coalitions may be waning. The coalitions between Blacks and Latinos of the 1960s came apart when policy preferences began to move in different directions. Latinos shifted their concerns to bilingual education, a policy that Blacks perceived as shifting resources from desegregation efforts (Falcón, 1988, 178). Blacks and Latinos also diverged on the "English Only" movement, employer sanctions, and the extension of coverage to Latinos in amendments to the VRA, resulting in increased tension between the groups (National Council of La Raza, 1990). In addition, Tedin and Murray (1994) found that both highly educated, higher income Black and Latino registered voters are less supportive of forming coalitions with each other than are lower educated, lower income, nonregistered Blacks and Latinos. They concluded, although tentatively, that more politically active and efficacious Blacks and Latinos are less likely to support biracial coalitions. These results held even after the introduction of socioeconomic controls. The findings of Tedin and Murray support earlier studies that showed an erosion of support for biracial coalitions, particularly among Mexican Americans (Ambrecht and Pachon, 1974; Browning, Marshall, and Tabb, 1984; Grebler, Moore, and Guzman, 1970; Henry, 1980).

Competition is another form of interminority group behavior. When there are differences among groups regarding political goals and outcomes, the potential for conflict exists. Competition may occur only in selective areas, leaving the potential open for coalitions in other areas, or competition may be present in most aspects of socioeconomic and political life, making the possibility of coalitions remote (Eisinger, 1976, 17-18).

Individuals and groups accrue power and status in a variety of ways. Some power contests involve group against group. Competition exists when two or more groups strive for the same finite objectives, so that the success of one may result in the reduced probability that another will attain its goals. Group competition can be viewed as power contests that occur when rivalry exists and groups have roots in different cultures. Furthermore, the greatest perceived competition can occur among near equal groups. This framework, while addressed to majority minority relations, also is useful in examining relationships among minority groups if it is recognized that not only status differences but status similarities (near equal groups) can become the bases for conflict (Blalock, 1967). Giles and Evans (1986) contend that greater competition and a stronger sense of group solidarity create more hostile attitudes. While this theory concerns Black-White dynamics, the same may hold true for interminority group relations.

Research from selected cities finds that Blacks, Latinos, and Asians compete for scarce jobs, housing, and government services (Oliver and Johnson, 1984; Johnson and Oliver, 1989; Falcón, 1988; MacManus and Cassell, 1982; Welch, Karnig, and Eribes, 1983; Mollenkopf, 1990). Survey data suggest a growing hostility and distrust among the three groups (Oliver and Johnson, 1984; Johnson and Oliver, 1989). While Blacks feel they have more in common with Latinos than with any other group, Latinos and Asians feel they have more in common with Whites (National Conference, 1993). The 1992 civil disturbances in Los Angeles highlighted the tensions that had emerged among Blacks, Latinos, and Asians (Koreans) in south central Los

Angeles (Abelmann and Lie, 1995; Stewart, 1993; Morrison and Lowry, 1994). Tensions are present in other cities as well: for example, in New York between Blacks and Koreans and between Blacks and Puerto Ricans; in Washington, D.C., between Blacks and Latinos; and in Miami between Blacks and Cubans and between Puerto Ricans and Cubans.

The 1996 election of a Dade County, Florida, mayor is illustrative of how tensions between Blacks and Cuban Americans trumped other presumed partisan and ideological differences. In that election, the moderate to liberal Democratic candidate was Cuban American Alex Penelas, and the conservative Republican candidate was Arthur Teele, a Black American. The conservative Republican Cuban American congressional delegation supported the moderate Cuban Democrat rather than the conservative Black Republican. Voting in the general election split along racial lines, with normally Republican Cubans voting for the Democrat and normally Democratic Blacks voting for the Republican. Penelas won the election. Examples of interminority group tensions are likely to increase in the future, particularly if the number of Whites residing in central cities continues to decline.

BLACK INSTITUTIONS: THE BLACK CHURCH

By far the most written about and identified institution in America's Black communities is the Black church. E. Franklin Frazier in his 1963 classic, *The Negro Church in America*, described the Black church as a "nation within a nation." For Frazier, "In providing a structured social life in which the Negro could give expression to his deepest feeling and at the same time achieve status and find a meaningful existence, the Negro church provided a refuge in a hostile White world" (44-45). Out of the church grew other organizing activities such as the pooling of economic resources for mutual assistance and insurance companies and "securing an education and building educational institutions" (Frazier, 1963, 83). Moreover, "The Negro church organization became the most important arena for political life among Negroes" (83). Other classic studies of the Black church also concluded that Black churches had been central to social and political activity in Black American communities for many years (DuBois, 1903; Woodson, 1921; Mays and Nicholson, 1933; Lincoln and Mamiya, 1990). It was in the churches that political information was disseminated, issues discussed, political strategies formulated, and church resources used for political activity. Despite Frazier's acknowledgment of the importance of the Black church to life in the Black community, he questioned whether it was possible for the church to be a vehicle for organizing challenges to the restrictions on Blacks in the world beyond the nation within a nation. He was not alone in his concern (Reed, 1986; Marx, 1967). Nevertheless, the weight of the evidence is on the side of the Black church as having served as an important political institution and resource for Black political activity.

As the 21st century begins, is the Black church still a major factor in political activity in America's Black communities? Does it continue to have significant influence on political mobilization in local and national elections?

Research is mixed on the answers to these questions. Tate (1993) found that Black religious institutions were still an important organizational resource for disseminating information about elections, encouraging church members to vote, providing a base for individuals to become involved in political campaigns, and contributing money to candidates. He concluded that "The church, compared to other Black institutions, has the most potential as a mobilizing agent within the Black community" (95). Harris (1995) noted that Blacks were more likely to receive political stimuli at their place of worship than were Anglo Whites, Latinos, and Jews. Dawson (1994) suggested that hearing political messages in church was weakly related to reinforcing the group political consciousness of Black congregants. According to Harris, Black religious institutions remain an important resource for Black political mobilization. At the same time, he identified an ambivalence on the part of the Black population toward the involvement of Black religious institutions in political activities.

The urban communities in which many Blacks live today, however, are not the same communities of a generation ago when the church was the focal point of community activity. With the lessening, although not the elimination of barriers to housing, many middle and upper income Blacks have migrated from the cities to surrounding suburbs. The result has been a concentration of lower income and poor Blacks in certain sections of major cities. Black churches, however, are not drawing their members from the community in which the church is physically located, since many who moved return to church on Sundays. Those most in need of outreach from the church probably are not members and are most likely less educated, poorer, and younger than the congregants. In addition, many previously predominantly Black communities are becoming home to other minority groups, specifically Latinos and Asians. Black churches, just like other Black organizations, are having to redefine their roles vis-à-vis the changing demographics of their surrounding communities.

PUBLIC POLICY CONCERNS

In 1968, the Kerner Commission Report warned that the United States was moving toward two societies, one Black, one White; 30 years later, the follow-up report is distressingly similar in tone (Harris and Curtis, 1998). While debate rages about the desirability of a "colorblind" society (a goal with broad support) and how to achieve it (controversy abounds), many realities indicate that Blacks and Whites in the United States experience different worlds and life chances. According to Abramson (1972), Blacks and Whites are exposed to different political realities that result in different political attitudes. He argues that many of the attitudes of Black Americans reflect an accurate response to the realities of Black political life in the United States. McClain (1982-83) extended Abramson's political reality concept to include objective social and environmental realities that may differ for Blacks and Whites—the social reality thesis. According to this argument, the objective reality of an individual's environment, in conjunction with the perceived reality of an individual's position, could be the basis upon which political attitudes are formed. What are some of the real and perceived differences? Do these differences result in different policy concerns for Black and White Americans? While space does not allow a full testing here of the social reality thesis or an analysis of all the policy areas of concern to Blacks that may be influenced by different social realities, one area with which Blacks are particularly concerned—violent crime—is explored.

Violent Crime

How much violent crime is there in the United States, and is it race-specific?[4] In 1992, based on crime victimization surveys, there were 6.6 million violent crimes, including 23,760 homicides (55 percent killed by handguns), 141,000 rapes, 1.2 million robberies, and 5.3 million assaults.[5] Five percent of all U.S. households had a member victimized by violence, and Americans had a greater chance of being involved in a violent crime than of being injured in a car accident (U.S. Department of Justice, 1994). While overall aggregate crime rates have been decreasing, they have not dropped for some segments of the population.

The differences in Black and White social realities are quite evident when violent crime is examined. The violent crime rate for Blacks was at its highest level in 1992, 50 per 1,000 persons, compared with 29.9 per 1,000 persons for Whites. Juvenile victimization rates are increasing. The overall aggregate victimization rate for those age 12 to 15 reached its highest level in 1992. Black males in this age group had the highest victimization rates for violent crime (113 per 1,000), while elderly White females had the lowest rate (3 per 1,000). Teenagers overall had very high rates: 90 per 1,000 for teenage White males, 55 per 1,000 for teenage White females, and 94 per 1,000 for teenage Black females (U.S. Department of Justice, 1994).

In 1991, homicide was the tenth leading cause of death for all Americans, but was the fourth leading cause of death for Blacks overall. Examining race and gender breakdowns for homicide victimization gives a clearer picture of Black/White different social realities. Black males had the highest homicide rate (72 per 100,000), followed by Black females (14 per 100,000), White males (9 per 100,000), and White females (3 per 100,000). Looking only at those between the ages of 15 and 24 but combining males and females, homicide was the third leading cause of death for Whites, exceeded only by accidents and suicide; for Blacks, however, homicide was the leading cause of death. Including all age and gender groups, Black males age 15 to 24 had the highest homicide rate (159 per 100,000) (U.S. Department of Justice, 1994).

Given these different Black/White realities, it is no surprise that 24.5 percent of Blacks identified crime, violence, guns, and gangs as the single most important problem when asked in a 1997 Joint Center for Political and Economic Studies survey to identify the most important problems facing the country today. The Blacks surveyed found the economy, jobs, and unemployment a distant second with 14.6 percent. The third most frequently identified problem was drugs (11.7 percent), a problem related to crime, violence, guns, and gangs. If added to the proportion of Blacks concerned about crime, 36.2 percent of Blacks were concerned about some aspect of crime and violence. Whites also listed crime, violence, guns, and gangs as the most important problem, but the level of concern was less than that of Blacks at 17.2 percent. Even with the 7.7 percent of Whites who thought drugs were a problem, the 24.9 percent of Whites concerned about crime was still significantly lower than that of Blacks. Whites found corruption and taxes the second most important problem at 12 percent. For Latinos, the economy, jobs, and unemployment were number one (15.6 percent), with crime, violence, guns, and gangs a close second (14.4 percent).

Racial differences in preferred policy options for addressing the issue of crime were also present in the Joint Center survey noted above. More than two-thirds (68.6 percent) of Whites and almost three-fourths (72.2 percent) of Latinos believed that the government should increase spending on prisons and law enforcement. Yet despite their higher levels of victimization, Blacks were split on the issue—a slim majority (51.1 percent) wanted increased spending on prisons and law enforcement, while more than two-fifths (44.9 percent) disagreed. Why were Blacks divided on this issue? Once again, Black policy preferences are rooted in their experiences. Notwithstanding increased vulnerability, Blacks have experienced less than equitable treatment from the police and the prison system in the United States, so they are not inclined to endorse them as crime control strategies. (On another dimension, while overwhelming percentages of Blacks, Whites, and Latinos supported stronger restrictions on the sale and use of handguns, Blacks were the most supportive) (Joint Center, 1997).

ISSUES THAT CONTINUE TO CONFRONT BLACK AMERICANS

Almost a century ago, DuBois (1903) observed that the fundamental political problem facing the United States was "the problem of the color line." DuBois's observation still rings true (Harris and Curtis, 1998). Race continues to be a "card" played in a variety of political settings, from elections to juries, at the same time that past opponents of racial equality and civil rights claim conversion to the gospel of colorblindness as articulated by Dr. Martin Luther King, Jr. Thus, the debates today have a common goal and disingenuously ignore the effects of history, the continuing discriminatory and exclusionary practices present in American society today and the fairly predictable effects of apparently racially neutral "rules of the game." These issues are no less important than those that DuBois and his colleagues contested in their efforts to reverse *Plessy* v. *Ferguson* (1896) and other legislation. Furthermore, the current debates are being held when the polity and the public are clearly antagonistic toward Black Americans and public policies that are perceived to work to the advantage of Blacks.

The rhetoric of the debates is often characterized by a fealty to individualism in liberal democratic thought and an aversion to recognizing people as members of a group. Blacks are accused of insisting on being classified as a group, thereby creating tensions with other Americans and undermining the individualistic visions of Dr. King and the nation's founders. To counteract this, color-conscious statutes and policies are identified and rooted out.

Implicit in this diagnosis is the idea that the responsibility for Black group identity lies with Blacks themselves and that by resisting the dismantling of hard-won protections and favorable policies, Blacks are working against their self-interests and the basic fabric of an ideal, colorblind society. Such ideas have currency in one form or another as the new century begins.

Blaming Blacks for group consciousness and cohesiveness reveals the lack of a sense of history. As an illustrative anecdote of the external source and the pernicious effect of Black group identification, consider the case of Gregory Howard Williams, Dean of Ohio State University's Law School. Williams, having the outward appearance of being White, was deemed to be bright, smart, and a future star until it was revealed that he was Black. Then the same adjectives no longer fit, and doors once open to him were closed (Williams, 1995). Individualism, however hallowed in liberal democratic theory, has had little relevance to how Blacks continue to be treated.

As noted, the debates ignore the evidence of ongoing racial discrimination. Racially based decisions continue in the very institutions that structure the opportunities for Black youths who aspire to individual achievement—the education system (Meier, Stewart, and England, 1989; Hall, 2000). Black students are less likely than White students to be provided the best educational opportunities and are more likely to be pushed out of schools. Such treatment can be mitigated, however, by the exercise of political power. Black representation on school boards is associated with Blacks gaining administrative positions. In districts where Blacks are administrators, there are more Black teachers. Where more Black teachers are employed, Black students fare better. Thus, there is a link between political representation and policy outcomes.

The present debates about mechanisms and policies to address the lingering effects of an earlier time also have clear ramifications for how the successor volume to this publication will read a century from now. If Blacks and Black interests cannot find representation in the political system, the electoral system and public policymaking will ultimately be judged to be unjust and illegitimate, and instability will likely follow.

The challenges facing Blacks in American politics in the 21st century are monumental—and some would argue, insurmountable. On a less pessimistic level, we can focus on what to do about the very real racial differences that continue to exist, and the list of what can be done is endless. Unfortunately, the debates about a colorblind society assume that existing racial differences are the result of the lack of individual initiative, thereby eliminating the necessity for public policy responses.

NOTES

1. Covered jurisdictions are those in which fewer than one-half of individuals eligible to vote were registered or voted in the 1964, 1968, or 1972 presidential elections *and* in which a discriminatory "test or device" was used in registration or voting. The states of Alabama, Alaska, Arizona, Georgia, Louisiana, Mississippi, South Carolina, Texas, and Virginia as well as 4 counties in California, 5 counties in Florida, 2 towns in Michigan, 10 towns in New Hampshire, 3 counties in New York, 40 counties in North Carolina, and 2 counties in South Dakota are covered jurisdictions.

2. North Carolina was only partially covered under the original act, as were Arizona, Hawaii, and Idaho. Alaska was fully covered.

3. This section is drawn from the election edition of McClain and Stewart (1999), pp. xiii-xviii.

4. The Federal Bureau of Investigation (FBI) defines violent crime in the United States as consisting of four offense categories—murder and nonnegligent manslaughter, forcible rape, robbery, and aggravated assault. All violent crimes involve force or threat of force (FBI, 1997, 10).

5. Tremendous differences exist between the official crime statistics reported by the FBI and the crime victimization surveys conducted by the Bureau of Justice Statistics. The survey data suggest higher levels of victimization in the United States than do the official statistics.

REFERENCES

Abelmann, N., and J. Lie. 1995. *Blue Dreams: Korean Americans and the Los Angeles Riots.* Cambridge: Harvard University Press.

Abramson, P.R. 1972. "Political Efficacy and Political Trust Among Black School Children: Two Explanations." *Journal of Politics* 34:1243-1275.

Ambrecht, B., and H.P. Pachon. 1974. "Ethnic Political Mobilization in a Mexican American Community: An Exploratory Study of East Los Angeles, 1965-1972." *Western Political Quarterly* 27:500-519.

Blalock, H.M. 1967. *Toward a Theory of Minority-Group Relations.* New York: John Wiley & Sons, Inc.

Bobo, L.D., and F.D. Gilliam. 1990. "Race, Sociopolitical Participation, and Black Empowerment." *American Political Science Review* 75:76-91.

Bobo, L.D., and V. Hutchings. 1996. "Perceptions of Racial Competition in a Multiracial Setting." *American Sociological Review* 61:951-972.

Bobo, L.D., C.L. Zubrinsky, J.H. Johnson, Jr., and M.L. Oliver. 1994. "Public Opinion Before and After a Spring of Discontent." In *The Los Angeles Riots: Lessons for the Urban Future.* Ed. M. Baldassare. Boulder, Col.: Westview Press, 103-133.

Bositis, D.A. 1996a. "Blacks and the 1996 Elections: A Preliminary Analysis." Unpublished paper.

———. 1996b. "African Americans and the Republican Party, 1996." Washington, D.C.: Joint Center for Political and Economic Studies.

Brown v. *Board of Education of Topeka.* 1954. 347 U.S. 483.

Browning, R.P., D.R. Marshall, and D.H. Tabb. 1984. *Protest Is Not Enough.* Berkeley: University of California Press.

————. 1990. "Has Political Incorporation Been Achieved? Is It Enough?" In *Racial Politics in American Cities*. Ed. R.P. Browning, D.R. Marshall, and D.H. Tabb. New York: Longman.

Bush v. *Vera*. 1996. 517 U.S. 952.

Cohen, G. 1982. "Alliance and Conflict Among Mexican Americans." *Ethnic and Racial Studies* 5:175-195.

Davidson, C. 1992. "The Voting Rights Act: A Brief History." In *Controversies in Minority Voting*. Ed. B. Grofman and C. Davidson. Washington, D.C.: Brookings Institution, 7-51.

Davidson, C., and B. Grofman, Eds. 1994. *Quiet Revolution in the South: The Impact of the Voting Rights Act, 1965-1990*. Princeton, N.J.: Princeton University Press.

Dawson, M.C. 1994. *Behind the Mule: Race and Class in African-American Politics*. Princeton, N.J.: Princeton University Press.

DuBois, W.E.B. 1903. *The Negro Church*. Atlanta: Atlanta University Press.

Dyer, J., A. Vedlitz, and S. Worchel. 1989. "Social Distance Among Racial and Ethnic Groups in Texas: Some Demographic Correlates." *Social Science Quarterly* 70:607-616.

Eisinger, P.K. 1976. *Patterns of Interracial Politics: Conflict and Cooperation in the City*. New York: Academic Press.

Espiritu, Y.L. 1992. *Asian American Panethnicity: Bridging Institutions and Identities*. Philadelphia: Temple University Press.

Estrada, L., F.C. Garcia, and R.F. Marcias. 1981. "Chicanos in the United States: A History of Exploitation and Resistance." *Daedalus* 110:103-132.

Falcón, A. 1988. "Black and Latino Politics in New York City." In *Latinos and the Political System*. Ed. F.C. Garcia. Notre Dame, Ind.: University of Notre Dame Press.

Federal Bureau of Investigation. 1997. *Crime in the United States—1997*. Washington, D.C.: U.S. Government Printing Office (GPO).

Finkel, S.E., T.M. Guterbock, and M.J. Borg. 1991. "Race-of-Interviewer Effects in a Preelection Poll: Virginia 1989." *Public Opinion Quarterly* 55 (Fall):313-330.

Frazier, E.F. 1963. *The Negro Church in America*. New York: Schocken Books.

Freer, R. 1994. "Black-Korean Conflict." In *The Los Angeles Riots: Lessons for the Urban Future*. Ed. M. Baldassare. Boulder, Col.: Westview Press, 175-203.

Giles, M.W., and A. Evans. 1986. "The Power Approach to Intergroup Hostility." *Journal of Conflict Resolution* 30(3):469-486.

Grebler, L., J. Moore, and R. Guzman. 1970. *The Mexican American People*. New York: Free Press.

Grofman, B., L. Handley, and R. Niemi. 1992. *Minority Representation and the Quest for Voting Equality*. New York: Cambridge University Press.

Guinier, L. 1994. *The Tyranny of the Majority: Fundamental Fairness in Representative Democracy*. New York: Free Press.

Guinn v. *United States*. 1915. 238 U.S. 347.

Gurin, P., S. Hatchett, and J.S. Jackson. 1989. *Hope and Independence: Blacks' Response to Electoral and Party Politics*. New York: Russell Sage Foundation.

Hall, P.Q. 2000. "Race, Representation, and Educational Opportunity in North Carolina Public Schools." Paper presented at the meeting of the National Conference of Black Political Scientists, March 9-12, 2000, Washington, D.C.

Harris, F.C. 1995. "Religious Institutions and African American Political Mobilization." In *Classifying by Race*. Ed. P.E. Peterson. Princeton, N.J.: Princeton University Press.

Harris, F.R., and L.A. Curtis, Eds. 1998. *Locked in the Poorhouse: Cities, Race, and Poverty in the United States.* Boulder, Col.: Rowman & Littlefield Publishers, Inc.

Henry, C.P. 1980. "Black and Chicano Coalitions: Possibilities and Problems." *Western Journal of Black Studies* 4:222-232.

Henry, C.P., and C. Muñoz, Jr. 1991. "Ideological and Interest Links in California Rainbow Politics." In *Racial and Ethnic Politics in California.* Ed. B.O. Jackson and M.B. Preston. Berkeley, Cal.: Institute of Governmental Studies.

Jennings, J. 1992. "Blacks and Latinos in the American City in the 1990s: Toward Political Alliances or Social Conflict." *National Political Science Review* 3:158-163.

Johnson, J.H., C.K. Jones, W.C. Farrell, Jr., and M.L. Oliver. 1992. "The Los Angeles Rebellion: A Retrospective View." *Economic Development Quarterly* 6:356-372.

Johnson, J.H., and M.L. Oliver. 1989. "Inter-Ethnic Minority Conflict in Urban America: The Effects of Economic and Social Dislocations." *Urban Geography* 10:449-463.

Johnson et al. v. *Mortham.* 1995. 915 F. Supp. 1529, N.D. F199.

Joint Center for Political and Economic Studies. 1997. *1997 National Opinion Poll—Politics.* Washington, D.C.: Joint Center for Political and Economic Studies.

―――.1998a. *Black Elected Officials: A Statistical Summary, 1993-1997.* Washington, D.C.: Joint Center for Political and Economic Studies.

―――. 1998b. *1998 National Opinion Poll—Politics.* Washington, D.C.: Joint Center for Political and Economic Studies.

Judd, D. 1979. *The Politics of American Cities.* Boston: Little Brown and Company.

Lincoln, C.E., and L.H. Mamiya. 1990. *The Black Church in the African American Experience.* Durham, N.C.: Duke University Press.

MacManus, S., and C. Cassell. 1982. "Mexican Americans in City Politics: Participation, Representation, and Policy Preferences." *Urban Interest* 4:57-69.

Marx, G.T. 1967. *Protest and Prejudice.* New York: Harper and Row.

Mays, B., and J.W. Nicholson. 1933. *The Negro's Church.* New York: Institute of Social and Religious Research.

McClain, P.D. 1982-83. "Environment of Risk and Determinants of Racial Attitudes Toward Gun Regulation: A Test of the Social Reality Thesis." *Journal of Environmental Systems* 12:229-248.

―――. 1993. "The Changing Dynamics of Urban Politics: Black and Hispanic Municipal Employment—Is There Competition?" *Journal of Politics* 55:399-414.

―――. 1996. "Coalition and Competition: Patterns of Black-Latino Relations in Urban Politics." In *The Politics of Minority Coalitions: Race, Ethnicity, and Shared Uncertainties.* Ed. W.C. Rich. Westport, Ct.: Praeger.

McClain, P.D., and A.J. Karnig. 1990. "Black and Hispanic Socioeconomic and Political Competition." *American Political Science Review* 84:535-545.

McClain, P.D., and J. Stewart, Jr. 1999. *Can We All Get Along? Racial and Ethnic Minorities in American Politics,* 2d ed. updated. Boulder, Col.: Westview Press.

McClain, P.D., and S.C. Tauber. 1994. "The Urban Mosaic: Interminority Group Relations in Urban Politics." Paper presented at the 1994 annual meeting of the Southern Political Science Association, Atlanta. November 2-6.

―――. 1995. "We Win! You Lose! Implications of Black, Latino, and Asian Socioeconomic and Political Resources for the Other Groups' Electoral Success in Urban Politics." Paper presented at the 1995 annual meeting of the American Political Science Association, Chicago. August 31-September 3.

―――. 1998. "Black and Latino Socioeconomic and Political Competition: Has a Decade Made a Difference?" *American Politics Quarterly* 26 (April):101-116.

McDonald, L., and j.a. powell. 1993. *The Rights of Racial Minorities: The Basic ACLU Guide to Racial Minority Rights,* 2d. ed. Carbondale: Southern Illinois University Press.

Meier, K.J., and J. Stewart, Jr. 1990. "Interracial Competition in Large Urban School Districts: Elections and Public Policy." Paper presented at the annual meeting of the American Political Science Association, San Francisco.

Meier, K.J., J. Stewart, Jr., and R.E. England. 1989. *Race, Class, and Education: The Politics of Second-Generation Discrimination*. Madison: University of Wisconsin Press.

Miller v. Johnson. 1995. 515 U.S. 900.

Mollenkopf, J.H. 1990. "New York: The Great Anomaly." In *Racial Politics in American Cities*. Ed. R.P. Browning, D.R. Marshall, and D.H. Tabb. New York: Longman, 97-115.

Morrison, P.A., and I.S. Lowry. 1994. "A Riot of Color: The Demographic Setting." In *The Los Angeles Riots: Lessons for the Urban Future*. Ed. M. Baldassare. Boulder, Col.: Westview Press, 19-46.

National Conference of Christians and Jews. 1993. *Taking America's Pulse: The Full Report of the National Conference Survey on Inter-Group Relations*. New York: Louis Harris and Associates.

National Council of La Raza. 1990. "Background Paper for Black-Hispanic Dialogue." Unpublished paper.

Nelson, W.E., Jr. 1992. "Black Mayoral Leadership: A Twenty-Year Perspective." *National Political Science Review* 2:188-195.

Oliver, M.L., and J.H. Johnson. 1984. "Inter-Ethnic Conflict in an Urban Ghetto: The Case of Blacks and Latinos in Los Angeles." *Social Movements, Conflicts, and Change* 6:57-94.

Olsen, M.C. 1970. "Social and Political Participation of Blacks." *American Sociological Review* 35:682-697.

Petrocik, J.R., and S.W. Desposato. 1998. "The Partisan Consequences of Majority-Minority Redistricting in the South, 1992-1994." *Journal of Politics* 60:613-633.

Plessy v. Ferguson. 1896. 163 U.S. 537.

Reed, A., Jr. 1986. *The Jesse Jackson Phenomenon*. New Haven: Yale University Press.

Reeves, K. 1997. *Voting Hopes or Fears? White Voters, Black Candidates, and Racial Politics in America*. New York: Oxford University Press.

Regalado, J.A. 1994. "Community Coalition-Building." In *The Los Angeles Riots: Lessons for the Urban Future*. Ed. M. Baldassare. Boulder, Col.: Westview Press, 205-235.

Rose, H.M. 1971. *The Black Ghetto: A Spatial Behavioral Perspective*. New York: McGraw-Hill.

Saito, L.T. 1993. "Asian Americans and Latinos in San Gabriel Valley, California: Ethnic Political Cooperation and Redistricting 1990-92." *Amerasia Journal* 19:55-58.

See, L.A. 1986-87. "International Migration and Refugee Problems: Conflict between Black Americans and Southeast Asian Refugees." *The Journal of Intergroup Relations* 14:38-50.

Shaw v. Hunt. 1997. 517 U.S. 899.

Shaw v. Reno. 1993. 509 U.S. 630.

Shingles, R.D. 1981. "Black Consciousness and Political Participation: The Missing Link." *American Political Science Review* 75:76-91.

Sigelman, L., and S. Welch. 1991. *Black Americans' Views of Racial Inequality: The Dream Deferred*. Cambridge: Cambridge University Press.

Smith v. Allwright. 1944. 321 U.S. 649.

Sonenshein, R.J. 1990. "Biracial Coalition Politics in Los Angeles." In *Racial Politics in American Cities*. Ed. R.P. Browning, D.R. Marshall, and D.H. Tabb. New York: Longman, 41-63.

———. 1993. *Politics in Black and White: Race and Power in Los Angeles*. Princeton, N.J.: Princeton University Press.

Stewart, E. 1993. "Communication Between African Americans and Korean Americans: Before and After the Los Angeles Riots." *Amerasia Journal* 19:23-53.

Tate, K. 1993. *From Protest to Politics: The New Black Voters in American Elections.* Cambridge, Mass.: Harvard University Press.

Tedin, K.L., and R.W. Murray. 1994. "Support for Biracial Political Coalitions among Blacks and Hispanics." *Social Science Quarterly* 75:772-789

Thernstrom, A.M. 1987. *Whose Votes Count? Affirmative Action and Minority Voting Rights.* Cambridge: Harvard University Press.

U.S. Bureau of the Census. 1993. "Voting and Registration in the Election of 1992." *Current Population Reports,* P20-466. Washington, D.C.: GPO.

———. 1995. "Voting and Registration in the Election of November 1994." Tables 2, 17. Available from http://www.census.gov/population/socdemo/voting/work/tab02txt (or /tab17.txt)

———. 1998a. "Table 1. Percent Reported Voted and Registered by Race, Hispanic Origin and Gender: November 1964 to Present." Available from http://www.census.gov/population/socdemo/voting/history/vot1.prn

———. 1998b. "Voting and Registration in the Election of November 1996." *Current Population Reports,* P20-504. Table 4. Washington, D.C.: GPO.

U.S. Commission on Civil Rights. 1968. *Political Participation.* Washington, D.C.: GPO.

U.S. Department of Justice. 1994. "Violent Crime: National Crime Victimization Survey." NCJ-147486, April. Washington, D.C.: Bureau of Justice Statistics.

Verba, S., and N. Nie. 1972. *Participation in America.* New York: Harper and Row.

Warren, C.L., J.G. Corbett, and J.F. Stack. 1986. "Minority Mobilization in an International City: Rivalry and Conflict." *Political Science and Politics* 19:626-634.

———. 1990. "Hispanic Ascendancy and Tripartite Politics in Miami." In *Racial Politics in American Cities.* Ed. R.P. Browning, D.R. Marshall, and D.H. Tabb. New York: Longman.

Welch, S., A.K. Karnig, and R. Eribes. 1983. "Changes in Hispanic Local Employment in the Southwest." *Western Political Quarterly* 36:660-673.

Williams, G.H. 1995. *Life on the Color Line: The True Story of a White Boy Who Discovered He Was Black.* New York: Dutton.

Williams, L.F. 1987. "Black Political Progress in the 1980s: The Electoral Arena." In *The New Black Politics: The Search for Political Power,* 2d ed. Ed. M.B. Preston, L. Henderson, and P. Puryear. New York: Longman, 97-135.

Woodson, C.G. 1921. *The History of the Negro Church.* Washington, D.C.: Associated Publishers.

Chapter 9

Race, Crime, and Punishment:
Old Controversies and New Challenges

by Darnell F. Hawkins
Professor of African American Studies, Sociology, and Criminal Justice,
University of Illinois at Chicago

and Cedric Herring
Professor of Sociology and Public Policy,
University of Illinois at Chicago

INTRODUCTION

This chapter explores several themes and debates that have been an integral part of U.S. history and the nation's legacy of race relations and that continue to pose major public policy challenges at the beginning of the 21st century. Focusing largely on trends during the decades since 1950, we seek to account for patterns of change and continuity in the level of ethnic and racial disparity within the nation's criminal justice system. At the center of our analysis is an assessment of trends in race-specific rates of imprisonment during a period of rapid societal transformation. We also provide data on racial differences in arrests for crime and in rates of criminal victimization. We conclude with a discussion of the social forces that undergird these phenomena, namely, the persistence of socioeconomic inequality and its racially disproportionate impact on American society. This discussion is framed in an assessment of the implications of our findings for public policy.

HISTORICAL OVERVIEW

For much of U.S. history, crime and punishment have provided some of the most publicly visible and horrific icons and symbols of the ethnic, racial, and social class inequality and conflict within U.S. society. From the vantage point of the early 21st century, these intergroup cleavages and their impact on crime and punishment are perceived largely in terms of Black versus White or Anglo versus Latino. Our analysis in this chapter will focus mainly on crime and justice across these contemporary racial and ethnic contrasts. However, it is important to place the discussion within the context of the broader ethnic and racial divisions and conflicts that have shaped American history for more than a century.

At the turn of the 20th century, the nation's most recent immigrants, largely from eastern and southern Europe, were disproportionately represented among those confined in state and local prisons, jails, and chain gangs. Decades earlier, such overrepresentation within the criminal justice system was the fate of immigrants of Irish ancestry. Euphemistically labeled the "foreign-born," members of these groups were frequently portrayed by the media and in government documents as prone to excessive involvement in crime, disorder, and other unacceptable conduct. Images of their criminality, perhaps even more than notions of their lesser intelligence or nonmainstream religious beliefs, drove the public policy campaigns that successfully curbed their entry into the United States from the late 1800s well into the 20th century. Although largely downplayed in historical accounts of the period, the question of ethnic and racial differences in rates of crime and administration of justice was central to many of the political and economic struggles at the turn of the century. Those struggles pitted Irish, Italians, Jews, Greeks, and Poles against the more established ethnic Europeans who preceded them (Brown and Warner, 1992; DuBois, 1904; Gould, 1981; Hawkins, 1993, 1994, 1995; Monkkonen, 1975; Nelli, 1970; National Commission on Law Observance and Enforcement, 1931; Rose, 1997; Steinberg, 1989; Takaki, 1987, 1993; U.S. Immigration Commission, 1911).

The years just before and after the beginning of the 20th century were also noted for extremes of racial disparity in crime and punishment. Much is known about the disproportionate presence of Blacks in southern prisons and jails during this period (e.g., see Adamson, 1983; Hawkins, 1985; Myers, 1995; Jaynes and Williams, 1989; Sellin, 1976). Rates of confinement for Blacks living in the northern states were also extremely high (DuBois, 1899). In the South, actions taken against African Americans within and outside the formal criminal justice system came to symbolize the racial bigotry of the period; such actions often provoked political and public policy debates reminiscent of earlier controversies surrounding the moral and legal acceptability of slavery. The most extreme of those widely noted injustices occurred before World War I. Yet even in the decades between World Wars I and II, lynchings, chain-gang style penal practices, and prosecutorial and judicial racial bigotry were commonplace (Adamson, 1983; Beck and Tolnay, 1995a, 1995b; Gunning, 1996; Myers, 1995; Kennedy, 1997).

The Scottsboro, Alabama, rape case of 1931-32 and similar instances of race-based "rush to judgment" tactics within the southern criminal justice system were stark reminders of the seemingly inextricable link between race and the administration of justice in the United States. Indeed, legal challenges to such abuses brought by or on behalf of criminal defendants of color were instrumental in shaping the "due process revolution" that changed American criminal procedural law during the past half-century. From *Powell* v. *Alabama* (1932) to *Miranda* v. *Arizona* (1966), the nation's criminal law reflects efforts to confront the legacy of racial and ethnic inequality.

African Americans are not the only people of color who have experienced substantial overrepresentation in the justice system. Members of other racial and ethnic minority populations have been imprisoned at very high rates and have been the target of some of the same miscarriages of justice. Many historical accounts of the period between the end of the Civil War and the early decades of the 20th century ignored the extent to which the criminal behavior of the foreign-born from Mexico, China, and Japan as well as that of Native Americans was used as justification for their exclusion or "pacification" (Sanborn, 1904; U.S. Immigration Commission, 1911; Wilson, 1980; Takaki, 1987; Knepper, 1989; Steinberg, 1989).

THE COLOR LINE AND AMERICAN CRIMINAL JUSTICE

As American society begins the new millennium, the legal, public policy, and social scientific debates over how race, ethnicity, and socioeconomic status affect crime and punishment—far from being artifacts of the past—continue largely unabated. Further, many of the themes and topics of debate at the turn of the 20th century are strikingly similar to those in today's public discourse. Some analysts have concluded that, despite perceptions to the contrary, perhaps very little has changed regarding race, crime, and punishment in the United States during the past century, especially when considering the plight of African Americans (Kennedy, 1997; Russell, 1998).

Yet it is equally clear that for some of the ethnic and racial groups noted above, much indeed has changed. Without exception, the disproportionate rates of arrest and imprisonment of White ethnic populations during the late 1800s and early 1900s significantly declined over time. So, too, did the levels of detention and confinement of Chinese and Japanese Americans. It is beyond the scope of this chapter to catalog all of the social changes that may have contributed to this shift. But a number of researchers have suggested that those groups' experiences with crime and punishment have potential relevance for efforts to understand the causes of current racial and ethnic disparity and to devise public policies aimed at reducing it (Steinberg, 1989; Hawkins, 1993, 1994).

It is clear that much of the drop in the rates of criminal justice system involvement of America's White ethnic immigrants stems directly or indirectly from their improved socioeconomic status. That proposition is a major tenet of our discussion of contemporary trends. Later in the chapter, we explore the link between socioeconomic conditions and the actual etiology of criminal conduct among contemporary African Americans. A group's improved social and economic standing also affects its level of representation within the justice system in other, more indirect ways.

For example, Brown and Warner (1992) observed that at the turn of the 20th century many of the newest immigrants were targeted by the police for surveillance, especially for public order offenses. That surveillance resulted in excessive and disproportionate rates of arrest and conviction. Part of the eventual decline in the rates of arrest and punishment of these targeted White ethnic groups not only resulted from changes in social behavior that accompany greater affluence, but also was linked to their successful entry into gatekeeping roles in the criminal justice system. The entry of large numbers of these groups into the ranks of the police, prosecutors, magistrates, and judges was likely a decisive factor in reducing their levels of official sanctioning for crime (Hawkins, 1994).

In addition, the ability of White ethnic groups to use their improved economic status to counteract the public policies and laws that provided a legal and ideological basis for their differential targeting also affected their level of criminal justice system involvement over time. Contemporary African Americans have used protest and politics to successfully dismantle many of the de jure manifestations of American racism. So, too, White ethnic groups used their political clout to fight the ethnic biases and anti-immigrant sentiments that fueled some of the ethnic disparity in crime and punishment at the beginning of the 20th century. As a result, political appeals and rhetoric that highlighted the criminality of White ethnic groups such as the Irish and southern and eastern Europeans and, to a lesser extent, people of Italian or Jewish ancestry were largely absent in the nation's public discourse by 1950 (Steinberg, 1989; Hawkins, 1993, 1994).

Similarly, the economic success of the earliest waves of Asian immigrants to the United States likely contributed significantly to the gradual decline in their rates of criminal justice system involvement. Sometimes labeled "model minorities" today, Japanese and Chinese Americans are now noted for their relative underrepresentation among people arrested, convicted, and punished for crime.

It is equally clear that the level of criminal justice involvement for other previously overrepresented groups, notably African Americans, Latinos, and Native Americans, has not changed as markedly during the past century. Indeed, events and developments of the past decade have raised anew concerns regarding the connection between race, ethnicity, and crime, with much of the focus on African Americans. Among the incidents most frequently noted are the use of the Willie Horton vignette by George Bush during the 1988 presidential election campaign, the police beating of Rodney King in 1991, the O.J. Simpson murder trial in 1996, and the beatings and shootings of Black citizens by New York City police between 1997 and 1999. Some analysts view these events and the reactions to them as evidence of a lack of progress in race relations and as cause for serious concern for the future of the nation (Hacker, 1992; Rowan, 1996). When seen against the backdrop of more routine, everyday patterns of crime, law enforcement, criminal punishment, and the public perceptions that accompany them, these incidents are frequently cited as proof of the racial chasm that divides American society. This backdrop includes:

- escalating rates of criminal violence and other crime within the nation's inner cities, especially among underclass youth (Fingerhut and Kleinman, 1990; Fingerhut, Ingram, and Feldman, 1992; Blumstein, 1995; Fox, 1996; Sickmund, Snyder, and Poe-Yamagata, 1997; Anderson, 1998; Cook and Laub, 1998; Fagan and Wilkinson, 1998);

- the racialization of the War on Drugs, as symbolized by the gross sentencing disparity between those convicted of possessing crack cocaine and those convicted of possessing powder cocaine, as well as the targeting of African American inner-city communities by law enforcement (Tonry, 1995; Chambliss, 1995; Miller, 1996; Kennedy, 1997; Russell, 1998); and

- the trend toward more punitive sentencing policies in recent decades, resulting in dramatic increases in the number of state and federal prisoners in the United States, with a growing overrepresentation of people of color (Tonry, 1995; Mauer, 1990; Mauer and Huling, 1995; Miller, 1996; Blumstein and Beck, 1999).

The explanatory dilemma posed by the contrast between the enormous progress made by ethnic Whites and Asians and the lack of significant progress by African Americans, Latinos, and Native Americans is evident in all of the chapters in this volume. As the historical sketch and outline of recent developments here have suggested, the dilemma is particularly acute in the study of race, crime, and punishment. The questions posed by this contrast include:

- Has the plight of African Americans, as measured by their involvement in crime and their exposure to the criminal justice system, improved or worsened over the past several decades?

- To what extent do race and ethnicity continue to shape patterns of crime and administration of justice in the United States today? Has there been change over time in the type of discrimination facing African Americans and other people of color in law enforcement and within the nation's criminal justice system?

- What is the connection between socioeconomic inequality and the overrepresentation of African Americans and other people of color within the criminal justice system?

- What has been the effect of the "new immigration" of recent decades on the racial/ethnic distribution of crime and punishment?

- What are the implications for public policy of the status of African Americans within the nation's criminal justice system? What public policy initiatives are needed to improve current levels of racial disparity in crime and punishment?

This chapter explores these and related questions. In many respects, the four and one-half decades between 1950 and 1995 offer an ideal temporal framework for assessing the extent of change and continuity in crime and justice. As other chapters in this volume document, American society since the 1950s has experienced important social, political, and economic transformation. Areas of societal change include the substantial alteration in the legal and political status of African Americans that resulted from the Civil Rights movement and the reforms in law and public policy that the movement brought about at the federal, state, and local levels. There is also evidence of significant change in the socioeconomic well-being of large segments of the nation's Black population and improvement in White attitudes toward Blacks during this period.

Many of these societal changes might be expected to have affected the level of inequality and disparity in crime and justice as well as other race-related outcomes and conditions. That potential was noted by early analysts of crime and justice. From the 1920s through the early 1970s, the criminological literature is replete with anticipation and advocacy of improvements in the legal and social well-being of African Americans. Most analysts shared the view that such improvements would lead to a decrease in levels of racial disparity for observed rates of criminal involvement and punishment. They attributed high rates of Black crime and punishment to the effects of economic deprivation and the lack of political influence. Improvements in the former were seen to decrease the "propensity" for criminal behavior among Blacks; economic progress and political clout were seen to reduce the effects of race on the administration of justice (Sellin, 1928; Shaw and Mackay, 1942; Branham and Kutash, 1949; Quinney, 1970; Wolfgang and Cohen, 1970; Chambliss and Seidman, 1971).

During more recent decades, crime analysts, like their counterparts in other areas of social research, have cast their discussions of race and crime within a different and less optimistic framework. They have highlighted both the post-1960s rise in crime and violence in the United States and the increasingly punitive response by lawmakers to this upward trend. Further, in contrast to the "rising tide lifts all boats" themes in the earlier literature, recent analysts have pointed to the growing socioeconomic schisms in American society. These include the widening of the gap between Blacks and Whites as well as the gaps among African Americans, most notably the split between the growing middle class and the inner-city poor.

This chapter assesses the effects of race on crime and punishment during decades characterized by two seemingly counteracting sets of causal forces: the liberating and racial inequity-reducing effects of the Civil Rights reforms of the early decades of the period; and the rise since 1970 of what Wilson (1987) and others have labeled the "urban underclass." The underclass is defined "in terms of attitudes and behavior, especially behavior indicating deviance from social norms—weak attachment to the labor force, bearing children out of wedlock, dependence on public assistance, and drug use and habitual criminal behavior" (Jargowsky and Bane, 1991, 236). We begin our examination of the fit between these sets of social forces and the empirical realities of race, crime, and punishment by analyzing imprisonment trends in the United States since 1950.

TRENDS IN IMPRISONMENT AND ARREST, 1950-95

In 1990, the American media reacted with alarm to the publication of a study conducted by the Sentencing Project, a Washington, D.C.-based research and advocacy group (Mauer, 1990). Perhaps the most widely cited finding from the report was Mauer's conclusion that during 1989, more Black males between the ages of 20 and 29 were under the control of the nation's criminal justice system (in jail or prison or on probation or parole) than were enrolled in institutions of higher education (609,690 versus 436,000). Mauer also reported that 23 percent of all Black men in this age range were in the grasp of the criminal justice system during 1989. A second report (Mauer and Huling, 1995, 3) showed that by 1994 this number had increased to 787,692, or 30.2 percent of all 20-29 year-old Black males in the United States.

For many observers, these statistics provided a handy reference point to illustrate the link between race and crime in the United States. For some, it provided more evidence of the legacy of racism in American society. For others, it was seen as proof of excessive and rapidly growing involvement in serious crime among America's urban, Black, and Latino youth. Table 9-1 is

TABLE 9-1

Race and Criminal Justice System Control, 20-29 Year-Olds, 1989 and 1994

Race/ Gender & Year	State & Federal Prisons	Jails	Probation	Parole	All	Rate[1] %
White Males						
1989	153,314	94,616	697,567	109,011	1,054,508	6.2
1994	180,915	110,585	640,956	136,620	1,069,076	6.7
Black Males						
1989	146,064	66,188	305,306	92,132	609,690	23.0
1994	211,205	95,114	351,368	130,005	787,692	30.2
Hispanic Males						
1989	42,457	24,357	134,772	36,669	238,255	10.4
1994	81,391	41,641	138,703	56,412	318,147	12.3
White Females						
1989	7,268	7,099	141,174	8,712	164,249	1.0
1994	9,875	11,872	177,360	15,802	214,909	1.4
Black Females						
1989	6,737	6,095	58,597	6,998	78,417	2.7
1994	12,138	10,876	96,481	14,921	134,416	4.8
Hispanic Females						
1989	1,997	2,036	29,850	3,210	37,093	1.8
1994	3,537	4,171	36,099	6,137	49,994	2.2

1. The percentage of all Americans in that gender/race/age group under the control of the criminal justice system.

Sources: Mauer (1990), Table 1, 8; and Mauer and Huling (1995), Table 1, 3.

a summary of data provided in the two aforementioned reports. It illustrates the overrepresentation of African Americans and Latinos among those under the control of the nation's criminal justice system in 1989 and 1994; it also shows the sizable increase in the number of people of color. During this five-year period, the rate of social control for Black males increased by nearly one-third, and the rate for Black females rose by 77 percent, whereas Whites experienced modest levels of social control and rates of increase. There has been considerable debate regarding the causes of the rise in racial disparity. Before turning to that debate, the extent of racial disproportionality in rates of control and confinement will be examined further.

Racial Disparities in Confinement Rates

The U.S. Department of Justice (1997a), in an annual report of correctional populations, presents data consistent with the temporal trends shown in Table 9-1. According to the report, during 1995:

- 5.4 million adults in the United States were under correctional supervision;

- 1.1 million were confined in state and federal prisons, and 499,000 were held in local jails; of these, 784,000 (49 percent) were White and 767,000 (48 percent) were Black;

- 3.8 million people were on probation or parole, including about 2.4 million (64 percent) Whites and about 1.3 million (35 percent) Blacks.

Given that African Americans were about 12 percent of the nation's overall population in 1995 and that males are the bulk of all people under criminal justice system control, these statistics show an alarming level of racial disparity. Black males, who constitute about 6 percent of the nation's population, are about 48 percent of all people in prison or jail—nearly eight times the rate expected on the basis of population size alone.

In light of the historical grounding of the beginning of this chapter, how do the racial disparities of the late 1980s and early 1990s compare with those of earlier decades? Table 9-2 shows the racial composition of federal and state prison populations at 10-year intervals between 1950 and 1980 and yearly between 1981 and 1995. Changes during this 45-year period are notable in several respects. Most striking is the remarkable growth in the overall size of the nation's prison population, a phenomenon that is unprecedented in the history of the nation (Blumstein and Beck, 1999).

The rise from 178,065 inmates in 1950 to 1,126,287 in 1995 represents a 633 percent increase. However, as Table 9-2 also illustrates, the trend toward increasingly higher imprisonment rates is not evident throughout the entire period; the 1960s were an exception to an otherwise steady rate of growth. In 1950, the overall confinement rate for Americans was 110 per 100,000 citizens. This rate increased to 119 in 1960, but declined to 97 by 1970. The 1970s, 1980s, and 1990s were marked by a continued rise in the rate of imprisonment. By 1981, the rate had reached 153/100,000 (U.S. Department

TABLE 9-2

Prisoners Under State and Federal Jurisdiction by Race, 1950-95

Year	Total	White	Black	% Black	Other[1]
1950	178,065	NA	NA	34	NA
1960	226,344	NA	NA	37	NA
1970	198,831	NA	NA	41	NA
1980	328,695	169,274	150,249	46	9,172
1981	368,772	190,503	168,129	46	10,140
1982	414,362	214,741	189,610	46	10,011
1983	437,238	225,902	200,216	46	11,120
1984	462,442	239,428	209,673	45	13,341
1985	502,507	253,599	220,700	44	28,208
1986	544,972	274,701	246,833	45	23,438
1987	585,040	291,606	262,958	45	30,476
1988	627,600	308,712	289,462	46	29,426
1989	712,364	343,550	334,952	47	33,862
1990	773,919	369,485	367,122	47	37,312
1991	825,619	385,347	395,245	48	45,027
1992	882,500	409,700	424,900	48	47,900
1993	970,444	444,100	473,300	49	53,044
1994	1,054,774	464,167	501,672	48	88,935
1995	1,126,287	455,021	544,005	48	127,261

1. Includes other races and persons for whom race was undetermined. Latinos are typically included with Blacks and Whites. Figures exclude jail inmates.

Sources: U.S. Department of Justice, year-end reports and other periodic publications. Titles vary. Racial breakdowns were not available in most of the reports for the period between 1950 and 1980. The "% Black" data for 1950, 1960, 1970, and 1980 were taken from a special Department of Justice study prepared by Cahalan (1986).

of Justice, 1983, 48). Counting both prison and jail inmates, U.S. incarceration rates climbed to 312/100,000 in 1985, to 460/100,000 in 1990, and to 598/100,000 in 1995 (U.S. Department of Justice, 1997a, 6).

The increase in the size of the U.S. prison population is also associated with a growing disparity over time between White and African American rates of confinement. In 1950, about one out of every three prisoners were African American. By 1995, Blacks were one out of every two inmates. As would be expected, the rise in the level of racial disparity for the year-end prison population is also reflected in the changing profile of yearly prison admissions. As shown in Table 9-3, the rate of Black admissions rose from 30 percent of all prisoners in 1950 to 44 percent in 1986. By 1995, the rate was 48 percent (U.S. Department of Justice, 1997a, 14).

TABLE 9-3

**Percentage of State and Federal Prison
Admissions by Race, 1950-95**

Year	% White	% Black	% Other Race
1950	69	30	1
1960	66	32	2
1970	61	39	–
1975	64	35	1
1980	58	41	1
1981	57	42	1
1982	55	44	1
1983	58	41	1
1984	58	41	1
1985	56	43	1
1986	55	44	1
1987	53	45	2
1988	49	50	1
1989	47	52	1
1990	48	51	1
1991	46	53	1
1992	46	53	1
1993	46	53	1
1994	47	52	1
1995	51	48	1

Sources: Langan (1991); U.S. Department of Justice (1997a).

Further evidence of the rising level of racial disparity in prison and jail confinement rates is seen in the more detailed examination of confinement rates per 100,000 residents found in Table 9-4. These data reveal a major increase between 1985 and 1995 in the confinement rate for Black males and females. There was also a substantial increase in the confinement rate for White females. Yet even with the increases for other race/gender groupings during this period, the Black male rate of imprisonment in 1995 was 7.5 times the White male rate, 102 times the White female rate, and 15 times the Black female rate.

Although informative, the data in Table 9-4 conceal other major changes in levels of ethnic and racial disparity in incarceration rates. These changes relate to the steady decrease during the 1980s and 1990s in the number of non-Hispanic Whites among those imprisoned.

The relatively sizable increase in the number of Whites incarcerated between 1985 and 1995 can be attributed partly to a growth in the per capita

TABLE 9-4

**Number of Adults Held in State or Federal Prisons
and Local Jails per 100,000 Adult Residents
by Race and Gender, 1985-95***

Year	White		Black	
	Males	Females	Males	Females
1985	528	27	3,544	183
1986	570	29	3,850	189
1987	594	35	3,943	216
1988	629	41	4,441	257
1989	685	47	5,066	321
1990	718	48	5,365	338
1991	740	51	5,717	356
1992	774	53	6,015	365
1993	805	56	6,259	403
1994	851	61	6,682	435
1995	919	68	6,926	456

* Data are based on the resident population of each group on July 1
of each year.

Source: U.S. Department of Justice (1997a), Table 1.7, 7.

rate of confinement for Whites of Hispanic origin. In Table 9-5, for example, Latinos were only 7.6 percent of the nation's prisoners in 1980, but 15.5 percent in 1995. The actual number of Hispanic prisoners increased almost sevenfold during this period, growing by 219 percent, an average increase of 12.3 percent each year (U.S. Department of Justice, 1997b). The rising rates of Latino confinement account for much of the growth over time in the number of White prisoners in Table 9-2. People of Hispanic origin are variably classified as Black or White. Yet, because most Latinos are classified as White, the use by analysts of official data such as those in Tables 9-2 through 9-4 may result in their failure to note the decrease in the non-Hispanic White portion of the prison population.

For example, if 100,000 of the Latino prisoners in 1995 shown in Table 9-2 are classified as "White," the actual number of non-Hispanic Whites imprisoned in that year would be around 355,000, or about 32 percent of all prisoners. Therefore, people of color and ethnic minorities constituted more than two-thirds of the nation's prisoners in 1995. As indicated in Table 9-3, Whites, most of whom were likely to be of non-Hispanic origin, were 69 percent and 66 percent of all prisoners in 1950 and 1960, respectively. This means that the proportion of non-Hispanic Whites among the nation's prisoners in 1995 was about one-half of that in the 1950s and 1960s. Further,

TABLE 9-5

Trends in Latino Incarceration Rates, State and Federal Prisons, 1980-95

Year	Number of Latinos	% Latino
1980	25,246	7.6
1981	29,087	7.8
1992	37,226	8.9
1983	41,088	9.4
1984	NA	NA
1985	54,672	10.9
1986	62,610	11.5
1987	69,810	12.0
1988	76,400	11.9
1989	90,383	12.7
1990	103,065	13.3
1991	112,520	13.6
1992	125,018	14.1
1993	138,699	14.6
1994	156,908	14.9
1995	174,292	15.5

Source: U.S. Department of Justice, periodic reports.

although the "other race" category of prisoners in Table 9-2 remains a small percentage of all inmates and includes some people for whom race was unknown, there is a steady increase in the absolute number of prisoners under this rubric between 1980 and 1995.

The media and the public largely ignore the increasing rate at which the American criminal justice system is becoming a site for the processing of fewer Anglo Whites and greater numbers of people of color other than Blacks. Yet this trend may have profound implications for race and ethnic relations and the political and economic development of the country in the 21st century. To answer a question posed earlier, the growing racial and ethnic diversity of the nation's population that has resulted from the most recent waves of immigration has not led to any reduction in the rate of African American imprisonment and social control. The decrease in the share of Anglo Whites in prison has come at the expense of increased rates of confinement for African Americans; it has also come at the expense of increases for Latinos and perhaps other smaller, recently arrived non-White racial/ethnic groupings.

The imprisonment and social control statistics presented above paint a disturbing picture of change and continuity in racial and ethnic disparities.

Already sizable in 1950, the gap between African Americans and Whites grew during a period of perceived "progress" in race relations and in the social and legal standing of Blacks in U.S. society. As Americans turned increasingly to the use of prisons in an effort to control crime, African Americans bore the brunt of this rising tide of punitiveness. As early as 1970, because of emerging changes in law enforcement, Blacks were 41 percent of the nation's state and federal prisoners (Table 9-2). But the upward trend in the Black share of the prison population was most pronounced between the late 1980s and 1995. Those years were marked by the "invention" and mass marketing of crack cocaine and, in response, an intensified War on Drugs. The latter has been expedited by major changes in federal and state sentencing guidelines that have resulted in less judicial discretion (Miller, 1996; Tonry, 1996; Kennedy, 1997). As the data in Table 9-3 illustrate, this period was also marked by a sharp rise in the Black share of prison admissions, a more sensitive barometer of changes in law enforcement.

The Impact of Drug Law Enforcement

Indeed, the impact of drug law enforcement can be seen in several U.S. Justice Department analyses of the sources of growth in the nation's prison population between 1985 and 1995. Prisoners sentenced to state prisons who were charged with a drug-related offense increased by 30.7 percent between 1985 and 1990 and by another 8.6 percent between 1990 and 1995. In 1985, 38,900 inmates were serving time for drug offenses. By 1995, the number had increased almost sixfold to 224,900 (U.S. Department of Justice, 1997b, 10). Blumstein and Beck (1999) report that by 1996, drugs constituted the single largest offense category among all state and federal prisoners. They note that the state incarceration rate for drugs had increased by a factor of 10, from 12 to 120 per 100,000 citizens, in that year.

Further, according to Blumstein and Beck (1999), Tonry (1995), Mauer and Huling (1995), Miller (1996), and numerous other observers, African Americans have been disproportionately affected by the legislative reforms, law enforcement changes, and judicial practices that have constituted the War on Drugs. Between 1985 and 1995, the number of Black inmates serving time for drug offenses rose by an estimated 117,400, whereas the number of White inmates increased by only 64,900. This rise in the number of drug offenders accounted for 42 percent of the total growth among Black inmates and 26 percent of the growth among White inmates (U.S. Department of Justice, 1997b, 10).

HIGHER RATES OF IMPRISONMENT AND RISING CRIME RATES: DOES THIS NEXUS ACCOUNT FOR INCREASED RACIAL DISPARITY?

As noted, the disproportionate presence of ethnic and racial minorities among those in U.S. prisons and jails has been widely observed for most of this century. Consequently, the questions of how much of the Black-White gap in rates of criminal punishment can be attributed to racial bias in the administration of justice and how much to racial differences in rates of criminal involvement are part of a century-old debate (DuBois, 1899, 1904; Sellin, 1928, 1935).

The most recent upsurge in levels of imprisonment and the apparent rise in racial disparity seen in Tables 9-1 through 9-5 have also been the source of scrutiny by criminologists and other social scientists. Beginning in the late 1970s and early 1980s, a number of researchers noted the steady rise in the rate of Black imprisonment and engaged in a scholarly and public policy debate about the causes of this increase (Dunbaugh, 1979; Christianson, 1981; Blumstein, 1982; Myers, 1984; Hawkins, 1985). In his discussion of "our Black prisons," Christianson insisted that racism in the administration of justice accounted for much of the racial imbalance. Blumstein, while not completely discounting the effects of discrimination, argued that racial differences in rates of serious criminal involvement must be considered a plausible explanation for much of the imbalance.

Despite widely publicized instances of racial bias in the administration of justice during recent years, a consensus has emerged among crime analysts that such bias alone cannot account for the wide racial disparity in the levels of criminal punishment in the United States. It is agreed that most, perhaps the overwhelming majority, of the disparity results from racial differences in actual criminal conduct (Hindelang, 1978, 1981; Blumstein, 1982; Jaynes and Williams, 1989; LaFree, Drass, and O'Day, 1992; LaFree, 1995; Tonry, 1995). However, challenging this apparent consensus is mounting evidence of current patterns of lawmaking and enforcement that result in racially disparate impacts (e.g., crack versus powder cocaine punishments, death penalty sentencing, and police surveillance tactics). Some observers also challenge the belief that conduct differences alone account for the racial disparities. Skepticism has been directed not so much at the overall levels of racial disparity, but rather at the widening of the racial gap in recent decades (Mann, 1993; Chambliss, 1995; Tonry, 1995, 1996; Miller, 1996; Kennedy, 1997; Russell, 1998).

For example, while acknowledging that high levels of Black criminal involvement account for much of the punishment gap observed between Blacks and Whites, Tonry (1995, 4) noted:

> Crime by Blacks is not getting worse. The proportions of serious violent crimes committed by Blacks have been level for more than a decade. Since the mid-1970s, approximately 45 percent of those arrested for murder, rape, robbery, and aggravated assault have been Black (the trend is slightly downward). Disproportionate punishments of Blacks, however, have been getting worse, especially since Ronald Reagan became President. Since 1980, the number of Blacks in prison has tripled. Between 1979 and 1992, the percentage of Blacks among those admitted to state and federal prisons grew from 39 to 54 percent.

The examination of national imprisonment trends in this chapter has shown the accuracy of Tonry's observations regarding the level of racial disproportionality. But what about his observations regarding the lack of conformity between levels of racial disparity in arrests versus imprisonment?

How consistent with imprisonment trends are the arrest rates for Blacks and Whites between 1950 and 1995? Other researchers have probed these precise questions and offer some insights.

Two studies by LaFree, Drass, and O'Day (1992) and LaFree (1995) examined arrest trends for Blacks and Whites in the United States that cover much of the time frame of this chapter. In their study of serious felony offenses that tend to drive imprisonment trends (i.e., homicide, robbery, and burglary), LaFree, Drass, and O'Day found a substantial increase in rates of arrests for both Blacks and Whites between 1957 and the early 1970s and a decline in rates from the late 1970s through 1988. However, of the three offense categories, only robbery showed a widening of the racial gap in arrests between 1957 and 1988.

The 1995 study by LaFree of arrests between 1946 and 1990 produced similar findings. He reported that, compared with 1946 data, the ratio of Black to White arrests was smaller in 1990 for aggravated assault, burglary, and theft. Further, from its peak in 1956 when the Black homicide rate was 16 times that of Whites, the homicide ratio had declined to 8.5 to 1 by 1990 (1995, 180-181). Thus, it appears that changes in the level of racial disparity for several serious crimes most likely to lead to confinement are somewhat at odds with the growing racial gap in imprisonment during the past half-century.

The research reported in this chapter traces the same terrain and reaches similar conclusions. Table 9-6, taken from Uniform Crime Reports for the same years in Table 9-1, supports the findings and observations of Tonry and LaFree and his associates. It shows the percentage of arrests by race for all index crimes and for violent crimes between 1950 and 1996. Little change is observed in the level of racial disproportionality for either of the aggregate offense categories. Indeed, as LaFree (1995) noted, Blacks were a larger share of violent offenders in 1960 and 1970 than in the next two decades.

Like many recent analysts, LaFree is not convinced that police discrimination can explain the large gap between arrests for Blacks and Whites and between arrests for Whites and other racial groups or the persistence of these disparities over time. The data he presents and the findings in Table 9-6 raise doubts for many observers as to whether patterns of arrest alone account for the widening gap in Black-White imprisonment rates. LaFree is correct in noting that differences by race vary by crime type and that the crimes traditionally associated with the risk of imprisonment—homicide, robbery, assault, and burglary—still show high levels of racial disparity. Nevertheless, it is also true that these offenses do so to a lesser degree than they did several decades ago (Blumstein and Beck, 1999).

As previously noted, an increasing number of researchers have observed that a rise in drug arrests, as opposed to arrests for involvement in more serious forms of criminal behavior, accounts for much of the recent increase in levels of racial disparity in arrests and imprisonment (Chambliss, 1995; Tonry, 1995; Miller, 1996; Kennedy, 1997). Blumstein's (1995) primary objective was to show the causal linkages among illicit guns, drug trafficking, and the sharp rise in youth homicide during the mid-1980s. He observed a

TABLE 9-6

Racial Differences in Arrests for Serious Crime, 1950-96

Year	Index Arrests	% White	% Black	% Other
1950[a]	223,036	64.9	34.1	1.0
	Violent	56.5	42.4	1.1
1960[b]	499,637	64.3	33.3	2.4
	Violent	44.4	54.3	1.3
1970[c]	1,199,073	61.6	36.4	2.0
	Violent	44.7	53.3	2.0
1980[d]	2,195,746	65.5	32.8	1.7
	Violent	54.4	44.1	1.4
1981	2,291,169	64.3	34.1	1.6
	Violent	53.0	45.7	1.4
1982	2,138,015	62.7	35.6	1.7
	Violent	51.9	46.7	1.3
1983	2,145,411	62.6	35.7	1.7
	Violent	51.2	47.5	1.4
1984	1,831,683	65.2	33.1	1.7
	Violent	53.2	45.6	1.2
1985	2,118,524	64.5	33.7	1.9
	Violent	52.2	46.5	1.3
1986	2,160,252	64.5	33.7	1.8
	Violent	52.2	46.5	1.3
1987	2,261,979	62.6	35.5	1.9
	Violent	51.2	47.3	1.4
1988	2,109,919	62.4	35.7	2.0
	Violent	51.7	46.8	1.5
1989	2,341,260	60.9	37.1	1.9
	Violent	50.8	47.7	1.4
1990	2,310,860	63.6	34.4	2.1
	Violent	53.7	44.7	1.6
1991	2,236,837	63.2	34.6	2.2
	Violent	53.6	44.8	1.6
1992	2,477,507	62.7	35.2	2.1
	Violent	53.6	44.8	1.7
1993	2,419,225	61.3	36.5	2.2
	Violent	52.6	45.7	1.8

(continued)

New Directions

TABLE 9-6 continued

Year	Index Arrests	% White	% Black	% Other
1994	2,381,534	61.4	36.3	2.3
	Violent	53.4	44.7	1.9
1995	2,237,062	61.9	35.7	2.4
	Violent	54.3	43.7	2.0
1996	2,051,110	62.0	35.3	2.7
	Violent	54.6	43.2	2.2

a. The term "index crimes" was not used in the 1950 or 1960 Uniform Crime Reports. For those two years, we created a listing of crimes that is roughly comparable to the index of serious criminal involvement used in later years. For 1950, this index consists of homicide, robbery, assault (both major and minor), burglary, larceny/theft, auto theft, and rape. Violent crimes are homicide, robbery, assault, and rape.

b. For 1960, index crimes were composed of murder, manslaughter, forcible rape, robbery, aggravated assault, burglary, larceny/theft, and auto theft. Violent crimes were murder, manslaughter, forcible rape, and aggravated assault.

c. For 1970, index crimes were criminal homicide, including murder and both negligent and nonnegligent manslaughter, forcible rape, robbery, aggravated assault, burglary/breaking and entering, larceny/theft, and auto theft. Violent crimes were criminal homicide, forcible rape, aggravated assault, and robbery.

d. For 1980, arson was added to the list of index offenses, and negligent homicide was dropped. Other index offenses and the listing of violent crimes were unchanged through 1996.

Source: U.S. Department of Justice, Federal Bureau of Investigation (1950-96).

major increase in the drug arrest disparity between Black and White youths between 1980 and 1990. Further, Blumstein and Beck (1999) show that arrests for drug offenses and, to a lesser extent, assaults explain the sharp rise in U.S. prison admissions during the past decade. Much of the increase in the size of the resident prison population can be attributed to growth in the amount of time that convicted persons must serve. Both observations may have implications for the shaping of public policies aimed at reducing racial disparity in criminal punishment.

THE COSTS OF DISPARITY: CRIME VICTIMIZATION AMONG AFRICAN AMERICANS

While the burgeoning victims' rights movement in the United States attests to the inattentiveness of American law to the plight of crime victims regardless of their race or ethnicity, the African American crime victim provides a case study in neglect and omission. In its review of the status of Black Americans, the National Research Council (NRC) observed that despite the widespread belief that racial disparity in crime and justice affects American race relations, few studies have examined the impact of crime and punishment on Blacks themselves and their communities (Jaynes and Williams, 1989, 464). Using data assembled by Myers and Sabol (1987), the NRC report stated: "The high volume of criminal activity in Black communities has meant that their victimization rates exceed those found in other communities. Furthermore, since the incidence of victimization is highest for persons who have incomes of less than $10,000 per year, the Blacks in the lower socioeconomic classes suffer especially" (Jaynes and Williams, 1989, 465).

In addition, the report noted that compared with other racial and ethnic groups, Blacks experience greater medical costs and more time away from work due to personal victimization such as assaults and suffer greater economic losses attributable to robbery and burglary. The NRC report also observed that the economic impact of crime on the Black community extends far beyond its effects on individual victims. Because crime affects the economic viability of minority-owned and other firms doing business in minority neighborhoods, it negatively impacts the economic viability of the communities in which most African Americans live (Jaynes and Williams, 1989, 464-472).

More recent evidence of racial disparity in rates of criminal victimization and its effects is presented by Walker, Spohn, and DeLone (1996, Chap. 2). Using data from the Bureau of Justice Statistics for 1992, they report that rates of victimization vary by gender and by place of residence, but that levels of victimization for Blacks exceed those of Whites for nearly all crime categories. For example, Blacks are more than three times as likely as Whites to be victims of robbery and more than twice as likely to be victims of assault or rape. Crimes of theft show less racial disparity, but Black rates still exceed White rates, especially Whites of non-Hispanic ancestry.

Indeed, it is likely that the actual size of the racial disparity in crime victimization is even greater than the two studies show. Both the NRC's findings and the study by Walker, Spohn, and DeLone (1996) used data from federal victimization surveys (National Crime Victimization Survey, or NCVS). Some critics of these surveys allege that, like most public opinion surveys, the NCVS tends to have higher response rates from people of middle class backgrounds, and lower response rates from the urban and rural poor and minorities.

Walker, Spohn, and DeLone (1996, 24-26) suggest that the tendency of politicians, researchers, and the media to highlight criminal offending among Blacks while ignoring their similarly disproportionate rates of victimization has a potentially negative impact on race relations. They assert that one consequence of such reporting of crime is the perception among much of the public that "the typical crime is a violent crime, . . . the typical crime victim is White, and . . . the typical offender is African American or Hispanic" (25). That perception has allowed American politicians to use the "race card" in most presidential election campaigns and many local contests over the past two decades. As Russell (1998) shows, this perception has also provided the basis for a series of "racial hoaxes" in which White offenders accuse Blacks of crimes that they themselves have committed. Russell (71-75) documents 67 instances of such hoaxes in the United States between 1987 and 1996.

Ignoring the Black Crime Victim

While images of the criminal offender of African ancestry are firmly etched into the consciousness and subconsciousness of Americans, the Black crime victim remains largely ignored, with perhaps one notable exception. The racialization of criminal violence in American society has meant that interracial crime is much more likely to catch the public spotlight than acts of intraracial offending. Since the Civil Rights movement, there has been greater public sensitivity to incidents involving police maltreatment of Black citizens, and such awareness has sometimes carried over to actual or alleged White-on-Black crime between ordinary citizens.

Yet despite greater public scrutiny of selected White-on-Black offenses, the media and the public continue to neglect many other serious crimes involving Blacks who are victimized by Whites. In addition, the far more typical Black-on-Black crime victims receive scant public notice. Even as the 21st century begins, evidence keeps mounting that convicted killers of Whites are much more likely than killers of Blacks to be sentenced to death (*McCleskey* v. *Kemp*, 1987; Kennedy, 1988, 1997; Paternoster, 1984; Baldus, Woodworth, and Pulaski, 1990, 1994). Beyond homicide, the race of the victim appears to play a major role in the punishment for many types of offenses (Hawkins, 1987a).

Even rising rates of homicide among youths during the late 1980s and early 1990s do not seem to have caused a sustained shift in attention to Black crime victims. Such violence, even more than violence among adults, has disproportionately affected African Americans. Despite the tendency to view youth violence as a public health problem and the sporadic media coverage of gangs and drive-by shootings, the tragic loss of life among disadvantaged children of color has led to public policy initiatives that have focused more on Black youth *offenders* than on young victims of violence. Further, when attention has been paid to violent youthful offenders of color, it has resulted in their "demonization" and the tendency to view violence as inherent in what it means to be poor and Black or Latino (Miller, 1996; Fishman, 1998; Rodriguez, 1998).

In contrast to the perceptions of violent Black youths, a White youth charged in 1998 with a widely publicized schoolyard killing was described by the media as "boyish and quintessentially American" (Dowdy, 1998, E1). Similar bias in newspaper reporting of homicide has been noted in other studies, which have shown that cases involving White victims are more likely than cases with Black or Latino victims to appear in the daily press (Johnstone, Hawkins, and Michener, 1994; Hawkins, Johnstone, and Michener, 1995).

Law Enforcement: A Pattern of Over- and Underenforcement

According to Hawkins (1987a, 1987b) and Fishman (1998), the tendency of the public and the legal system to demonize Black criminal offenders while simultaneously devaluing the lives of their Black victims has tremendous implications for public policy. This perception may affect law enforcement by creating a pattern of both over- and underenforcement (Kennedy, 1997). Such a legal response may lead to high detention rates of Black males accused of acts of violence against Whites or of drug trafficking, while minimizing the protection afforded to Black women who are victims of domestic assault. The propensity of law enforcement officials to perceive all young Black males as potential violent offenders may also limit the extent to which these youths can rely on the police for protection. This creates a self-help, vigilante-like cycle of violent homicidal retribution (Hawkins, 1983; Black, 1983, 1993; Anderson, 1998; Fagan and Wilkinson, 1998).

A recent study also suggests that ignoring the minority victims of crime is not limited to victims of crimes against the person. Warner (1997) found that community poverty rates in Boston are associated with police recording of burglary incidents reported by citizens. Poverty increases the likelihood that an incident will not be recorded. While poverty appears to matter more than race, neighborhoods with a large number of Black residents are most affected by both poverty and subsequent nonrecording of burglaries.

Findings and insights such as these prompted Kennedy (1997) to observe:

> Like many social disasters, crime afflicts African-Americans with a special vengeance; at most levels of income, they are more likely to be raped, robbed, assaulted, and murdered than their White counterparts. Thus, at the center of all discussions about racial justice and criminal law should be the recognition that Black Americans are in dire need of protection against criminality. A sensible strategy of protection should include efforts to ameliorate the social ills that contribute to criminality, including poverty, child abuse, and the deterioration of civic agencies of social support. A sensible strategy of protection should also include, however, efforts aimed toward apprehending, incapacitating, deterring, and punishing criminals. To accomplish those essential tasks requires a well-functioning system of law enforcement (11,12).

Kennedy continued by specifically acknowledging the difficulties of achieving the goal of more effective law enforcement. He accused some contemporary social commentators of being "unduly hostile to officials charged with enforcing criminal laws, insufficiently attentive to victims and potential victims of crime, and overly protective of suspects and convicted felons" (12).

Kennedy's policy pronouncements are useful in exposing the dilemma facing African Americans and those who attempt to reduce current levels of racial disparity. However, to the extent that he merely reframes the perennial contrast between the "law and order" political right and the "soft on crime" left wing, his work offers only limited guidance for efforts to develop public policies aimed at redressing the myriad social correlates of crime.

Several decades ago, Wilson (1975), a commentator who leans toward conservative positions on many issues, noted the errors made by both political liberals and conservatives in confronting the nation's crime problem. In a discussion of interactions between the police and inner-city neighborhoods, Wilson said:

> In sum, when questioned closely, the community and the police tend to agree as to the source of their difficulties, though clearly they disagree over who is to blame. The chief problem is to be found in the relations between young males, especially young Black males, and ghetto police officers. But if this is true, why is there not a tacit alliance between older Black residents, interested in better police protection and fearful of rising rates of crime (especially juvenile crime), and police officers who are concerned about crime and who want "more cooperation" in ending it (119)?

Wilson continued by saying that he believed such a convergence between the views of Black citizens and the police did exist. He noted:

> One night spent in a ghetto police precinct will provide graphic evidence of the extent to which older Black residents, especially the women, regularly turn to the police for help. But to a considerable degree the alliance is never forged, at least not to the extent one finds in a middle-class White suburb. The reasons are skin color and the conditions of ghetto life (119).

On the need for more police protection in Black communities, Wilson identified the dilemma facing those who attempt to heed appeals for greater protection of Black citizens, such as the effort made by Kennedy (1997):

> Thus, if the law-abiding majority in a Black community demand "more police protection," they are likely to be calling for police activity that will increase the frequency of real or perceived police abuses. If, on the other hand, they demand an end to "police harassment," they are likely to be ending police practices that have some (no one knows how much) crime prevention value (Wilson, 1975, 121).

In much of Kennedy's (1997, 136-166) discussion of the same issues, he urged precisely such a call for modification of police practices that lead to the harassment of Black citizens. He specifically targeted the use of racial profiles as part of the determination of criminal suspects by law enforcement officials. While Wilson (1975) seems to be skeptical of the success of this "give and take" approach to law enforcement, Kennedy sees such changes as a necessary and doable part of the policy reform needed to protect Black citizens and establish racial justice.

On the current public policy front, developments in two large U.S. cities seem to offer support for the stances taken by both Kennedy and Wilson. The recent and ongoing success in reducing youth homicide rates in Boston through police-community cooperation appears to support Kennedy's contention that such change need not come at the expense of civil liberties. On the other hand, the major decline in crime and violence in New York City since the mid-1990s seems to be associated with a rise in the abuse of police authority, with African Americans the primary victims. This latter observation does not bode well for efforts to devise public policies that reduce crime without resorting to racist forms of law enforcement.

We will return briefly to these policy issues at the end of the chapter. We examine next the implications for public policy of another social ill that is correlated with racial disparity in the rates of crime and punishment—namely, socioeconomic status.

CRIME, THE UNDERCLASS, AND SOCIOECONOMIC INEQUALITY

One of the first casualties of the cultural/race wars that have historically permeated the assessment of race, crime, and justice in the United States has been candid and honest discussion of the precise nature and magnitude of the crime problem and how it can be solved. That discourse has become extremely polemicized and politicized in recent years with the emergence of labels such as "predatory crime," "superpredators," "crack babies," and "gang bangers," all of which allude in various ways to the criminality of people of color. In a curious turn, discussions of race and crime appear to have been more candid near the beginning of the 20th century and shortly thereafter than they are today (DuBois, 1899, 1904; Sellin, 1928, 1935). According to Tonry (1995), during recent decades, discourse about race often takes the form of "subtext" in analyses of crime and justice. Such lines of discourse do little to advance the goal of designing public policy to address this race and crime nexus.

Few observers, regardless of their race or ideological orientation, can deny that racially disproportionate rates of crime and punishment remain a major American social problem. Further, as noted above, America's recent epidemic of crime and punishment has hit its citizens of African ancestry with a vengeance (Kennedy, 1997). At the beginning of this chapter, we suggested that the progress of White ethnic groups in reducing their rates of crime and punishment was the result of their improved economic, social, and political standing within American society. In the same vein, we propose that much of the failure of African Americans to achieve similar levels of economic and social standing is a result of their continuing exposure to poverty and reduced economic opportunities. By taking such a position, we acknowledge a related question encountered increasingly in the race relations and criminal justice literature: Why have African Americans not achieved levels of economic progress and betterment similar to the levels achieved by White ethnic groups and some Asian Americans over the past half-century?

For many observers, this question lies at the heart of the polemicized debates over crime and justice and other social policies (e.g., affirmative action and welfare reform) in the United States today. Although it is beyond the scope of this chapter to pursue this question in detail, the concluding section explores the etiological links between socioeconomic inequality and the persistence of comparatively high rates of crime and punishment for African Americans.

Wilson's *The Truly Disadvantaged* (1987) placed the discussion of urban poverty squarely within public policy discourse and provided an important bridge toward understanding high rates of crime and punishment among African Americans. An important strand of this research attempts to identify the effect of neighborhoods on underclass behavior (Jencks and Mayer, 1991; Cohen and Dawson, 1993; Crane, 1991a, 1991b). This "neighborhood effects" literature seeks to measure the impact of neighborhoods on the behavioral characteristics of their residents. By comparison, much of the traditional literature on crime and justice tends to focus on attributes of the individual offender or victim.

The Relationship Between Crime and Community

Beginning with the work of Shaw and Mackay (1942), the link between community conditions and criminal behavior is well established, but not always well understood or specified. Typically, communities with large concentrations of low income people score high on an assortment of indexes of social dysfunction, including criminal activity. For many years, social researchers have posited a relationship between group and individual socioeconomic status, the level of social disorganization found in the community, and elevated rates of crime and punishment. Shaw and Mackay believed that community/neighborhood effects in Chicago accounted for high rates of crime among White ethnic groups as well as among African Americans and Mexican Americans. The departure of these groups from "disorganized" areas was said to coincide with sharp declines in their rates of criminal involvement.

Yet under dispute are several aspects of the relationship between crime and community, many of which may have implications for the formulation of policies to reduce racial disparity in crime. For example, still unresolved is the question of whether poverty and social decay foster increasing risk of crime, or whether crime fosters decay and concentrations of poverty (as investors and residents flee in reaction to crime). Flight and blight are likely self-reinforcing. As high income people leave inner-city communities for the suburbs, the concentration of poverty and social problems in inner-city communities worsens. In turn, as the concentration of poverty and social problems grows, high income residents increasingly move to the suburbs.

Similarly, researchers have only recently begun to specify the social and developmental processes that may link community disadvantage to varying rates of criminal behavior. They are seeking a better understanding of the role played by individual (or group) characteristics versus community and neighborhood contexts in accounting for racial differences in rates of criminal offending and victimization (Sampson and Lauritsen, 1994; Sampson and Wilson, 1995; Sampson, 1997). It is still unknown why some communities that are similar in their ethnic/racial and social class composition sometimes have quite different rates of crime and violence. From a policy perspective aimed at reducing racial disparity, understanding these dynamics may be quite consequential.

In addition, researchers who focus mainly on the link between crime and characteristics of individuals take varying paths, all of which have implications for understanding racial differences and what can be done about them. For example, some of these analysts cite the lack of a work ethic as the source of criminal activity, poverty, and other social problems. Freeman and Holzer (1986) argue that a lucrative underground economy has weakened the incentive for young Black men to enter mainstream employment. Illegal activities such as trade in illicit drugs, illegal gambling, smuggling, prostitution, selling stolen merchandise, illegal bartering of goods and services, perpetrating confidence games, and hustling make it possible for those not involved in the formal, mainstream economy to survive without legitimate work.

Other analysts attempt to develop more explicitly the causal link between individuals' involvement in crime and the social impediments they face. These analysts focus on the fact that people from poorer neighborhoods are more likely to encounter blocked opportunities for upward mobility. Because they lack opportunity through legitimate channels, they turn to more expedient means of making a living. Most of these analysts share a research tradition attributed to the work on opportunity and crime conducted by Merton (1957). With the increasing emphasis on racial differences in rates of violence and serious offending among youths, an even more diverse assortment of etiological perspectives has emerged. Many of these are grounded in research on the situational, psychological, developmental, and neurobiological determinants of criminal conduct. An effort is often made to examine the role of the family in determining the level of criminal involvement (Loeber and Farrington, 1998; McCord, 1997).

Despite their seeming dissimilarities, all of these approaches to the study of crime and racial disparity have one thing in common: acknowledgment of the importance at some level of socioeconomic status and inequality in explaining racial and ethnic differences in rates of crime and punishment. In an attempt to understand the documented changes in levels of arrests and imprisonment for African Americans over the past several decades, we will review some of the basic changes in their socioeconomic condition. Of particular interest is the extent to which the widely noted social changes of the past decades have led to economic gains for the average African American.

RACE AND SOCIOECONOMIC CHANGES

As noted at the beginning of this chapter, in examining the patterns of change in the social and economic status of African Americans, there are areas of dramatic and steady improvement that would be expected to lead to decreased, rather than increased, levels of crime and punishment over the past four and one-half decades. A notable example of these changes can be found in the area of educational attainment. African Americans have steadily increased their levels of educational attainment, from an average of 5.8 years of education in 1940 to an average of 12.4 years in 1990. Accordingly, the educational attainment gap between Blacks and Whites dwindled to less than one-half a year by 1990 (Thomas, Herring, and Horton, 1996).

In American society, education is often depicted as the vehicle, equally accessible to all citizens, through which various occupational goals and levels of earnings can be achieved. Thus, improved educational attainment is said to be associated with reduced criminal involvement, especially property crime borne of economic deprivation. Yet the educational gains of African Americans between 1940 and 1990 have not resulted in the kind of increased earnings that might mitigate involvement in crime. In 1996, Blacks had personal earnings that were about 67 percent those of Whites. Earnings differences persist even after accounting for educational attainment, as earnings gaps occur for each educational attainment level.

Figure 9-1 presents changes in average personal earnings by level of educational attainment for Black and White men from 1980 to 1996. The figure shows that mean income generally increased for each race with additional years of education. The increment to earnings varied dramatically by subgroup, however. For each level of educational attainment, White men earned more than Black men. In other words, racial differences in earnings become greater over time even after accounting for levels of educational attainment.

Trends in family income reveal additional grim news for African Americans. As Figure 9-2 illustrates, in 1953, Black families earned about 56 percent as much as White families ($2,450 versus $4,406). By 1996, Black families still earned only 59 percent as much as White families ($26,522 versus $44,756). Even more telling is the fact that Black income as a percentage of White income in 1996 had fallen from 61 percent in 1970, following the height

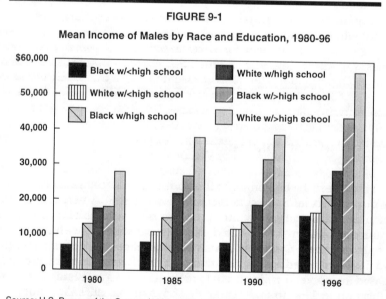

FIGURE 9-1

Mean Income of Males by Race and Education, 1980-96

Source: U.S. Bureau of the Census (1980, 1985, 1990, 1996). Income figures refer to the year prior to the survey years.

FIGURE 9-2

Changes in Median Family Income by Race, 1953-96

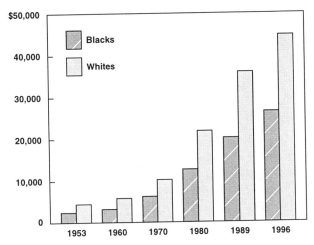

Source: U.S. Bureau of the Census (1953, 1960, 1970, 1980, 1989, 1996), "Historical Income Tables," Table F-5.

of the Civil Rights movement. This pattern reflects modest progress and subsequent retrenchment.

Changes in the occupational structure of the African American community suggest that Blacks have made progress in upgrading the kinds of jobs in which they are employed. As Figure 9-3 demonstrates, however, this general improvement in occupation does not mean that the income gap between Blacks and Whites has closed, as Whites have also substantially enhanced their occupational standing since 1940. The percentage gap between Blacks and Whites remained virtually constant for over half a century. The largest relative gains for African Americans occurred in the middle, or "transitional," occupations such as craft workers, operatives, and laborers.

The change from goods production to knowledge production and the increased use of technology have also had consequences for rates of Black unemployment and labor force participation. Since 1960, the Black unemployment rate has typically been at least twice that of Whites. A slight exception occurred in the early 1970s. Since then, however, the ratio has approached 2.5 to 1.

Figure 9-4 shows that educational differences cannot account for the racial gap in unemployment rates. In all cases since 1980, the unemployment rates of African Americans exceeded those of Whites with comparable levels of educational attainment. In 1997, Blacks with college degrees had levels of unemployment (7 percent) that surpassed those of Whites with high school diplomas (5 percent).

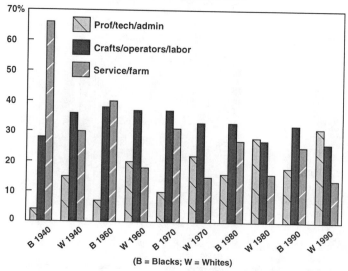

FIGURE 9-3

Percentage of Black and White Males in Selected Occupational Types, 1940-90

(B = Blacks; W = Whites)

Source: Integrated Public Use Microdata Samples from the U.S. decennial censuses.

A final indicator of the social and economic status of African Americans is the poverty rate. In 1959, the proportion of people living below the official poverty line was 22 percent. Despite public perceptions to the contrary, the poverty rate in the United States fell rapidly during the War on Poverty, which began in 1964. Until the 1990s, the incidence of Black poverty fell each decade, but the poverty gap between Blacks and Whites did not narrow. Black poverty rates were triple those of Whites during the 30-year period. In 1960, more than 55 percent of African Americans lived below the poverty line compared with 18 percent of Whites. In 1970, the rates were 34 percent and 10 percent, respectively. In 1996, the poverty rate for Blacks was 28 percent compared with 9 percent for Whites.

Educational differences alone cannot account for the racial differences in poverty. Figure 9-5 shows that Black adults at all levels of education are more likely than White adults to be impoverished. For example, in 1996, Blacks with some college were more likely to live in poverty (10 percent) than were Whites with only a high school diploma (8 percent).

IMPLICATIONS FOR PUBLIC POLICY

Much of the failure of African Americans to convert educational gains into a reduction in the economic gap vis-à-vis Whites is the result of the

FIGURE 9-4

Percentage of Males Unemployed by Race and Education, 1980-97

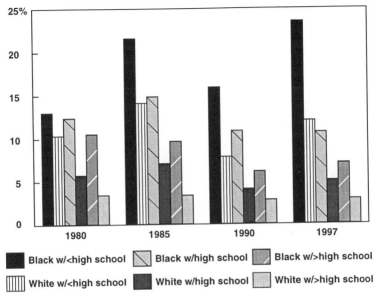

Source: U.S. Bureau of the Census (1980, 1985, 1990, 1996). Income figures refer to the year prior to the survey years.

persistence of discrimination aimed at Black workers. However, the lack of greater movement toward racial parity, especially during recent decades, has resulted in the more or less steady decline in the economic and social well-being of the nation's inner-city poor. The well-documented overrepresentation of the urban poor among those involved in crime and punished for it has many obvious, and some less obvious, implications for the development of private initiatives and public policies to address the status and functioning of African Americans.

As consistently noted here, economic disadvantage has long been acknowledged as a likely precipitant of criminal involvement. Many analysts and policymakers have thus suggested that prevention of crime and reduction of racial inequality in rates of punishment will be possible only to the extent that the living conditions of the disadvantaged are upgraded. We believe that some changes in public policy alternatives short of a major change in the economic status of the nation's underclass can help reduce racial disparity in crime and punishment. Yet it is the link between poverty or relative deprivation and crime that must be addressed to achieve any lasting change in the gap between Whites and non-Whites in crime and punishment.

FIGURE 9-5

Percentage of Males in Poverty by Race and Education, 1980-96

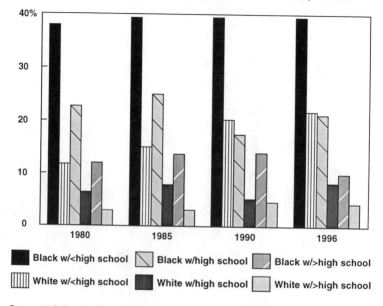

Source: U.S. Bureau of the Census (1980, 1985, 1990, 1997). Income figures refer to the year prior to the survey years.

As observed earlier, much of the current literature that attempts to explain racial differences in rates of crime is derived from the work of Wilson (1987) on the impact of social isolation on dysfunctional underclass behavior. Although weak labor force participation is viewed as a marker of underclass status and a strong correlate of criminal involvement, relatively little is known about the nature of that relationship. It is known, however, that the relationship is certainly not one-way. Labor force participation affects the likelihood of individual criminal involvement, and high rates of crime and punishment affect a group's rate of entry into the labor force. Freeman (1989) found that male criminality is likely to have large labor force effects. He reports that for males of all ages and races, those under the supervision of the criminal justice system are 7 percent of the male labor force. For males 18-34 years old, the share is 11 percent. For Black males 18-34 years old, the proportion is 59 percent.

On the other side of the coin, social scientists generally agree that persistent unemployment leads to poverty and that residential concentrations of poverty lead to higher crime. However, studies about the relationship between unemployment and crime have produced inconsistent results. Johnson and Herring's (1989) work incorporates aspects of the dual labor market theory, which distinguishes between "good" and "bad" jobs. Primary sector jobs pay reasonably well, have good benefits, and offer future economic advantages. Secondary sector jobs are low paying, have few benefits, and offer few prospects for upward mobility. Primary sector jobs offer a "stake in conformity" because employees think that there is something to lose in leaving such a job. The authors considered variables that included the poverty rate, income inequality, percentage of the population represented by young males, percentage who were African American, and rate of labor market instability (a combination of the unemployment rate and the percentage of the workforce in service sector jobs).

The analysis revealed that neighborhoods with high levels of labor market instability had significantly higher rates of violent crime, property crime, poverty, and income inequality. High rates of poverty or income inequality alone could not predict violent crime or property crime. Unemployment and marginal employment appeared to have direct effects on criminal involvement.

For 18-24 year-olds, those employed in secondary sector jobs spent more time out of the labor market than those employed in primary sector jobs. Time out of the labor force and expected job duration were modest, but significant predictors of criminal involvement. Young people in this age group who were students were significantly less likely to be involved in crime. Generally, a tendency toward criminal activity could be predicted by an individual's time in the labor force coupled with the percentage of nearby adults who were outside the labor force. However, this relationship held only in areas with high unemployment rates. Similar findings have been reported by Crutchfield (1989, 1995).

The problem with much of the underclass discussion is precisely one of miscasting the link between social deviance, work, and poverty. It is possible, for example, that aspects of the criminal justice system are also causal agents in poverty and community dysfunction. Researchers have begun to examine the impact of social control, especially detention and imprisonment for long periods, on the well-being of disadvantaged young males, their communities, and the nation. Analysts now question the wisdom of current laws and practices, which in many American cities result in the social control of more than one-half of all young Black males on any given day of the year.

This fact may help account for the tendency of Blacks to be somewhat less confident in the criminal justice system than Whites. Survey data from the Gallup Organization (American Correctional Association, 1997) suggest that 46 percent of Blacks express very little or no confidence in the criminal justice system compared with 39 percent of Whites. Similarly, 24 percent of Blacks say they have very little or no confidence in the police compared with 9 percent of Whites. Survey data from the American Correctional Association (1995) indicate that a higher percentage of Blacks (43 percent) than Whites (30 percent) strongly agree that "a balanced approach of prevention, punishment, and treatment is better at controlling and reducing crime than imprisonment alone." This is despite the fact that a higher percentage of Blacks (91 percent) than Whites (83 percent) believe it is extremely important that more money be spent on reducing violent crime (American Correctional Association, 1997). A higher percentage of Blacks (76 percent) than Whites (54 percent) also believe it is extremely important that more money be spent on reducing illegal drug use among adults.

CONCLUSION

Our review suggests that the problems surrounding crime and justice in the United States at the beginning of the 21st century are enormous and challenging. While there are no quick fixes, there are a number of viable public policy options, many of which we have alluded to in this chapter, that may begin to narrow the nation's racial divide in the crime and punishment arena. Although we have argued that a reduction in levels of socioeconomic inequality is a sine qua non for achieving any meaningful and lasting progress, public policies and legal reforms aimed at other, more symptomatic aspects of crime and justice are well worth considering. For example, along with economic reforms designed to give all citizens viable alternatives to a "life of crime," we believe that social policies aimed at reducing racial bigotry in the administration of justice are much needed. The social divide has generated the racial profiling of crime suspects, a tendency to devalue the lives of people of color, and race-based "get tough on crime" policies. That divide is as much a barrier to progress in reducing racial inequity in crime and punishment as are the social forces that lead to poverty and disproportionate numbers of single, female-headed households in urban minority communities.

REFERENCES

Adamson, C.R. 1983. "Punishment After Slavery: Southern State Penal Systems, 1865-1890." *Social Problems* 30 (June):555-569.

American Correctional Association. 1995. *Sourcebook of Criminal Justice Statistics Online, 1995.* Washington, D.C.: American Correctional Association.

———. 1997. *Sourcebook of Criminal Justice Statistics Online, 1997.* Washington, D.C.: American Correctional Association.

Anderson, E. 1998. "The Social Ecology of Youth Violence." In *Youth Violence,* Vol. 24, *Crime and Justice: A Review of Research.* Ed. M. Tonry and M.H. Moore. Chicago: University of Chicago Press, 65-104.

Baldus, D.C., G. Woodworth, and C.A. Pulaski, Jr. 1990. *Equal Justice and the Death Penalty: A Legal and Empirical Study.* Boston: Northeastern University Press.

———. 1994. "Reflections on the 'Inevitability' of Racial Discrimination in Capital Sentencing and the 'Impossibility' of Its Prevention, Detection, and Correction." *Washington and Lee Law Review* 51.

Beck, E.M., and S.E. Tolnay. 1995a. "Violence Toward African Americans in the Era of the White Lynch Mob." In *Ethnicity, Race, and Crime: Perspectives Across Time and Place.* Ed. D.F. Hawkins. Albany: State University of New York Press, 121-144.

———. 1995b. *A Festival of Violence: An Analysis of Southern Lynchings, 1882-1930.* Champaign: University of Illinois Press.

Black, D. 1983. "Crime as Social Control." *American Sociological Review* 48:34-45.

———. 1993. *The Social Structure of Right and Wrong.* San Diego: Academic Press.

Blumstein, A. 1982. "On the Racial Disproportionality of the United States's Prison Populations." *The Journal of Criminal Law and Criminology* 73 (Fall):1259-1281.

———. 1995. "Youth Violence, Guns, and the Illicit-Drug Industry." *The Journal of Criminal Law and Criminology* 86 (Fall):10-36.

Blumstein, A., and A.J. Beck. 1999. "Factors Contributing to the Growth in U.S. Prison Populations." In *Crime and Justice: A Review of Research,* Vol. 26. Ed. M. Tonry. Chicago: University of Chicago Press.

Branham, V.C., and S.B. Kutash. 1949. "The Negro in Crime." In *Encyclopedia of Criminology.* New York: Philosophical Library, 267-277.

Brown, M.C., and B.D. Warner. 1992. "Immigrants, Urban Politics, and Policing in 1900." *American Sociological Review* 57:293-305.

Cahalan, M. 1986. *Historical Corrections Statistics in the United States, 1850-1984.* NCJ-102529, December. Washington, D.C.: U.S. Department of Justice, Bureau of Justice Statistics.

Chambliss, W.J. 1995. "Crime Control and Ethnic Minorities: Legitimizing Racial Oppression by Creating Moral Panics." In *Ethnicity, Race, and Crime: Perspectives Across Time and Place.* Ed. D.F. Hawkins. Albany: State University of New York Press, 235-258.

Chambliss, W.J., and R.B. Seidman. 1971. *Law, Order and Power.* Reading, Mass.: Addison-Wesley.

Christianson, S. 1981. "Our Black Prisons." *Crime and Delinquency* 27:364-375.

Cohen, C.J., and M.C. Dawson. 1993. "Neighborhood Poverty and African American Politics." *American Political Science Review* 87:286-302.

Cook, P.J., and J.H. Laub. 1998. "The Unprecedented Epidemic in Youth Violence." In *Youth Violence,* Vol. 24, *Crime and Justice: A Review of Research.* Ed. M. Tonry and M.H. Moore. Chicago: University of Chicago Press, 27-64.

Crane, J. 1991a. "Effects of Neighborhoods on Dropping Out of School and Teenage Childbearing." In *The Urban Underclass.* Ed. C. Jencks and P.E. Peterson. Washington, D.C.: Brookings Institution, 299-320.

———. 1991b. "The Epidemic Theory of Ghettos and Neighborhood Effects on Dropping Out and Teenage Childbearing." *American Journal of Sociology* 96:1226-1259.

Crutchfield, R.D. 1989. "Labor Stratification and Violent Crime." *Social Forces* 68:588-608.

———. 1995. "Ethnicity, Labor Markets, and Crime." In *Ethnicity, Race, and Crime: Perspectives Across Time and Place.* Ed. D.F. Hawkins. Albany: State University of New York Press, 194-211.

Dowdy, Z.R. 1998. "Who Pulled the Trigger? RACE." *Boston Globe,* June 21, E1-2.

DuBois, W.E.B. 1899. *The Philadelphia Negro: A Social Study.* Philadelphia: University of Pennsylvania Press (1996).

———, Ed. 1904. *Proceedings of the Ninth Atlanta Conference for the Study of the Negro Problems,* Vol. 2. Atlanta: Atlanta University.

Dunbaugh, F.M. 1979. "Racially Disproportionate Rates of Incarceration in the United States." *Prison Law Monitor* 1 (March):205, 219-222.

Fagan, J., and D.L. Wilkinson. 1998. "Guns, Youth Violence, and Social Identity in Inner Cities." In *Youth Violence,* Vol. 24, *Crime and Justice: A Review of Research.* Ed. M. Tonry and M.H. Moore. Chicago: University of Chicago Press, 105-188.

Fingerhut, L.A., D.D. Ingram, and J.J. Feldman. 1992. "Firearm Homicide Among Black Teenage Males in Metropolitan Counties." *Journal of the American Medical Association* 267 (June 10):3054-3058.

Fingerhut, L.A., and J.C. Kleinman. 1990. "International and Interstate Comparisons of Homicide Among Young Males." *Journal of the American Medical Association* 263 (June 27):3292-3295.

Fishman, L.T. 1998. "The Black Bogeyman and White Self-Righteousness." In *Images of Color, Images of Crime*. Ed. C.R. Mann and M.S. Zatz. Los Angeles: Roxbury, 109-125.

Fox, J.A. 1996. *Trends in Juvenile Violence: A Report to the United States Attorney General on Current and Future Rates of Juvenile Offending*. Washington, D.C.: U.S. Department of Justice, Bureau of Justice Statistics.

Freeman, R.B. 1989. "The Employment and Earnings of Disadvantaged Male Youths in a Labor Shortage Economy." Paper presented at a conference on "The Truly Disadvantaged," Northwestern University, Evanston, Ill., October 19-21.

Freeman, R.B., and H. Holzer. 1986. *The Black Youth Unemployment Problem*. Chicago: University of Chicago Press.

Gould, S.J. 1981. *The Mismeasure of Man*. New York: W.W. Norton and Company.

Gunning, S. 1996. *Race, Rape, and Lynching*. New York: Oxford University Press.

Hacker, A. 1992. *Two Nations: Black and White, Separate, Hostile, Unequal*. New York: Scribners.

Hawkins, D.F. 1983. "Black-White Homicide Differentials: Alternatives to an Inadequate Theory." *Criminal Justice and Behavior* 10:407-440.

———. 1985. "Trends in Black-White Imprisonment: Changing Conceptions of Race or Changing Patterns of Social Control?" *Crime and Social Justice* 24:187-209.

———. 1987a. "Beyond Anomalies: Rethinking the Conflict Perspective on Race and Criminal Punishment." *Social Forces* 65:719-745.

———. 1987b. "Devalued Lives and Racial Stereotypes: Ideological Barriers to the Prevention of Family Violence Among Blacks." In *Violence in the Black Family: Correlates and Consequences*. Ed. R.L. Hampton. Lexington, Mass.: D.C. Heath, 189-205.

———. 1993. "Crime and Ethnicity." In *The Socio-Economics of Crime and Justice*. Ed. B. Forst. New York: M.E. Sharpe, 89-120.

———. 1994. "Ethnicity: The Forgotten Dimension of American Social Control." In *Inequality, Crime, and Social Control*. Ed. G.S. Bridges and M.A. Myers. Boulder, Col.: Westview Press, 99-116.

———. 1995. "Ethnicity, Race, and Crime: A Review of Selected Studies." In *Ethnicity, Race, and Crime: Perspectives Across Time and Place*. Ed. D.F. Hawkins. Albany: State University of New York Press, 11-45.

Hawkins, D.F., J.W.C. Johnstone, and A. Michener. 1995. "Race, Social Class, and Newspaper Reporting of Homicide." *National Journal of Sociology* 9:113-140.

Hindelang, M.J. 1978. "Race and Involvement in Common Law Personal Crimes." *American Sociological Review* 43:93-109.

———. 1981. "Variation in Rates of Offending." *American Sociological Review* 46:461-474.

Jargowsky, P.A., and M.J. Bane. 1991. "Ghetto Poverty in the United States, 1970-1980." In *The Urban Underclass*. Ed. C. Jencks and P.E. Peterson. Washington, D.C.: Brookings Institution, 235-273.

Jaynes, G.D., and R.M. Williams, Jr. 1989. *A Common Destiny: Blacks and American Society*. Washington, D.C.: National Research Council.

Jencks, C., and S.E. Mayer. 1991. "The Social Consequences of Growing Up in a Poor Neighborhood: A Review." In *The Urban Underclass*. Ed. C. Jencks and P.E. Peterson. Washington, D.C.: Brookings Institution, 321-341.

Johnson, R.J., and C. Herring. 1989. "Labor Market Participation Among Young Adults: An Event History Analysis." *Youth & Society* 21:3-31.

Johnstone, J.W.C., D.F. Hawkins, and A. Michener. 1994. "Homicide Reporting in Chicago Dailies." *Journalism Quarterly* 71:860-872.

Kennedy, R. 1988. "*McCleskey* v. *Kemp*: Race, Capital Punishment, and the Supreme Court." *Harvard Law Review*, 1388-1433.

————. 1997. *Race, Crime and the Law.* New York: Pantheon Books.

Knepper, P. 1989. "Southern-Style Punitive Repression: Ethnic Stratification, Economic Inequality, and Imprisonment in Territorial Arizona." *Social Justice* 16 (Winter):132-149.

LaFree, G. 1995. "Race and Crime Trends in the United States: 1946-1990." In *Ethnicity, Race, and Crime: Perspectives Across Time and Place.* Ed. D.F. Hawkins. Albany: State University of New York Press, 169-193.

LaFree, G., K.A. Drass, and P. O'Day. 1992. "Race and Crime in Postwar America: Determinants of African-American and White Rates, 1957-1988." *Criminology* 30:157-188.

Langan, P.A. 1991. *Race and Prisoners Admitted to State and Federal Institutions, 1926-86.* NCJ-125618. Washington, D.C.: U.S. Department of Justice, Office of Justice Programs, Bureau of Justice Statistics.

Loeber, R., and D.P. Farrington, Eds. 1998. *Serious and Violent Juvenile Offenders: Risk Factors and Successful Interventions.* Thousand Oaks, Cal.: Sage.

Mann, C. 1993. *Unequal Justice: A Question of Color.* Bloomington: Indiana University Press.

Mauer, M. 1990. *Young Black Men and the Criminal Justice System: A Growing National Problem.* Washington, D.C.: Sentencing Project.

Mauer, M., and T. Huling. 1995. *Young Black Americans and the Criminal Justice System: Five Years Later.* Washington, D.C.: Sentencing Project.

McCleskey v. *Kemp.* 1987. 481. U.S. 279.

McCord, J. 1997. *Violence and Childhood in the Inner City.* New York: Cambridge University Press.

Merton, R.K. 1957. *Social Theory and Social Structure.* Glencoe, Ill.: Free Press.

Miller, J.G. 1996. *Search and Destroy: African-American Males in the Criminal Justice System.* New York: Cambridge University Press.

Miranda v. *Arizona.* 1966. 384 U.S. 436, 86 S. Ct. 1602, 16 L. Ed. 2d 694.

Monkkonen, E.H. 1975. *The Dangerous Class: Crime and Poverty in Columbus, Ohio, 1860-1885.* Cambridge, Mass.: Harvard University Press.

Myers, M.A. 1995. "The New South's 'New' Black Criminal: Rape and Punishment in Georgia, 1870-1940." In *Ethnicity, Race, and Crime: Perspectives Across Time and Place.* Ed. D.F. Hawkins. Albany: State University of New York Press, 145-168.

Myers, S.L., Jr. 1984. "Race and Punishment: Directions for Economic Research." *American Economic Review* 74 (May):288-292.

Myers, S.L., Jr., and W.J. Sabol. 1987. "Crime and the Black Community: Issues in the Understanding of Race and Crime in America." Paper prepared for the Committee on the Status of Black Americans, National Research Council, Washington, D.C.

National Commission on Law Observance and Enforcement. 1931. *Report on Crime and the Foreign-Born.* Washington, D.C.: U.S. Government Printing Office (GPO).

Nelli, H.S. 1970. *Italians in Chicago, 1880-1920.* New York: Oxford University Press.

Paternoster, R. 1984. "Prosecutorial Discretion in Requesting the Death Penalty: A Case of Victim-based Racial Discrimination." *Law and Society Review* 18:437-478.

Powell v. *Alabama.* 1932. 287 U.S. 45, 53 S. Ct. 55, 77 L. Ed. 158.

Quinney, R. 1970. *The Social Reality of Crime.* Boston: Little Brown.

Rodriguez, L.J. 1998. "The Color of Skin Is the Color of Crime." In *Images of Color, Images of Crime.* Ed. C.R. Mann and M.S. Zatz. Los Angeles: Roxbury, 130-133.

Rose, P.I. 1997. *They and We: Racial and Ethnic Relations in the United States.* New York: McGraw-Hill.

Rowan, C.T. 1996. *The Coming Race War in America.* Boston: Little Brown/CTR Productions.

Russell, K. 1998. *The Color of Crime.* New York: New York University Press.

Sampson, R.J. 1997. "The Embeddedness of Child and Adolescent Development: A Community-Level Perspective on Urban Violence." In *Violence and Childhood in the Inner City.* Ed. J. McCord. New York: Cambridge University Press, 31-77.

Sampson, R.J., and J. Lauritsen. 1994. "Violent Victimization and Offending: Individual-, Situational-, and Community-level Risk Factors." In *Understanding and Preventing Violence,* Vol. 3, *Social Influences.* Ed. A.J. Reiss and J.A. Roth. Washington, D.C.: National Academy Press, 1-15.

Sampson, R.J., and W.J. Wilson. 1995. "Toward a Theory of Race, Crime, and Urban Inequality." In *Crime and Inequality.* Ed. J. Hagan and R. Peterson. Stanford, Cal.: Stanford University Press.

Sanborn, F.M. 1904. "Negro Crime." In *Proceedings of the Ninth Atlantic Conference for the Study of Negro Problems.* Vol. 2. Ed. W.E.B. DuBois. Atlanta: Atlanta University.

Sellin, T. 1928. "The Negro Criminal: A Statistical Note." *Annals of the American Academy of Political and Social Science* 140:52-64.

———. 1935. "Race Prejudice in the Administration of Justice." *American Journal of Sociology* 41:312-317.

———. 1976. *Slavery and the Penal System.* New York: Elsevier.

Shaw, C.R., and H.D. Mackay. 1942. *Juvenile Delinquency and Urban Areas.* Chicago: University of Chicago Press.

Sickmund, M., H.N. Snyder, and E. Poe-Yamagata. 1997. *Juvenile Offenders and Victims: 1997 Update on Violence—Statistics Summary.* Washington, D.C.: Office of Juvenile Justice and Delinquency Prevention.

Steinberg, S. 1989. Updated ed. *The Ethnic Myth: Race, Ethnicity and Class in America.* Boston: Beacon Press.

Takaki, R., Ed. 1987. *From Different Shores: Perspectives on Race and Ethnicity in America.* New York: Oxford University Press.

———. 1993. *A Different Mirror: A History of Multicultural America.* Boston: Little Brown and Company.

Thomas, M., C. Herring, and H.D. Horton. 1996. "Racial and Gender Differences in Returns to Education." In *Race and Ethnicity in America: Meeting the Challenge in the 21st Century.* Ed. G. Thomas. New York: Taylor and Francis Publishers, 239-252.

Tonry, M. 1995. *Malign Neglect: Race, Crime, and Punishment in America.* New York: Oxford University Press.

———. 1996. *Sentencing Matters.* New York: Oxford University Press.

U.S. Bureau of the Census. 1980, 1985, 1990, 1996, 1997. Current Population Surveys, March Demographic Supplements.

———. 1953, 1960, 1970, 1980, 1989, 1996. Current Population Surveys, March Demographic Supplements. "Historical Income Tables."

U.S. Department of Justice, Federal Bureau of Investigation. 1950, 1960, 1970, 1980-89, 1990-96. *Crime in the United States—Uniform Crime Reports.* Washington, D.C.: GPO.

U.S. Department of Justice. 1977-82. *Prisoners in State and Federal Institutions on December 31.* Titles may vary. Washington, D.C.: Bureau of Justice Statistics.

———. 1983. *Prisoners in State and Federal Institutions on December 31, 1981—Sentenced State and Federal Prisoners at Year End, 1925-1981.* National Prisoner Statistics Bulletin, SD-NPS-PSF-8, NCJ-86485, March. Washington, D.C.: Bureau of Justice Statistics.

————. 1997a. *Correctional Populations in the United States, 1995.* NCJ-163916, May. Washington, D.C.: Office of Justice Programs, Bureau of Justice Statistics.

————. 1997b. *Bulletin: Prisoners in 1996.* NCJ 164619, June. Washington, D.C.: Office of Justice Programs, Bureau of Justice Statistics.

U.S. Immigration Commission. 1911. *Immigration and Crime.* Vol. 36. Washington, D.C.: GPO.

Walker, S., C. Spohn, and M. DeLone. 1996. *The Color of Justice: Race, Ethnicity, and Crime in America.* Belmont, Cal.: Wadsworth Publishing Company.

Warner, B.D. 1997. "Community Characteristics and the Recording of Crime: Police Recording of Citizens' Complaints of Burglary and Assault." *Justice Quarterly* 14 (December):631-650.

Wilson, J.A. 1980. "Frontier in the Shadows: Prisons in the Far Southwest, 1850-1917." *Arizona and the West* 22:323-342.

Wilson, J.Q. 1975. *Thinking About Crime.* New York: Basic Books.

Wilson, W.J. 1987. *The Truly Disadvantaged: The Inner City, the Underclass, and Public Policy.* Chicago: University of Chicago Press.

Wolfgang, M., and B. Cohen. 1970. *Crime and Race: Conceptions and Misconceptions.* New York: Institute of Human Relations Press.

Chapter 10

African American Prospects in the 21st Century: A Framework for Strategies and Policies

by James S. Jackson

Director, Research Center for Group Dynamics and Program for Research on Black Americans, Institute for Social Research, Center for Afroamerican and African Studies, and Daniel Katz Distinguished University Professor of Psychology, University of Michigan

INTRODUCTION

This book presents data and analyses on the status of African Americans as the 21st century begins. From this mass of information, one fact is clear—Blacks have suffered the most persistent forms of individual and institutionalized racial discrimination, and for a longer period, than any definable group in American history. This systematic and sustained discrimination is at the heart of a syndrome of disadvantage that lowers life chances and circumstances for individuals and families in the Black population. As the preceding chapters show, disadvantage is evident in almost every aspect of American society—individual and family income; occupational, marital, and health status; educational opportunity and attainment; and housing and living arrangements. In those rare areas of life where Blacks have come to dominate, such as professional sports, controversy abounds regarding possible race-related genetic differences. The authors in this volume conclude that Black disadvantage is due to a confluence of factors—historical accumulation of disparity, the legacy of slavery, de jure and de facto segregation in their caste-like manifestations, and abiding discrimination and racism.

The authors highlight the extensive demographic, political, economic, and social changes that are likely in the diversified nation and global village of the 21st century. They outline future programs and policies in the context of a rapidly changing ethnic and racial diversity that will affect relationships among African Americans and other groups in the United States. The intent of this final chapter is to provide a road map for the development of policy options to address the major racial issues discussed in the preceding chapters.

The following broad recommendations for policymakers, private organizations, and citizens are based on the findings of the authors in this volume:

- development of a sustained, comprehensive focus by government and private and public organizations on providing greater economic

I would like to express my deep appreciation to Margaret C. Simms, Vice President for Research, Joint Center for Political and Economic Studies, for her constructive comments on this chapter.

opportunities in education, employment, and intergenerational transfer of wealth;

- enforcement of existing Civil Rights legislation and regulations to eliminate continuing, persistent racial and ethnic discrimination in housing, employment, schooling, and the criminal justice system; and

- identification of common objectives among racial and ethnic minority groups to produce workable, long-lasting coalitions.

CHANGE AND THE 21st CENTURY

What are the prospects for African Americans in the future, when the United States will be a truly demographic multiracial society? Demographic projections forecast a racially and ethnically diverse America with no one group having a substantial numerical majority. Based on the Middle Series Census Bureau projections, by about 2050, Whites will represent only a slight majority (53 percent) of the population. According to the projections, that population of 394 million will be almost 25 percent Hispanic, 14 percent Black, 9 percent Asian, and 1 percent Native American.

Net immigration may substantially increase during some periods in the 21st century. The future may also differ because of unanticipated high intermarriage rates among many racial and ethnic groups and the attendant change in identities or assimilation of descendants. The future may be further affected as the perception and meaning of race and ethnicity change (Farley, this volume).

The demographic, geographic, economic, social, and political realities of life among racial and ethnic groups suggest a range of possible relationships. While it is apparent that America cannot function merely in a Black-White context, it is uncertain what elements will evolve in a new ethnic and racial paradigm. How will current and forthcoming demographic changes affect racial ideologies and our thinking of race? What will the changes mean for race relations among all groups?

Possible trajectories of the new ethnic and racial diversity are directly tied to the position of minority groups. Corporate or Balkanization approaches would allocate resources to racially distinct minority groups based on their relative proportion in the population (Gordon, 1994). Competitive approaches view these groups as fighting over available social, economic, and political resources. McClain and Stewart in this volume present a somewhat more pessimistic view. They argue that the hard-fought political victories of African Americans in the 1950s and 1960s may be eroded if the country remains deeply divided racially and if Blacks do not make consistent efforts to continue to accumulate and wield political power. Cooperative approaches envision traditional minority groups coming together with a unified voice to further the common good of all in social, economic, and political arenas. It is possible that the elimination of race as a defining issue on which minorities base their quest for economic and political well-being may bring about the embracing of ethnicities as social categories, rather than as groups haggling over power and resources (Gordon, 1994).

Three Visions for Future Race Relationships

Current and historical relationships among ethnic and racial groups lead to several visions of a possible future society. The first is a "colorblind civil society" that ignores racial and ethnic differences and attempts to exist as "one people." This vision may be more utopian than realistic; even the assimilative experience of European immigration took many generations. The wide scope of continuing and future immigration and the broad diversity of the overall demographic mix make this alternative unlikely.

"Multiracial conflict" is a second and more dire vision that postulates combative struggles along racial and ethnic lines to further the interests of individual groups rather than the larger society (Gordon, 1994). This vision is also unlikely. Current patterns of geographic dispersion and intermarriage rates suggest that considerable assimilation, at least among non-Black ethnic and racial groups, will occur over the next several generations. However, because of many historical and contemporary reasons, Hochschild and Rogers (this volume) point out that Blacks may become "odd people out," excluded from coalitions of other ethnic and racial groups.

The third vision is a "multiracial civil society" in which pluralistic coexistence is the hallmark (Hochschild and Rogers). This vision seems the most likely. A multiracial civil society cherishes and embraces racial and ethnic differences as groups work together to further society's common good. This model is not predicated upon assimilation, either geographic or through intermarriage.

A future of racial division or harmony in the United States depends strongly on the extent to which ethnicities and races are included in society. Events of the past 40 years have shown that the removal of legal barriers does not necessarily result in full and equal participation (McClain and Stewart). As pointed out throughout this study, large and abiding inequalities in work, income, education, political participation, and family life act against the full incorporation of many ethnic and racial groups. There are also other bases for societal cleavage that are not completely tied to race or ethnicity. Factors such as religion, gender, age, recency or timing of immigration, and political ideology can contribute to either division or coalition building (Hochschild and Rogers).

On the other hand, many White Americans have deep feelings that some assimilation and amalgamation are necessary to maintain a strong, united country (Gallup, 1997). Many view the explosion of immigration and the changing ethnic mix as a threat to basic values. The authors in this volume advocate a more pluralistic vision in which equality of opportunity is not bound by race or ethnicity (Hochschild and Rogers; LaVeist). This pluralistic perspective need not encroach in any way on a united, strong America that has a continuing, renewed commitment to democratic values, industry, and individual success.

A direct canvas of beliefs about the nature of racial and ethnic life shows wide differences among racial and ethnic groups (Gallup, 1997). In recent surveys, Blacks and Whites strongly disagree about whether Blacks continue to experience racism and discrimination in jobs, housing, the media, and the criminal justice system (Hochschild and Rogers; Hawkins and Herring, this volume). Whites are consistently more likely to see progress than regression. It is noteworthy that these perceptions are diverging over time. A declining proportion of Blacks believe that racial equality is increasing—from between 50 percent and 80 percent in the mid-1960s to between 20 percent and 45 percent in the 1990s. Whites generally believe that African Americans are as well off or better off than Whites in jobs, access to health care, and education, and almost 50 percent of Whites hold the same views regarding income and housing. Again, African Americans disagree.

A Changing Approach to Policymaking

As a discriminated against minority, the Black population has suffered the indignity of being "protected" by the government with respect to much of its material and social well-being. In a society whose core values are self-determination, industry, and hard work, African Americans have endured the humiliation of appearing to be occupational and income wards of the state, dependent upon government jobs, subsidized housing, and various forms of welfare transfers. The fate of Blacks has all too often been dictated by how the state has defined and implemented policies that respond to the changing priorities of the general public. The relatively low level of Black participation in free market investments and in the development of private enterprise is an impediment to economic advancement in a nation that values the free market and capitalism. This obstacle has social and psychological as well as material consequences. For a population group for whom most demographic and socioeconomic status markers point to disadvantage (Council of Economic Advisers, 1998), the country debates whether public policies should be race sensitive or race neutral (Hochschild and Rogers). Given the 400-year history of public policies that favored Whites, it is ironic that such a debate should be conducted at the beginning of the 21st century.

Nevertheless, there are strong differences of opinion about race-sensitive and race-neutral policies that have important implications for the future of government programs that may benefit African Americans. A similar debate changed the targeted policies of the War on Poverty in the 1960s to ones (if there were replacement policies) that focused more broadly on socioeconomic disadvantage. Similarly, education policies were changed in the 1960s and 1970s, following significant rulings to rectify the historical gaps in educational opportunities for Blacks. As discussed by Nettles and Orfield (this volume), for the past 25 years this set of education policies has been debated and, more recently, legally challenged.

America begins the new century with a less focused and less effective policymaking approach to addressing the circumstances of Black Americans than it had 40 years ago. It is as if Blacks were once again at the starting line of a footrace with one leg hobbled (Kerner and Lindsay, 1968).

THE POLITICS OF RACE IN A DIVERSIFIED AMERICAN SOCIETY

In this volume, Farley documents the significant changes that have occurred over the past 30 years in the economic and social status of African Americans. The incredible growth of the U.S. economy during the decade of the 1990s has helped, but not completely addressed, implementation of the full employment policies that may be fundamental to African American economic survival. Economic expansion has begun to move even groups previously considered unemployable (e.g., the "underclass") into the mainstream economy. Past experience indicates that the Black underclass is the last to be affected by a booming economy and the first to be fired when the business cycle bottoms out. Whether growth will continue through the next business cycle cannot, of course, be predicted. But the economy cannot grow indefinitely, and government should not continue to rely on the market to provide a surrogate full employment policy.

Policies for Blacks in the 21st Century

Historically, the development and implementation of public policies and strategies that focus on racial issues in the United States have proceeded slowly and indirectly. The issue of race has been debated more than any social, political, or economic problem in America's history. The debate continues in the 21st century, but unless there is greater attention to concrete remedies, the outcome may be no different than it was in the 20th century: continued institutionalized discrimination (Clark, 1993). While Black Americans today are more advanced socially and better off economically than the Black populations of the 17th, 18th, and 19th centuries, this is not a valid comparison. A more useful comparison is with contemporary ethnic minorities, most of whose family histories in America are considerably shorter than those of Blacks and many of whom experienced severe disadvantages after their arrival (Council of Economic Advisers, 1998).

African Americans are, of course, not the only group to have faced bigotry, discrimination, and racism. The history of the United States is replete with groups (e.g., Chinese, Irish, and Poles) who have suffered from negative attitudes and discrimination. Nevertheless, many of these ethnic and racial groups, particularly ethnic Whites, made substantial progress during the 20th century in improving their socioeconomic status (Hawkins and Herring). Blacks, however, have not made the same kind of progress, in part because most U.S. public policies have not been designed to create equal circumstances for African Americans compared with the rest of the U.S. population. Prior policies have not addressed the fundamental reasons for the continuing negative status of African Americans.

Furthermore, because of sustained discrimination, group solidarity, an important element in a group's initial rise to economic viability and equality, has not accelerated African Americans' fortunes as it has those of other groups in America. The difficulties facing Blacks are relatively simple to assess, but they demand complex solutions. Group advancement in any society and for any period of time is a function of social and economic opportunities and material, social, and psychological resources. The success of Black advancement in the 21st century will depend on developing these opportunities and resources.

Strategies and policies for Black advancement must focus on two fronts to succeed. The first includes policies that are universally applicable, to be developed at federal, state, and local government levels. The second includes policies that are group specific, to be developed by private and public organizations nationally and locally. However, the prognosis for public policies that target African Americans is poor in today's political climate because of the heterogeneous goals and interests of a diversifying American population (Darity and Myers, this volume). Nevertheless, the lack of political will and waning public support for race-based policies do not diminish the opportunities for grassroots groups, national Black and other organizations, and private corporations and foundations; these groups can play a major role in the development of targeted strategies, in concert with complementary universal government policies, to assist African Americans. Public policies developed in one area of life, or in one historical era, or for one age group may profoundly influence other areas of life, or subsequent time periods, or other age groups. For example, public policies have had unanticipated positive effects (e.g., Medicare on the well-being of older African Americans) as well as negative outcomes (e.g., Aid to Families with Dependent Children on the functioning of the African American family) (Hamilton and Hamilton, 1997).

CROSS-CUTTING POLICY THEMES

Several cross-cutting policy themes in the preceding chapters lead to the policy conclusions and recommendations of this book:

- the necessity of a broad-based focus by government and private and public organizations on providing a wide range of economic opportunities to improve, among other areas, family support systems, to finance education reform, and to allow for intergenerational wealth accumulation;

- the imperative of eliminating ongoing racial and ethnic discrimination through more vigorous monitoring and enforcement of antidiscrimination laws in housing, employment, schooling, and the criminal justice system; and

- the importance of finding common objectives among racial and ethnic minority groups as a basis for building effective coalitions.

Developing Wide-Ranging Economic Policies

Wilson (1987, 1996, 1999) has consistently called for full employment economic strategies. The recent sustained economic expansion (Farley) and new census data (U.S. Bureau of the Census, 2000), indicating that Black poverty is at its lowest level since the Census Bureau began collecting this information, demonstrate that a full employment environment can benefit Blacks in particular. If, as many have argued (e.g., Wilson, 1999), Black under- and unemployment are caused mainly by the lack of available good jobs, general government policies that move the country toward sustained full employment would mitigate this problem.

Reform in the financing of American education is crucial. Vast differences exist in the education of minority and nonminority children (Nettles and Orfield), as made abundantly clear by the college selection experiments in Texas and California to replace affirmative action policies. Lack of coordination in financing public education is but one problem area. As has become apparent in many states, neighborhood financing policies do not work in a society that tolerates housing discrimination. America's disastrous experiments with racially based busing showed that busing also does not work; the social and psychological costs are intolerable.

Alternative methods of equalizing educational opportunities must be found. Increased state and federal financing of education may be one answer. African Americans today strongly support the use of vouchers in public education (Center for Joint Studies, 1999). This support does not reflect a philosophical rejection of public education, but rather a profound understanding that the current system has failed the African American community. There is a serious need to rethink public financing and the role of the federal government in providing support for public schools.

U.S. higher education is the envy of the world, but the U.S. public K-12 system falls below almost all other advanced nations in reading and mathematics. As Nettles and Orfield urge, education reform, especially at the K-12 level, must be undertaken soon. This will benefit all Americans, particularly racial and ethnic minorities.

Another important economic area that government must address is the provision of better family support systems. The African American family bears tremendous burdens. Over the past four decades, substandard housing, lack of jobs, poor transportation, and availability of drugs have seriously eroded the ability of the Black family to serve as an important buffer in the lives of African Americans as a group and individually (Tucker, this volume). A concerted family assistance plan would create nonstigmatized support for family formation and subsistence (Moynihan, 1973). While an organized family policy would benefit all Americans, it would exceedingly improve Black lives (Hill, 1997). Similarly, a combination of tax credits, negative income tax, direct payments for child support, and better child-care facilities would help every American family.

While experts debate what to do with budget surpluses and whether and how to reduce taxes, the future of Blacks might be better served by increasing investments in human capital. The lack of progress in this area has contributed to Blacks having the lowest average material attainment of any racial and ethnic group in U.S. society. New investments would help rebuild dilapidated schools, replace aging housing stock, and upgrade inefficient transportation systems between cities and suburbs.

Darity and Myers suggest a direct redistribution of wealth to eliminate racial economic inequality. Historically, wealth redistribution has been a taboo for the American electorate, nor is it clear that reparations are a policy option with much likelihood of quick passage. Nevertheless, a viable beginning could be a government apology and formal recognition of the fact that African Americans have suffered and continue to struggle because of the long history of slavery, segregation, and discrimination.

A first step could be calculation of the "damages" resulting from hundreds of years of public policies that have discriminated against African Americans. The government could begin to redress these wrongs through a systematic program for economic revitalization. Under this program, funds could be transferred to communities in the form of low and no interest loans for upgrading housing, transportation systems, schools, child-care facilities, and other areas. This comprehensive plan would address the tremendous material requirements of poor neighborhoods more effectively than did the 1960s' War on Poverty and the more recent highly publicized but incomplete "enterprise zones." At the same time, the program would meet the public's clear preference for policies that are not race specific. Not only would such a plan help rebuild communities and create jobs for local residents of all racial and ethnic backgrounds, but it would also give social and psychological cohesion to neighborhoods (Harris and Curtis, 1998). This recommendation is based on the fact that conditions of life for African Americans are the product of the historical treatment of generations of Blacks and the continuation of discrimination. A government-led, neighborhood-based economic revitalization plan would provide opportunities and resources to address the root causes of African American disadvantage.

In the context of the "new political culture" (Clark and Martinot, 1998), which envisions new coalitions among government and private and public organizations, this chapter proposes a broad-based economic opportunity rights movement. It would focus on elimination of economic barriers and provision of work opportunities for all ethnic and racial groups. This approach could appeal to a large cross-section of a greatly diversified America.

Antidiscrimination Legislation and Enforcement

The authors argue for vigorous enforcement of existing antidiscrimination laws and regulations. Given the continuation of widespread discrimination, "blame" for the poor status outcomes of racial and ethnic minorities cannot be reliably allocated to either systemic or individual and group behaviors. Thus, the authors advocate increased enforcement of antidiscrimination regulations not only for African Americans, but also for other ethnic and racial populations (Darity and Myers; Hochschild and Rogers; McClain and Stewart). The authors emphatically agree that every American must be assured an equal opportunity to succeed within the system.

Coalition Building

The theme of coalition building has less to do with government policies and more to do with local and private strategies and cooperation among groups. Almost every chapter points to the necessity for African Americans to build formal and informal coalitions with other racial and ethnic groups and Whites. The authors note, however, the difficulties in forming coalitions that racial and ethnic minorities consider to be in their best interests or that all groups together envision as useful (see especially McClain and Stewart; Hochschild and Rogers). Building effective coalitions will not be an easy task and will demand the trust and good will of groups that historically have not cooperated. Although cases of positive coalition building across racial and ethnic lines can be found at the national level, especially during the Civil Rights era of the 1960s (e.g., Wilson, 1999), regional and local coalition building will be more likely in the 21st century. As pointed out by the authors, coalitions among diverse ethnic and racial populations may require forming and reforming, depending on the particular needs of the groups involved and the strategies necessary to address common concerns.

CONCLUSIONS: RACE AND POLICIES IN THE NEW AMERICA OF THE FUTURE

Long-term poverty and the absence of positive life chances characterize the lives of African Americans. Although Blacks have made substantial improvement in some areas such as education and median income, the data documented in this volume demonstrate their continuing poor relative status in many areas (Farley; Darity and Myers). As just one example, Hawkins and Herring present an alarming statistic: while African American males make up 6 percent of the population, they constitute 48 percent of all people in prisons and jails. Ongoing disparities demand concerted attention and new policy directions at the beginning of the 21st century.

Academicians, policymakers, and the general public have difficulty understanding the continuing poor position of Blacks relative to Whites and certain recent immigrant groups. Policymakers and social critics have sought a single explanation for the lack of general Black advancement. One explanation highlights the importance of individual and group "deficiencies"; another emphasizes a systematic lack of structural opportunities in, for example, education and employment. However, lack of progress may be due to the fact that many fundamental aspects of life for the majority of Blacks are essentially negative. These negative factors are found in family formation, job opportunities, exercise of the voting franchise, health and health care, living arrangements, housing, wealth, and criminal justice. No factor alone is the cause of ongoing African American material and social disadvantage, but in combination and over a long period, these negative circumstances form a daunting set of obstacles. The authors conclude that African Americans as a group have few true advantages in society today. The reasons are difficult to establish, given the complex combination of structural factors—such as job availability, economic conditions, and personal and family wealth—and individual and group behaviors. The persistence of prejudice and discrimination undoubtedly contributes to the observable negative outcomes that continue to afflict the Black population.

Some of the authors have used public opinion surveys to show that race-targeted policies are not politically acceptable today nor will they be in the future (Darity and Myers; Hochschild and Rogers). The authors present a wide range of recommendations for new strategies that are needed for the nation to prosper and move forward in the changed demographic landscape of the 21st century. These include school vouchers in the short term (Nettles and Orfield); direct redistribution of wealth (Darity and Myers); multiracial coalitions (Hochschild and Rogers); universal health insurance coverage (LaVeist); nondifferential sentencing (Hawkins and Herring); and a new social policy for Black families (Tucker). As discussed, the most common theme among the recommendations is the imperative of coalition formation among racial and ethnic groups that historically have not been good partners. Survey data and voting patterns (McClain and Stewart) suggest that new immigrant groups have much in common with Blacks—as well as many differences. The key will be to minimize the differences and maximize the shared interests within a common democratic framework.

Racial progress was indeed made in the last half of the 20th century. The Civil Rights movement resulted in a sea change in the beliefs and attitudes of the majority of Americans. The changes in the national consensus produced the political climate and basis for the legislation of the 1960s that brought about far-reaching protections not only for Blacks, but also for a broad array of America's minorities and women. The success of that movement, a model in coalition building, had much to do with timing, economic conditions, effective grassroots organizations, and the special will of a few elected officials. However, it is doubtful that a national consensus exists today that would establish social, political, and economic equality among all racial and ethnic groups in the 21st century.

Most of the study's authors are not optimistic about a narrowing of Black-White economic, political, or social gaps in the foreseeable future (Darity and Myers; Farley; Hochschild and Rogers; McClain and Stewart). The lack of commitment to ensure greater equality and the strong consensus in favor of reduced transfer programs may result in a continuation of, or even an increase in, existing inequalities.

In summary, this chapter argues for the need to conduct an unparalleled assault on economic deprivation, perhaps through a society-wide economic opportunity rights movement, coupled with a comprehensive, universal government attack on economic inequality. At the heart of the agenda are: (1) vigorous enforcement of racial and ethnic antidiscrimination laws in education, employment, housing, politics, health services, and criminal justice; (2) development of a comprehensive government and private sector plan that addresses the long history of unequal racial treatment; (3) rebuilding of neighborhoods and central cities; (4) creation of programs that strengthen family formation and maintenance; (5) implementation of educational and work opportunities for all; and (6) provision of transportation systems that permit access to good jobs and decent living conditions. This approach requires a strong commitment by government and the private sector to eradicate existing inequalities. It calls for the formation of new infrastructures to create equal economic, social, and political opportunities for the racially and ethnically diverse America that is unfolding in the new century.

BIBLIOGRAPHY

Austin, R.W., Ed. 1996. *Repairing the Breach.* Dillon, Col.: Alpine Guild, Inc.

Bell, D. 1993. "Remembrances Past: Getting Beyond the Civil Rights Decline." In *Race in America: The Struggle for Equality.* Ed. H. Hill and J.E. Jones, Jr. Madison: University of Wisconsin Press, 73-82.
Bobo, L.D. 1997. "The Color Line, the Dilemma, and the Dream." In *Civil Rights and Social Wrongs.* Ed. J. Higham. University Park: Pennsylvania State University Press, 31-55.
Bowen, W.G., and D. Bok. 1998. *The Shape of the River: Long-Term Consequences of Considering Race in College and University Admissions.* Princeton, N.J.: Princeton University Press.
Burman, S. 1995. *The Black Progress Question: Explaining the African American Predicament.* Thousand Oaks, Cal.: Sage Publications.

Chalmers, D. 1991. *And the Crooked Places Made Straight: The Struggle for Social Change in the 1960s.* Baltimore, Md.: Johns Hopkins University Press.
Chase-Lansdale, P.L., and J. Brooks-Gunn, Eds. 1995. *Escape from Poverty: What Makes a Difference for Children?* New York: Cambridge University Press.
Chideya, F. 1999. *The Color of Our Future.* New York: William Morrow and Company.
Clark, K.B. 1993. "Racial Progress and Retreat: A Personal Memoir." In *Race in America: The Struggle for Equality.* Ed. H. Hill and J.E. Jones, Jr. Madison: University of Wisconsin Press, 3-18.
Clark, T.N., and V. Hoffman-Martinot, Eds. 1998. *The New Political Culture.* New York: Westview Press.
Clayton, O., Jr., Ed. 1996. *An American Dilemma Revisited: Race Relations in a Changing World.* New York: Russell Sage Foundation.
Cose, E. 1993. *The Rage of a Privileged Class.* New York: HarperCollins.
———. 1997. *Color-Blind: Seeing Beyond Race in a Race-Obsessed World.* New York: Harper-Collins.
Council of Economic Advisers. 1998. *Changing America: Indicators of Social and Economic Well-Being by Race and Hispanic Origin.* Washington, D.C.: U.S. Government Printing Office (GPO).
Currie, E. 1998. "Race, Violence, and Justice Since Kerner." In *Locked in the Poor House: Cities, Race, and Poverty in the United States.* Ed. F.R. Harris and L.A. Curtis. New York: Rowman & Littlefield.
Curry, G.E., Ed. 1996. *The Affirmative Action Debate.* New York: Addison-Wesley.

Curtis, L.A. 1998. "Policy for the New Millennium." In *Locked in the Poor House: Cities, Race, and Poverty in the United States*. Ed. F.R. Harris and L.A. Curtis. New York: Rowman & Littlefield.

Danziger, S.H., and D.H. Weinberg, Eds. 1986. *Fighting Poverty: What Works and What Doesn't*. Cambridge, Mass.: Harvard University Press.

Danziger, S.H., and P. Gottschalk. 1995. *America Unequal*. New York: Russell Sage Foundation.

Darity, W.A., Jr., and S.L. Myers, Jr. 2000. "Languishing in Inequality: Racial Disparities in Wealth and Earnings in the New Millennium." In *New Directions: African Americans in a Diversifying Nation*. Ed. J.S. Jackson. Washington, D.C.: National Policy Association (NPA), Chap. 4.

DuBois, W.E.B. 1903. *The Souls of Black Folk*. New York: Vintage.

Entine, J. 2000. *Taboo: Why Black Athletes Dominate Sports and Why We're Afraid to Talk About It*. New York: PublicAffairs.

Farley, R. 1996. *The New American Reality*. New York: Russell Sage Foundation.
———. 2000. "Demographic, Economic, and Social Trends in a Multicultural America." In *New Directions: African Americans in a Diversifying Nation*. Ed. J.S. Jackson. Washington, D.C.: NPA, Chap. 2.

Farley, R., S. Danziger, and H.J. Holzer. 2000. *Detroit Divided*. New York: Russell Sage Foundation.

Feagin, J.R. 2000. *Racist America: Roots, Current Realities and Future Reparations*. New York: Routledge.

Feagin, J.R., and M.P. Sikes. 1994. *Living with Racism: The Black Middle-Class Experience*. Boston, Mass.: Beacon Press.

Featherstone, M., Ed. 1990. *Global Culture*. Newbury Park, Cal.: Sage Publications.

Fischer, C.S., et al. 1996. *Inequality by Design*. Princeton, N.J.: Princeton University Press.

Fix, M., and M.A. Turner, Eds. 1999. *A National Report Card on Discrimination in America: The Role of Testing*. Washington, D.C.: Urban Institute Press.

Franklin, D.L. 1997. *Ensuring Inequality: The Structural Transformation of the African American Family*. New York: Oxford University Press.

Freeman, R.B., and W.M. Rodgers, III. 2000. "Area Economic Conditions and the Labor Market Outcomes of Young Men in the 1990s Expansion." In *Prosperity for All? The Economic Boom and African Americans*. Ed. R. Cherry and W.M. Rodgers, III. New York: Russell Sage Foundation.

Gallup Organization. 1997. *The Gallup Poll Social Audit on Black/White Relations in the United States*. Princeton, N.J.: Gallup Organization.

Gerard, H.B., and N. Miller. 1975. *School Desegregation*. New York: Plenum.

Gilroy, P. 2000. *Against Race: Imagining Political Culture Beyond the Color Line*. Cambridge, Mass.: Harvard University Press.

Gordon, A.F., and C. Newfield, Eds. 1996. *Mapping Multi-Culturalism*. Minneapolis: University of Minnesota Press.

Gordon, M.M. 1994. "Models of Pluralism: The New American Dilemma." In *Race and Ethnic Conflict*. Ed. F.L. Pinchus and H.J. Erlich. Boulder, Col.: Westview Press, 186-193.

Gordon-Reed, A. 1997. *Thomas Jefferson and Sally Hemings: An American Controversy*. Charlottesville: University of Virginia Press.

Gramlich, E.M. 1998. *Is It Time to Reform Social Security?* Ann Arbor: University of Michigan Press.

Hacker, A. 1992. *Two Nations: Black and White, Separate, Hostile, Unequal*. New York: Charles Scribner's Sons.

Hamilton, D.C., and C.V. Hamilton. 1997. *The Dual Agenda: The African American Struggle for Civil and Economic Equality.* New York: Columbia University Press.

Harris, F.R., and L.A. Curtis, Eds. 1998. *Locked in the Poor House: Cities, Race, and Poverty in the United States.* New York: Rowman & Littlefield.

Harrison, R. 1998. *What the Social Sciences Know about Race and Race Relations.* Paper presented at the American Sociological Association Conference on Race and Ethnicity, Washington, D.C.

Harrison, R. J., and C.E. Bennett. 1995. "Racial and Ethnic Diversity." In *State of the Union: America in the 1990s.* Ed. R. Farley. New York: Russell Sage Foundation.

Hawkins, D.F., and C. Herring. 2000. "Race, Crime, and Punishment: Old Controversies and New Challenges." In *New Directions: African Americans in a Diversifying Nation.* Ed. J.S. Jackson. Washington, D.C.: NPA, Chap. 9.

Hawley, W.D., and A.W. Jackson, Eds. 1995. *Toward a Common Destiny: Improving Race and Ethnic Relations in America.* San Francisco: Jossey-Bass Inc.

Hernstein, R.J., and C. Murray. 1994. *The Bell Curve: Intelligence and Class Structure in American Life.* New York: Free Press.

Hill, R.B. 1997. *The Strengths of African American Families: Twenty-Five Years Later.* 2nd ed. Lanham, Md.: University Press of America.

Hochschild, J.L. 1995. *Facing Up to the American Dream: Race, Class, and the Soul of the Nation.* Princeton, N.J.: Princeton University Press.

Hochschild, J.L., and R.R. Rogers. 2000. "Race Relations in a Diversifying Nation." In *New Directions: African Americans in a Diversifying Nation.* Ed. J.S. Jackson. Washington, D.C.: NPA, Chap. 3.

Holzer, H.J. 1995. *Employer Hiring Decisions and Anti-Discrimination Policy.* Research Report 96-356. Ann Arbor: University of Michigan, Population Studies Center.

———. 1996. *What Employers Want: Job Prospects for Less-Educated Workers.* New York: Russell Sage Foundation.

Jaynes, G.D., and R.M. Williams, Eds. 1989. *A Common Destiny: Blacks and American Society.* Washington, D.C.: National Research Council.

Kaus, M. 1992. *The End of Equality.* New York: Basic Books.

Kerner, O., and J.V. Lindsay. 1968. *Report of the National Advisory Commission on Civil Disorders.* New York: Bantam Books.

Kinder, D.R., and L.M. Sanders. 1996. *Divided by Color: Racial Politics and Democratic Ideals.* Chicago: University of Chicago Press.

LaVeist, T.A. 2000. "African Americans and Health Policy: Strategies for a Multiethnic Society." In *New Directions: African Americans in a Diversifying Nation.* Ed. J.S. Jackson. Washington, D.C.: NPA, Chap. 6.

Lewis, J., and P. Onuf, Eds. 1999. *Sally Hemings and Thomas Jefferson: History, Memory, and Civic Culture.* Charlottesville: University of Virginia Press.

Massey, D., and N.A. Denton. 1993. *American Apartheid: Segregation and the Making of the Underclass.* Cambridge, Mass.: Harvard University Press.

Maynard, R.A. 1997. *Kids Having Kids: Economic Costs and Social Consequences of Teen Pregnancy.* Washington, D.C.: Urban Institute Press.

McClain, P.D., and J. Stewart, Jr. 2000. "An Overview of Black American Politics and Political Participation Since the Civil Rights Movement." In *New Directions: African Americans in a Diversifying Nation.* Ed. J.S. Jackson. Washington, D.C.: NPA, Chap. 8.

Miller, J.G. 1996. *Search and Destroy: African American Males in the Criminal Justice System.* New York: Cambridge University Press.

Morenoff, J.D., and R.J. Sampson. 1997. "Violent Crime and the Spatial Dynamics of Neighborhood Transition: Chicago, 1970-1990." *Social Forces* 76:31-64.

Moynihan, D.P. 1973. *The Politics of a Guaranteed Income: The Nixon Administration and the Family Assistance Plan.* New York: Vintage Press.

———. 1986. *Family and Nation.* New York: Harcourt Brace Jovanovich.

Munnell, A., L.E. Browne, J. McEneaney, and G.M.B. Tootel. 1992. *Mortgage Lending in Boston: Interpreting HMDA Data.* Working Paper 92-7. Boston: Federal Reserve Bank of Boston.

Myrdal, G. 1944. *An American Dilemma: The Negro Problem and Modern Democracy.* New York: Harper.

Nettles, M.T., and G. Orfield. 2000. "Large Gains, Recent Reversals, and Continuing Inequality in Education for African Americans." In *New Directions: African Americans in a Diversifying Nation.* Ed. J.S. Jackson. Washington, D.C.: NPA, Chap. 5.

Ogbu, J. 1978. *Minority Education and Caste: The American System in Cross-Cultural Perspective.* New York: Academic Press.

Oliver, M.L., and T.M. Shapiro. 1995. *Black Wealth/White Wealth: A New Perspective on Racial Inequality.* New York: Routledge.

Patterson, O. 1997. *The Ordeal of Integration: Progress and Resentment in America's "Racial" Crisis.* Washington, D.C.: Civitas Counterpoint.

Pedraza, S., and R.G. Rumbaut, Eds. 1996. *Origin and Destinies: Immigration, Race, and Ethnicity in America.* New York: Wadsworth.

Rodgers, H.R., Jr., Ed. 1988. *Beyond Welfare: New Approaches to the Problem of Poverty in America.* Armonk, N.Y.: M.E. Sharpe, Inc.

Sandefur, G.D., and M. Tienda, Eds. 1988. *Divided Opportunities: Minorities, Poverty, and Social Policy.* New York: Plenum.

Smith, R.M. 1997. *Civic Ideals.* New Haven, Ct.: Yale University Press.

Sniderman, P.M., and E.G. Carmines. 1997. *Reaching Beyond Race.* Cambridge, Mass.: Harvard University Press.

Sniderman, P.M., P.E. Tetlock, and E.G. Carmines, Eds. 1993. *Prejudice, Politics, and the American Dilemma.* Stanford, Cal.: Stanford University Press.

Thernstrom, S., and A. Thernstrom. 1997. *America in Black and White: One Nation, Indivisible.* New York: Simon & Schuster.

Tomasson, R.F., F.J. Crosby, and S.D. Herzberger. 1996. *Affirmative Action: The Pros and Cons of Policy and Practice.* Washington, D.C.: American University Press.

Tucker, M.B. 2000. "Considerations in the Development of Family Policy for African Americans." In *New Directions: African Americans in a Diversifying Nation.* Ed. J.S. Jackson. Washington, D.C.: NPA, Chap. 7.

U.S. Bureau of the Census. 1996. *Current Population Reports.* P60-193. Washington, D.C.: GPO.

———. 1997. *Current Population Reports.* P60-198. Washington, D.C.: GPO.

———. 2000. *Money Income in the United States: 1999.* Washington, D.C.: GPO.

Williams, P.J. 1995. *The Rooster's Egg: On the Persistence of Prejudice.* Cambridge, Mass.: Harvard University Press.

Wilson, W.J. 1978. *The Declining Significance of Race: Blacks and Changing American Institutions.* Chicago: University of Chicago Press.

———. 1987. *The Truly Disadvantaged.* Chicago: University of Chicago Press.

———. 1996. *When Work Disappears: The World of the New Urban Poor.* New York: Alfred A. Knopf.

————. 1999. *The Bridge Over the Racial Divide: Rising Inequality and Coalition Politics.* Berkeley: University of California Press.

Wong, P., Ed. 1999. *Race, Ethnicity, and Nationality in the United States: Toward the Twenty-First Century.* Boulder, Col.: Westview Press.

Yinger, J. 1995. *Closed Doors, Opportunities Lost: The Continuing Costs of Housing Discrimination.* New York: Russell Sage Foundation.

Program for Research on Black Americans, University of Michigan

The Program for Research on Black Americans (PRBA) was established in 1976 at the University of Michigan's Institute for Social Research by an interdisciplinary team of social scientists. They were convinced that high quality national data on African Americans was critical for advancing academic scholarship and developing effective public policy. In keeping with that vision, PRBA seeks to collect, analyze, and interpret empirical data on African Americans as well as international data on people of African descent. A second important goal is to provide research and training opportunities for social scientists and students of color. PRBA's primary areas of study are mental health, aging and human development, and race and political participation.

Today, PRBA is a center of scholarship and research, with more than 90 scholars, research assistants, and graduate students from a wide array of disciplines committed to distinctive research. Researchers affiliated with the program serve on advisory panels for philanthropic foundations, government policymaking bodies, and other policy advisory groups to acquaint a broad audience with the implications that PRBA research findings may have on national policy that affects African Americans.

PRBA's published books include *Life in Black America* (1991); *Aging in Black America* (1993); *Mental Health in Black America* (1996); and *Family Life in Black America* (1997). PRBA also publishes in-house documents, including a newsletter, *African American Research Perspectives*, Occasional Reports, and Working Paper Series.

To obtain these in-house publications, please contact:

Program for Research on Black Americans, University of Michigan
5006 Institute for Social Research
Ann Arbor, Michigan 48106-1248
Tel (313) 763-0045   Fax (313) 763-0044
www.isr.umich.edu/rcgd/prba

National Policy Association

The National Policy Association was founded in 1934 by distinguished business and labor leaders who believed that the private sector should actively participate in the formulation of public policy. NPA's goal is to seek common ground on effective and innovative strategies that address a range of issues vital to the prosperity of America.

NPA is one of the nation's principal nonpartisan, nonprofit organizations promoting informed dialogue and independent research on major economic and social problems facing the United States. NPA brings together influential business, labor, agricultural, and academic leaders to identify solutions to these emerging challenges. Through its policy committees, NPA provides a broad-based arena where members hear differing viewpoints and gain new insights on issues of mutual concern and national importance. The policy groups include the Committee on New American Realities, the Food and Agriculture Committee, the Global Economic Council, and the North American Committee.

NPA-sponsored research addresses fundamental questions related to strengthening U.S. competitiveness and productivity in a context of justice, equity, and basic human values. Through its research and other projects, NPA seeks to develop pragmatic solutions to the structural and technological changes impacting an increasingly interdependent world. Topical publications, seminars, and conferences help disseminate the conclusions and recommendations of NPA's work.

National Policy Association
1424 16th Street, N.W., Suite 700
Washington, D.C. 20036-2229
Tel (202) 265-7685   Fax (202) 797-5516
npa@npa1.org   www.npa1.org

Selected NPA Publications

Income, Socioeconomic Status, and Health: Exploring the Relationships, ed. James A. Auerbach and Barbara Kivimae Krimgold (NPA/Academy for Health Services Research and Health Policy: Forthcoming 2000), NPA #299.

Improving Health: It Doesn't Take a Revolution, by James A. Auerbach, Barbara Kivimae Krimgold, and Bonnie Lefkowitz (NPA/Academy for Health Services Research and Health Policy: Forthcoming 2000), NPA #298.

New Directions in Thinking About Race in America: African Americans in a Diversifying Nation, *Looking Ahead* (October, 1998, $10.00), Vol. XX, No. 3.

Affirmative Action: A Course for the Future, *Looking Ahead* (August, 1996, $10.00), Vol. XVIII, No. 2.

China's WTO Accession: America's Choice, by Richard W. Fisher (16 pp, 2000, $8.00), NPA #296.

Ensuring Global Food Security, by Charles S. Johnson (16 pp, 1999, $5.00), NPA #295.

The Challenges of Globalization for U.S. Development Assistance, by Emmy Simmons (16 pp, 1999, $5.00), NPA #294.

Creating an International Development Framework, by James D. Wolfensohn (20 pp, 1999, $8.00), NPA #293.

Employment Practices and Business Strategy, ed. Peter Cappelli. A New American Realities Committee-commissioned study available from Oxford University Press (240 pp, 1999, $29.95).

The Future Stakes for U.S. Food and Agriculture in East and Southeast Asia, ed. Steven A. Breth, James A. Auerbach, and Martha Lee Benz (176 pp, 1999, $15.00), NPA #291.

How Public Education Must Respond to Meet the Challenges of a Global Society, by Donald P. Nielson (24 pp, 1998, $5.00), NPA #292.

An Agnostic Examination of the Case for Action on Global Warming, by Murray Weidenbaum (16 pp, 1998, $5.00), NPA #290.

Through a Glass Darkly: Building the New Workplace for the 21st Century, ed. James A. Auerbach (148 pp, 1998, $15.00), NPA #289.

Ordering Information

To order NPA publications
and to find out about NPA's Membership Program,
visit NPA's Web site, www.npa1.org
or contact:

National Policy Association

1424 16th Street, N.W., Suite 700
Washington, D.C. 20036-2229
Tel (202) 265-7685   Fax (202) 797-5516
npa@npa1.org   www.npa1.org